POLITICS AND SOCIETY IN WALES

Language and Governance

POLITICS AND SOCIETY IN WALES SERIES

Series editor: Ralph Fevre

Previous volumes in the series:

Paul Chaney, Tom Hall and Andrew Pithouse (eds), *New Governance – New Democracy? Post-Devolution Wales*

Neil Selwyn and Stephen Gorard, *The Information Age: Technology, Learning and Exclusion in Wales*

Graham Day, *Making Sense of Wales: A Sociological Perspective*

Richard Rawlings, *Delineating Wales: Constitutional, Legal and Administrative Aspects of National Devolution*

Molly Scott Cato, *The Pit and the Pendulum: A Cooperative Future for Work in the Welsh Valleys*

Paul Chambers, *Religion, Secularization and Social Change in Wales: Congregational Studies in a Post-Christian Society*

Paul Chaney, Fiona Mackay and Laura McAllister, *Women and Contemporary Welsh Politics: The First Years of the National Assembly for Wales*

Elin Royles, *Revitalising Democracy? Devolution and Civil Society in Wales*

The Politics and Society in Wales series examines issues of politics and government, and particularly the effects of devolution on policy-making and implementation, and the way in which Wales is governed as the National Assembly gains in maturity. It will also increase our knowledge and understanding of Welsh society and analyse the most important aspects of social and economic change in Wales. Where necessary, studies in the series will incorporate strong comparative elements which will allow a more fully informed appraisal of the conditions of Wales.

POLITICS AND SOCIETY IN WALES

Language and Governance

Edited by

COLIN WILLIAMS

School of Welsh
Cardiff University

Published on behalf of the University of Wales

UNIVERSITY OF WALES PRESS
CARDIFF
2007

© The Contributors 2007

All rights reserved. No part of this book may be reproduced, stored in a retrieval system, or transmitted, in any form or by any means, electronic, mechanical, photocopying, recording or otherwise, without clearance from the University of Wales Press, 10 Columbus Walk, Brigantine Place, Cardiff, CF10 4UP.
www.uwp.co.uk

British Library Cataloguing-in-Publication Data

A catalogue record for this book is available from the British Library.

ISBN 978–0–7083–2112–6

Typeset by Column Design
Printed in Great Britain by Antony Rowe Ltd, Wiltshire

Contents

Preface

While there are several volumes which deal with issues of governance and another rich literature which deals with the formulation of language policy, there is, I believe, no single volume providing a coherent interpretation of the relationship between language and governance.

This volume represents the fruits of a continued dialogue between active participants in the formulation and implementation of language policy. The key issues analysed in this volume were first discussed at two closely related conferences held over four days at the National Assembly for Wales and Cardiff University from 29 November to 2 December 2001. The initiators and academic organizers were myself and Professor Linda Cardinal of the University of Ottawa, who first met as a result of our mutual close friendship with Charles Castonguay. The National Assembly event was organized in an exemplary manner by Pierre Boyer, then of the Forum of Federations, and Mark Williams of the National Assembly for Wales. The Cardiff University event was co-organized by myself and Professor Alistair Cole, School of European Studies, Cardiff University. We are grateful to the ESRC who sponsored the event and for their support in relation to two research projects on 'The Bilingual Context, Policy and Practice of the National Assembly for Wales' (Grant no. R 00022 2936) and on 'Devolution and Decentralisation in Wales and Brittany' (Grant no. L 219 25 2007).

A second opportunity was provided for several of the contributors to continue their dialogue as they participated in a conference on the theme of 'Languages and Constitutionalism' hosted by the School of Law, Ottawa University and the Law Society of Upper Canada, November 2004. A third opportunity was provided by participation at a conference on 'Debating Language Policies in Canada and

Europe' hosted by the Centre of Governance, Ottawa University, March, 2005. Each of these conferences allowed a genuine exchange of views and has greatly informed the resultant contributions published in this volume. Subsequently Cardinal, Dunbar, Loughlin, Nic Craith and Williams have maintained this regular intellectual interchange as members of the Language, Policy and Planning Research Unit of Cardiff University.

My initial interest in Canadian Studies was nurtured by working with Charles Whebell and Don Cartwright of the Department of Geography, the University of Western Ontario, where I remain an Adjunct Professor of Geography. I am grateful to the former Head of Department, Professor Roger King and the current head, Professor Dan Shrubsole for making Western a very special academic home for me. The Canadian Studies in Wales Group and the Welsh Language Board have also been instrumental in fostering collaboration and I am grateful to both organizations for their support. My thanks to colleagues within the School of Welsh, Cardiff University, and in particular, Professor Sioned Davies, for maintaining so intellectually supportive an environment within which to work. I should also like to thank Thomas Charles Edwards, Jesus College, and Anthony Lemon, Mansfield College and the School of Geography, who co-hosted my visiting fellowship at Oxford University during the academic year 2001–2 when some of the planning and groundwork for this volume was undertaken.

The Social Sciences Committee of the Board of Celtic Studies has sponsored this publication. I am grateful to Dr. Richard Wyn Jones, chair of the Committee, and to Prof. Ralph Fevre, Series Editor of the 'Politics and Society in Wales Series', for their encouragement and professional advice. I also wish to thank the staff at the University of Wales Press for their diligence in bringing this volume to publication.

Colin H. Williams
School of Welsh, Cardiff University

List of contributors

Dyane Adam is the former Commissioner of Official Languages, Ottawa.

Linda Cardinal is a Professor of Political Science, Centre of Governance, Ottawa University.

Guy Dumas is Associate Deputy Minister, Language Policy Secretariat of Quebec.

Robert Dunbar is Reader in Law and Celtic Studies, Aberdeen University.

Gerard Finn is the former Director General, Office of the Commissioner of Official Languages, Ottawa.

Will Kymlicka is Professor of Philosophy at Queen's University, Kingston.

Jean-Francois Lisée is Director of Cérium, Université de Montréal.

Diana Monnet is Deputy Secretary, Official Languages Division, Treasury Board Secretariat, Ottawa.

Norman Moyer is Assistant Deputy Minister, Canadian Identity, Department of Canadian Heritage, Ottawa.

Warren Newman is General Counsel, Department of Justice, Ottawa.

Máiréad Nic Craith is Professor at the Academy for Irish Cultural Heritage, Ulster University.

Leachlain S. Ó Catháin is a solicitor and member of Foras na Gaeilge.

John Loughlin is Professor of Politics at the School of European Studies, Cardiff University.

Rt Hon. Rhodri Morgan is the First Minister, the National Assembly for Wales.

Rhodri Glyn Thomas is the Heritage Minister of the National Assembly for Wales.

Winston Roddick, QC is the former Counsel General of the National Assembly for Wales.

Colin H. Williams is Research Professor, School of Welsh, Cardiff University and a Member of the Welsh Language Board.

List of illustrations

Figures

Tables

For Charles

Part I

Languages in Social, Legal and Political Context

1

Language, Law and Governance in Comparative Perspective

COLIN H. WILLIAMS

Introduction

The fate of so-called lesser-used languages and the corresponding pressure on governments exerted by various organizations within civil society has been a persistent feature of many states in the modern period. Within the UK issues of language and governance are a relatively new field of activity made more urgent by the transfer of direct responsibilities to devolved administrations in Northern Ireland, Scotland and Wales. Historically they have an older provenance in Canada, Ireland and several parts of Europe. Nevertheless, systematic analysis of these various experiences has been limited and thus I believe it is timely that a specific concentration on language and governance be initiated. There are three reasons for this conviction. The first derives from my own cross-cultural explorations of Canadian–European approaches to language policy. I initially researched Canadian–Quebecois aspects of language politics and policy formulation in 1973–4 and have been a frequent return visitor to Canada using the resultant insights from my fieldwork to inform my analysis of European situations. The second is a pressing need to advise, cajole, encourage and boost the confidence and, at times, the committed interest of politicians and public servants charged with formulating and discharging new language-related policies in increasingly multicultural contexts. The third is the real possibility that the rich Canadian and western European experience will offer approaches, models and policies of critical interest to politicians and others in central and eastern Europe as they grapple with the urgent business of consolidating official languages, identifying languages of instruction at different levels in the educational system, specifying the rights and obligations of their constituent citizens and launching new systems of governance within multi-level polities.

By inviting leading practitioners, politicians, senior civil servants and academics from Canada and Europe to contribute to this volume, I hope to increase the level of mutual understanding of responsible participants as they explore the relationships between language, law and governance. I believe that the resultant perspectives reflected in these pages is a remarkably original contribution to this dialogue. I want to influence, to strengthen and to empower the speakers of the target languages discussed herein, but I want to do so from the perspective of a critical participant rather than an apologist. Thus my aim is to situate key trends in language policy development within the larger debates of social and economic change. I am convinced that far too little detailed analysis of our respective condition and genuine comparative analysis is undertaken in these fields and far too much propaganda and generalized, uncritical acceptance of the worth of 'foreign' models is projected in what passes for political debate on lesser-used languages. A second conviction is the need to move way from the lazy categorization of language policy issues as being unique, residual and essentially cultural in orientation. A more holistic, integrated approach to language policy and evaluation is needed. Several robust examples of such an approach are provided in this volume, but they are all too often accompanied by lacklustre governmental practices which dent their effectiveness.

Given these convictions, this volume seeks to present contemporary assessments of the relationship between language and governance in parts of the European Union (EU) and North America. It also seeks to present arguments concerning the fundamental issues which underlie the determination of official language policy in an increasingly multicultural world order. There is no doubt that issues of both governance and diversity are handled differently either side of the Atlantic, but that bespeaks a wider divergence related not only to historical trajectories but also to current world views. Many EU-based critics fondly conceive of Canadians as being North Americans who are moderated by a more communitarian, social democratic outlook so redolent in parts of Europe. But to deny or to downplay the influence of the US on Canadian thought and practice is an unwise move. Canadian society is heavily infused with American mores, expectations, daily contact, familial and corporate relationships. Thus how the US perceives itself in relation to the world's diversity is critical also for interpreting Canadian choices and freedom of action. This has been made more acute recently by the significant increase within North America generally of Pacific Rim-oriented economies, technologies and inter-cultural contacts. Kagan puts it thus:

> It is time to stop pretending that Europeans and Americans share a common view of the world, or even that they occupy the same world. On the all-important questions of power – the efficacy of power, the morality of power – the desirability of power-American and European perspectives are diverging. Europe is turning away from power, or to put it a little differently, it is moving beyond power into a self-contained world of laws and rules and transnational negotiations and cooperation. It is entering a post-historical paradise of peace and relative prosperity, the realization of Immanuel Kant's 'perpetual peace.' Meanwhile the United States remains mired in history, exercising power in an anarchic Hobbesian world where international laws and rule are unreliable, and where true security and the defence and promotion of the liberal order still depend on the possession and use of military might. (Kagan, 2003: 3)

Reid (2004) argues that Americans should wake up to the new European superpower, not just because of Europe's collective economic and political influence on the world stage, but also because of the manner in which internal reform has strengthened the pursuit of 'ever closer union' without necessarily abandoning its diverse constituent particulars. Many Europeans are not so sanguine. Although they may be protected within the apparatus of liberal democracy's institutions and norms, they do not necessarily expect or welcome a world system dominated by variants of liberal democracy fashioned according to American or British hegemonic principles. True, many in the central and eastern parts of Europe welcomed the restoration of their all too brief democratic experience and rejoiced at the events of 1989 when participation, representation, human rights and the 'return to Europe' signalled a revolution in their political architecture. Still others in the atrophying Yugoslav polity had to cope with the virulent manifestations of fascist and totalitarian genocide as Serb nationalism in turn targeted Slovenes, their former Croat allies, Muslims and others in Bosnia and finally the Albanians of Kosova (Berman, 2004). But dissenters today agitate against the sweeping tides of globalization, sociocultural uniformity, state centralism and American-inspired cultural mores and modes of behaviour. It may be that globalization has brought some significant shifts in governance and has made the democratic impulse all the more possible for many previously excluded groups, but it does not necessarily follow that the messages encoded within globalization, the pressures of a free market or the appeal of democracy chime in the charnel house of state socialism.

Central to this, of course, is the role of the English language and of Anglo-American values and business practices. Revulsion for liberal economies and global markets manifests itself in countless ways in both new and old democracies, from workers' strikes to the boycotting of certain goods and violent protests at G8 summit meetings. Dahrehdrof, echoing most commentators, suggests that such sentiments formed one of the motives for 'the French and perhaps even the Dutch to reject the European Union's Constitutional Treaty, which some regarded as too "Anglo-Saxon" in its economic liberalism' (Dahrendorf, 2005: 1). Yet there is no doubting the impact of 'ever closer union' on the constitutional autonomy and freedom of action of the EU's constituent states. In the United Kingdom, although membership of the EU has presented constitutional and political difficulties, it has also brought into sharp focus the inadequacies of our 'Customary Constitution', especially in regard to the specification of citizen obligations and the relationship between the rule of law and the rights of citizens. It has also prompted the question as to whether there should be a written constitution, as a counterweight to the claims of 'elective dictatorship' and 'mandated majority rule'.

At the close of his remarkable book, *Reshaping the British Constitution*, Nevil Johnson outlines the implications of the drift towards a written constitution:

> Such steps would in turn imply qualification of the doctrine of parliamentary sovereignty, brought about not by stealth or neglect, but explicitly . . . This in turn might entail some degree of separation of Parliament from the Executive to reduce the latter's power over the former . . . There could be a place for a new second chamber elected on a different basis from the House of Commons and acknowledging in some degree the desirability of bringing nations and regions more explicitly into the constitutional framework of the United Kingdom. One of the consequences of such a change might then be the need for amendment of the present devolution settlements to resolve the anomalies in them regarding English political rights as well as to affirm a general obligation to sustain the Union and further its interests. (Johnson, 2005: 314)

These trends echo several of the arguments put forward in the Canadian constitutional debate of more than twenty years ago, which saw the patriation of their constitution from the United Kingdom. Then, issues of national unity and political stability were wedded to the equality of French and English in federal institutions and this in turn became a cornerstone of the Canadian Charter of Rights and Freedoms in 1982 in which, as we shall see, 'the principles contained in the *Official Languages Act* were seen by many as generous ideals rather than legal requirements' (Adams, chapter 3). In many ways Canada has experimented with managing issues which the UK has yet to tackle and by contrast the UK has been forced to deal with other issues which Canada does not as yet consider to be pressing problems. Even so, by bringing British–Canadian approaches into sharp relief, the present volume's central themes reveal the complexity of the relationship between citizen, language and governance.

Contributors to this volume raise concerns related to the nature of evolving federal systems, the implication of devolutionary measures for the UK and by extension Ireland, the EU and Canada/Quebec, the underlying tension in Canada between official bilingualism and pluralism (especially as it impacts on native peoples and minority language groups), the nature of community rights and community empowerment, questions on how to devise policies to integrate newcomers without denying or damaging their fundamental sociocultural and economic rights, the central role of the civil service within the transition programmes of the devolved administrations, the tension between 'top down' and 'bottom up' language planning initiatives, and the inadequacy of corpus language planning for minority languages used in different levels of administration. Underlying all of these topics is the manner in which external pressures, such as American influence on Canada and the UK's membership of the EU, influence not only the formal constitutional revisions under review, but also the ways in which 'generic' continent-wide policies are put into practice at the local level. Here the governance of language policy is used as a surrogate for far wider issues related to the protection of individual freedoms and minorities, the political limitations on executive power and the guarantees which constitutional reform, devolved government and a new rights-based regime can offer the historically beleaguered subjects and citizens of increasingly multicultural democracies.

Consequently four areas of this complex relationship are given special attention in our work. Part I deals with Languages in Social and Political Context; Part II offers a comparison of Legislative and Institutional Frameworks; Part III assesses Policies and Programmes; while Part IV concerns Language Policies, National Identities and Liberal-Democratic Norms. Each of these parts reveal the details of specific policy changes over time, but they all nevertheless deal with responses to more universal issues, such as the need to belong to a relevant collectivity, the differential impact of the forces of globalization, democratic transitions, language vicissitudes, empowerment and governance. Times change, as do political priorities in multilingual societies. Let us therefore address several of these overarching themes.

Belonging

Fundamentally, of course, both citizenship and participatory democracy have been subject to immense pressure of late as a result of complex processes related to globalization, Europeanization and the transformation of government. There is now a rich literature on the rules and implications of membership in increasingly multicultural societies. Of particular interest are those studies which entreat with the connections between concepts such as race, ethnicity and nationality, such as Fenton and May (2002), the role of minorities in history, such as Hepburn (1978), the rights of minorities in plural societies, such as Kymlicka (1995) and (Harff and Gurr, 2004), and the meaning of identity in the modern world, such as Taylor (1989). Yet there remains the basic political puzzle, namely how best to interpret the various bases upon which membership in the polity is based. Conventionally in western Europe the two concepts of *jus sanguini* and *jus soli* have been used as alternative principles in law to determine how people belong to states. *Jus sanguini*, as interpreted, for example, in Germany, avers that membership of the state is related to ancestry, while *jus soli,* exemplified by the French Republic, asserts that membership is related to territory and is a political compact. Lo Bianco (2005) reminds us that the one and indivisible French Republic derives from the French revolution motto: 'one state, one nation, one language'. Consistent with this and despite the contentious politics surrounding immigration, he argues that France maintains relatively liberal citizenship laws:

> French scholars also cite Article 27 of the International Covenant on Civil and Political Rights in which immigrants can claim as individuals (not minority collectivities) the right to practise their first language and to form cultural associations. To acquire French citizenship, foreign residents must have lived in France for 5 years, have a regular income, accommodation, show respectable life and customs ('bonnes vie et moeurs') and demonstrate 'assimilation to French community'.

But interestingly a tested knowledge of French is not a requirement for citizenship.

Lo Bianco (2005) also reminds us that citizenship rights granted to new arrivals are different depending on the ultimate legal character of the idea of being a citizen. In reality neither system excludes totally, nor includes automatically. However, as we shall see in chapter 4, these principles of citizenship imply quite radically different ways of thinking about language policy, entitlements and rights, and the construction of language regimes in various states of the European Union?

How these principles are interpreted is a matter of great significance for member states of the EU. Lo Bianco, in discussing French state policy, draws out an important distinction between language rights and language needs. He argues that after many centuries of resistance the Breton and Occitan languages have managed to gain limited political status because they belong to French territory.

> Hence a Breton can claim language rights whereas an immigrant can only claim language needs. The notion essentially being that lacking the national language constitutes a need and a disadvantage while lacking the opportunity to maintain and transmit to younger generations the ancestral, non-national, language is constituted as a right if that language can be found to have a soil, or territory, connection with the republic. (Lo Bianco, 2005)

But, as reported in chapter 4 even elements of this level of recognition are contested within the French legal system, especially in relation to the deliberations surrounding the Breton Diwan school system.

Similarly, some relaxation of the *jus sanguini* principle is evident in German proposals whereby the then Chancellor Gerhard Schroder's centre-left government sought to ease citizenship restrictions imposed on those of non-German ancestry. Lo Bianco (2005) reports that the Dual Nationality Law would have liberalized existing citizenship procedures significantly, by reducing the residency requirements and liberalizing partner rights in inter-cultural marriages. A language requirement would remain, but dual passport rights would be conceded. However, the continuing strong opposition from conservatives who oppose the law suggests to Lo Bianco that *jus sanguinis* will probably remain the basis of

German citizenship. More generally the movement towards a greater specification of the various relationships between citizen, state and immigrant, which lay at the heart of the drive to establish a European Convention, has signalled a new context within which these principles become exercised and challenged. Although the Convention's momentum has been halted, the issues which it sought to address will grow inexorably and encourage fresh attempts and new solutions.

Globalization

While there is much agreement about the significance of globalization, there is less agreement as to its origins and effects. Globalists tend to adopt a benign attitude to its growth, while anti-globalists invest in globalization most of the evils of advanced capitalism and the 'malaise of modernity', to use Charles Taylor's phrase. One of the key triggers for the expansion of global financial markets, and hence new patterns and processes of globalization, was the pressure from Western governments, the International Monetary Fund (IMF) and the World Bank to liberalize global trading and to reduce the role of the state in economic affairs. Both features have had their effects on globalization and on the growth of governance alongside government. Powerful institutions, such as the IMF, for example, sought to encourage a high level of fiscal and monetary discipline, to advance reforms leading towards market economies and to encourage free trade, free capital flow and economic cooperation among countries (Haynes, 2005: 140). In tandem with the Bank for International Settlements and the World Bank, new arrangements for regulating the flow of money, the conditions under which global capitalism operates and the oversight function of networked agencies, such as the Financial Stability Forum (FSF), have been put in place. In part this has also lead to an increase in the need for global governance and for an injection of a greater degree of transparency and direct control of governments in international economic affairs (Woods, 2002: 42).

The political economic thrust required to bolster the international monetary system and advance the spread of economic globalization has necessitated the following key steps:

- cut government spending, including on health and welfare;
- cut wage levels or at least severely constrain wage rises in order to reduce inflation and make exports more competitive (Brecher and Costello, 1994: 56–7);
- expand the role of the private sector through privatization of state assets;
- liberalize foreign trade;
- liberalize control of capital, capital movement and money markets, including the lifting of restrictions on foreign investment;
- protect weaker sectors of society by strengthening social safety nets. (Haynes, 2005: 140)

It is within this context that new patterns of language and governance have to be calibrated. Globalization and its myriad patterns for inter-lingual communication comprise a new set of elements within the system, some of which are predictable while others are less so. Thus influential commentators, such as Phillipson (2003: 103), aver that while trends such as globalization and Europeanization inevitably favour English-speakers, what is less obvious is the manner in which integrating the needs of the various language dimensions into the reform of the EU system may create new opportunities for several of the less dominant languages. Different types of opportunities have also been created by the rise of so-called meso-level government, in the shape of regional assemblies and devolved administrations, where lesser-used languages, have received increased attention both as a policy focus and as an instrument for communication. This has led to new forms of governance at regional and local levels, involving the rise of new substantive and participatory demands.

Democracy

Regime change and the democratization of vast parts of the world have also brought into fresh view reworked concepts such as civil society, social capital, political empowerment and participatory democracy. Added to this is the switch in more mature liberal democracies from vertical to horizontal forms of government. New actors, domestic interest groups and transnational organizations are increasingly influential in determining agendas and in highlighting inequities within existing structures of government. Drawing on the work of Loughlin (1999), and Loughlin and Williams (chapter 4 below) we concur with Denters and Rose (2005) that, while the traditional model of democracy, at both local and regional level,

> has been based on a *general, undifferentiated relation* between the community of local citizens and an elected council that represented the community, new relations between citizens and their local government are characterized by a higher degree of functional differentiation inasmuch as they allow for citizen participation directed at *particular (sets of) decisions.* (Denter and Rose, 2005b: 260)

The differentiation of the represented, as, for example, different language groups, raises new and complex issues for governance. Cardinal has dubbed this a new pressure for horizontal governance in Canada, with all its attendant difficulties both for representation and for mass democracy. Implicit in this shift is also a concern for the manner in which different groups of citizens interconnect with government. This implies not only that the responsible governments have to be more adaptive and responsive, but also that the manner in which language pressure groups and official agencies interact must also become more sophisticated in tone and holisitic in character.

Language Policy

Language policies in Canada have been influenced by a 'majoritarian' approach to participation and identity construction at both the federal and the Quebecois level. Indeed, the Quebec–rest of Canada dialogue has dominated the political and constitutional debate as to what role French and English should play in the construction of a reformulated 'national' culture. It is the constitution, statute and secondary legislation which defines the contours of the official languages landscape. The court system is critical and central to the operation of policy. Official language rights are clearly enunciated and several agencies exist to enforce legislation both for the whole of Canada and within Quebec itself. Hence the relationship between language, law and governance is better developed in Canada than in most European cases. However, Cardinal in chapter 16, has demonstrated how official language minorities in Canada have been able to use the dominant paradigm of national unity and governance to promote their own ideas. Yet, while they have succeeded in influencing the development of language policies and planning, they have also had to face their own reality of internal schisms, atrophying networks and increasing fragmentation in far too many communities. In consequence, despite the extensive machinery put in place to allow members of the respective official linguistic minorities to transmit their languages and engage with officialdom in several respects, there is the feeling that societal bilingualism has not yet established itself as the essential element of Canadian life. At first sight this is a surprising discovery for non-Canadians who assume that Canada's long-term commitment to official bilingualism automatically incorporates the goal of societal bilingualism.

Robert Dunbar (chapter 5) demonstrates how and why the Canadian state has explicitly refrained from declaring itself committed to the achievement of societal bilingualism. The constitution says nothing about the acquisition by the linguistic majorities of the language of the minority. Neither is the Canadian educational system geared toward the production of fully functional bilinguals. Canada also evinces a somewhat different approach to language maintenance and to 'reversing language shift'. Language equality appears to be the overriding principle with its concomitant emphasis on the articulation of clearly defined language 'rights'.

Thus in many respects European language activists, anxious to emulate the Canadian success in promoting official bilingualism, soon learn to temper their admiration. They engage in a judicious combination of selecting and rejecting aspects of the Canadian experience and end up grafting on to their own beleaguered situations only the most promising and appealing aspects, rather than the system writ large. In part this reflects the pragmatic nature of the exchange, but it also reflects a failure to comprehend how the various policy-related elements relate the one to the other. My aim is to improve this comprehension by providing here a forum for a remarkably original collection of writings both in terms of ideas and comparative analyses.

Languages

Languages in both Canada and the UK, the core of this volume, may be divided into three categories. First, there are the aboriginal languages; some fifty-two such languages (in twelve separate language families) are currently spoken by Canada's indigenous peoples. The 2001 Canadian census indicated that 198,595 people, or about 0.6 per cent of the Canadian population, claim an aboriginal language as a mother tongue. This represented a 3.5 per cent decline from 1996, when 205,800 persons reported themselves as having an aboriginal tongue as their mother language (Statistics Canada, 2003a). However, for most of these languages, mother-tongue competence – and use – tends to be much greater amongst older than younger people, and only three such languages, Cree (spoken in 2001 by 77,285 as a mother tongue), Inuktitut (29,695) and Ojibway (21,980), can be considered to have a reasonably good chance of survival as spoken community-based languages. (Drapeau, 1998).

Second, there are the 'official' languages, French and English, the languages of the two major European powers which colonized what is now Canada in the sixteenth to eighteenth centuries. Unlike the languages of Canada's aboriginal peoples, these are languages spoken by tens of millions of people worldwide, are the dominant and/or majority language in dozens of states, and have considerable prestige in a wide range of international institutions. According to the 2001 Canadian census, 82 per cent of the Canadian population claimed one of these two languages as their mother tongue. An even higher percentage, 89.5 per cent, claimed one of these two languages as the language spoken most often at home, and over 98 per cent of Canadians claim to be able to speak and understand at least one or the other of these languages. However, speakers of French are, as demonstrated by the foregoing statistics, a minority within the Canadian state, as well as in nine of the ten provinces and in all three territories, and English-speakers are a minority in the province of Quebec. The francophone minority is proportionally largest in New Brunswick, where its 239,400 members constitute about a third (33.2 per cent) of the population; while there are more francophones in Ontario – 509,265 – they constitute only 4.5 per cent of the provincial population. In other provinces, the francophone communities are small both in absolute and proportional terms, and in all cases number fewer than 65,000 and constitute less than 5 per cent of the population (Statistics Canada, 2003b).

While neither French nor English is remotely threatened with extinction, the French linguistic minorities in most provinces are in decline, both in absolute and proportional terms, and the complete assimilation of such *linguistic communities* within various provinces is in some cases a very real possibility and a very serious threat. This is what animates Cardinal's analysis in chapter 16 and serves to underpin several of the criticisms levelled at the Canadian system by Dunbar in chapter 5. In a few provinces, such as Alberta and British Columbia, the francophone population is growing significantly, but part of the increase is due to the migration of francophones looking for work, and whether they will form self-sustaining linguistic communities is doubtful. The anglophone minority in Quebec is in no immediate danger of disappearance, and while it has declined somewhat in both absolute and percentage terms, this is due to, in considerable measure, the outward migration of anglophones to other provinces, rather than assimilation into the francophone majority; furthermore, while there is some evidence that a larger number of Quebec anglophones have become fluent in French, assimilation is rare, and subtractive bilingualism, the norm for many francophone minority communities, does not hold for the anglophone minority of Quebec. (Statistics Canada, 2003b).

Third, there are a large number of languages spoken by successive waves of immigrants to Canada, generally known as 'heritage' languages in Canada. According to the 2001 Canadian census, 5,334,770 persons, or 18.0 per cent of the Canadian population – about one sixth – claimed one of these heritage languages as a mother tongue, though a smaller percentage, 10.5 per cent, claimed such a language as a language of the home (Statistics Canada, 2003b). Almost 872,400 persons claimed Chinese as their mother tongue, making it the third most widely spoken language in Canada, while very large numbers of Canadians also claimed Italian and German, Portuguese, Spanish, Greek and Ukrainian as mother-tongue languages. The fastest growing heritage languages were Punjabi, with 32.7 per cent more speakers in 2001 than in 1996, Arabic, up by 32.7 per cent, Urdu, and, almost double its 1996 level, Tagalog, up by 26.3 per cent, and Chinese, up by 18.5 per cent. While intergenerational retention of heritage languages has been more marked in rural communities – as, for example, in the case of Scottish Gaelic in eastern Nova Scotia – the general pattern appears to be similar to that of speakers of 'immigrant' languages in the United States, namely, assimilation within the majority language community within three generations.

Similarly, there are languages that are indigenous to the British Isles and Ireland—'autochthonous' languages, in the terminology of the Council of Europe's European Charter for Regional or Minority Languages (the 'Languages Charter'), and these would include the UK's Germanic languages, such as English, of course, together with Scots and Ulster Scots, as well as its Celtic languages, such as Welsh, Scottish Gaelic, Irish, Cornish and Manx. English is the de facto 'official language' of the UK (population estimate in 2006, 59,834,300) and occupies that second category in this language typology, as does Welsh arguably in relation to the devolved institutions of Welsh government. According to the 2001 British census, 575,640 people in Wales identified themselves as being able to speak Welsh, representing 20.52 per cent of the population aged three and over. The demographic position of the other Celtic languages is weaker; for example, according to the 2001 British census, some 167,490 people, or 9.98 per cent of the population of Northern Ireland, claimed to have an ability to speak Irish, and some 58,652 people, or 1.2 per cent of the population of Scotland, reported themselves being able to speak Scottish Gaelic (Scotland's Census, 2001). The number of speakers of Cornish is likely to be in the hundreds (Payton, 2000), and of Manx just over one thousand (Isle of Man Census, 2002).

In Ireland by 2002, as is discussed in chapter 6 below, total Irish-speakers had risen to 1,570,894 (41.9 per cent of the population) and the language enjoys the full privileges of being the first official language of a sovereign state. Even this, however, does not guarantee survival and the full employment of Irish in everyday situations.

The current weakness of the Celtic languages should not detract from the fact that they have a very long association with law and government, if not governance. One need only cite the impact of the Laws of Hywel Dda, the grandson of Rhodri Mawr, who from 942 AD ruled most of Wales. His decision to codify Welsh law and to apply customary principles in the administration of justice has been heralded both as a unifying instrument in the making of the nation and as a unique contribution to the emergence of European law. Some forty manuscripts of Welsh law are extant, dating from the thirteenth to the sixteenth centuries. While six are in Latin most are in Welsh which acts a gentle correction to those commentators who claim that, following devolution, laws are being drafted in Welsh for the first time ever. A more voluminous record is that of the codification of Irish law and the employment of the Irish language in the affairs of successive kingdoms as described in the works of Thomas Charles Edwards (1989; 1992; 1993; 2003).

Governance

Governance has come to the fore in the fields of comparative politics and international relations, often as an attempt to answer central questions such as 'who rules, in whose interests, by what mechanism and for what purposes?' (Held and McGrew, 2003: 8). As an analytical approach governance, whether at global or local level, is preoccupied by process, by rule systems and by interaction across multiple levels of authority. The key features of the institutional architecture of global governance have been described by Held and McGrew as follows:

- It is *multilayered* in the sense that it is constituted by and through the structural enmeshment of several principal infrastructures of governance: the suprastate (such as the UN system), the regional (EU, MERCOSUR, ASEAN, etc.), the transnational (civil society, business networks and so on), and the substate (community associations, and city governance) (Scholte, 2000). Sandwiched between these layers is national government.
- It is often described as polyarchic or *pluralistic* since there is no single locus of authority. This is not to imply any equality of power between the participants but simply to acknowledge that political authority is decidedly fragmented.
- It has variable *geometry* in so far as the relative political significance and regulatory capacities of these infrastructures vary considerably around the globe and from issue to issue.
- The system is *structurally complex*, being composed of diverse agencies and networks with overlapping (functional and/or spatial) jurisdictions, not to mention differential power resources and competencies.
- Far from national governments being sidelined in this system, they become increasingly crucial as *strategic sites* for suturing together these various infrastructures of governance and legitimizing regulation beyond the state. (Held and McGrew, 2003: 9)

One feature which has brought governance, rather than government, to full focus has been the reconfiguration of authority between the various layers of responsibility and the opening up of hitherto formal boundaries which prohibited many actors in society from having access to political decision-making. This is not to say that all the polities treated in this volume are open, transparent and fully responsive entities. However, the rise of network societies has undermined the exclusive authority of states to arbitrate and solve complex issues. By the same token it has empowered many interest groups, agencies, non-governmental organizations (NGOs) and transnational actors to engage with bureaucracies, government departments and state institutions. Information overflow on a crowded international stage is now the norm, leading some, such as Roseneau, to propose simplifying typologies of governance as in Table 1.1.

Table 1.1: Rosenau's six types of governance

	PROCESSES *(type of collectivities involved in this form of government)*	
	unidirectional (vertical or horizontal)	multidirectional (vertical or horizontal)
Formal	**Top-down governance**	**Network governance**
	(governments, TNCs, IGOs)	*(governments, IGOs, NGOs*
		INGOs – e.g. business alliances)
STRUCTURES		
informal	**Bottom-up governance**	**Side-by-side governance**
	(*mass publics, NGOs, INGOs)*	*(NGO and INGO, governments)*
mixed	**Market governance**	**Mobius-web governance**
formal	*(governments, IGOs, elites*	*(governments, elites, mass*
informal	*markets, mass publics, TNCs)*	*publics, TNCs, IGOs, NGOs, INGOs)*

Source: Roseneau, 2003: 81.

The key feature of this typology is that it allows for network analysis and horizontal communications to be treated alongside the more familiar top-down hierarchical ordering of events. As we shall see throughout this volume it has been bottom-up pressure which has placed language issues, recognition and rights on the political agenda. This has impacted especially on local and regional government levels, mainly by the adoption of New Public Management practices. Denters and Rose have identified three major changes at the lower levels of political responsibility, namely 'a widespread adoption of NPM and public-private partnerships; involvement or organized local associations, interest groups and private actors in policy partnerships; and introduction of new forms of citizen involvement' (Denters and Rose, 2005b: 261). Both economic efficiency and democratic quality have been hugely affected by 'multi-agency working, partnerships and policy networks which cut across operational boundaries' (Leach and Percy-Smith, 2001:1). This form of governance is in turn impacted upon by the major pressures involved in urbanization, globalization, Europeanization and in new substantive demands and new participatory demands. The range of influence of these five factors on local governance is well illustrated in Table 1.2. The questions asked here by Denters and Rose relating to the interplay of local and meso-level tiers of government, whether in the regions of Europe or the provinces of Canada, force us to look afresh at the suturing together of policy and governance in the responsive state.

A feature often emphasized in the literature is the need for coordination of activities at all levels in the spatial hierarchy. This involves a closer examination of the institutionalization necessary to make coordination of policy and efforts work. The sheer complexity of handling the relationship between many languages and various systems of governance in places such as India, China or the EU is daunting. But it is nonetheless challenging also for mature democracies such as Canada, Ireland and the UK. What compounds the difficulties is the fact that many civil servants and politicians within these latter states, let alone the wider international system, may be characterized as reluctant reformers in a process of governance without conviction when it comes to matters of minority language promotion. Happily no such charge can be laid at the feet of our first two contributors who by their leadership and conviction have encouraged the professional practice of language governance.

Table 1.2: Comparing local governance: major trends, challenges and questions.

Trend	Challenge	Questions
Urbanization	Coordination of activities of various sub-national governments	1. Have there been any changes in the relations between governments or at the local and meso-level of local government systems?
Globalization	Development of new division of labour in the territorial state to meet the socio-economic consequences of globalization	2. Have there been any changes in relations between local governments and higher tiers of government?
Europeanization	Secure or even increase the role of local government in the newly emerging European polity	3. What are the major implications (direct and indirect) of the rise of the EU for local governments and systems of local government?
New substantive demands	Increase local capacity for effectively and efficiently solving community problems	4. What are the major changes in systems of local government management and community partnerships?
New participatory demands	Respond to new participatory demands and secure the responsiveness of local government	5. What are the major changes in the system of local democracy?

Source: Denters and Rose, 2005a: 8.

Part I: Languages in Social and Political Context

Chapter 2 presents the views of the Rt. Hon. Rhodri Morgan, First Minister, National Assembly for Wales on the theme of 'The Challenge of Language Equality' while chapter 3 presents the views of Dyane Adam, Commissioner of Official Languages of Canada who retired in July 2006, on 'Language and Governance in Canada'. Rhodri Morgan traces the forces which influence the fortunes of Welsh in an Anglocentric world. Chief of these have been political integration, mass emigration and rapid industrialization. More recently proactive language policies have sought to promote bilingualism within Wales. In contrast to Canada, the Welsh approach relies less on detailed legislation and the courts system to specify the rights and obligations of citizens and government alike. Rhodri Morgan acknowledges that recent legislation providing language choice 'on the basis of equality' is not the same as granting equal status to Welsh and English. Neither is legislation sufficient to guarantee the survival of Welsh. Nevertheless, he has committed the government to tackling several of the more worrying trends underlying language erosion. Evidence of this resolution are the principles enunciated in *Iaith Pawb* (2003) which underpins current government language policy, and which was in turn based on the recommendations of enquiries by the Culture and Education Committees of the National Assembly for Wales (NAfW, 2002). This policy and the accompanying process, critiqued in chapters 12 and 15 below, indicate a more comprehensive approach to language planning and policy. The long-term goal is the creation of societal bilingualism, whereby people may choose to live their lives through either Welsh or English or both. As Dunbar (chapter 5) notes in his critique of the Canadian and British approaches, this 'implies that all Welsh people should be equipped with the capacity to make that choice, and that implies a sufficiently strong command of both languages'. These aims have been integrated into the revised Welsh Language Board's strategic directives, which will need to be complemented by vigorous action to promote Welsh across all aspects of public life. This remains a challenge for government and civil society alike. Yet, because of the devolution experience, Rhodri Morgan argues that Wales is well placed to contribute to the public debate on the increasingly pluralist basis of society. Active membership of the British–Irish Council within which his government seeks to promote diversity in a positive manner throughout these isles, is but one reflection of this trend.

In chapter 3 Dr Dyane Adam, former Commissioner of Official Languages (COL), outlines the Canadian experience of language legislation. Dr Adam cautions that aspects of the Canadian federal model may not necessarily be exportable to the other contexts discussed in this volume without significant modification, as it has been designed to serve a particular set of circumstances. The Commissioner's Office is well placed to discharge its functions and responsibilities because, although an agent of the Canadian Parliament, it is independent of government and exercises an oversight role to ensure that public bodies comply with both the spirit and the letter of the law. The prime duty is to respond to violations of linguistic rights and to find solutions to the ever-changing problems which arise within the system, a challenge which has been met by her successor Graham Fraser. Dr Adam is particularly exercised by the need to work in a concrete fashion with partner agencies, such as the Department of Canadian Heritage, and to ensure that the official language communities remain vibrant and vital entities. Her argument is that the Canadian Parliament has a particular opportunity to make a difference to the demographic reality of most official language communities and to allow them fully to express their culture, history and identity. Since the strengthening of the law in 1994 it could be said that the project of creating a bilingual country is a work in progress. Over the thirty years of the COL's existence, real progress had been made in doubling the number of bilinguals and in the change of attitude toward official bilingualism which is now seen as a bridge rather than a barrier between communities. The outstanding challenge is the persuasiveness of the new media, which poses severe difficulties for francophone minorities. The federal government can ameliorate some of these threats if it is guided by law in a spirit of tolerance following Lord

Acton's maxim that the most certain test of freedom is the security enjoyed by minorities.

Following these introductory chapters, which are based upon the active principles of leadership, conviction, legal oversight and equality of treatment, we turn to consider the intellectual foundations of governance and state transformation. In chapter 4 John Loughlin and Colin Williams discuss the origin and force of governance, global transformation and the communitarian social state as they relate to the determination of language policy in Europe and Canada. Claims and counter-claims of the demise of the nation-state and the transformation of civil society in Europe by processes such as supra-national integration, advanced capitalism and the spread of instantaneous means of communication impact upon the formulation of public policy. However, little of this discussion has influenced the debate on the relationship between governance and language policy, especially those aspects which relate to so-called minority languages. Chapter 4 aims to remedy this situation to a certain extent by focusing on four aspects of this relationship. First, the authors attempt a conceptual clarification of key terms such as governance and the transformation of civil society. Secondly, they describe a major paradigm shift from the welfare state to the neo-liberal state and speculate on the emergence of a third paradigm, which they term the social state. Thirdly, they address the way in which each of these state paradigms has dealt with issues related to minority language representation in contradistinction to the promotion and defence of the hegemonic, state language. Finally, they explore the various opportunities and challenges for minority languages which are posed by the current transformation of the European state system.

Taken together, these experiences and paradigm shifts amount to a significant transformation of the nation-state and of its component parts – nation and state – over the past fifty years. This transformation has occurred under the influence of three major factors:

1. those forces operating from 'above', particularly globalization and Europeanization (itself largely a response to globalization);
2. the reform of the state from 'within' with the adoption of new models of public administration such as the New Public Management, etc.;
3. pressures from 'below' with the strident emergence on to the public arena of sub-national authorities, both regions and cities, summed up in the phrase 'the new regionalism'.

To these processes of changes may be added the new geopolitical situation following the collapse of the Berlin Wall, the transformation of the Soviet empire, the enlargement of the European Union and the prospect of Turkey's accession, and, to an as yet unknown extent, the 11 September attacks on the World Trade Centre and the Pentagon, together with the related invasion and 'reconstruction' of Iraq which heralds unanticipated consequences for global security.

Each of the principal thematic dimensions of the transformed nation-state within western Europe has been subject to a particular disciplinary focus, as follows:

- The transformation of the concept and practice of sovereignty (political science and public law).
- The loss of control over fundamental areas of public policy: economic, financial, environmental, industrial (political science and public administration/public policy, economics).
- Incapacity to control and master technological changes (sociology, public policy).
- Loss of the monopoly over culture, language and identity (sociology, anthropology, socio-linguistics, public policy).
- Reordering of international and intergovernmental (both between national governments and between national and sub-national governments) relations leading to new paradigms of diplomacy (international relations, comparative politics).
- The shift in conceptions of state territory from an analysis of the ordering of politically bounded space to a recognition of the closure effects of space and time producing

interdependent flows of information, people, goods and services (geography, regional science).

Recognizing that these three state paradigms are still in a state of flux, the authors turn to an analysis of how language and language policy are conceptualized and translated into public policy terms in each of them. This innovative chapter thus establishes the intellectual context for the more detailed explorations of individual language–governance experiences in the chapters which follow.

In chapter 5, Robert Dunbar surveys the genesis and operation of language rights regimes, with a particular reference to Canadian and British experience. In spite of the obvious historical socio-political affinities, the legal framework for the management of language issues in the two countries shows a significant degree of variation. By comparing and contrasting the variety of approaches taken by state, provincial and national-level government towards linguistic issues, he is able to assess the relative practical value of language rights in broader linguistic revival initiatives. The striking difference between the general approaches surveyed in Canada and the UK, is the much greater reliance in Canada on a rights-based model. Very few defensible minority language rights obtain within the UK system but in Wales, at least, a comprehensive and holistic approach to minority language maintenance and revival has been possible. Stealth rather than legislation has produced gains, but as discussed in chapter 15 there are growing demands in Wales for a Charter of the Welsh Language, an Office of Official Languages and the passage of new legislation to cover language services and expectations in the private and voluntary sectors (Williams, 2005). A final focus is on current European initiatives viz. the operation of the European Charter for Regional or Minority Languages within the Council of Europe Framework which sets a new context for the outworking of the relationship between rights, governance and language planning.

In chapter 6, Professor Máiréad Nic Craith, discusses the implications of new forms of governance for citizen empowerment and raises a number of fundamental issues as regards the meaning of equality of language rights in a European context. Her analysis deals with the management of language-related tensions within communities, and the urgency of guaranteeing protective measures to endangered language communities. Prof. Nic Craith warns against complacency as regards the hegemonic position of English as the world language. The author concludes with an appeal to recast lesser-used language speakers, not as a minority group, but as an ever-increasing international community with well-established contacts whose cumulative pressure can work to persuade governments to reconsider their attitudes towards the 'cost' of linguistic diversity.

Part II: Comparing Legislative and Institutional Frameworks

In chapter 7 Gérard Finn, former Director General, Office of the Commissioner of Official Languages of Canada, explains the evolution of the distribution of powers within the Canadian federal system before specifying in detail recent reforms influencing the treatment of official language communities by the Canadian state. The context for such reforms is a recognition that the reduction in expenditure on the official languages programme in the 1990s threatened to undermine much of the force of language-related gains made since the early 1970s. This reinforces the relevance of treating the issues of language and governance in a wider political economic context as the Canadian state was seeking to adjust to the pressures identified above in terms of global economic trading and fiscal reductions in government expenditure. Data-based systematic comparisons between anglophones and francophones on items such as rates of language retention, average income levels, relative gaps in levels of education and labour market participation rates are then presented. All users of language-related data in Canada would recognize the need for new, more comprehensive data to allow sophisticated comparisons to be undertaken between respective language groups. They would also heed Finn's advice that it is too early to judge to what extent the injection of over $751 million dollars of new funds into the Official Languages programmes over a five-year period will halt the erosion of the Official Languages Program. As several contributors to this volume make clear *The Next Act: New Momentum for Canada's Linguistic Duality* has identified education, community development and a bilingual public service as priorities for action, but it is debatable as to whether or not the community of speakers themselves has been empowered by this transformation and rededication of government commitment.

In chapter 8, Warren Newman, General Counsel of the Justice Department, Canada, provides a detailed legal history and expert analysis of the evolution of Canadian federal language rights law. The protection of minorities is, as the Supreme Court of Canada held in the *Quebec Secession Reference* (SCR 1998), one of the basic structural principles of Canada's constitutional framework. Some of these provisions, such as those of s. 23 of the Charter which guarantee minority language education rights, are restricted in their application to linguistic minorities; other language rights, however, may be seen to benefit both linguistic minorities and majorities (Newman, 2004) This principle is reflected in the guarantees afforded to minorities by the Charter of Rights and other provisions of the Constitution, notably those that entrench and protect rights in relation to the use of the English and French languages.

'The importance of language rights', the Supreme Court stated eloquently in the *Manitoba Language Rights Reference*, 'is grounded in the essential role that language plays in human existence, development and dignity.'

> It is through language that we are able to form concepts; to structure and order the world around us. Language bridges the gap between isolation and community, allowing humans to delineate the rights and duties they hold in respect of one another, and thus to live in society. (Manitoba Language Rights, 1985)

In turn Newman's analysis evaluates milestones in the evolution and interpretation of federal language rights. These include the constitutional power over language rights and the principle of advancement as detailed in the Official Languages Act of 1969; the 1973 parliamentary resolution and the scope of the declaration of equal status; the 1982 Charter of Rights; the 1988 Official Languages Act; and the federal government's various commitments under the terms of the Act.

Newman concludes that the legal and constitutional framework relating to official languages law and policy in Canada is characterized by a complex web of federal, provincial and territorial legislative, regulatory and policy measures. But he argues that this is to be expected in a modern federal state where two languages, English and French, are in common use amongst millions of Canadians every day. The experiential nature of language rights in Canada should not be undervalued for they are shaped by history, geography and demography, as well as by deeply held conceptions of individual, group and national identity. Efforts to respect and accommodate the place of the two official language communities in Canada and the minority communities within them go to the heart of the Canadian experience and its model constructs of bilingualism and multiculturalism. He avers that the federal Official Languages Act is a key element of that framework.

In chapter 9 Diana Monnet of the Official Languages Division, Treasury Board, Secretariat of Canada, illustrates one of the key implications of the Official Languages Act, namely its influence on governance and departmental policy. She provides an excellent account of the manner in which government departments have been forced to take a more serious approach to the issue of language equality within their respective domains. Evidence of a more robust commitment was given by the tone and content of the Speech from the Throne, 30 January 2001:

> Canada's linguistic duality is fundamental to our Canadian identity and is a key element of our vibrant society. The protection and promotion of our two official languages is a priority of the Government – from coast to coast. The Government reaffirms its commitment to support sustainable official language minority communities and a strong French culture and language. And it will mobilize its efforts to ensure that all Canadians can interact with the Government of Canada in either official language.

Monnet argues that the Government of Canada wanted to signal its reaffirmation of promoting linguistic duality, position itself as an ally of the French language, demonstrate that it wanted to take into account the priority needs of official language minority communities, and strengthen the service delivery in both official languages. On 30 September 2002, in a new speech from the Throne, the government made a commitment to strengthening the Official Languages Program. The Official Languages Action Plan released on 12 March 2003, was developed to meet that commitment.

But how was it to achieve such aims? Primarily through the network of governance which mainstreamed its ideas through such agencies as the Standing Joint Committee on Official Languages; the Commissioner of Official Languages; Canadian Heritage; the Department of Justice Canada; the Privy Council Office; the Public Service Commission of Canada. In turn these agencies would be infused with new ideas and additional energy derived from the Network of Champions and the Advisory Committees on Official Languages. Horizontal governance was to be encouraged by a greater emphasis on revitalizing bilingual services to the public, by reinvigorating community development and vitality and by sharing the federal government's vision of a bilingual state.

Yet all too often within multilingual states one of the biggest barriers to the realization of sympathetic and, at times, quite radical visions, is the opposition of the civil service. Consequently the sociolinguistic character of the federal workforce is a major determinant of success. As the Canadian model is predicated on a rules-based approach to institutional bilingualism, not individual bilingualism, it is imperative that the conditions of the language of work for civil servants are constantly monitored and reformed, or periods of stagnation and regression would return. The recent 'Modernisation of Government' initiative has increased greater respect for the official languages within the ministries and has ushered in a more pragmatic, user-friendly, yet highly professional, climate of work. This judgement and the underlying philosophy is in turn critiqued in chapter 16 by Linda Cardinal who analyses the effectiveness of horizontal governance for the operation of the Canadian official languages regime.

In chapter 10 the emphasis shifts from the federal to the provincial level, as Guy Dumas, of the Language Policy Secretariat of Quebec, presents a detailed account of the challenges facing the French language within Quebec. Based on the Charter of the French Language and subsequent legislative reforms he sketches the operation of a rights-based approach to key domains of socio-economic life. Insightful illustrations are drawn from the language of the workplace, of trade and commerce, of public administration. Attention is also given to the effectiveness of agencies supporting current language policy, such as the Office de la langue française, the Commission of Toponomy, the Conseil de la langue française and the Commission de protection de la langue française.

He argues that the main effect of language policy has been the restoration of Quebec's French character and the availability of services in French to clients. The three outstanding challenges are: the greater use of French in information and communication technology; the increased use of French in the workplace despite the pressure of globalizing forces; and the pursuit of the integration of immigrants into francophone society. It is likely that sociolinguistic and commercial pressure to switch to English will remain; consequently, even more language legislation will be required to regulate behaviour. Dumas argues that official unilingualism is not inconsistent with the protection of minority languages, including English. His analysis has resonance for not only francophone communities elsewhere in Canada, but also the many significant linguistic minorities within the EU who press for a greater specification of their rights, often within designated geographically demarcated spaces.

In chapter 11, Winston Roddick, QC, former Counsel General, National Assembly for Wales, sets out the legislative context for the treatment of Welsh and English on the basis of equality. He traces the historical development of the status of the Welsh language in the governance of Wales, arguing that Welsh lost its legal and official status through the 'unabashed cultural cleansing' brought about by successive Acts of Parliament. Elements of a partial reconstruction of that status have been implemented with the passage of the Welsh Courts Act 1942, the Welsh Language Act 1967 and the Welsh

Language Act 1993. Taken together these acts constitute a framework of common law which could act as a fourth pillar, supplementing the support of the public sector, the private sector and popular goodwill, to sustain a strategy for the Welsh language. However, modern legislation relating to the language is flawed because it has failed to tackle the fundamental issue, namely the enforceability of language rights. There has not been an acceptable balance between rights and remedies. Several improvements ushered in by institutional devolution and by the establishment of the National Assembly in 1999 have created new challenges and opportunities for a legally binding framework in a bilingual society. These include a marked strengthening of the administration of justice in Wales, improvements in the training and education of the judiciary in the use of Welsh and the use of this language throughout the whole criminal process. But there remain serious structural impediments to the articulation of language rights in Wales. These include the lack of true equality between English and Welsh, the lack of an independent language ombudsman, and the difficulty in finessing the precise relationship between the government of Wales and the government of the UK. Winston Roddick reminds us that ultimately it is the UK Parliament and the British legal system which will exercise the lasting influence on the future relationship between the Welsh language and governance.

In chapter 12, Leachlain S.Ó. Catháin, Board Member, Foras na Gaeilge, surveys the development of legislation and programmes to support the Irish language. He argues that the initial dependence on good will and political rhetoric has been unable to halt the decline in the use of Irish during the twentieth century. Of crucial importance was the lack of enthusiasm shown by successive Cabinets and civil servants to implement thoroughgoing reforms to promote bilingualism within the public sector. Attempts to introduce a new Irish Language Act, based on the Welsh experience, had been stalled at every occasion, but finally succeeded in 2003 and has been accompanied by the establishment of a Language Ombudsman, The first incumbent, Seán Ó Cuirréain has proved to be a remarkably dynamic and effective *An Coimisinéir Teanga*.The author concludes with a call for an urgent enactment of a robust legislative initiative which is essential in order to provide a platform for citizen choice and other sociolinguistic reforms.

The seven chapters in this section provide rich comparative material but also demonstrate the need for policies and programmes to be monitored effectively and to secure a role for civil society to offer an independent critique of language-related initiatives. The third part presents such a critique both from within the system and from critical, if engaged, commentators.

Part III: Assessing Policies and Programmes

Establishing an appropriate infrastructure for operating in two or more official languages is a difficult enough task. Regulating the behaviour and effectiveness of such systems is even more challenging. In chapter 13, Norman Moyer, Assistant Deputy Minister, Canadian Identity, Department of Canadian Heritage, evaluates the promotional programmes of his ministry. The key operational instrument is a concordat established by the federal government with each province, capable of being articulated and integrated within a wider government strategy as monitored by the Official Languages Commission. The chapter focuses on the practical difficulties in realizing the aims of the ministry, which include both financial constraints and negative attitudes on behalf of the English-speaking majority. A series of detailed cameos illustrate the range of the department's responsibilities, and confirm the necessity for constant interdepartmental dialogue and cajoling for, as the author makes clear, minority linguistic survival requires a constant injection of energy to ensure 'that the mainstream does not submerge the minority stream'. As such it offers a practioner's perspective on the process of articulating language rights in the delivery of programmes and services.

In chapter 14 Rhodri Glyn Thomas, former Chair of the Culture Committee, National Assembly for Wales, argues that the co-equality of languages in Wales has worked well in institutional terms, but less well in interpersonal transactions.

The cross-party consensus to depoliticize the language issue had been sustained in the first term of the NAfW (1999–2003), while the second term has been preoccupied with implementing the broader measures to realize the creation of a bilingual nation. Uncertainty over the future of the Welsh Language Board and of the government's implementation of its *Iaith Pawb* strategy has repoliticized the language issue (if in reality it was ever not politicized). The chapter critiques the policy-review process from an influential insider's perspective and charts the likely developments of bilingual policy in Wales over the medium term. As Heritage Minister the author is now in a position to implement many of his, and his party's ideas, as a result of the coalition government Plaid formed with the Labour Party following the May 2007 National Assembly elections. When read alongside the account given by Roddick (chapter 11) and Williams (Chapter 15) a rich interpretation of the devolution settlement in Wales is provided.

In chapter 15, Colin H. Williams, a member of the Welsh Language Board, identifies the four challenges facing Welsh, as being to increase the number of Welsh-speakers; to provide opportunities to use the language; to change people's patterns of language use, and to encourage more people to take advantage of the opportunities which currently exist; and to strengthen Welsh as a community language. He outlines the board's evolving strategy and illustrates various successful initiatives in design and marketing, bilingual education and community development. Language policy in Wales has attracted some of the more edifying virtues of deliberative democracy, despite counter-evidence that the public domain of citizenship, equity and service is atrophying as a result of the processes analysed superbly in David Marquand's *The Decline of the Public* (2004). The danger, of course, is that language revitalization has become too closely linked with the public domain. The chapter proceeds with an analysis of government policy as enunciated in *Iaith Pawb* (2003), the debate surrounding the integration of the Welsh Language Board into the National Assembly for Wales and the implications of current coalition government in Wales. A most pressing issue is the need to revise the legislative arrangements and framework surrounding the operation of language policy.

The key implication of his analysis is that neither the UK government nor constitutional experts have given much thought to the post-devolution settlement. His critique of the multilayered nature of authorities exercising some statutory influence on language policy is a classic illustration of the fragmented nature of the post-devolutionary practices and processes. This makes it both more difficult to locate the source of authority in particular circumstances and to rule in matters of complaint and lack of compliance. A strategy of ambitious reform would reduce this element of confusion and obfuscation while a major step forward would be the declaration of a Charter for the Welsh Language, together with a new round of Welsh legislation in relation to education and bilingual service provision. The chapter concludes with a set of recommendations which, if implemented, would enable the Welsh Assembly Government better to realize its stated policy aims.

In chapter 16, Linda Cardinal, concentrates on the variety of language-related issues facing citizens and policy-makers alike. Her far-sighted chapter on horizontal governance and official languages in Canada tackles several incongruities in the operation of official bilingualism. Her argument is that the new form of governance has opened up unchartered possibilities for official language minorities. In particular it should help the organizational capacity and collective intelligence of minorities in Canada. Attention is also focused on the lack of a sustained dialogue between representatives of the First Nation peoples and francophones; the need for flexibility in the handling of the structural relationship between minorities and government and the medium-term implications for governance of decentralization measures. Many of her key points illustrate the simultaneous operation of different types of governance, identified by Roseneau in Table 1.1. The opening up of new spaces afforded by horizontal governance in Canada and devolution in the UK would appear to favour an increase in side-by-side governance. Thus the chapter's arguments and perspectives have ramifications for state–minority relations in a number of other contexts also.

In chapter 17, Jean-Francois Lisée, asks whether Quebec has given up its historical quest for autonomy and is seeking to become a North American Region State. The implications for language and governance are spelled out for an increasingly fluid society with an open border and the chapter charts the differential effect of closer union with the USA on both francophone and anglophone communities. The second part of the chapter deals with the economic and political prospects for governance change, especially in respect of federal redistributive policies, which have an impact on all provinces but are particularly acute in determining Ottawa–Quebec relations. Explicit in his analysis is the profound effect of economic change and government policy on the survival of French-speakers outside Quebec, the role of extraterritoriality and internationalism on the multiple identities of residents within Quebec, and the fundamental impact which economic globalization is having on the capacity of the Quebecois society to regulate its own affairs. Lisée's interpretation is an excellent illustration of the myriad factors which conduce to the transformation of systems of governance identified in Table 1.1. The telling point is that, while the world changes profoundly, leading politicians and commentators, let alone academic specialists, still insist on treating national communities as if they remained self-contained, self-regulating autonomous entities.

Part IV: Language Policies, National Identities and Liberal-Democratic Norms

In Part 4 Will Kymlicka's concluding chapter offers a response to the principal issues and debates raised by the contributors and provides his own perspectives on the relationship between language policies and governance in selected multicultural societies. His first observation is that the strengthening of the status of the French language in Canada, and of Celtic languages in the United Kingdom and Ireland, applies to historic language groups, rather than immigrant groups. Thus while assimilationist projects with respect to historic minorities are now largely delegitimized, the same cannot be said of assimilationist projects regarding immigrants, at least in respect of language. Kymlicka asks why historic language communities are being singled out for legal protection. The answer he provides has to do with consent, a sense of historic injustice and the manner in which historic minorities have been able to draw upon ideas of 'nationhood'. Until relatively recently claims to nationhood by so-called non-state nations were historically rejected by most Western states, but they have become increasingly accepted, as have the more specific claims that are seen as flowing from nationhood, such as regional autonomy, the maintenance of distinct educational and legal systems and the protection and use of national languages. Consequently, issues of language and governance should be seen as one component of a much broader phenomenon of the revindication of ethno-national identities in the post-war era, and the rebirth of the 'nations within' as self-consciously political actors and movements. Yet the precise role of language within such nationalist projects varies immensely, and Kymlicka offers some useful comparisons between Quebec and the Celtic cases under review, most of which turn around the notion of self-government. Given that a common argument for devolving power to 'nations within' is that they need some degree of self-government over issues of language and culture, Kymlicka suggests that other questions need to be raised about the linkages between language policy and national autonomy. It is often said that national groups require self-government in order to maintain their language and culture. But the causal relationship can also go the other way. He cites the work of Rainer Baubock, in that 'rather than self-government being a means to preserve cultural difference, this difference is more often preserved as a means to justify the claim to self-government' (Baubock, 2000: 384). As peoples are continually required to explain why they deserve self-governing powers, possession of a distinct language or legal tradition provides one possible answer.

Yet there is a major difference, he notes, between the practice and justification for such defence in Canada/Quebec as compared with the Celtic cases. He argues that

> in Canada, the legitimacy of the Quebecois project stems in part from the fact that it relies on a fairly familiar model of a national political community, defined by a common language that is dominant over a particular territory. Official bilingualism at the federal level, on this model, is necessary to ensure that both language communities are equally represented in the central government, and equally able to access its services. But the assumption is that most individuals will continue to live their lives in relatively monolingual societies, each of which is institutionally complete. Keeping a country together with two parallel, institutionally complete and territorialized language communities is not easy, but part of what holds it together is precisely the fact that each community can see the other as forming a separate but 'normal' liberal-democratic national political community built around a common language and territory.

He identifies a quite different model for societal bilingualism emerging in the diverse Celtic contexts:

> In the Celtic cases, by contrast, the main goal of language policy is not to create two parallel and largely monolingual societies – a separate Welsh-speaking or Gaelic-speaking society alongside the English-speaking society. Rather, the goal is to encourage greater bilingualism in everyday life, so that most citizens will feel comfortable operating in either language in a wide range of functions . . . Viewed in this light, the Celtic cases offer the promise of a genuinely new model of a single bilingual national political community (in contrast to the sort of binational federation of two distinct monolingual political communities that we see in Canada or Belgium). (Kymlicka, chapter 18)

This volume presents a tightly integrated argument for the need to move beyond treating language rights as *sui generis* and for integrating language-related needs into the fabric of government decision-making at all levels where appropriate. Both the Canadian and the European cases demonstrate that it is possible to mainstream language issues, but that it is difficult both to maintain the political momentum and to guarantee that local communities benefit in full from the resultant policies. There is a certain irony that as the socio-legal position of many of the language groups treated herein improves, the actual range of social contexts within which the target language is used becomes rather attenuated, forcing language promoters to adopt a more tempered and qualified stance. Nevertheless, in the more promising circumstances there is a cautious optimism that an effective system of language governance can offer an institutional bridge to a more democratic, inclusive and purposeful treatment of long-beleaguered language minorities.

ACKNOWLEDGEMENT

I acknowledge the help received from Canadian friends, in particular colleagues at the Universities of Western Ontario, Toronto, Laval and Ottawa. Rob Dunbar provided many of the Canadian language statistics. I also want to thank the British Association for Canadian Studies, the Canadian Studies in Wales Group, the Quebec Délégation Général in London and the many public officials in Canada who agreed to be interviewed and share their insights on the operation of language policy.

REFERENCES

Baubock, R. (2000) 'Why stay together: a pluralist approach to secession and federation', in W. Kymlicka and W. Norman (eds), *Citizenship in Diverse Societies*, Oxford: Oxford University Press.

Berman, P. (2004) *Terror and Liberalism*. New York: W. W. Norton & Co.

Bogadnor, V. (2003) *The British Constitution in the Twentieth Century*, Oxford: Oxford University Press.

Brecher, J. and Costello, R. (1994) *Global Village or Global Pillage: Economic Reconstruction from the Bottom Up*, Cambridge, MA: South End Press.

Dahrendorf, R. (2005) *Back to the Politics of Cultural Despair*. available at *www.project-syndicate.org*. London: Project Syndicate.

Denters, B. and Rose, L. E. (2005a) 'Local governance in the third millennium: a brave new world?' in B. Denters and L. E. Rose (2005), *Comparing Local Governance*, Basingstoke: Palgrave, pp. 1–11.

Denters, B. and Rose, L. E. (2005b) 'Towards local governance?' in B. Denters and L. E. Rose (2005), *Comparing Local Governance*, Basingstoke: Palgrave, pp. 246–62.

Drapeau, L. (1998) 'Aboriginal languages: current status', in J. Edwards (ed.), *Language in Canada*,. Cambridge: Cambridge University Press.

Edwards, T. C. (1989) *The Welsh Laws*, Cardiff: University of Wales Press.

Edwards, T. C. (1992) 'The pastoral role of the church in the early Irish laws', in J. Blair and R. Sharpe (eds), *Pastoral Care Before the Parish*, Leicester: Leicester University Press.

Edwards, T. C. (1993) *Early Irish and Welsh Kinship*, Oxford: Oxford University Press.

Edwards, T. C. (ed.) (2003) *After Rome*, Oxford: Oxford University Press.

Fenton, S. and May, S. (eds) (2002) *Ethnonational Identities*, Basinstoke: Palgrave.

Harff, B. and Gurr, T. R. (2004) *Ethnic Conflict in World Politics*, Boulder: Westview.

Haynes, J. (2005) *Comparative Politics in a Globalizing World*, Cambridge: Polity Press.

Hepburn, A. C. (ed.) (1978) *Minorities in History*, London: Arnold.

Held, D. and McGrew, A. (eds) (2003) *Governing Globalization*, Cambridge: Polity Press.

Isle of Man Census Report 2001 (2002) *Volume 2, Economic Affairs Division*, Douglas: Isle of Man Government Treasury, March 2002, pp. 37–8, available at http://www.gov.im/lib/docs/treasury/economic/census/reportvolume2.pdf.

Kagan, R. (2003) *Paradise and Power. America and Europe in the New World Order*, London: Atlantic Books.

Kymlicka, W. (1995) *The Rights of Minority Cultures*, Oxford: Oxford University Press.

Kymlicka, W. and Patten, A. (eds) (2003) *Language Rights and Political Theory*, Oxford: Oxford University Press.

Leach, P. and Percy-Smith, J. (2001) *Local Governance in Britain*, Basingstoke: Palgrave.

Lo Bianco, J. (2005) *International Issues in Languages Policy*, Edinburgh: Scottish CILT.

Loughlin, J. (1999) *Regional and Local Democracy in the EU*, Luxembourg: Office for Official Publications of the European Communities.

MacCaluim, A. and McLeod, W. (2001) *Revitalising Gaelic?* Edinburgh: Celtic Studies Edinburgh University.

MacKinnon, K. (2003) *Gaelic Analysis and Graphical Illustration for Comunn na Gàidhlig*. Black Isle: SGRÙD Research.

Manitoba Language Rights (1985) *Manitoba Language Rights Reference* (1985) S. C. R., Ottawa: Supreme Court.

Marquand, D. (2004) *Decline of the Public*, Cambridge: Polity Press.

National Assembly for Wales (2003) *Iaith Pawb: A National Action Plan for a Bilingual Wales*, Cardiff: Welsh Assembly Government.

Newman, W. J. (2004) 'Understanding language rights, equality and the *Charter*: towards a comprehensive theory of constitutional interpretation', *National Journal of Constitutional Law*, 363, 1–15.

Payton, P. (2000) 'Cornish', in G. Price (ed.), *Languages in Britain and Ireland*, Oxford: Blackwell, pp. 109–1.

Philipson, R. (2003) *English-only Europe?* London: Routledge.

Quebec Secession Reference (1998) *Reference re Secession of Quebec* (1998) 2 S. C. R. 217, Ottawa: Supreme Court.

Reid, T. R. (2004) *The United States of Europe: The New Superpower and the End of American Supremacy*, New York: The Penguin Press.

Roseneau, J. N. (2003) 'Governance in a new global order', in D. Held and A. McGrew (eds), *Governing Globalization*, Cambridge: Polity Press, pp. 70–86.

Scholte, J. A. (2000) *Globalization: A Critical Introduction,* Basingstoke: Palgrave.

Scotland's Census 2001 (2003) The Registrar General's Report to the Scottish Parliament, available at http://www.gro-scotland.gov.uk/grosweb/grosweb.nsf/pages/file5/$file/rg_report_parliament.pdf, Edinburgh: The Scottish Parliament.

Statistics Canada, (2003a) *Aboriginal Peoples of Canada: A Demographic Profile*, 2001 Census: Analysis Series, Ottawa: Ministry of Industry.

Statistics Canada (2003b) *Profile of Languages in Canada: English, French and many others*, 2001 Census: Analysis Series, Ottawa: Ministry of Industry.

Taylor, C. (1989) *Sources of the Self: The Making of Modern Identity*, Cambridge, MA: Harvard University Press.

Woods, N. (2002) 'Global governance and the role of institutions', in D. Held and A. McGrew (eds), *Governing Globalization*, Cambridge: Polity Press, pp. 25–45.

Williams, C. H. (ed.) (2000) *Language Revitalization. Policy and Planning in Wales*, Cardiff: University of Wales Press.

Williams, C. H. (2003) 'Language, law and politics', in W. J. Morgan and S. Livingstone (eds), *Law and Opinion in Twentieth-century Britain and Ireland*. Basingstoke and New York: Palgrave Macmillan. pp. 109–40.

Williams, C. H. (2005) *Ymateb Colin Williams i Ddeddf Iaith Newydd: Dyma'r Cyfle,* Aberystwyth: Cymdeithas yr Iaith.

2
The Challenge of Language Equality

RHODRI MORGAN

It is a pleasure to provide a chapter in this volume, which has developed from the interchange of ideas initiated at the Language and Governance Conference held at Cardiff in November 2001 and continued in successive conferences in Canada and the UK. The first conference was an unparalleled opportunity to compare experiences and expertise in the field of language and governance on an international level. It was also extremely timely in terms of policy development, in informing the National Assembly for Wales's Culture and Education Committees' review of language policy and *Iaith Pawb*, the Welsh government's language policy document which appeared as a result of this review.

The present foundation of our statutory language policy in Wales is the Welsh Language Act (1993), which establishes the principle of language equality in public life. There is a need to examine a little of the background to language policy in order to understand why language equality is so much of a challenge in Wales.

The Acts of Union of England and Wales 1536 to 1543 included a clause which, more or less, forbade Welsh-speakers from holding legal or administrative posts. This meant that English was the official language although Welsh was the language of more than 90 per cent of the population. This, therefore, set the tone for the following centuries, with Welsh having a subordinate official status, and the gentry and the ruling classes turning their backs on the language whilst Welsh still remained the language of the majority of the population.

The advent of the industrial revolution, with Wales at its forefront, saw immigration on a large scale throughout the nineteenth century. This is what created Cardiff. The arrival of the industrial revolution meant that there was no need to migrate on a large scale as was the case with Irish- and Gaelic-speakers. But, by 1901, only 50 per cent of the population, approximately one million people, spoke Welsh. The total of one million Welsh-speakers at the time, of course, was much higher than the total of speakers a century earlier in 1801. The increase in the numbers of speakers enabled the Welsh language to sustain books and magazines, unlike at any time previously. But the decline in the percentage of Welsh-speakers contained dangers for the future of the language. This is the reason for the debate that is continuing today with regard to the contribution of the industrial revolution: was it positive or negative for the fate of the Welsh language? Another more recent factor that was dividing the language was the presence of the television in every family home. Welsh was seen to be inferior and economically worthless by many, but clearly not by all for the language continued to be used in more limited functions. English was the language 'to get ahead in the world'. English was the language of the education system from the official beginning in the 1870s. A consistent decline was seen in the percentage of Welsh-speakers throughout the twentieth century; this occurred as a result of a number of factors, such as the low official status afforded to the Welsh language, substantial immigration and migration as occurred during the depression in the 1930s.

Notwithstanding this pattern of decline, in the last quarter of the century, and in a number of areas, there was a change for the better in the profile and the status of the Welsh language. Driving this change was the demand from parents for education through the medium of Welsh, something that is continuing to grow and develop throughout Wales. The language movement gave rise to other important changes. The 1967 Welsh Language Act gave parity to the Welsh language in some restricted areas such as the use of Welsh in the legal system, whilst the establishment of a state Welsh-language television channel in 1982 gave credibility and a 'young profile' to the language in, arguably, the most important medium of all. The 1990 Education Act reinforced the Welsh language's position and established it as a core part of the curriculum throughout Wales. Then, in 1993, another Welsh Language Act was passed which established a statutory Welsh Language Board whose function was to promote the use of Welsh in the public sector and, in legal terms at least, gave equal status to Welsh and English in public life in Wales.

Perhaps any legislation is a product of its time and circumstances, and this was certainly the case with the 1993 Act. One of the main considerations of the Act was to make good the injustice done to the minority without raising the hackles of the majority. Arguably, taking measures beyond what the country was ready for could have caused problems and a negative reaction. It was also important that the Act was flexible, in order to acknowledge the vast variations in the situation of the language, in different areas of Wales.

The result was a uniquely Welsh model, which grew organically from what was happening in Wales at the time. The Act established the principle of 'treating both languages on the basis that they were equal', but this principle comes to life only through Welsh-language schemes. Public bodies have to prepare a scheme which explains how they will implement the principle when conducting public business in Wales. The Act places responsibilities on bodies rather than giving rights to the individual. This is frustrating for some individuals. But in the context of trying to build a consensus about the language, it was much better to follow this direction. I argue that it would not have been good to see the Welsh language as a bone of contention in the courts all the time, as this would have polarized opinion rather than create harmony.

The flexibility of the 1993 Act is reflected in the resultant schemes. Every organization prepares its own unique scheme which gives effect to the principle of equality 'as far as it is appropriate under the circumstances and is reasonably practicable'. Therefore, the schemes which are negotiated with and subsequently approved by the Welsh Language Board are designed to reflect the bilingual services offered by an organization.

The 1993 Act reflects the language challenge which faces us in Wales. Whilst one in five are able to speak Welsh, nearly everyone in Wales is able to speak English, the most widely spoken language in the world and the language of business and popular culture. They have access to services in English, and every Welsh-speaker is bilingual. Therefore, in practice, there was, and there is, no language equality in Wales. This is the fundamental and awesome challenge which faces us, and the 1993 Act was a practical step to transforming practices and attitudes.

To date, over 353 Welsh-language schemes have been approved by the Welsh Language Board and the position of Welsh in the sector has been transformed, over a ten-year period. This is certainly a positive step for the Welsh language but it must be borne in mind that a change in attitude and language balance is no minor matter. The demographic reality of Welsh-speakers' being in a minority within a country which experiences significant amounts of both immigration and outmigration, and practices which have been formed over decades, if not centuries, have meant that there is inequality, and that the Act on its own cannot change this situation. To this end, the Welsh Language Board has undertaken various activities to support and promote the Welsh language in every sector and across all ages throughout Wales, and has done this by aiming to take the non-Welsh-speaking population with it.

There are positive indications that, as a government, we are succeeding in this and are developing a general consensus and widespread support for the language. For example, in 2000, the Welsh Language Board commissioned a survey which said that 83 per cent of those questioned stated that the Welsh language was something of which everyone in Wales could be proud; 80 per cent stated that the Welsh language belonged to everyone in Wales. It is vitally important to retain this goodwill. For a long time, Welsh has been considered as something which could separate us. I am confident that this old fault line has decreased – it is important that we create respect for diversity and use the language to bring people together.

Of course, since the 1993 Welsh Language Act was passed, the constitutional and political situation has been transformed with limited self-government and the establishment of the National Assembly in 1999. What will be the long-term effects of devolution on language and language equality in Wales? There are two hypotheses. The first is that devolution will weaken the Welsh language. The basis for this hypothesis is that devolution means that Welsh people will not be as dependent on the language as a means of expressing their separate identity. There are echoes of this in the experiences of Ireland and Scotland. Religion in the former and national institutions in the latter fulfilled the same requirement with the result that the native languages were neglected.

However, I agree with the second hypothesis, namely that devolution is providing – and will provide – a new momentum for the language. The evidence to date fully supports this opinion. It is certain that devolution has raised the profile of the Welsh language in public life. The devolution statute, Government of Wales Act (1998), complements the principle of equality between English and Welsh in the work of the Assembly, and Welsh is visible and audible in the work of the Assembly. This is all-important in emphasizing the relevance of Welsh in the world of work and in public life in Wales. It is also worth emphasizing that constitutional reform has virtually reinvented Welsh as a language of law and government administration as was demonstrated so well in Rawlings *Delineating Wales,* (2003).

However, my feeling as First Minister is that what is more important than all of this is the contribution that the National Assembly and the Welsh Assembly Government has made to the development of a language policy in Wales. In the Assembly's first term (1999–2003), the Assembly Government published *Iaith Pawb*, its national action plan for a Bilingual Wales. This was developed as a result of a valuable review of the Welsh Language by the cross-party Assembly Culture and Education Committees over the period of a year. This review was a means of having a mature and constructive debate and aimed to develop a political consensus about the direction that a language policy should take at the start of a new century.

Iaith Pawb is an all-important step for language policy in Wales (see chapter 15 below). It is a definitive statement of political commitment and is totally clear about the Assembly Government's vision, namely to create a Wales that is truly bilingual. For the first time, also, we see the government dealing with the field of language policy in an holistic way and being committed to ensuring that the Welsh language is being considered across all areas of work of the Assembly. It is only by exploring all aspects which affect the language, such as the economy, housing, planning and education, that we ensure a thriving future for the Welsh language in the context of the forces of globalization. The needs of the Welsh language and the implications for the Welsh language will be core considerations for new policies and initiatives, be they in the field of education, health, agriculture etc., and *Iaith Pawb* indicates clearly the necessary steps which will be taken to support the Welsh language across a wide range of the Assembly Government's work and that of its major partners.

One of the main themes of *Iaith Pawb* is to promote the use of Welsh. The 2001 census is quite positive about Welsh, with approximately 600,000 of the Welsh-domiciled population indicating that they can speak Welsh. This increase since the 1991 results suggests that we have reversed the decline of the Welsh language, but our work is only just beginning. It is vitally important that we promote and enable people to use the Welsh language in all aspects of the nation's life and in our communities, and this is reflected throughout *Iaith Pawb*. As a government, we also stress the importance of creating opportunities to learn the language, by building on our foundations in the field of education and promoting Welsh and its use amongst our young people. Hand in hand with applying the Welsh Language Act to its maximum power by extending it to the utilities such as the former publically owned gas, water and electricity providers, it is vitally important that we support community activity which will strengthen the position of the Welsh language through the work of the Mentrau Iaith (local language enterprise agencies) and the Urdd (the Welsh League of Youth). The emphasis which the Assembly Government is placing on this policy is being reflected in the significant additional investment in the funding which is used to support Welsh. The budget of the Welsh Language Board has been doubled over the past three-year period to £16 million per annum and there is significant investment in the promotion of Welsh in other fields such as education and the arts.

There are obvious advantages to bilingualism, both in terms of allowing people to choose between alternative cultures and in gaining valuable linguistic and communicative skills, and it is important that we convey those advantages, and create the opportunities for people to avail themselves of the language, in order to secure the growth of the language. The challenge of doing this, in the face of international linguistic tendencies is enormous, but I am confident that as a government we can play a leading role in ensuring language equality and a bright future for the Welsh language in every part of Wales.

In this regard, it is important to realize that many countries and languages throughout the world face the same challenges as Welsh, and that we all benefit from the development of international linguistic planning. There is a wealth of information, research, innovation and good practice in the field. It is important that we share this and to this end the original conference and the subsequent meetings which have informed the discussions in this volume were an important catalyst. I feel that we, in Wales, should continue to benefit from the experience and expertise of other places. And, in the same way, we are keen to contribute our experiences to others. In this regard, I am extremely proud of the role that Wales plays within the British–Irish Council by taking the lead role in the work of native and minority languages, and the praiseworthy work of the Welsh Language Board on a European level also offers firm foundations for policy development in Wales. I know that the comparative discussions held in and since the Cardiff conference – which are the basis of this volume – will be profitable and challenging, and I have pleasure in recommending this volume and encourage more cooperation in the future in this vitally important field.

3
Language and Governance in Canada: The Role of the Commissioner of Official Languages

DR. DYANE ADAM

Language Rights: The Canadian Experience

With its two official languages and extensive experience in language planning, and as a member of both the Commonwealth and francophonie families of countries, I believe Canada has much to contribute to the study, definition and implementation of language policies. In so doing, I fully recognize that the Canadian model of language management is probably not exportable.

In a sense, Canada was born a bilingual country. Our founders rejected the traditional model of the nation-state, which still governed our two mother countries and most of Europe in the nineteenth century, to embrace the idea of a federation based on respect for diversity and accommodation of differences. In 1867, when the largely French-speaking province of Quebec and the largely English-speaking provinces of Nova Scotia, New Brunswick and Ontario joined to form the Canadian Confederation, both languages were allowed in our first Parliament and in federal courts, as well as in the Quebec legislature and Quebec courts.

As Canada grew, absorbing new provinces and territories, this concept remained the basis of our federation. This is not to say, however, that language rights evolved naturally and smoothly throughout our history. There were many instances of popular resistance or official indifference and even some setbacks when acquired rights were withdrawn in certain provinces. But since confederation to this day, minority language communities across our vast country have expressed a strong determination to protect, preserve and develop their own cultures while striving towards common goals. In fact, every generation of Canadians has had to contend with the challenge of making room for the two founding languages within their national institutions and within Canadian society.

The Official Languages Act, introduced in Parliament in October 1968 and adopted the following year, included provisions to establish the status of English and French as the official languages of Canada and set out for the first time the language rights of citizens in their dealings with Parliament, the federal government and federal institutions and the duties of those institutions toward the citizen in matters of language. Another major advance toward the equality of the two languages came from the proclamation of the Canadian Charter of Rights and Freedoms in 1982, which accompanied the patriation of our constitution from Great Britain. From then on, the equality of French and English in federal institutions was rooted in the very constitution of the country, whereas the principles contained in the Official Languages Act were seen by many as generous ideals rather than legal requirements.

The Office of the Commissioner of Official Languages

The fundamental objectives and underlying principles of a new official languages policy, then, were clearly set out and duly legislated. Their implementation, however, rested on untested instruments. One of these was the Office of the Commissioner of Official Languages, created by the 1969 Act, with the following mandate:

> To take all actions and measures within the authority of the Commissioner with a view to ensuring recognition of the status of each of the official languages and compliance with the spirit and intent of this Act in the administration of the affairs of federal

institutions, including any of their activities relating to the advancement of English and French in Canadian society.

Like my four predecessors, when I was appointed in 1999 I saw my first duty as responding to specific violations of language rights within my stated mandate. This is still the most important part of my mandate. But investigation and redress of individual complaints cannot be carried out in a narrow, isolated manner when one is charged with such a broad mandate. That is why I have sought to use the hundreds of complaints filed each year to create momentum for change. Investigations into violations of language rights must address the very root of the violations in order to achieve lasting solutions, and to resolve especially complex problems a comprehensive study of their causes and ramifications may be in order. In the case of recurring complaints, I believe consultations should be held among interested parties to explore the possibility of using new methods.

My priority, then, has always been to perform the Commissioner's traditional role as an ombudsman with vigilance, but I also remain determined to expand this protective role and serve as an educator, to better inform the Canadian people of their rights, and to consolidate the place of linguistic duality at the heart of Canadian identity. In my view, only by effectively acting as both an agent of change and an ombudsman can the Commissioner of Official Languages fully address the three main objectives of the Official Languages Act, namely:

- the equality of English and French in Parliament, within the Government of Canada, the federal administration and institutions subject to the Act;
- the preservation and development of official language communities in Canada;
- the equality of English and French in Canadian society.

Can a Commissioner of Official Languages, even the most proactive one, hope to achieve these objectives single-handedly?

Of course not. Linguistic duality calls for a major commitment that involves promoting not only the equal status of the two official languages, but also the quality of services offered to the public in English and French, employees' ability to work in their preferred language in the public service, the equitable participation of both language groups in the public service, development of minority official language communities, and access to health and education services in both official languages. Since the growth and vitality of minority official language communities depend on so many factors – such as education, immigration, municipal services, health services and broadcasting – it follows that the government must necessarily adopt a coordinated approach.

In Canada, for example, our Department of Canadian Heritage oversees a broad programme involving all government departments and agencies to encourage the development of the official language minority communities: francophones outside Quebec and anglophones in Quebec. All federal departments are included in this programme, and all activities that fall under the priorities of the official language minority communities are eligible. These may include, among others, activities in arts and culture, economic development and tourism, human resources development, new technologies, and health and social services.The area of responsibility of the Canadian Commissioner of Official Languages is vast and varied. I think it is vital that the Commissioner be able to intervene on behalf of the greatest number of people, not only where they work, but also where they learn and live. Indeed, what sense would it make if official language minorities were allowed to use their native tongue while working in federal institutions but were prevented from doing so in their own community? In Canada, the particular situation of Quebec as the homeland of North America's only majority French-speaking population demands special attention. In a flexible and open federation, this situation can and must be addressed with understanding and a spirit of cooperation. In the last decade, for example, the Government of Canada has worked with Quebec to defend French language and culture, among other things, by signing agreements on immigration and manpower training.

While political leadership and administrative cooperation are indispensable, in my view, more – much more – is required to give the two official languages truly equal status in our society, simply because language is much more than a demographic or political reality. Language is the expression of a culture and a part of the common identity and heritage of all citizens of a federation. What is required is a collective effort and the Commissioner of Official Languages must exercise authority in stimulating and channelling this collective effort.

The 1988 Official Languages Act, which modernized and strengthened the first Official Languages Act, confirms the Commissioner's duty to be an agent of change. Going beyond institutional bilingualism, the Act now includes a formal commitment by the federal government 'to enhancing the vitality of the English and French linguistic minority communities in Canada and supporting and assisting their development; and fostering the full recognition and use of both English and French in Canadian society'. Such is, in a nutshell, the legal and constitutional framework within which the Canadian Commissioner of Official Languages operates, and that is how I see my mandate.

Future Challenges

There can be no doubt that this framework and the action of successive Commissioners of Official Languages allowed Canada to come a long way towards ensuring language equality for its citizens over the last thirty years.

Various numbers point to this reality; for example, the number of bilingual Canadians has doubled during that period. More important, attitudes have changed and at long last, for a new generation of Canadians, language is no longer seen as a barrier between communities but as a bridge between people. But we cannot take equality of linguistic opportunity for granted; nor can we avoid the profound structural changes that are transforming societies around the world. Societies evolve and languages evolve with them, more rapidly and more profoundly today than ever before. Most industrialized countries have experienced radical policy shifts, significant budget cuts, government restructuring, privatization, new trade agreements and greater reliance on information technologies as they have sought to adapt to the new global realities.

As new priorities emerge, it is crucial that we do not jettison hard-won rights and values, including language rights. This is vitally important for Canada, where our bilingual and multicultural character and our respect for our aboriginal heritage help to shelter us from domination by the powerful cultural influence of our American neighbour. The words 'vitality,' 'development' and 'fostering' are terms that call for action. The pervasiveness of the new media is also cause for concern when seen from a minority-language perspective.

It was a Canadian, Marshall McLuhan, who in the early 1960s predicted that we soon would all be living in a 'global village'. It is perhaps not surprising, then, that Canada is today the most 'wired' country in the world, where approximately five million Canadian households, or 40 per cent, have access to the Internet. I do not think that we can turn a blind eye to the effects of the new media on minority languages. Nor do I think we are powerless to intervene. For example, in 1999, my office published a special study urging the federal government to make a greater contribution to French-language content on the Internet. Since then, the government has taken a number of initiatives in this direction, and federal services will be available on the web everywhere in Canada in both official languages, regardless of how great the demand may be.

In conclusion, I fear that I might have raised more questions than I have provided answers. But I will be content if I have succeeded modestly in demonstrating that wherever we come from, wherever we live, we can act in favour of language equality and cultural vitality. Our mandates and means differ, but our responsibility is the same: we are the custodians of one of our respective countries' most precious legacy: their different languages. I believe we will not succeed if we see equality as only a legal or political question. It is above all a question of justice. We must be guided not only by the law but by the spirit of compromise and tolerance. In this there can be no better guide than the celebrated British historian Lord Acton, who wrote: ‘The most certain test by which we judge whether a country is really free is the amount of security enjoyed by minorities.’

4

Governance and Language: The Intellectual Foundations

JOHN LOUGHLIN AND COLIN H. WILLIAMS

Introduction

One of the major debates within contemporary social science surrounds the impact of globalization on a range of human activities, not the least of which is the practice of statecraft. Claims and counter-claims of the demise of the nation-state and the transformation of civil society in Europe by processes such as supra-national integration, advanced capitalism and the spread of instantaneous means of communication impact upon the formulation of public policy. Little of this discussion, however, has influenced the debate on the relationship between governance and language policy, especially those aspects which relate to so-called minority languages. We aim to contribute to filling this lack by focusing on four aspects of this relationship. First, we attempt a conceptual clarification of key terms such as governance and the transformation of civil society. Secondly, we describe a major reconfiguration of the state as it moves from the 'welfare' to the 'post-welfare' state, in which at times 'neo-liberal' elements and at other times 'communitarian' elements are dominant. Thirdly, we address the way in which each of these reconfigurations has dealt with issues related to minority-language representation in contradistinction to the promotion and defence of the hegemonic, state language. Finally, we explore the various opportunities and challenges for minority languages which are posed by the current transformation of the European state system. This chapter thus sets the intellectual context for the more detailed explorations of individual language-related experiences in the successive chapters which follow.

That the world economy has changed profoundly in recent decades is not subject to dispute. Clearly a transformation of sorts has occurred. But the claim that there is a specifically new kind of globalization which emerged at the beginning of the 1980s, and is profoundly modifying the nature of the nation-state, made by authors such as Cerny (1995), Held (1999), Habermas (2001) and Beck (2000) has been countered by influential authors such as Hirst and Thomson (1996), who assert that a form of globalization has been with us at least since the end of the nineteenth century, when capitalism had a truly global reach. Earlier writers, following Wallerstein's (1974, 1979) influential world-system theory, such as Knox and Agnew (1989), Williams (1986) and Taylor (1985), have examined the implications of globalization for the dynamics of the world economy and global–local relations and have confirmed that the nation-state has survived by transforming itself in the recent period. In similar vein, Garrett and Lange (1991) sought to show that, despite claims that the nation-state was no longer the most important arena of social and party mobilization, the 'partisan-ideological' thesis, that is, the continuing importance of Left–Right party competition within national political systems, still held up. Furthermore, the claim that accelerated European integration leads to a new kind of European governance system, as put forward by Gary Marks *et al.* (1996), Beate Kohler-Koch (1999) or Wallace and Wallace (2000), is countered by liberal intergovernmentalists, such as Andrew Moravcsik (1993) or Alan Milward (2000), who assert that this allegedly new system is scarcely more than a strong international regime which has modified but little the role of national governments and actors within national states. Yet again those who point to a new role for regions in a post-national and post-sovereign Europe such as Michael Keating (1998) or John Loughlin (2000; 2001) are countered by Patrick Le Galès and Christian Lequesne who deny that the region has any great significance and hold up instead the city as the key political unit of territorial politics (1998). In broader terms postmodernist authors such as Jean Baudrillard (1990) who point with approval to what they claim is the fragmentation of both epistemological and ontological dimensions of society are countered by Alain Touraine's critique of modernity (1992) or Peter Wagner's sociology of modernity (1994), who, while both accepting some of the postmodernist diagnosis, seek to rescue and update the concept of modernity itself.

Much of this literature fails to interpret exactly *what* has changed, *why* these changes, if any, have occurred, and *what* is their significance. Neither are the various conceptualizations of governance explained in any systematic way by the different dimensions of transformation whether cognitive or empirical. Indeed, the notion of transformation itself can be analysed in at least three different ways: as a patina of substantive change, as an Incremental Evolutionary Transformation (IET) and as a Revolutionary Transformation (Loughlin 2004). In short there is much disputation about the key concepts and paradigms we wish to employ in this volume, none more so than the central concern with governance.

Governance

Kooiman (1993) helps to clarify the conceptual difficulties raised by the term governance by distinguishing between the concepts of *governing*, *government* and *governance*. It is Incremental Evolutionary Transformation, that is, gradual tinkering and *bricolage*, punctuated by moments of epochal or paradigmatic change, that best describes the processes of change in Western capitalist states and it is probably this which is captured by the exploding number of 'governance' titles referred to above. 'Governance', like the term 'transformation', is often used in a vague and fuzzy way.

Government and governance are both ways of governing society yet while government relates to the forms associated with liberal representative democracy, the traditional state, governance involves a much wider set of actors, including elected politicians and public officials, but also various non-elected interest and pressure groups (Rhodes, 1997). The main thrust of the argument of governance theorists is that, as society becomes more complex and differentiated, the traditional method of governing from above – government – becomes more difficult. This leads to governance, understood as steering rather than directing, which it is claimed supplements or at times even replaces government. Governance is allegedly more bottom-up than top-down and involves a partnership between government and non-governmental elements of civil society. Within this same 'bottom-up' perspective, Rhodes asserts that 'governance refers to self-organizing, interorganizational networks' (1997: 53), which is distinct from government. Implicit in the arguments promoting governance is the notion of transformation: modes of governing go from simply government to a wider system of governance. Kohler-Koch (1999), in analysing the European Union as a political system, postulates an 'evolution and transformation' of the EU into a system of *network governance*. Comparing different kinds of states with each other and with the EU, she proposes a typology of modes of governance (Figure 4.1).

Figure 4:1: A typology of modes of governance

	–	**Organizing principle of political relations**	
	–	**Majority Rule**	**Consociation**
Constitutive logic of the polity			
	Common good	Statism	Corporatism
	Individual interests	Pluralism	Network governance

Source: Beate Kohler-Koch (1999).

In this schema, which combines typologies elaborated by Lijphart and Lehmbruch, systems of governing may be categorized as being organized according to basic principles: the way in which political relations are organized – majority rule or consociation (Lijphart) and the way in which the basic logic of the polity is conceptualized – according to a principle of the common good or of individual interests (Lembruch). This leads to a matrix of four possible modes of governance each with its own country or system exemplar: statism (France); corporatism (Switzerland and Germany); pluralism (United States); and network governance (EU). Kohler-Koch's typology is useful both in so far as it illustrates that there exists a variety of state traditions and also that the EU is not simply a system of governance *sui generis* but can be analysed comparatively in the context of these state traditions. She also argues that governance coexists with government, in contrast to approaches that suggest that governance is replacing it. What is not clear, however, is whether 'network governance', which characterizes the EU, is also becoming predominant within the national systems. In other words, is it at least modifying French statism, Anglo-American pluralism and German or Dutch corporatism? We argue here that all states have been subjected to common pressures which have indeed led to a certain convergence, but that this has also been shaped by the traditional modes of governance: statism, consociationalism, or pluralism.

It might be argued that governance has always been part of government in the sense that there have always been interest groups from outside the official political system involved in policy-making. The vast body of literature devoted to the policy sciences, policy analysis and policy communities and, indeed, the debates on relations of political power which have involved elitists, pluralists, Marxists and neo-corporatists, were all concerned with what is now referred to as governance. The key question is how they relate to each other and whether we are now experiencing a new *configuration*, or even a paradigm shift in the relationships between government and governance, state and economy, state and civil society. A reconfiguration occurs when both the cognitive and empirical elements of one paradigm are replaced by another – an epochal change, in Cerny's term. Such a reconfiguration also affects the mode of governance, as it redefines the role and nature of government and its relationship with the wider civil society.

We can identify at least two significant reconfigurations within this global transformation. The first was the setting up of welfare states during the period which the French call the *Trente Glorieuses* (1945–75); the second occurred following the hegemony of the neoliberal model, which seriously challenged the welfare state model and has led to what we might term 'post-welfare states', which is characterized by a variety of forms. The contending paradigms seek to explicate the interrelationships between state, market and society and their respective implementation of key concepts of democratic theory and practice such as sovereignty, responsibility, and accountability. Each paradigm also implies a particular understanding of public policy, public administration and the nature of institutions. All of these elements add up to what we have defined as governance.

The Welfare State Model

Although the welfare state predates the period following the Second World War and has its roots in the programmes of the nineteenth-century Bismarkian state, the policies of the British Liberals at the turn of nineteenth and twentieth centuries, and the 1930s Swedish Social Democrats, it established its hegemony as part of the post-war political, social and economic reconstruction of western Europe. The welfare state was accepted by both moderate social democratic or labour parties and centre-right conservative and Christian Democratic parties. Crouch (1999) has dubbed this the 'mid-century consensus'.

It was accepted by most elites, as well as by civil society generally, that the state not only could but also *ought* to intervene in the economy and civil society in a Keynesian approach to economic governance. Empirically, during this period, everything was expanding: the economy, citizen's needs and the policy programmes, administration and public spending designed to meet those needs. This led to the development of a particular kind of state whose characteristics were: centralization to assist redistribution, standardization to ensure equality, and a bureaucratization of civil and economic life. Welfare state governance thus became typified as elitist, neo-corporatist and top-down (Lehmbruch and Schmitter, 1982), and represented the culmination of the nation-state as the political system most closely associated with modernity within a liberal, representative democracy (Touraine, 1992; Habermas, 2001). According to Wagner (1994), it was the final phase of 'organised modernity', as opposed to the 'liberal modernity' of the nineteenth and early twentieth centuries. In its ulterior form, modernity was 'organized' by state forces unable to tolerate the disruptive potentialities of 'liberal' modernity as found in the explosion of market forces in the nineteenth and early twentieth centuries, which Polanyi labelled 'the Great Transformation' (1957).

Yet the functional operation of the welfare state produced critiques from both the left and the right. The most systematic critique from the left came from the Frankfurt School led by Adorno (1969), Horkheimer (1972) and Marcuse (1972). This was based on the notion that 'organized modernity' suffocated the human spirit and produced 'one-dimensional man', subject to bureaucratic pressures and reduced to a state of passivity. These critiques especially that of Marcuse, eventually fed into the student revolts of the 1960s and were important elements in the later partial disintegration of 'organized modernity' and the emergence of 'postmodernism'. The left-wing critique of welfarist modernity would not have rejected the role of the state as such, but rather this kind of centralized and bureaucratic state.

The more telling critique derived from the New Right, a form of right-wing libertarianism, with a stinging attack involving economic (Friedman, 1961), bureaucratic (Niskanen, 1971) and philosophical (Nozick, 1974), analyses directed at the state itself. Such authors claimed that welfare states were ultimately 'ungovernable' and stifled the freedom and entrepreneurial spirit necessary for human beings to realize their full social and economic potential. Thus, during the period of welfare state pre-eminence, three main competing models coexisted, namely the welfare state of the moderate labour and conservative movements, the left-wing libertarianism of the New Left, and the right-wing libertarianism of the New Right.

Offe (1984) claims that these critiques from both left and right were rooted in a similar analysis of 'the contradictions of the Welfare State', being based on the notion that it is impossible to realize both bourgeois democracy *and* ever-increasing welfare provisions. However, the model experienced a serious crisis at the end of the 1960s and the beginning of the 1970s. This involved a weakening of confidence in the 'fordist' capitalist methods of production, which, coupled with the oil crisis of 1973, led to an economic crisis which the Keynesian approach was incapable of solving. This put even greater strains on the welfare state as unemployment rocketed; industrial production plummeted, producing an important fiscal crisis of the state.

One response to the crisis derived from what we may call, perhaps retrospectively, the 'neo-liberal movement' which greatly influenced the administrative and industrial elites still in control of the economic and political systems. While the May 68ers were experimenting with being *homo ludens,* those at the centre of power were being won over to the arguments of the neo-liberals. Meanwhile, society itself was undergoing profound social and economic transformations to the extent that, as Mendras (1984) argues, traditional social classes and even 'social movements' in Touraine's meaning of the term ceased to exist. The end result, which occurred between the mid-1970s and the early 1980s, was the gradual replacement of the hegemony of the welfare state with an emerging neo-liberal paradigm.

In all welfare state systems, state, market and society are, theoretically, *congruent* but with the state dominant and, to some extent, attempting to control in a top-down manner society and market. Sovereignty is also theoretically exercised in an absolute manner by central governments on behalf of their national populations within clearly defined territorial boundaries. In Hirschman's terms, *exit* opportunities are reduced (that is opportunities to escape across borders), *loyalty* is emphasized and *voice* is encouraged (Hirschman, 1970). This closure was the culmination of processes of nation-state building that had begun at least two centuries earlier. Governance, during this period, might be described as hierarchical, top-down and technocratic, flowing from the operation of the state as the dominant actor, which corresponds to Kohler-Koch's category of statist governance (figure 4.1). This is true of all welfare states even if the institutional expression is consistent with each state's particular political culture and state tradition.

The Post-Welfare State

Although the welfare state model of the state took different forms, there were a certain number of underlying principles and features that all welfare states held in common, closely related to the Beveridgian and Keynesian models of social and economic policy respectively: equity and equality for both individuals and territories and, to achieve these, a high degree of centralization and uniformity. The Keynesian/Beveridgian state, however, came under pressure from a number of directions. First, it found itself incapable of maintaining the level of services to which citizens had become accustomed. This was exacerbated by the economic crises of the late 1960s and the oil crisis of 1973, which led to a new economic phenomenon: stagnation *and* inflation (stagflation) as well as rapidly rising unemployment. All of this put enormous strains on public finances. Secondly, there were the rapid changes associated with globalization and the rise of new technologies, as well as accelerated European integration, which can be seen as ways by which international capital responded to the economic crises. But globalization meant that national governments were no longer capable of exercising sovereignty in such a pristine manner as in times past. Increasing areas of public policy slipped from their grasp and sovereignty became an increasingly empty concept, whether it was understood as referring to the position of national governments in international relations or to the exercise of internal control within the boundaries of the state. What had been perceived as a zero-sum game – exclusive definitions of identity, citizenship and sovereignty – increasingly became viewed as positive-sum– multiple identity, joint citizenship and shared sovereignty. Thirdly, in western Europe, while the European Union took over many core functions, there was also a general phenomenon of regionalization and decentralization, at least in the larger states, as central governments were incapable of performing the many tasks expected of them (Loughlin, 2001). Governance became more complex as society itself diversified from the highly stratified and structured version of the 1950s and early 1960s to one that was more fragmented and atomized. This in turn led to the rise of single-issue campaigns, and their attendant actors, together with a new recomposition of political movements and parties which have been forced to rethink and reformulate their political projects. The old left/right cleavage is now less relevant as new issues and concerns have emerged that are mainly about lifestyle or identity issues which tend to overshadow the traditional concerns with deep structural questions involving the organization of the state and society.

We sometimes label the dominant political ideology of this period as 'neo-liberalism', although at the time it is unlikely that the new politicians such as Reagan and Thatcher had a clearly formulated ideological agenda. 'Neo-liberalism', rather, evolved in a piecemeal and ad hoc manner in response to the challenges of the time. But, in what eventually became the neo-liberal paradigm of governance, the *market* was dominant and market-based approaches have been increasingly introduced into public administration and policy. The state was reduced to 'facilitating', or 'steering', and governance is now seen as a bottom-up, pluralistic process involving a myriad of groups. In effect, the new governance corresponds closely to Kohler-Koch's *pluralist* mode of governance and is similar to Esping-Anderson's (1990) Anglo-American form of welfare capitalism. However, the new neo-liberal governance is different from these in that it operates in a very different political, economic and ideological context from that which prevailed during the heyday of the welfare state. This is a world of economic, social and cultural globalization, deregulation and open borders. To a large extent, then, the new governance has been imposed by necessity on nation-states, but they in turn have sought to welcome it as a means of easing the burdens of governing.

The 'Third Way' State Paradigm

While experiments in neo-liberal governance spread across the developed world, it also influenced many of the states of Latin America and the newer post-Soviet states in the 1980s and early 1990s. During the 1980s and 1990s, a series of irreversible reforms, inspired by neo-liberal approaches, and supported by international organizations such as the OECD, the World Bank and the International Monetary Fund, were implemented in most countries. These included privatization, deregulation, regional pacts which lowered tariff barriers (as with NAFTA) and abolished frontiers (as in the Schengen group of the EU) and reforms of public administration which was opened up to internal competition and in effect adopted a new operating culture.

Nevertheless, neo-liberalism was not universally accepted and, indeed, the political left and some of the political centre actively opposed it. The response was what came to be called the 'Third Way', most strongly espoused by the UK Prime Minister Tony Blair and his Chancellor of the Exchequer Gordon Brown but already present in President Clinton's reinventing government movement and given some intellectual respectability by authors such as Amitai Etzioni (1993) and Anthony Giddens (2000) who differ in their interpretation of the 'Third Way'. The notion of a Third Way is, however, far older and traceable to the intellectual roots of Christian Democracy, to Catholic social philosophy, which sought to find a third or middle way between the totalitarian systems of communism and fascism and the individualistic capitalism of the 1930s (Hanley, 1994). In Wales this Catholic philosophical tradition influenced Saunders Lewis, the founder of Plaid Cymru, and a convert to Catholicism after his experiences in France as a soldier during the First World War. The Plaid vision of Wales as a 'community of communities' is also related to Catholic philosophy although there are clearly strong influences also from nonconformist Protestantism.

The German social market of the 1950s and 1960s and the Dutch 'polder model' might also be seen as examples of a third way between market and state-dominated approaches or between balanced public and private sectors. These older versions would not have fully accepted the role of the market popularized by contemporary neo-liberalism. Today's version of the Third Way, however, accepts the irreversibility of the neo-liberal reforms, while at the same time attempts to add a social, communitarian or solidaristic elements to these. European socialists and social democrats such as Jospin and Schröder have also felt it necessary to elaborate their own 'national' versions of the Third Way. Jospin's would accept more state intervention than Blair's while Schröder's would be more concerned to preserve some of the *acquis* of the welfare state. All, however, accept some injection of market principles into these systems. In Spain, the centre-right government of Aznar was ideologically not so far removed from Blair's New Labour and the British Tories and US Republicans are today speaking of 'compassionate conservatism'. In essence, then, the various third ways seem to be attempts to bring together once again state, market and society but this time with a greater emphasis on 'society'.

A crucial difference between these attempts and the earlier pre-war and immediate post-war third ways is that society itself has been fundamentally transformed. Then, there were recognizable social classes with reasonably clearly defined roles in the system of production. Today, social classes have been transformed into 'constellations' (Mendras, 1994), families, although still the most common form of human cohabitation have become less patriarchal and are now more democratic (Giddens, 2000), while the old rural and working-class communities have given way to less cohesive groupings of residents. There is today a new individualism and a willingness to tolerate living arrangements that were execrated in the past. It is this new societal context that has necessitated the 'new governance' as governments try to find public policy approaches which can respond to its complexity. At the same time, both progressives and conservatives are worried that social fragementation has gone too far and wish to rebuild 'community', despite the ambiguities surrounding this term. The third way approaches fit into this communitarian perspective. This is a sea change when compared to the heyday of neo-liberalism under Mrs Thatcher, who thought that 'society' did not exist, only families and individuals. None of these approaches is completely free of contradictions as both Thatcherite neo-liberalism and Blairite Third Wayism have encouraged the freedom of individuals and neither has been particularly friendly to the traditional family.

The Third Way approaches are different from the neo-liberal paradigm and are not simply neo-liberalism dressed in fancy social democratic clothes. This becomes clear when we examine the mode of governance that is associated with them. Neo-liberalism attempted to reduce or marginalize the state and to give predominance to the market. It tended to deny the existence of society and concentrated on entrepreneurial individuals. The new approach accepts the market but gives an important role to the state, albeit one that is based on 'facilitatation' and partnership rather than top-down interventionism. It also accepts the reality of 'society'. Thus, the relationships between the three entities of state, market and society are reconfigured differently from either the welfare state or the neo-liberal models and are based the principles of partnership and subsidiarity. In Kohler-Koch's model, this is called *network governance*, but, in our conception, it is a feature of governance within member states as well as within the European Union.

Is there any evidence to support this argument? It could be argued that in the UK, one of the originators of the neo-liberal model, the reforms that were carried out by the Blair government are very much along the lines outlined in the previous paragraphs: devolution to Scotland and Wales and, possibly in the future, to the English regions; the power-sharing arrangements in Northern Ireland and between the Republic of Ireland and the UK; the reforms of local government, all along the lines of partnership and subsidiarity are very different from what could have happened under the previous Tory governments. In Italy, significant reforms are taking place to improve regional and local democracy. In France, there have been important reforms and experimentation also at local government level and decentralization has entered a new phase. In Spain, several of the Autonomous Communities are experimenting with local democratic participation. Ireland's economic miracle is largely based on this partnership approach. The European Union itself is promoting 'network governance' through programmes such as LEADER (the rural development programme). One could multiply examples.

Of course, it is also possible to argue that the neo-liberal reforms were less radical than is being claimed here and that, in practice, they were in fact what we have just described. We accept that the neo-liberal programme was never fully implemented nor, perhaps, could it have been. Nevertheless, it did exist at the level of discourse, of analysis and of political ideology and it did have real effects in the transformation of political and policy systems. What has changed is the discourse, which has been replaced by the programme outlined above and this, in turn, is the basis of further experimentation and reform in policy and administration. What has also changed is the context with a quite different economic, social and geopolitical situation today compared to the early 1980s. Thus, although much more empirical research is needed, it is argued that real transformations have occurred and are still taking place.

Explaining the Transformations

The notion of Incremental Evolutionary Transformation, with long periods of *bricolage* punctuated by shorter-term more fundamental paradigmatic is a good description of the changes outlined above. The question remains: what has brought about these changes? Epochal change occurs when there are contradictory forces at work which undermine either the legitimacy or the effectiveness of a given set of political, administrative and social institutions. These underlying forces are usually new forms of economic activity and relationships that are best served by particular forms of organization and which other forms hinder. Spruyt (1994) argues that, in the fourteenth and fifteenth centuries, the new economics of trade and urban development was hindered by the older feudal system, as well as by the Holy Roman Empire and the papacy. The three more 'modern' forms of political organization were the city-states, the city-leagues and the sovereign territorial state (the forerunner of the modern nation-state). In fact, it was the latter which proved in the end victorious as best suited to the emerging forces of mercantile and industrial bourgeois capitalism. Polany (1957) in *The Great Transformation* made a similar argument pointing to the necessity of markets to break down the older forms of social and political organization to create the nation-state. Today, we are witnessing a similar transformation as the nation-state is finding it increasingly difficult to provide either a suitable framework of welfare democracy – its internal function – or of operating as a sovereign entity on the level of international relations (Ruggie, 1993) – its external function. According to Cerny, ' . . . the state is being not only eroded but also fundamentally transformed within a wider structural context . . . The international system is no longer simply a states system; rather, it is becoming increasingly characterized by a plural and composite . structure.' (2000: 595) The same author identifies paradigmatic change as occurring 'when the requirements for providing . . . both public goods and private goods in some workable combination increase beyond the capacity of the institutional structure to reconcile the two over the medium-to-long term' (p. 602).

The most probable explanation of the forces driving the changes is that these were economic: the crisis of the capitalist model of the 1930s which contributed to the Second World War and the adoption of the Beveridgian/Keynesian model which led to the welfare state; the economic crisis of the 1970s which led to the subsequent crisis of this model and to the success of neo-liberalism, deregulation and globalization; the costly societal and economic dysfunction of the strong version of neo-liberalism in the 1990s which led to its modification in the form of the Third Way. Political and administrative elites have responded to these changes by reinventing government with new modes of governance each corresponding to the challenges of the particular paradigm: statist during the welfare state; pluralist during the neo-liberal period; network during the social state period. In the period of growth of the welfare state, the concerns were the management of growth and the effectiveness of policy programmes and 'fordist' models, mirroring the large-scale corporation, were adopted. In the neo-liberal period, the concern was the management of contraction and efficiency with the adoption of 'post-fordist' management models emphasizing 'flexibility' and customized variation. In the current phase of evolution, flexibility and customization are tempered by concerns of partnership and social solidarity. Wider changes in society, culture and values both fed into and were influenced by these economic, political and administrative changes.

Thus the main argument of this chapter is that there has, indeed, been a transformation, or even several transformations, of governance in Western states since 1945. However, the social science literature has been deeply divided with regard to the significance of these changes and, indeed, whether anything has really changed at all. In this chapter we argue that there has been at least one paradigm shift – from the welfare state to the neo-liberal state – and that we are witnessing yet another towards what has been called the Third Way but which, in fact, is a plurality of types of Third Way, each dependent on a particular state tradition and set of political conditions in particular countries, but influencing each other. International organizations such as the EU, OECD and the IMF have also been important conveyors of these new models although an organization such as the EU may itself be divided among competing positions. The transformation of governance is really one manifestation of a wider set of transformations: of the economy, of the state, of society and of culture. These transformations signalled the collapse of at least one conception of the modern nation-state and have profound implications for political democracy and the nature of our political systems. Thus we need to refound the basic concepts of democracy and to reflect on the kinds of political, economic and societal institutions that might be necessary to give this expression. Within each of these state traditions, the place of language and language policies are conceptualized in distinct ways, which we identify as belonging to a French, Germanic and Anglo-Saxon state tradition respectively.

The French (Jacobin) State Tradition

The French conception may be summed up in the phrase the 'one and indivisible Republic', which refers to the unity and indivisibility of both the nation and the state. In practice, this has meant uniformity and standardization in political and administrative structures but also in culture and language. The problem for the French statists was and remains, as Fernard Braudel (1986) has illustrated, that France is composed of a great variety of landscapes, cultures and languages. Although this process of nation-building has been successful in the sense that today the vast majority of French citizens now speak French and identify primarily with the French nation, it is still not complete. Today, two hundred years after the Revolution, there are still millions of French people who speak languages other than French – Corsican, Breton, Flemish, Alsatian/German, Catalan, Basque, and the various dialects of Occitan as well as other dialects of French itself such as *gallo* in Brittany and *picard*.

The function of the state, therefore, was to bring about the unity and indivisibility required to create the nation. Initially, as Weil (2002) has shown, the French state chose *jus sanguini* (in 1803) in preference to *jus soli*. Ties of blood, of ancestry and of ethnic membership were gradually conceived as smacking of a feudal value system whereby people belonged to specific places. Nineteenth-century demographic change, occasioned by industrialization and urbanization, and the need to incorporate by force immigrants' children motivated the adoption of *jus soli* in 1889 (Mamadouh, 2005).

The French state tradition also gave rise to a particular concept of citizenship based on the idea of *jus soli* (literally soil), whereby residence within the national space territory is the basis for citizenship and thus in theory, the French citizen is devoid of any ethnic, racial, gender, or religious characteristics, and speaks only French.He or she relates directly to the state without passing through any intermediary bodies such as the Church or other corporatist associations. This conception of citizenship was formulated at least partly in opposition to the situation prevailing in France's regions whose inhabitants were dominated (or at least so it was thought) by the Catholic Church, and where society was organized in a distinctly hierarchical and corporatist way. Regional populations related to the state via their hierarchical superiors, whether clerical or lay. It was in these regions, too, that there was greatest opposition to the principles of the Revolution, to republicanism and even to democracy itself. These contextual differences retain their purchase today as regards the governance of language issues in France. These have included: the insertion into the constitution that France is the language of the people (originally against the threat of the English language but subsequently used against France's minority languages); the difficulties with signing the European Charter of Regional and Minority Languages; the recognition of the existence of the 'Corsican people' in the 1991 revision of that island's statute by the then Minister of the Interior, Pierre Joxe and the opposition to the current laws on Corsica which give its *collectivité territoriale* some modest legislative powers and make the teaching of Corsican obligatory in the state school system; the attempt to incorporate the Breton diwan schools into the national education system by the Minister of Education Jack Lang; etc. This new cleavage has split almost every party in France and became an issue in the 2002 presidential elections with the candidature of Chevènement, whose *pôle républicain* attracted traditionalists from across the political spectrum from the extreme left to the extreme right. The *souverainistes,* in general, have opposed both the move towards greater European integration (as well as 'globalization') and the move towards greater plurality within France, seeing French sovereignty, unity and indivisibility as threatened by this double movement.

Many of the recent measures to recognize the ethnolinguistic diversity of France have been seized upon by traditional statists and by both the Conseil d'Etat and the Conseil Constitutionnel, which judged them to be unconstitutional. In effect, the measures and the reactions to them have given rise to a new cleavage (or perhaps the resurrection of an old cleavage – that between the Jacobins and the Girondins) in French politics: *souverainistes* vs. *pluralistes*.

Despite these considerations the French model diffused to other European states either as a result of conquest during the

Napoleonic Wars, as happened on the Iberian Peninsula, or as a consequence of imitation by newly formed nation-states such as Italy during the nineteenth and early twentieth centuries. Two other groups adopted a loose version of the French state model. First, the small, largely homogeneous states of Greece and Portugal, which have emphasized the unitary character of the state. While Portugal granted a high degree of autonomy to its island possessions, the Azores and Madeira, the mainland population, although having regionally distinctive populations, is linguistically homogeneous and all attempts at political regionalization have been rejected by the population. In Greece, too, although large parts of the country consists of islands and there are some linguistic minorities on the mainland such as the Arvanitians, the emphasis has been on centralization and a very robust policy of opposing internal ethno-linguistic distinctiveness (Williams, 1992) clearly related to the tradition of *henosis* (Loughlin, 2001).

The second group consists of Belgium, the Netherlands, Luxembourg and Finland. Belgium, riven by its linguistic-related conflict between Flemish and Walloons, has passed from being a Jacobin unitary state dominated by French-speakers to being a federal state, with a complicated decentralized system of economic regions and linguistic communities (including the small German-speaking minority and officially bilingual Brussels). In reality Belgium has largely abandoned its French Napoleonic heritage as its federal state apparatus is almost a residual state, with most power residing in the regions and communities, albeit in an asymmetrical form, with Flanders being the strongest, having decided to combine the community and the region, while Wallonia has kept them separate. The Netherlands inherited the Napoleonic system of the unitary state but, its 1848 constitution, written by the statesman Thorbecke, while retaining the external features of this system, was imbued with the spirit of German administrative theory, which gave it a much more corporatist and quasi-federalist meaning. A further modification was the introduction of 'pillarization' (*verzuiling*) which meant that the religious and ideological groups coexisted peacefully in toleration of each other. *Verzuiling* refers to the situation after the 1917 pacification process, a deal in which socialists obtained voting rights for workers and confessionals received state subsidies for religious schools. Virginie Mamadouh, in a personal communication (2005), remarks that the tolerance of the Dutch state needs some qualification especially since the 2000 debate on the multicultural drama, the effects of 9/11 and of the events of 2 November 2004 and the aftermath. What is without doubt is that the state financing of Islamic schools has major implications for Dutch and possibly other EU states' interpretation of honouring the rights of its multicultural citizens.

Consequently, although the Netherlands was a fairly homogeneous society, linguistically and ethnically, it has been capable of a great deal of generosity towards its linguistic minority, mainly the Friesians in the north of the country. The same open-minded tolerance and generosity has been shown both to English, which is in effect the second language of the country, and to those immigrants speaking Arabic, Turkish or Moluccan who have settled in the country.

Finally, Finland, which, on becoming independent in 1918, adopted the French model, has shown a very un-Jacobin attitude towards its linguistic minorities, mainly Swedish-speakers, who number only about 6 per cent of the population but whose language is one of the two official languages of the country, although any minority language could have this status. Furthermore, the Finns recognize bilingual communes, with all the services in both languages, if 8 per cent of the population speak the minority language. Finally, on the Finnish Aaland Islands, where 98 per cent speak Swedish, there is a system of 'regional citizenship' designed to protect the culture, language and property of the islanders, which is based, in part, on the ability to speak Swedish, and where Finnish is an optional language. Regional citizenship was first defined by a committee of the League of Nations in 1921 which sought to resolve the problem of the Aalanders' wish to secede from Finland to join Sweden. The League judged that the islands did not have a right to self-determination but that they were entitled to protect their language and culture. The notion of regional citizenship gives expression to this right and is based on being resident on the islands for at least five years, having Finnish nationality and having a good command of Swedish. Mastery of Finnish is not necessary. (Loughlin and Daftary, 1999; Loughlin and Olivesi, 1999). Nothing could be further from the Jacobin spirit as is evident if we try to imagine such an arrangement on the island of Corsica!

The Germanic and Scandinavian State Traditions

The foundation of German nationalism was the notion of a common cultural and linguistic heritage summed up in the term *Kulturnation*, despite the great political and administrative diversity largely inherited from the German Holy Roman Empire. In effect, this political and administrative situation left a legacy of both federalism and corporatism in Germanic conceptions of the state. Nevertheless, given the overriding importance of language in this national and state tradition, it was inevitable that there should be a linguistic homogenization with the formation of *Hochdeutsch,* which became the standard form of German.

At the same time, this homogeneous high German has coexisted relatively easily with the various dialects of German such as *Bayerisch* or *Limburgisch* and, indeed, with other languages such as Danish, Schwabian or Frisian. The arrangements for the accommodation of Danish-speakers on the German side of the border with Denmark in Schleswig-Holstein and the reciprocal arrangements on the Danish side are exemplary in this regard. In effect, these arrangements display a positive attitude on the part of the state, paralleling the Netherlands, with its constructive approach to the treatment accorded to the Frisian minority as well as to immigrant communities. Among the Scandinavian countries, we have already referred to Finland. Similar remarks could be made about the treatment of the Sami peoples by the Swedes and Norwegians as well as the Finns, but while Finnish-speakers in Sweden are well organized, and for the most part are immigrants or descendents of immigrants, one native population of Finns, the Tornedalen Finns, are struggling to have its disputed code of Meänkieli fully recognized and developed within the Tornadalen Valley.

The Anglo-Saxon State Tradition

This state tradition displays a curious mixture of both centralization and administrative and cultural diversity. In contradistinction to states, which are held to embody the soul of the nation, the UK, and its derivative states, have been dominated by various conceptions of 'government' rather than statehood. These have been called society-centred states rather than state-centred societies. At the same time, at least in the UK, the doctrine of the sovereignty of Parliament has had the effect of a strong centralization with political and economic power being concentrated in London and its hinterland, the south-east of England, while at the same time the continued existence of nations and distinct administrative arrangements in its constituent parts is tolerated.

During the nineteenth century, English succeeded in imposing itself as the dominant language in those nations where a Celtic language had previously been dominant. As we shall see in this volume, the various attempts at revitalizing the Celtic languages within their historical homelands have met with only limited success. Indeed, one of the justifications for this volume's comparative treatment of language and governance in the UK, Ireland, the EU and Canada was to provide practical policy measures by which this revitalization process could be strengthened. In the peculiar Anglo-Saxon tradition of tolerance mixed with repression, the tolerance was probably more important than the repression but, at the same time, vast forces of social and economic change associated with the Industrial Revolution were closely identified with the English language. These engulfed Great Britain and Ireland and encouraged the changeover of key elites to that language. On the other hand, the relatively tolerant attitude of the British authorities permitted at least a partial revival of these languages, especially Welsh, and to a lesser extent Irish in Northern Ireland, from the 1960s onwards.

Language in Public Policy

Crucially for this chapter, the conceptualization of language and the governance of minority languages has also changed. Taken together, these shifts amount over a period of about 50 years to a significant transformation of the nation-state and of its component parts – nation and state. We have already, in the first part of this chapter, outlined the shifts in conceptions of state organization and public policy and given some explanations as to why the shifts occurred. To these may be added the new geo-political situation following the collapse of the Berlin Wall and the Soviet empire and to an as yet unknown extent, the 11 September 2001 attacks on the World Trade Centre and the Pentagon together with their consequences for global security. Recognising that these competing state paradigms are still in a state of flux, we now turn to an analysis of how language and language policy are conceptualised and translated into public policy terms in each of them.

The Welfare State Model

With its emphasis on centralization, egalitarianism and redistribution, the welfare state also tended to have a homogenizing effect, particularly on minority languages and cultures which were conceptualized in a distinct manner, as follows:

- Regional cultures, with distinctive languages and values, were deemed to be 'unmodern', traditional and unprogressive, and were usually regarded by central elites, but sometimes also by regional elites, as an obstacle to regional development. They were therefore devalued and often reduced to mere 'folklore' for consumption by tourists. Reaping the seeds sown in earlier decades, the period between 1950–1980 witnessed significant language switching by minority-group members to Europe's hegemonic languages and their associated cultures. Attempts to revitalize lesser-used language communities were criticized as being parochial, irrelevant and misguided for they condemned such communities to remain at the traditional end of the traditional–modern continuum. Little thought was given then to the possibility that individuals within such communities could be ultra-modern in overlapping cultural and economic spheres, deploying their linguistic skills to enhance the quality of their lives.

- Such language activism as existed tended to be undertaken by rather small elites and their attendant student and youth movements (notable exceptions are Flanders and Catalonia). By and large the majority of citizens were indifferent and, among the generality of the linguistic minority, only a small number of parents fought for their children's right to a bilingual education.
- The classical left – Socialist, Labour and Communist Parties – tended to be hostile to these autochthonous languages and cultures, as was the (majority) nationalist right. Ethno-regionalist parties tended to claim a monopoly concern with the plight of threatened and endangered languages.
- It was only during the end of the period of welfare state hegemony that the left, or rather sections of the extreme left, began to take up the issue of regional and national minorities and their languages as part of a wider critique of both the welfare state and the capitalist system.
- Concerns with the failure of language transmission in the family, the atrophying of vibrant language communities and the harmful effects of demo-linguistic transformations were interpreted as the inevitable consequences of modernization. They were to be regretted, but politicians argued that such concerns lay outside the influence of orthodox, interventionist government policies.

The New Right/Neo-Liberal Model

The principles underlying the neo-liberal model of the state amount to an almost exact reversal of the principles of the welfare state model with a strident emphasis on less state intervention and bureaucracy, more individual freedom, and the abandonment of the goal of equality. The processes of deregulation and marketization encouraged a shift in the nature of the global economy, referred to as globalization.

During this period of neo-liberal hegemony a fundamental shift occurred in the conceptualization of culture and language both with regard to the state and with regard to models of economic development. Most states, even France, began to accept the necessity of certain pluralism in language policy. To some extent, this was an outworking of the emergence of English as a new lingua franca in diplomacy, academia and scientific research as well as in the popular media and the new technological developments and the predominance of the anglophone United States in these. The arrival of the Internet as a popular and widespread means of communications reinforced this Americanization of culture, with English as the lingua franca. However, it was also due to the growing importance of the European Union as a multilingual system of governance, where competence in more than one language was deemed necessary to participate fully in this new system. All of this relativized the notion of a *national* language, although there were some rearguard actions such as the insertion into the French constitution that there is only one language in France, the French language. Originally a means of protection against English, this clause was subsequently used against France's minority languages. Nevertheless, even in France there is now among the political class, with the exception of the *souverainistes* and the *mouvements laïques*, a much greater willingness to accept that minority languages may also be part of a nation's cultural heritage. These changes, related to the broader changes in the transformation of the state, outlined above, may be summarized as follows:

- A rethinking of the notion of *national* culture and language in the context of a multilingual and culturally diverse Europe, officially recognized in the Treaty of Maastricht.
- A growing appreciation of 'culture' as a variable in economic development – probably connected to the realization of the importance of knowledge and learning in a new paradigm of economic development.
- Related to this is a new appreciation of the opportunities

for regional cultures – the Catalans, the Flemish and the Québécois have all promoted this with great success.
- A new way of conceiving Europe as a mosaic of different cultures was developed, particularly by the Flemish government with the concept of cultural diversity and its project of a Europe of the Cultures in 2002.

Of course, much of the above remains at the level of discourse and it is difficult to demonstrate empirically that there is a positive relationship between the existence of a distinct culture and economic development. Nevertheless, this discourse has had the effect of finding expression in concrete public policy approaches.

The 'Third Way' Model: The 'Enabling' State

Britain is the pre-eminent exemplar of this model, and while British experience is, to a large extent, influenced by the United States it is, in turn, exciting great interest in other European countries. The state is modelled in a more positive way than in neo-liberalism, but the emphasis is now on partnership – between central and local and between public and private – as well as on subsidiarity. A good example of this partnership arrangement in terms of language and governance is the National Assembly for Wales's conception of the triangular relationship between the Welsh Language Board, its various sponsored partners, such as the National Eisteddfod, Yr Urdd, Mentrau Iaith Cymru, and the general public.

With regard to culture and values, there is a continuing acceptance of individualistic trends and toleration of a variety of lifestyles but, as outlined above, this is tempered by a new emphasis on 'community'. At least, there is a sense that certain valuable forms of community have been lost and that there is a worrying disintegration of society. Hence the recognized need to tackle housing issues, transport and regional development initiatives and most of all the creation of appropriate employment within atrophying Welsh-speaking areas in the north and west of Wales, and to a lesser extent within similar contexts in Ireland and Scotland. There is also a concern that decisions are taken at too great a distance from the ordinary citizen. Hence the partial justification for devolutionary measures within the United Kingdom. Nevertheless, these concerns do not seem to be translating themselves into political or social action at the local level. The picture here is one of apathy if not necessarily ignorance on the part of the general public as witnessed in the ow electoral turnout for the second term of the devolved Welsh and Scottish assemblies in the spring of 2003 that was maintained in the May 2007 National Assembly for Wales election.

European Perspectives and Trends

How do these various state traditions in turn impact on common European trends? European language policies are in a state of flux. Commercial and technological pressures empower hegemonic languages, medium-sized states struggle with strategic decisions over which language(s) of wider communication to employ in higher education, science and research endeavours, so-called lesser-used languages struggle to maintain a niche in their respective contexts while languages of non-European origin figure more prominently in issues of access to public services, calls for separate, often religiously enframed, education and basic citizenship entitlements.

It is only rather recently that linguistic minorities have been accorded special attention in international law. A basic difficulty stems from the extension of the individual human rights tradition, established after the French Revolution of 1789 whose rallying call was 'Liberty, Equality and Fraternity', into the realm of collective rights. The ensuing debate has focused on whether the use of a particular language in specified contexts is guaranteed by basic civil and political rights, such as the right to freedom of expression, and the right to respect for private and family life under instruments such as the European Convention on Human Rights.

However, recognition of rights derived from mutual tolerance, respect for diversity and social inclusion does not assuage the worries of those minorities who require strong support for the maintenance of minority linguistic identity.

This requires the state to act in respect of minority needs in public services, education, the legal system etc. so that the target language may be used as a means of meaningful communication and employment. The further extension of political support in respect of language planning requires specification as to whether personality or territorial rights (or an admixture of both) are to be implemented (Nelde, *et al.* 1992; 2001).

Whereas the United Nations has never separated out the national minorities from other linguistic groups, the Council of Europe has established this division between national minorities and immigrant groups in a very explicit manner (Ahtisaari, 2002). Within the purview of the Council of Europe, the Framework Convention for the Protection of National Minorities (1998) and the European Charter for Regional and Minority Languages, (1998) seek to establish minimum standards. To date, the charter has been signed by thirty states, seventeen of which have ratified it. Following a review between 2005–6 the current political concern is to harmonize Council of Europe and EU conventions in these matters. Blair (2002) argues that the Council of Europe has made an important contribution to the development of the *acquis communautaire* primarily through its legal instruments giving force to basic values, its work to integrate new member states and the consolidation of democratic stability in central and eastern Europe.

Similarly the Organisation for Security and Co-operation in Europe (OSCE) has been active in the specification of minority rights, most especially in the Hague Recommendations regarding the Education Rights of National Minorities, 1998, OSCE; the Oslo Recommendations regarding the Linguistic Rights of National Minorities, 1998; the final paragraphs of the Copenhagen Conference on the Human Dimensions Related to Linguistic Issues together with various documents released by the OSCE High Commissioner for National Minorities. Despite these advances it is difficult to describe the details of what has emerged as an apparent consensus among the larger European institutions and organizations as to what constitutes an appropriate set of language policies.

A basic difficulty in reconciling various language polices is the degree to which the target language reflects power differentials particularly within the EU and beyond. Support for languages of wider communication, such as English, French or German, derive in part from their strategic role as contributors to a former colonial, imperial past and to current state hegemony. Such support is not considered either as a direct subsidy or as an illogical intervention into the marketplace but as normal policy and practice to execute daily socio-economic functions. Far greater support is offered by international commerce, science and technology for such languages are purveyors of global knowledge, information and entertainment. All this reinforces the discourse of universalism and strengthens 'rational', normative expectations and behaviour. However, when it comes to support for historical language minorities exceptionalism rules, and the logic of such support is nearly always couched in moral, cultural and group identity terms rather than in strict instrumental, functional terms. In such cases language, culture and economy are treated as autonomous spheres of influence and activity. They are not necessarily seen as mutually binding or as constituting a sustainable alternative to the hegemonic language. And when any major case for structural reform is made it is nearly always advanced by language-related agencies rather than economic agencies in tandem. This makes it doubly difficult to mainstream language issues into political economic schemas, regional development programmes and the like. For so often language planning agencies can be accused of satisfying the interests of a small minority of citizens and of engaging in special pleading. This is an understandable, if regrettable state of affairs.

The Determination of Language Policy in the European Union

The governance of European languages has never been subject to a grand design, but has evolved in an epiphenomenal way. Up until 2004 the EU had eleven official and working languages and a plethora of vital languages spoken among the then 380 million citizens of EU states. Language policies have to deal with a varying geometry of multilingualism that is well known. Following Van Els (2001) a basic distinction can be made between the 'institutional' and 'non-institutional' aspects of EU policy. The statutory basis for the institutional use of languages is Article 217 of the Treaty of Rome, which charges the Council of Ministers to enframe all regulations. Theoretically three broad principles govern institutional usage. First, all official documents are translated into all official EU languages and gain purchase in a member state when they are produced in the officially recognized language of that state. Second, all citizens communicating with central EU institutions are entitled to a response in the official language of their choosing. Third, the EU's terminology database gives full coverage only in the languages designated as official EU languages. (Labrie, 1996: 5, quoted in Van Els, 2001: 320)

What is not recognized so well is what Mamadouh (2002) has termed the dual influence of language diversity on national identities and on the ability of citizens to access supra-national and transnational decision-making processes. The comparative perspective we adopt in this volume can assist in examining such structures of equality and inequality across space by undertaking a simultaneous analysis at seven scales, namely: 1. pan-European; 2 macro-regional; 3. state; 4. national/regional; 5. metropolitan/local; 6. ethnic, cultural or interest group; 7. individual citizen/subject/immigrant. At each level in the scale hierarchy a different combination of ecological, holistic and geolinguistic applications will be required to facilitate policy. Agencies as varied as state governments, the European Union and Parliament, multilateral interest groups and regional level authorities contribute both to the policy agenda and to the construction of the infrastructure whereby languages can be accommodated within this complex system of agencies. Thus network governance is both widened and deepened by the need to operate at all levels of the hierarchy.

However, Mamadouh has argued that the most compelling question facing EU decision-makers today is: 'How should the mediation between speakers of different languages be organized?' She has explored an answer by reference to grid-group cultural theory and has demonstrated how polices and practices are the result of competition between different rationalities and therefore depend on the influence, strategies and alliances of their adherents (Mamadouh, 2002). One of the competing rationalities we champion in this volume combines linguistic diversity, holistic thinking and ecological perspectives as developed by Williams (1991, 2002). Why then do we believe that linguistic diversity is a valuable thing, and what conditions are necessary for it to thrive? Part of the answer lies with the unravelling of European history. The Basques, Catalans and Welsh, for example, have long and rich histories which at various epochs since Roman times has made them more or less central to the whole course of European developments. The fact that none of their respective languages have official status at an all-EU level does not detract from the inherent worth of their respective cultures and regional economies. Similarly, it may be asked, why do lesser-used language networks seek to promote an alternative vision of European linguistic diversity to that which is advanced by the major economic actors and international organizations? Edwards (2002) asserts that this is done because it is recognized that diversity is good in itself, because it involves a preference for heterogeneous landscapes and an aesthetic appreciation that values multidimensional perspectives. He also provocatively asserts that guilt is a powerful motivating factor at work when the champions of such diversity often emanate from outside the communities concerned! But is diversity in and of itself an inherently valuable thing? A provocative challenge to the diversity-at-all-costs line is provided by Van Els who asserts that there are at least two myths which need to be deconstructed:

> It is a myth that the great diversity of languages and cultures as such is a good thing and that, consequently, its present manifestation in the EU represents a great richness, a treasure that should be defended at all costs. It is one of the myths that co-determine current EU policy on institutional language use.(Van Els, 2001: 349)

> Another myth is that changes in language policy in one domain, in this case the EU institutions, should necessarily have consequences for other domains, in this case particularly for the language use in member states themselves. (Van Els, 2001: 350).

The difficulties of language reproduction are by now very well known, but the central justification for introducing greater holistic perspectives is that maintenance and revitalization efforts rely on much more than language, education and culture. And yet too few official language planning agencies are really able to grapple with the multifaceted elements required, being limited primarily to social mobilization programmes, educational initiatives and marketing campaigns Too often they are bereft of any structural, and hence lasting, influence on issues of mainstream economic growth, regional development policy, labour migration, investment strategies and the like, all of which influence the vitality (or morbidity) of language networks and communities. Language planners conventionally cite the extra-linguistic impediments to effective policy implementation, but rarely engage such factors head on, presuming that they fall within the remit of other professional disciplines. Language planners within minority communities face the additional problem of having to resist a dominant rationality which places their efforts at revitalization within an exceptionalist reference frame. This is all the more daunting for them to resolve if we place such considerations alongside several outstanding questions which have yet to be tackled adequately by policy analysts within the EU.

Unresolved Questions

- How is European language policy decided upon? What time frame is envisaged and with what implication for the various macro-programmes devised by agencies such as the EU, the Council of Europe and NATO?
- What is the legal framework within which decisions about language policy and planning are made at the international level?
- What are the core needs for language development in Europe?
- Will multicultural cities such as Frankfurt, Paris, Brussels and London develop more multilingual policies which stress their comparative similarities, qua multi-ethnic nodes in a European metropolitan network, which will

separate them further from 'national' curricula and training requirements?

- Will a federal state of Europe be established in the near future with proscribed language regimes? This is unlikely. What is more likely is the creation of a system of multi-level governance in a post-sovereignty era. This will stand in direct contrast to both the nation-state system as discussed above, and the idealistic federal-regional system advocated by many.
- How will language policies relate to a reformed supranational territorial system? This is difficult to imagine at present, but it is clear that the more strident and better organized sub-state nationalities, such as the Catalans, Basques and Welsh, have made significant, if insufficient, advances at the regional and international level in the promotion of their common cause.
- Given metropolitan networking and globalized economic trends, will lesser-used language heartland regions and socio-economic structures be inevitably subject to issues of internal fragmentation and collapse in the face of social modernization?
- How can geolinguistic analysis assist in the definition of target communities of interest, map the overlapping functional spaces and measure the socio-economic impact of language plans?

The Enlarged European Union: New Language Contact Areas

As a result of the latest rounds of EU enlargement in 2004 initially ten new states and nine new official languages and in 2007 a further two states and three official languages have been added to the socio-linguistic diversity of the new European order. While conventionally language policy has been the preserve of the individual state, there is increasing evidence of the effect of EU and Council of Europe policy statements impacting on the range and mix of languages honoured and used both within and between individual states. Philipson argues that although the EU is committed to maintaining linguistic diversity there are severe structural problems in achieving this political goal.

> For this to be achieved presupposes giving language policy a much higher profile, and an infrastructure in member states and in EU institutions that is well qualified to implement and monitor language policies. This is not the position at present. In fact there is a serious risk, at both the national and the supranational levels, of language policy remaining entrenched in linguistic nationalism, and obscured by a false faith in English serving all equally well. Language policy at the EU level is politically sensitive. (Philipson, 2003a)

Within intergovernmental organizations the default trend may be moving toward the selection of a very limited number of transnational working languages. But there are other implications for an enlarged Europe which have more to do with direct citizen-to-citizen and company-to-company interaction.

The nature and pace of such change at the macro level can best be measured by focusing on those historical language contact areas, such as the Baltic Region or the Julian Alps where representatives of major language families such as the Slavic, Germanic and Latin come together. Language border areas can be used as a geo-strategic temperature gauge for the degree of intercultural cooperation and conflict which exists within cultural realms beyond the frontier. Borders, boundaries and frontiers are integral both to the geographer's trade and to the resolution of conflict within the European Union. In language border areas research has focused on simultaneous interlingual contact operating at a number of different scales ranging from the inter-state level, through intermediate trade, social and cultural organizations to the level of the individual. Much of this concern with borders and cultural transition zones has to do with respecting the minority linguistic rights of settled communities either side of the international or regional boundary (Cartwright, 1991, 1998). In consequence, the major challenge of such transition zones will be how to organize internal processes which will maximize the utility of all languages within the zones. Such zones can also act as bridges in the New World Order and thus symbolize a spirit of partnership and integration, wherein the free flow of goods and people may be encouraged. Bi- or tri-lingual inhabitants of such zones are set fair to act as critical elements in the integrative process. However, because such zones are also strategically significant and have a history of periodic violence, it is imperative that we fully understand the various sociolinguistic dynamics, which accompany such integrative measures.

Slovenia is a fascinating example of a rapidly modernizing society attempting to maintain its national language within a dynamic globalizing world. It straddles three of Europe's major culture regions, the Romance, Germanic and Slavic realm, where all of its neighbours possess powerful languages of wider communication, in addition to which, of course, it has had to come to grips with the demands of global English. Initial, fascinating enquiries have concentrated on the linguistic, migratory and ethno-political adjustments of the Slovene border areas and we now have an excellent range of detailed case studies by Klemencic and Klemencic (1997) on the north Adriatic border region 1521–1918; Bufon (1993; 1994) on the Slovene–Italian border population movements and sociolinguistic adjustments; Bufon (1997) on the ethnolinguistic structure of the upper Adriatic, 1910–91; Zupancic (1996, 1998) on issues of region, language and identity in Carinthia; together with Gosar and Klemincic (1994) on similar issues along the Slovene–Croatian border. Researchers at Ljubljana and Primorska (Koper) are undertaking vital work on the readjustment process of former state socialist societies seeking to be fully incorporated within the enlarged European Union.

A second impulse is the need is to measure the effect which globalization and the transnational transmission of culture by electronic means has upon language A new geography of language and communication is being fashioned, based upon networks and real-time interaction, with enormous consequences for power relations, entertainment and sport together with commercial transactions across borders.

Selected governments have also been very active in the application of Geographic Information Systems (GIS) to contextual analysis, none more so than the Basque and Catalan authorities. Following a real measure of autonomy after Franco's death, both governments have invested heavily in sociolinguistic data collection and analysis so as to underpin their active language planning and policy. The Basque government has a very sophisticated social survey capacity with state-of-the-art geolinguistic analysis which it employs to good effect both in pursing its public policies and in encouraging the linguistic micro-planning undertaken by the private, commercial sectors. Ultimately, as with any scientific/technological development, computer-aided cartography is only as good as the quality and integrity of its designers, interpreters and users. However, the Basque context demonstrates that such GIS applications can provide a frame within which governmental, commercial and communal contributions can coalesce to impact on language policy.

A few other issues require detailed investigation. First, the way in which the experiences generated within the most recent member states of the EU will impact on the plurilingual character of educational and public administrative services, together with the local government and legal system of the recently enlarged EU, is a vital challenge. This is especially so in the Hungarian–Slovene–Italian, Polish–German, Czech–German–Austrian, Slovak–Austrian, Finnish–Latvian–Lithuanian–Estonian cross-border regions. These sites are particularly acute in the construction of a new geography of communication, interaction and governance. Secondly, there is a need to analyse fluctuations in the economic demand for a skilled bilingual/multilingual workforce in several sectors of the European economy. Little comparative work has been undertaken on the linguistic training needs of general or specialized occupations. Neither is it known to what extent bilingual working practices, for example in Catalonia or Wales, offer a model for subsequent parallel developments in a range of multilingual contexts within other European regions, for example; either in respect of several European languages or selected non-European languages such as Arabic, Urdu, Hindi or variants of Chinese languages of wider communication. Thirdly the adoption of interactive media and Internet-based communication is especially significant for the functional diversity of many smaller languages right across Europe. Profound issues of citizenship and alienation, inclusion and exclusion, commonality and diversity relate to the new patterns of behaviour as consumerism, media patterns, information packaging and cultural orientation all challenge the post-Enlightenment rationalities and values of civil society.

Equality and Pragmatism as Basic Principles

Given these trend of language diversity, political integration and economic globalization, some would argue it is spurious to insist that all languages are to be treated equally within both the market and the institutions of the EU, for, as Van Els comments, 'The core problem is the fundamental equality of all EU languages as EU working languages. There is no linguistic insight that opposes the abandonment of this principle. Neither are the arguments for maintaining this principle tenable from a linguistic perspective.' (Van Els, 2001: 349)

In relation to EU language policy, Van Els argues that the following basic principles need to be discussed:

- the principle of equality for all 'official' languages, also as 'working languages' of the EU, will be abandoned formally;
- the basic principle will be, or remains, that none of the crucial interests of any member state or citizen of the EU may be harmed as a result of their language background;
- another basic principle will be that individual pragmatic solutions will be sought for the language communication problems in each of the sub-domains of the EU organization. (Van Els, 2001: 350)

However in yielding responsibility for language policy there is always the second issue of weakened participative democracy and lack of empowerment, by which we mean the danger that citizens and communities will be relegated to the role of passive recipients of top-down political decisions and language planning. Thus in institutional language planning at various scales in the spatial hierarchy we should always seek to:

- involve the target speakers/users of services as much as possible in the language planning decision-making process;

- engage the participation of inter-departmental agencies to realise language planning aims and programmes;
- seek to introduce horizontal forms of governance where feasible, but expect only partial success given the tendency to centralise and bureaucratize language-related activity;
- anticipate and resolve to overcome the barriers, vested interests, traditional thought and practice which arise from inter-departmental turf-wars and boundary disputes. (Williams, 2002 p. 18)

Governance and Language: Opportunities and Challenges

While the EU will have to come to a compromise arrangement for the relationship between the official and the working languages, the emerging governance paradigm outlined here also presents challenges and opportunities for less powerful, non-state languages. Among the opportunities may be listed:

- The European Union provides a new context which *may* provide opportunities, including the gaining of political influence, new partnership organizations and networks together with additional financial resources to support their languages and cultures.
- The weakening of the nation-state means also the weakening of the hegemony of *national* languages thereby giving minority languages a new legitimacy, if not necessarily an automatic boost to their actual use within civil society.
- The emphasis on community, subsidiarity, regional devolution and local democracy provides a set of opportunities to develop distinctive political and institutional forms to give expression to their identities.
- The possession of a minority language and culture *may* be an important asset in new models of regional economic development and it is encouraging that minority languages and cultures are now not dismissed as *obstacles* to such development.

- The establishment in 2007 of the European Language Planning Network provides an institutional forum by which regional and minority languages may be promoted within the EU.

The challenges include the following:

- The weakening of the nation-state is not an unmixed blessing as the nation-state is, in important respects, a bulwark against trends, such as cultural globalization, that are even more harmful to minority languages and cultures.
- The nation-state is also in possession of important resources, financial, administrative and policy in nature, that may be important for the preservation of minority languages whose populations and administrative structures will often lack these resources.
- Similarly, it is difficult for local and regional communities to possess all the resources necessary to transform their distinctive features from obstacles to social and economic development to being assets in this development – if governance means less government, it also means less allocation of public policy resources to such communities.
- ‘Communitarism’, like ‘multiculturalism’ may be inward-looking, reactionary and stultifying and the mobilization necessary to turn minority cultures into outward-looking, progressive and dynamic is difficult to achieve. What might be interesting is the notion of ‘interculturalism’, as advanced by certain Québécois scholars as a way of reconciling the assimilationist approach of traditional Jacobinism and the separatist or apartheid approaches typical of Anglo-Saxon or Germanic approaches. As we shall see in chapters ten and sixteen below, Québécois interculturalism makes French the vehicle of public discourse and activity, while other languages and cultures are allowed full rein in the private sphere.
- Partnership in terms of governance often introduces new actors into the policy-formation process. This is a positive move if additional resources are released which allow such partnerships to work. However, insufficient resources can often stifle the full impact of the transfer of

responsibility from central control to local agencies resulting in a local culture of 'blame' and 'complaint' directed not at government itself but at the responsible partner.

- A new emphasis on 'capacity-building' within the lesser-used language communities has to overcome structural difficulties in realizing the promise of service innovation, empowerment and institutional trust, the new leitmotifs of policies of social inclusion.
- New technologies may provide different forms of networking and interaction which in turn may release additional energies and give rise to synergy and economies of scale in bi- or multi-lingual communication.
- The skilling or commodification of language can provide new resources which appeal to the information society and increase the economic purchase of bi- or multi-lingual employees.
- Community vitality and revitalization can be achieved through a linguistic-led programme of socio-economic intervention.

In all these instances it is extremely difficult to isolate the patterns of cause and effect. Much of the dynamism behind these changes seems to originate in *economic* developments and in the avalanche of new technologies which have developed over the last forty years and which is now accelerating at an incredible rate. However, these economic changes are also dependent on other factors such as new values and attitudes in society and new forms of state activity and design, with new roles, functions and types of relationships with other levels of government and with the private sector and society.

We also believe that it is important to isolate another contextual feature of the changes: the macro-context represented by globalization and Europeanization. In fact, Europeanization is both a response to the threat of globalization and an expression of globalization. Nevertheless, we might conclude that there is a need to rethink our political concepts and practices: nation and state and their combination into nation-state; democracy; representative government; institutions. To put it in a nutshell, it might be said that we are starting the twenty-first century with political and administrative institutions inherited from the nineteenth-century nation-state, which were built on the principles of the eighteenth-century Enlightenment.

These transformations present minority languages and cultures with a number of challenges and opportunities. Among the challenges is the very real danger that many cultures and languages will be engulfed by the vast economic and cultural forces at work in our globalized and hi-tech world. On the other hand, the loosening up of the nation-state and the possibilities of new kinds of institutional design may also give these minorities the opportunity to adopt institutional and public policy models of social and economic development that will allow them, in collaboration with national and supra-national levels of governance, to confront the changes and both protect and develop themselves.

Conclusions

We have argued that language issues are directly related to questions of citizenship, identity, education, socialization and participation in the public sphere. In both political and organizational terms there is tremendous pressure on institutions within the EU to simplify and harmonize the range of services offered within a particular suite of languages. Countering such measures by formal language planning for smaller language communities becomes increasingly difficult. This is because the post-Enlightenment notions of inclusive citizenship are breaking down in the face of market segmentation and apparent consumer empowerment. This leads to a basic tension between commonality and fragmentation, between the basic needs of state socialization, including communicative competence in state-designated languages, and the reality of individual choices and the community orientation of many interest groups. Added to this is the post-enlargement issue of grappling with the sheer diversity of competing claims for recognition, rights and resources on behalf of those beleaguered groups who hitherto have not benefited from the institutional arrangements constructed by sovereign states in pursuit of plurinational democracy. The cases which follow, derived from British, Irish and Canadian experience, demonstrate that, even when relatively favourable conditions for sound governance in language policy matters are in place, there is no guarantee that empowerment and success will follow. It is even harder to envisage such empowerment taking place within political structures which are antipathetic to ethno-linguistic diversity let alone increasing communicative competence. But this is the common challenge we face as European citizens.

REFERENCES

Adorno, T. (1960) *The Authoritarian Personality*, New York: Norton.

Ahtisaari, M. (2002) '*Opening Statement*,' Conference on Creating a Common Structure for Promoting Historical Linguistic Minorities within the European Union, Finnish Parliament, Helsinki, Folktinget, 11–12, October 2002.

Beck, U. (2000) *What is Globalization?*, Malden, MA: Polity Press.

Blair, P. (2002) '*Promotion of Linguistic Diversity Through the European Charter for Regional and Minority Languages*,' Conference on Creating a Common Structure for Promoting Historical Linguistic Minorities within the European Union, Finnish Parliament, Helsinki, Folktinget, 11–12, October.

Braudel, F. (1986) *L'identité de la France*,Paris: Athaud Flammarion.

Bufon, M. (1993) 'Cultural and social dimensions of borderlands: the case of the Italo-Slovene transborder area', *GeoJournal*, Vol. 3, pp. 235–40.

Bufon, M. (1994) 'Per una geografica delle aree di confine:il caso della regione transconfinaria Italo-Slovene nel Goriziano', *Rivista Geografica Italiana*, Vol. 101, pp 477–605.

Bufon, M. (1997) 'The Political and Ethnic Transformations in the Upper Adriatic Between Conflicts and Integration Perspectives', *Anali ze istrske in mediteranske studije*, Vol. 10, pp. 295–306.

Bufon, M. (2001) 'Ćezmejne Prostorske Vezi Na Tromeji Med Italijo, Slovenijo in Hrvaśko', *Anali za istrske in mediteranske študije*, 11, 2, pp. 283–300.

Burns, T. R. and Carson, M. (2002) 'Actors, Paradigms and Institutional Dynamics', in J. R. Hollingsworth, K. H. Muller and E. J. Hollingsworth, (eds) *Socio-Economics: An Institutionalist Perspective*, Lanham, MD: Rowman and Littlefield.

Cartwright, D. (1991) 'Bicultural Conflict in the Context of the Core-Periphery Model'. In C. H. Williams, (ed.), *Linguistic Minorities, Society and Territory*, Clevedon, Avon: Multilingual Matters, pp. 219–46.

Cartwright, D. (1998) 'French-Language Services in Ontario: A Policy of "Overly Prudent Gradualism"?' In T. Ricento and B. Burnaby, (eds), *Language and Politics in the United States and Canada*, Mahwah, New Jersey: Lawrence Erlbaum, pp. 273–300.

Cerny, P. (1995) 'Globalization and the Changing Logic of Collective Action', *International Organization,* Vol. 49, no. 4, Autumn, pp. 595–625.

Crouch, C. (1999) *Social Change in Western Europe*, Oxford: Oxford University Press.

Dahl, R. (1967) *Pluralist democracy in the United States: conflict and consent,* Chicago: Rand McNally.

Dalby, D. (1998) *The Linguasphere:Register of the World's Languages and Speech Communities*, Vol. 1. Hebron, Wales: Linguasphere Observatory.

Dunbar, R. (2001) 'Minority Language Rights Regimes: An Analytical Framework, Scotland and Emerging European Norms', in Kirk, J. and D. O. Baoill, (eds), *Linguistic Politics*, Belfast: Queen's University. 231–54.

Esping-Anderson, G. (1990) *The Three Worlds of Welfare Capitalism*, Cambridge: Polity Press.

Etzioni, A. (1993) *The Spirit of Community: rights, responsibilities, and the communitarian agenda,* New York: Crown Publishers.

European Commission, (2001) *European Governance: a White Paper*, Luxembourg: Office of Publications of the EC.

European Cultural Foundation, (2000). *Which Languages for Europe?* Amsterdam, European Cultural Foundation, Vol. 1. (1999). Vol. 2 . (2000).

Extra, G. and Gorter, D. (ed.). (2001) *The Other Languages of Europe*, Clevedon, Avon: Multilingual Matters.

Farràs i Farràs, J., Torres i Pla, J. and Vila i Moreno, F. X. (2000). *El Coneixement del Català, 1996*, Barcelona, Publicacions de l'Institut de Sociolingüítica Catalana.

Garrett, G. and Lange, P. (1991) 'Political responses to interdependence: what's "left" for the left?' *International Organization*, 45, (4), Autumn: 539–564.

Generalitat de Catalunya, (2000). *Catalunya-Quebec: Legislació i polítiques lingüístiques,* Barcelona : Publicacions de l'Institut de Sociolingüítica Catalana.

Giddens, A. (2000) *The Third Way and its Critics*, Cambridge: Polity Press.

Gosar, A. and Klemencic, V. (1994) 'Current problems of border regions along the Slovene-Croatian border'. In W. A Gallusser (ed.), *Political Boundaries and Co-existence*, Bern, Peter Lang, pp. 30–42.

Habermas, J. (2001) *The Post-national Constellation: political essays*, Cambridge, MA: MIT Press.

Hanley, D. (1994) (ed.), *Christian Democracy in Europe: a Comparative Perspective,* London: Pinter Publishers.

Held, D. (1999) *Global Transformations: politics, economics and culture*, Cambridge: Polity Press.

Hirst, P. and Thompson, G. (1996) *Globalization in question: the international economy and the possibilities of governance*, Cambridge: Polity Press.

Hirschman, A. (1970) *Exit, voice, and loyalty: responses to decline in firms, organizations, and states*, Cambridge, (Mass.): Harvard University Press

Horkheimer, M. (1972) *Critical theory; selected essays*, New York: Herder and Herder.

Keating, M. (1998) *The New Regionalism in Western Europe: Territorial Restructuring and Political Change*, Cheltenham: Edward Elgar.

Keating, M., Loughlin, J. and Deschouwer, K. (2003), *Culture, Institutions and Regional Development: a Study of Eight European Regions: a Comparative Analysis*. Cheltenham: Edward Elgar.

Klemencic, V. (1992) 'Priseljevanje prebivalcev z obmoeja nekdanje Jugoslavije v Slovenijo', *Geografija v soli*, 2, 14–26.

Klemencic, V. (1994) 'Uberlensemoeglichkeiten der nichtankerennted Minderheit der Slowenen in der Steiermark, Steirische Slowenen.' Zweispraechigkeit zwischen Graz und Maribor, 81–90.

Klemencic, M. and Klemencic, V. (1997) 'The Role of the Border Region of the Northern Adriatic', *Anali za istrske in mediteranske studije*, Vol. 10, pp. 285–94.

Knox, P. and Agnew, J. (1989) *The Geography of the World Economy*, London: Arnold.

Kohler-Koch, B. (1999) 'The Evolution and Transformation of European Governance', in B. Kohler-Koch and R. Eising (eds.), *The Transformation of Governance in the European Union*, London and New York: Routledge, pp. 14–35,

Kooiman, J. (ed.), (1993) *Modern governance: new government-society interactions*, London: Sage.

Labrie, N. (1996) 'The historical development of language policy in Europe', In P. Ó. Riagáin and S. Harrington, (eds), *A Language Strategy for Europe, Retrospect and Prospect*, Dublin: Bord na Gaeilge, pp. 1–9.

Le Galès, P. and Lequesne C. (1998) (eds), *Regions in Europe*, London: Routledge.

Lehmbruch G. and Schmitter, P. (1982) *Patterns of corporatist policy-making*, London: Sage.

Lindblom, C. (1965) *The intelligence of democracy: decision making through mutual adjustment*, New York: Free Press London: Collier-Macmillan.

Lo Bianco, J. (2005) *International Issues in Languages Policy*, Edinburgh: Scottish CILT.

Loughlin, J and Daftary, F. (1999) *Insular Regions and European Integration: Corsica and the Åland Islands compared*. Flensburg: European Centre for Minority Issues, Report #5.

Loughlin, J. and Olivesi, C. (eds), (1999) *Autonomies Insulaires: vers une politique de différence pour la Corse.* Ajaccio: Editions Albiana.

Loughlin, J. (2000) 'Regional Autonomy and State Paradigm Shifts', *Regional and Federal Studies: an International Journal.* 10, (2), Summer 2000: 10–34

Loughlin, J. (2001) *Subnational Democracy in the European Union: Challenges and Opportunities,* Oxford: Oxford University Press.

Loughlin, J. and Peters, B. G. (1997) 'State Traditions, Administrative Reform and Regionalization', in M. Keating and J. Loughlin, (eds) *The Political Economy of Regionalism,* London: Frank Cass, pp. 41 – 62.

Mamadouh, V. (2001) 'The Territoriality of European Integration and the Territorial Features of the EU: The First 50 Years.' *T.E.S.G.* Vol. 92, no. 4.

Mamadouh, V. (2002) 'Dealing with multilingualism in the European Union', *Journal of Comparative Policy Analysis,* June.

Mamadouh, V. (2005) personal communication, 2nd March.

Marcuse, H. (1972) *One Dimensional Man*, London: Abacus.

Marks, G., Scharpf, F., Schmitter P. and Streek W. (1996) *Governance in the European Union,* London: Sage.

Mendras, H. (1994) *La Seconde Révolution Française: 1965–1984*, Paris: Gallimard.

Metcalfe, L and Richards S. (1990) *Improving Public Management.* 2nd edition, London: Sage.

Moravcsik, A. (1993) 'Preferences and Power in the European Community: a Liberal Intergovernmentalist Approach', *Journal of Common Market Studies.* 31, (4): 473–524.

Natali D. and Rhodes, M. (2002) 'Analysing Reforms of the Bismarckian Welfare State: Some Theoretical and Empirical Suggestions', mimeo, European University Institute,.

Nelde, P., Labrie, N. and Williams, C. H. (1992) 'The Principles of Territoriality and Personality in the Solution of Linguistic Conflicts', *Journal of Multilingual and Multicultural Development*, Vol. 13, No. 5, pp. 387–406.

Nelde, P. (2001) 'Perspectives for a European Language Policy" in D. Graddol, (ed.), *Applied Linguistics for the 21st Century*, AILA Review 14, pp. 34–48.

Niskanen, W. (1971) *Bureaucracy and Representative Government*, Chicago: Aldine.

Nozick, R. (1974) *Anarchy, State and Utopia*, Oxford: Blackwell.

Offe, C. (1984) *Contradictions of the Welfare State*, London: Hutchinson.

Phillipson, R. (2003a) *English-Only Europe?* London: Routledge.

Philipson, R. (2003b) Union in need of language equality, *The Guardian Weekly*, January.

Polanyi, K. (1957) *The great transformation: the political and economic origins of our time,* Boston, Mass.: Beacon Press.

Pridham, G. (2000) *The Dynamics of Democratization: a Comparative Approach*, London and New York: Continuum.

Rhodes, R. A. W. (1997) *Understanding Governance: Policy Networks, Governance, Reflexivity and Accountability*, Buckingham and Philadelphia: Open University Press.

Ruggie, J. G., (1993) 'Territoriality and Beyond: Problematizing Modernity in International Relations', *International Organization*, 47, (1), Winter: 139–174.

SOAS (1993), *The Linguasphere Programme*, London, School of Oriental and African Studies.

Spruyt, H. (1994) 'Institutional selection in international relations: state anarchy as order', *International Organization*. 48, (4): 527–57.

Taylor, P. J. (1985) *Political Geography: World-Economy, Nation-State and Locality*, Harlow: Longman.

Touraine, A. (1992) *Critique de la Modernité*, Paris: Fayard.

Van Els, T. J. M. (2001) 'The European Union, its Institutions and its Languages: Some Language Political Observations.' *Current Issues in Language Planning*, vol. 2, no. 4. 311–60.

Van der Merve, I. (1993) 'The Urban Geolinguistics of Cape Town'. *GeoJournal,* 31,409.

Wagner, P. (1994) *A Sociology of Modernity: Liberty and Discipline*, London: Routledge.

Walker, N. (2002) 'The Idea of Constitutional Pluralism', *Modern Law Review*, 65, pp. 317–359.

Wallace, H. and Wallace W. (eds), (2000) *Policy-making in the European Union*, 4th edn Oxford : Oxford University Press.

Wallerstein, I. (1974) *The Modern World System I*, New York: Academic Press.

Wallerstein, I. (1980) *The Modern World System II,* New York: Academic Press.

Williams, C. H. (1986) 'The Question of National Congruence', in R. J. Johnston and P. J. Taylor, (eds), *World in Crisis?* Oxford: Blackwell.

Williams, C. H. (1988) 'An Introduction to Geolinguistics', in C. H. Williams, (ed.), *Language in Geographic Context*, Clevedon, Avon.pp. 1–19.

Williams, C. H. (1991) 'Language Planning and Social Change: Ecological Speculations', in D.F.Marshall, (ed.), *Language Planning: Focusschrift in honor of Joshua A. Fishman,* Amsterdam: John Benjamins.

Williams, C. H. (1992) 'On the Recognition of Minorities in Contemporary Greece,' *Planet,* No 94, pp. 84–90.

Williams, C. H. (2002) The Importance of Holistic Language Planning for the Promotion of *Minority Languages*, Conference on Creating a Common Structure for Promoting Historical Linguistic Minorities within the European Union, Finnish Parliament, Helsinki, Folktinget, 11–12 October.

Williams, C. H. and van der Merve, I. (1996) 'Mapping the Multilingual City: A Research Agenda for Urban Geolinguistics', *Journal of Multilingual and Multicultural Development,* Vol. 17, No. 1, 49–66.

Zelinsky, W. and Wiliams, C. H. (1988) 'The Mapping of Language in North America and the British Isles', *Progress in Human Geography*, 12, 3, pp. 337–68.

Zupancic, J. (1996) *Slovenci v Avstriji:Sodobni Socialnogreografski Procesi in Ohranjanje Identitete,* Unpublished Ph.D. University of Ljubljana.

Zupancic, L. (1998) 'Identiteta Je Merljiva Prispevek K Metodologiji Proucevanja Etnicne Identitete', *Razprave in gradivo*, Ljubljana, vol. 33, pp. 253–68.

5

Diversity in Addressing Diversity: Canadian and British Legislative Approaches to Linguistic Minorities, and Their International Legal Context

ROBERT DUNBAR

The title to this chapter is ambiguous and perhaps slightly mischievous and, as such, needs some clarification. First, there is no one single 'Canadian' approach to linguistic minorities, but many, depending on which jurisdiction is being considered. Here, the focus will primarily be on the federal regime, but the approaches of other jurisdictions, in particular the provinces of Quebec and New Brunswick and the territories of Nunavut and North West Territories, will also be considered. Second, there is also no one single 'British' approach, but differing approaches in Wales, Scotland and Northern Ireland; indeed, there is arguably no 'British' legislative approach at all outside of the context of the so-called 'Celtic Fringe'. Again, all of these approaches will be considered. Third, the approach in Canada, at least, is not only a 'legislative' one, in the sense of an act or series of acts of a legislature, but is also constitutionally mandated. Both constitutional provisions and acts of legislatures will be considered, as will secondary legislation, but enactments of other bodies, such as municipalities, and less legally formal means of linguistic intervention will not be. Such provisions will be set against the backdrop of international legal norms which apply to both states.

In this chapter, I explore the surprising diversity of approaches to the question of legislating in respect of linguistic minorities – 'surprising', because of the historical closeness of the two states. Canada is, after all, a former British colony, and its political and legal history is heavily shaped by the British connection. While the private law of Quebec and Scotland has been described as being that of a 'mixed' jurisdiction,[1] having civilian and common law aspects,[2] the private law of other jurisdictions in the two states is based to a considerable degree on English common law. The Canadian constitution of 1867 was an enactment of the British Parliament, and Canadian constitutional law and broader public law incorporates a wide range of British legal concepts. Canada and Britain are both constitutional monarchies sharing the same monarch, and Canada and its provinces have adopted a British parliamentary model for their legislatures. English is the most widely spoken language in both states, although anglophones are a minority in one Canadian province, Quebec. Yet, in spite of these many similarities, the various Canadian approaches to linguistic minorities on the one hand and the various British approaches on the other differ markedly from each other (the various approaches *within* both states also differ in some important respects). In this chapter, I explore these differences, and also highlight some important similarities. In considering these matters, and in setting them against the international legal context in which both states operate – this context is often forgotten, particularly in Canada – I hope to show that none of the approaches is free from either theoretical or practical difficulties, and that the combined experience of the various jurisdictions in both states can provide some significant lessons.

Before turning to these matters, it may be useful briefly to consider the linguistic complexion of both states. As identified in chapter 1, both Canada and the UK are linguistically diverse states, and always have been. In Canada, there are fifty-two aboriginal languages (grouped in twelve separate language families) currently spoken by 198,595 people, or about 0.6 per cent of the Canadian population (2001 Canadian census.) There are two official languages, English and French, and the 2001 census reported that 82 per cent of the Canadian population claimed one of these two languages as their mother tongue.[3] An even higher percentage, 89.5 per cent, claimed one of these two languages as the language spoken most often at home,[4] and over 98 per cent of Canadians claim to be able to speak and understand at least one or the other of these languages.[5] The French linguistic minorities in most provinces are in decline, both in absolute and proportional terms, and the complete assimilation of such *linguistic communities* within various provinces is in some cases a very real possibility and a very serious threat.[6]

In addition to those who speak an aboriginal language or one of the two official languages, a further 5,334,770 persons, or 18.0 per cent of the Canadian population – about one sixth – claimed a language other than French, English or an aboriginal language – referred to as 'heritage languages' in Canada – as a mother tongue, though a smaller percentage, 10.5 per cent, claimed such a language as a language of the home.[7] Almost 872,400 persons claimed Chinese as their mother tongue, making it the third most widely spoken language in Canada, while very large numbers of Canadians also claimed Italian, German, Portuguese, Spanish, Greek and Ukrainian as mother-tongue languages. The fastest growing heritage languages were Punjabi, with 32.7 per cent more speakers in 2001 than in 1996, Arabic, up by 32.7 per cent, Urdu, almost double its 1996 level, Tagalog, up by 26.3 per cent, and Chinese, up by 18.5 per cent.[8]

In the United Kingdom, there are, as in Canada, languages that are indigenous to the British Isles and Ireland – 'autochthonous' languages, such as English, Scots and Ulster Scots, as well as Celtic languages such as Welsh, Scottish Gaelic, Irish, Cornish and Manx. All but English are minority languages. English is, of course, the single largest mother tongue in Britain, by a very wide margin, and is spoken by an overwhelming majority of the population. It is also the de facto 'official language' of the UK, although as we shall see, Welsh is also an 'official language', at least as regards the devolved institutions of Welsh government. According to the 2001 British census, 575,640 people in Wales identified themselves as being able to speak Welsh, representing 20.52 per cent of the population aged three and over.[9] There do not appear to be any monoglot Welsh-speakers, however, and the language has, until the 1981 census, suffered from a prolonged period of decline in numbers of speakers. The demographic position of the other Celtic languages is weaker, according to census data: for example, according to the 2001 British census, some 167,490 people, or 9.98 per cent of the population of Northern Ireland,[10] claimed to have an ability to speak Irish, and some 58,652 people, or 1.2 per cent of the population of Scotland, reported themselves being able to speak Scottish Gaelic.[11] Unlike the Canadian census, which solicits considerable amounts of information on linguistic competence and use for all languages spoken in Canada, the British census only solicits information on Welsh in Wales, Scottish Gaelic in Scotland and Irish in Northern Ireland; thus, it is very difficult to make statements which are as definitive and clear about speakers of all other languages, including English. However, both Cornish and Manx are revived languages; the number of speakers of Cornish is likely to be in the hundreds,[12] and of Manx exceeds one thousand.[13] It is thought that Scots and Ulster Scots are more widely spoken, but because of their linguistic similarity to English, it is not clear how many people use either as the sole or primary medium of communication, and if so used, in how many different domains.[14]

As is the case in Canada, a large number of other languages, referred to in the UK as 'community' rather than 'heritage' languages, are also spoken, brought by successive waves of relatively more recent immigration. Once again, the UK censuses do not solicit information on any of these languages, and therefore no definitive statements can be made; the censuses do solicit information on ethnicity, and the 2001 census revealed that 7.9 per cent of the population of the UK belonged to ethnic minorities.[15] However, not all persons who identify themselves as belonging to an ethnic minority community necessarily speak the language of that community, and 'ethnic' affiliation identified on the census (for example, Indian, Pakistani, Indian, Bangladeshi, Chinese, Black African, Black Caribbean, etc.) can itself hide a considerable range of linguistic affiliations. Recent research in London, however, reveals the huge linguistic diversity of the capital, and this pattern will be replicated, at least to some degree, in many other major British cities.[16]

Beneficiaries

In spite of this huge linguistic complexity, both Canada and the UK strictly limit the number of languages which benefit from constitutional and/or legislative protection. In Canada, French and English receive special recognition in the constitution, and in a number of pieces of important legislation, notably the Official Languages Act 1988.[17] In particular, subsection 16(1) of the Canadian Charter of Rights and Freedoms (the 'Charter') of 1982[18] provides that English and French are the *official languages* of Canada and have equality of status and equal rights and privileges as to their use in all institutions of the Parliament and government of Canada. Building on section 133 of the Constitution Act 1867,[19] the Charter also guarantees the right to use either English or French in any debates and other proceedings of Parliament,[20] requires that all statutes, records and journals of Parliament be printed and published in English and French, provides that both language versions of such documents are equally authoritative,[21] and provides that English or French may be used by any person in, or in any pleading in or process issuing from any court established by Parliament,[22] which includes the Federal Court, Trial Division, the Federal Court of Appeal and the Supreme Court of Canada.

Subsection 20(1) of the Charter provides that any member of the public in Canada has the right to communicate with and receive services from any head or central office of an institution of the Parliament *or government* of Canada[23] in English or French, and has the same right with respect to any other office of such institutions where there is a significant demand for communications with and services from the office in such language or, due to the nature of the office, it is reasonable that communications with and services from that office be available in English and French. These various constitutional requirements are clarified and particularized in the Official Languages Act 1988.[24] However, this act goes beyond the Charter in providing in Part V rights to federal civil servants to use English or French in the workplace.

Section 23 of the Charter is of particular importance because it relates to an area, primary and secondary education, which is within the exclusive legislative competence of the provinces;[25] but for section 23, the education of linguistic minorities in the provinces would be a matter for the provincial legislatures, bodies in which the linguistic majority are dominant. The right to minority language education is limited to the children of specific classes of beneficiaries: first, parents whose mother tongue is that of the official language minority of the province (that is, native English-speakers in Quebec and native French-speakers elsewhere); second, parents who received their primary school education in the minority official language anywhere in Canada (for example, a Canadian citizen who was educated in English in Ontario and who moves to Quebec); and third, parents any of whose children received primary or secondary instruction in the minority official language anywhere in Canada (for example, a Canadian citizen who had a child educated in English in Manitoba and who moves to Quebec can have all of his or her children educated in English there). Thus, the section 23 right is not an unlimited one. Significantly, it does not create a right to immersion education: a native English-speaking parent who was educated in Ontario does not have the right, under section 23, to have his or her children educated in Ontario through the medium of French. Thus, the minority language education right is contingent upon some pre-existing linkage to the linguistic minority; it effectively rations access to minority language education to those having such a link to the linguistic minority. The key point here, however, is that minority language education is constitutionally guaranteed only for English- and French-speaking linguistic minorities.

The Canadian constitution makes no explicit reference to any language other than English or French, and the same is generally the case under other federal legislation. Section 22 of the Charter provides that nothing in sections 16 to 20 of the Charter abrogates or derogates from any legal or customary right or privilege acquired or enjoyed either before or after the coming into force of the Charter with respect to any language other than English or French. It is not clear, however, whether any other language does, in fact, enjoy any such rights. Section 27 of the Charter provides that the Charter shall be interpreted in a manner that is consistent with the preservation and enhancement of the multicultural heritage of Canada. However, this section is one which guides interpretation, and does not create substantive rights; it certainly does not create any rights for languages other than English and French.[26] Subsection 35(1) of the Charter may be of some relevance for speakers of aboriginal languages. It provides that the existing aboriginal and treaty rights of the aboriginal peoples of Canada (defined in subsection 35(2) to include the Indian, Inuit and Métis peoples of Canada) are recognized and affirmed. Subsection 35(1) makes no specific reference to languages, but may yet be relevant to the constitutional status of aboriginal languages in Canada. It has, for example, been suggested that the concept of 'aboriginal rights' includes everything necessary for the survival of aboriginal peoples as such, and includes rights to land, language, economy, culture, law and government.[27] Canada has witnessed a virtual explosion of case law, including a large number of fundamentally important Supreme Court of Canada decisions, which have clarified considerably the content of the concepts 'aboriginal rights' and 'treaty rights'; however, there have, as yet, been no decisions which explore the extent to which either concept may embody a right to language, or what the content of such a right might be.

The picture at the provincial level is broadly similar. Under the Charter, English and French are the official languages of one province,[28] New Brunswick, and the Charter guarantees the right to use either language in the debates and other proceedings of the New Brunswick legislature[29] and in the New Brunswick courts,[30] and ensures that the statutes, records and journals of the legislature are bilingual.[31] Subsection 20(2) of the Charter goes further than subsection 20(1) in respect of bilingual services from the federal Parliament and government, in that it contains an unqualified right to communicate with and receive available services from any office of an institution of the legislature or government of New Brunswick in either English or French.[32] Furthermore, subsection 16.1(1) of the Charter provides that the English linguistic community and the French linguistic community in New Brunswick have equality of status and equal rights and privileges, including the right to distinct educational institutions and such distinct cultural institutions as are necessary for the preservation and promotion of those communities. French and English also have enhanced constitutional status in two other provinces. Section 23 of the Manitoba Act 1870[33] provides that either English or French may be used in the debates of the provincial legislature, that both languages shall be used in the records and journals of the legislature, that the Acts of the legislature shall be printed and published in both languages, and that either language may be used by any person or in any pleading or process in or from any court of the province.[34] Although the Charter of the French Language[35] made French alone the official language of Quebec, section 133 of the Constitution Act 1867 contained similar guarantees with respect to the use of French *and* English as section 23 of the Manitoba Act 1870,[36] and section 7 of the Charter of the French Language was amended accordingly, to reflect the protections set out in section 133.[37]

In addition to these constitutional provisions, there is a wide range of provincial legislation which provides special recognition to French and English; space does not permit a discussion of all such enactments, but in virtually all cases, legislative recognition is extended only to French and English. However, in two territories, the Northwest Territories and Nunavut, recognition is given to certain aboriginal languages, as well as English and French. The preamble to the Northwest Territories' Official Languages Act[38] recognizes that the existence of aboriginal peoples constitutes a fundamental characteristic of Canada, that aboriginal peoples, speaking aboriginal languages, constitute the Territories a distinct society within Canada, that the languages of the aboriginal peoples should be given recognition in law, and notes a commitment to the preservation, enhancement and development of such languages. Section 4 provides that Chipewyan, Cree, English, French, Gwich'in, Innuinnaqtun, Inuktitut, Inuvialuktun, North Slavey, South Slavey and Tlichô are the official languages of the Northwest Territories, and section 9 provides that everyone has the right to use any of these official languages in the debates and other proceedings of the territory's legislative assembly. However, this legislation does not, in practice, confer equal status on the various aboriginal languages with English and French. For example, while subsection 14(1) provides that any member of the public may communicate with and receive services from any head or central office of any institution of the government of the Northwest Territories in English or French, subsection 14(2) provides that any member of the public may communicate with and receive services from any regional, area or community office of the government in any official language other than English or French only where there is a 'significant demand' for communications and services in such languages. As a result of sections 29 and 38 of the Nunavut Act,[39] the Official Languages Act of the Northwest Territories is incorporated into Nunavut law. Quebec's Charter of the French Language gives very limited recognition to aboriginal languages.

In the United Kingdom, there is no single constitutional document, and there is no constitutionally mandated 'official language'. English, however, is the de facto official language, and its position in public institutions has from time to time been legislatively reinforced, sometimes at the expense of the autochthonous languages. The Act of Union of 1536, for example, which formally incorporated the Principality of Wales into England, reinforced by further legislation in 1542, provided that English would be the language of the courts in Wales and that only those able to speak English could hold public office; the aim was to create a uniform, English-speaking legal and administrative system throughout England and Wales. The Courts of Justice Act of 1731 required the use of English in all courts in England and Wales, and in the court of Exchequer in Scotland, and the Administration of Justice (Language) Act (Ireland) of 1737 had the same effect with respect to the courts of Ireland.[40] The Education Act of 1870 for England and Wales and the Education (Scotland) Act of 1872 introduced universal, state-supported education, but only through the medium of English. As a result, the English language achieved an even greater institutional dominance in the UK than in Canada.

Against this backdrop, the status of the Welsh language has, primarily in the latter years of the twentieth century, been legislatively recognized in Wales; Scottish Gaelic in Scotland and Irish in Northern Ireland have also recently received a measure of recognition. Four pieces of legislation have been particularly important in establishing the status of the Welsh language. The first is the Broadcasting Act 1980, which, together with the Broadcasting Act 1981, established Sianel Pedwar Cymru (S4C), the Welsh-language television channel which started broadcasting in 1982.[41] The second is the Education Reform Act 1988,[42] which ensured Welsh a fundamental place in the national curriculum for Wales; in particular, the curriculum for students between five and sixteen must include core and foundation subjects,[43] and Welsh is a core subject in Welsh-speaking schools and a foundation subject in non-Welsh-speaking schools.[44] The third piece of legislation, the Welsh Language Act 1993, is perhaps the most important. It created a statutory body, Bwrdd yr Iaith Gymraeg, the Welsh Language Board, which has the general function of 'promoting and facilitating the use of the Welsh language', together with more specific functions.[45] The Welsh Language Act 1993 will be considered in greater detail below. The final piece of legislation is the Government of Wales Act 1998 (subsequently amended by the Government of Wales Act 2006 c.32) which created devolved government in Wales through the establishment of the National Assembly for Wales. This act provides that the Assembly shall, in the conduct of its business, give effect, so far as is both appropriate in the circumstances and reasonably practicable, to the principle that English and Welsh should be treated on a basis of equality.[46] The Assembly also has the power – but is not required – to pass subordinate legislation in both English and Welsh, and where it does so, both versions are equally authoritative.[47] Finally, this act provides that the assembly may 'do anything it considers appropriate to support the Welsh language',[48] and, while the Assembly may have been able to take such measures even in the absence of this provision,[49] it is at least of symbolic importance in highlighting the importance attached to the support of the Welsh language under devolution. These measures have been modified and, indeed, enhanced in the Government of Wales Act 2006; in this regard, sections 35 and 78 are particularly important. Section 35 provides that the National Assembly for Wales must, in the conduct of its proceedings, give effect to the principle that English and Welsh should be treated on the basis of equality (at least 'so far as is both appropriate in the circumstances and reasonably practicable'). Section 78 requires Welsh Ministers in the newly-created Welsh Assembly Government to adopt a strategy on how they propose to promote and facilitate the use of the Welsh language. It also requires them to adopt a scheme specifying measures which they propose to take as to the use of Welsh in the provision of services to the public, for the purpose of giving effect to the principle that in the conduct of public business in Wales English and Welsh should be treated on a basis of equality.

Scottish Gaelic has also been recognized and given support through a number of pieces of legislation; however, such legislative support has, to date, been less dramatic than that for Welsh. Scottish Gaelic does not yet enjoy a stand-alone television station like Welsh, although the Broadcasting Act 1990 and 1996 gave recognition to Gaelic through the creation of a Gaelic Broadcasting Committee ('Comataidh Craolaidh Gàidhlig', or 'CCG') empowered to fund the production of Gaelic television and radio programming. Under the Communications Act 2003, the CCG was replaced by a new body, the Gaelic Media Service ('Seirbhis nam Meadhanan Gàidhlig', or 'SnamMG'), and its powers were expanded to create programming as well as to fund it. There has been some recognition of Gaelic in education legislation, but Gaelic generally has a much more tenuous and marginal place in the education system than Welsh in Wales. There was no mention of Gaelic in the Scotland Act 1998, which created the devolved institutions in Scotland. In April, 2005, though, the Scottish Parliament passed the Gaelic Language (Scotland) Act 2005, a piece of legislation that was modelled to a certain extent on the Welsh Language Act 1993, and which gives Bòrd na Gàidhlig (Alba) (the 'Gaelic Language Board') a statutory basis. This new legislation is discussed further below. The legislative status of Irish in Northern Ireland is less developed still; however, although Irish enjoys little formal legislative support in Northern Ireland, the UK has assumed particular international obligations in respect of the language, and these will be explored below.

Thus, in the UK, as in Canada, very limited legislative recognition is given to the great linguistic diversity that actually exists. In Canada, significant constitutional and legislative recognition is given to English and French only. This is due in part to history: these are the languages of the two European powers that colonized the country, the languages of Canada's 'founding peoples'.[50] It is also a matter of political expediency: the 1867 constitutional settlement was designed to knit together a linguistically diverse country,[51] and subsequent legislative enactments, from the Official Languages Act 1969 to the 1982 Charter were in part in response to linguistic tensions, including the rise of the secessionism in Quebec. Furthermore, it is also a matter of expediency. While, as noted in the initial section of this chapter, roughly one sixth of the Canadian population has a mother tongue other than English or French, the number of French-speakers still significantly outnumbers the speakers of all other languages (except English) combined. And while the vast majority of allophones (persons whose mother tongue is neither English nor French) also speak French or English, a majority of French-speakers in Canada and a large majority of English-speakers speak only their mother tongue.

In the UK, English has no obvious legislative or constitutional status at all, but is, as a matter of practice and tradition, the dominant language for all formal governmental purposes. Recognition of other languages has been relatively recent, and limited to three of the UK's 'autochthonous' languages; the greatest measures of recognition and support have been taken in respect of the demographically strongest and, arguably, the most politicized of these, Welsh, with lesser status accorded to Scottish Gaelic and Irish.[52] In the UK, however, there are very different historical, political and practical expedients. In particular, the autochthonous language communities in the UK have historically been dominated, and therefore have not had to be accommodated.

Unlike Quebec nationalism, Irish nationalism has not been primarily language based (though language has played a role), and this is even more true of contemporary Scottish nationalism. Thus, in its strategies for addressing nationalist sentiment in Northern Ireland and Scotland, the UK has generally not had to attach much weight to linguistic questions. In Wales, language has generally been a much more salient factor in the question of nationalism, and this may in part explain the more rigorous regime there. And, in terms of practicalities, each of the autochthonous language communities is a minority even in their nations, and a tiny minority in the UK as a whole: even Welsh-speakers, by far the largest autochthonous linguistic minority, make up less than 1 per cent of the British population. All speakers of autochthonous languages in the UK are fluent in English. However, in each case, the autochthonous linguistic minority has a special claim: each are, as noted, indigenous to the three nations (Wales, Scotland and Northern Ireland), and have been historically dominant there; although census figures are not kept for languages other than Welsh, Gaelic and Irish, it is likely that the numbers of speakers of each are greater than the numbers of speakers of all other minority languages in each of the respective nations combined;[53] speakers of each of these languages have engaged in increasingly more determined campaigns to ensure legislative recognition of their languages; and, finally, each of these languages benefits from international legal commitments recently entered into by the UK.

The non-recognition of the languages of migrants – whether recent migrants or more long-standing migrant communities – is, of course, the norm in the vast majority of states, but the justifications for this are less obvious, particularly in states such as Canada and the UK which give a measure of recognition to certain linguistic minorities. The question of whether and to what extent the linguistic claims of migrants and their descendants should be recognized is one with which legal theorists and political philosophers have been grappling in recent years; space does not permit an assessment of the developing literature on this issue.[54]

Structure: 'Coercion', Rights and Administrative Planning Approaches

There are, however, several striking differences between the various approaches to minority language maintenance taken in Canada and in Britain (and particularly, in Wales). The first of these is the much greater emphasis placed on the articulation of relatively clearly defined language 'rights' in Canada. By contrast, 'rights' do not figure nearly so prominently in British approaches. The second is the differing concepts of bilingualism that underlay legislative measures in Canada and Britain, a contrast which is particularly clear in the case of Welsh. The third is the somewhat different salience attached to language maintenance and, in particular, to 'reversing language shift'.

A 'Rights' Framework

In Canada, the various protections afforded to French and English are, as we have seen, generally conceived of in terms of rights. Perhaps the three most important provisions, in terms of the daily lives of members of the French and English linguistic minorities, are those set out in subsection 19(1) of the Charter, relating to the federal courts, subsection 20(1) of the Charter, relating to communication with and services from institutions of the Parliament and government of Canada, and section 23 of the Charter, relating to primary and secondary education. The subsection 20(1) right to communicate with and receive services from the federal Parliament and government has, as noted, been further articulated in the Official Languages Act 1988, but that legislation also treats access to services as a matter of rights. As discussed above, both the right to communicate with and receive services in French or English and the right to primary and secondary minority language education are subject to certain limitations. With regard to the right to communicate and receive services in French or English, that right is absolute when dealing with the head or central office of any federal institution or any other office or facility of such institutions located in the National Capital Region;[55] with regard to other offices, the right is conditional on the existence of 'significant demand' for such communications and services, and such demand is defined by detailed regulations prepared by the government of Canada.[56]

The section 23 right to minority language education is subject to a range of limitations, some of which were described above and will be considered further below, but it, too, is subject to a condition of sufficient demand. In particular, paragraph 23(3)(a) provides that the right to minority language education applies only wherever in a province 'the number of children of citizens who have such a right is sufficient to warrant the provision to them out of public funds of minority language instruction'. In Canada, education is a matter for which the provinces rather than the federal government have sole legislative authority, and so the duty implied by the section 23 right is one which ultimately falls on the provinces, and it is the provinces which, in practice, set out in legislation and/or regulations the basis for determining demand sufficiency. However, the consistency of such provincial rules with the requirements of section 23 is subject to the scrutiny of the courts, and the principles by which demand sufficiency is to be determined have been articulated in a series of important decisions of the Supreme Court of Canada.[57]

The approach to minority language provision at the provincial and territorial level also tends to be conceived of as a matter of rights. This is certainly the case with respect to French and English in New Brunswick, as was described above. Although Ontario, the province with the numerically largest francophone minority community, is not officially bilingual by virtue of the constitution or an official languages act, it has developed a fairly comprehensive model for the protection of the francophone minority, and this model is framed primarily in terms of rights. Under the French Language Services Act,[58] for example, subsection 5(1) provides that everyone has the *right* to communicate in French with, and to receive available services from, any head or central office of a government agency[59] or institution of the legislature, and has the same right in respect of any such agency or institution located in or serving an area of the province designated in a schedule to the Act. The right to French-medium education set out in section 23 of the Charter is recognized and amplified upon in the Education Act.[60] With regard to the provincial courts, section 125(1) of the Courts of Justice Act[61] provides that the official languages of the courts of Ontario are English and French, but subsection 126(1) creates an arguably more extensive right than that contained in the Charter in respect of the federal courts, in that it provides that a party to a proceeding who speaks French has the *right* to require that it be conducted as a bilingual proceeding.[62]

The approach in the UK, as exemplified by the situation with respect to Welsh in Wales – the strongest of the minority language regimes in the UK – is strikingly different in this respect, as the use of a rights-based model is almost completely eschewed. In the Education Act 1988, for example, there is an element of compulsion – as Welsh is made part of the national curriculum, all students must take it as a subject from the age of five to sixteen – but aside from this requirement, there is no right created to receive one's education through the medium of Welsh. In practice, Welsh-medium education is very widely available, but its provision is based on decisions voluntarily taken by local education authorities and, since the creation of the Welsh Language Act 1993, through the development of language schemes (to be discussed momentarily) with the assistance and subject to the approval of the Welsh Language Board.

The Welsh Language Act 1993 itself creates few recognizable language 'rights'. The centrepiece of the approach taken under this Act is the creation of Welsh-language schemes by public bodies under which the use of the Welsh language in the public sector is to be advanced. The Welsh Language Board plays a crucial role in this process. Under section 5 of the act, every public body[63] to which a notice is given by the Board must prepare a Welsh-language scheme that specifies the measures the public body proposes to take as to the use of Welsh in connection with the services it provides. In specifying such measures, the public body is to give effect to the principle that, in the conduct of public business and the administration of justice in Wales, the English and Welsh languages should be treated on the basis of equality. This obligation is not, however, absolute; public bodies need implement the principle only 'so far as is both appropriate in the circumstances and reasonably practicable'.[64] The application of the general principle and the determination of scope of this qualification are not left to public bodies themselves, however; the act provides that the Board must issue guidelines as to the form and content of schemes[65] to which each public body must have regard in preparing their scheme,[66] that the public body must carry out consultations in the preparation of the scheme,[67] and the scheme must be submitted to the Board for approval.[68] The Board published its guidance to public bodies in 1996,[69] and this guidance requires that Welsh-language schemes set out the measures that public bodies will take in relation to: dealing with the Welsh-speaking public, including such matters as correspondence, telephone communication, the conduct of meetings and so forth; and, the public face of the organization, including its corporate identity, signage, publishing and printing material directed to the public, forms and explanatory material, press notices, publicity and advertising, and official notices.[70]

Once approved, the Welsh-language plans are potentially enforceable, and therefore they create binding commitments for the public bodies which have created them. They do not, however, create 'rights' to obtain minority language services in the classic sense. Members of the public can make complaints to the Welsh Language Board that a public body is not implementing its Welsh-language scheme; however, they cannot claim that their 'right' to a Welsh-language service has been infringed or denied, and, in the absence of action taken by the Board, as provided for in the Act, it is not clear that a member of the public has any obvious remedy, a point to which further consideration will be given below.

Indeed, the closest any of the core pieces of legislation relating to the Welsh language come to creating a clearly expressed right is subsection 22(1) of the Welsh Language Act 1993, relating to the use of Welsh in the courts, and even that provision does not refer explicitly to a 'right', but uses permissive language to express the entitlement; it provides that 'in any legal proceedings in Wales the Welsh language may be spoken by any party, witness or other person who desires to use it', subject to such prior notice as may be necessary. As already noted, the Government of Wales Acts of both 1998 and 2006, mirroring the language of the Welsh Language Act 1993, provide that the National Assembly for Wales must, in the conduct of its business give effect, so far as is both appropriate in the circumstances and reasonably practicable, to the principle that the English and Welsh languages should be treated on the basis of equality; however, neither the 1998 nor the 2006 Act make explicit provision for the use of the Welsh language in the work of the Assembly, and does not purport to create any rights. The 1998 Act does require that the standing orders – the Assembly's rules of procedure – to be made in both English and Welsh,[71] and also provides that the English and Welsh texts of any subordinate legislation made by the Assembly shall be treated as being of equal standing (although, curiously, it does not require that such legislation be made in both languages) (this provision was carried forward and expanded in section 156 of the 2006 Act to also cover any primary legislation which the Assembly may in future be empowered to create). However, all of these provisions do not relate to the rights of individuals.[72] The ability to use Welsh in the Assembly is guaranteed, but in the standing orders, and not explicitly in the 1998 or in the 2006 Acts themselves, and, even there, the provisions are permissive and avoid the language of rights: Members *may speak* in English or Welsh, and simultaneous interpretation facilities shall be provided for speeches made in Welsh.[73]

As we shall see in the next section, the limited use of a rights-based approach has implications for the ways in which the Welsh-language regime is implemented and enforced. However, the Welsh approach is, at least in this respect, markedly different from that which has generally been taken in Canada. In Wales, considerable power with respect to the nature and extent of the language regime is essentially left to a semi-autonomous public body, the Welsh Language Board, appointed by and ultimately accountable to the Welsh Assembly Government. Members of the Welsh-speaking public generally do not have a clear idea from the legislative framework of the nature and extent of the public services that they will enjoy, have no clear idea of what entitlements they have, and have very few rights which they themselves can rely upon and enforce.

In Canada, although bodies which are broadly similar to the Welsh Language Board are created – for example, the Office of the Commissioner for Official Languages under the Official Languages Act 1988 – they generally have a very different role in the language regime. Such bodies have relatively little control over the ultimate shape of the language regime – that is generally determined by the constitution, statute and secondary legislation – and the prime focus of their activities is to assist in enforcement of the legislation. They can and do monitor implementation of the language regime, and can and do provide valuable language planning advice to public sector bodies and more generally. Members of the official language minorities do, however, have a reasonably clear idea of their entitlements, and have fairly clear rights which they can have enforced.

It is not altogether clear why such differing approaches emerged in two states which, as noted at the outset, share so many common values and principles. Space does not permit anything but the broadest generalizations, but part of the reason for the differing approaches may be attributable to the broader legal climate in the two states at the time the minority language regimes were being created. From the late 1950s, if not before, a fairly robust 'rights culture' was emerging in Canada, as evidenced by the adoption in 1960 of the Canadian Bill of Rights; though this enactment did not have constitutional status, and was only a federal statute, applicable to federal laws and institutions, it did represent a significant break from the British legal tradition of leaving civil liberties to be protected by the moderation of legislative bodies themselves and the rules of the common law.[74] The idea that the regulation of language was a matter of rights has an even older pedigree in Canada, dating, as we have seen, back to the Constitution Act 1867, in provisions such as section 133. Thus, it was not surprising that a firmly rights-based approach should have been taken in the first Official Languages Act of 1969, or in the 1982 constitution, which, as we have seen, introduced a constitutionally based rights document, the Charter. Although British lawyers were amongst the drafters of the European Convention on Human Rights, and although the UK was the first state to ratify that important human rights treaty, the UK does not have a constitutionally entrenched Bill of Rights in the Canadian or American senses, and the introduction of a more limited rights document into domestic law by way of parliamentary statute took place only in the last few years, with the passage of the Human Rights Act 1998. All of the key Welsh-language legislation, save for those limited (though nonetheless important) provisions relating to language in the Government of Wales Acts of 1998 and 2006, long predated this rights statute, and is a function of broader historical, political and practical considerations.

The Welsh-language regime represents a challenge to the notion that a minority language regime cannot be effective unless it is based on a clearly articulated set of enforceable language rights. In the decade and a half since the passage of the Welsh Language Act 1993, well over 350 Welsh-language schemes have been created, and now all education authorities and local councils, and a wide range of other public bodies, including national UK bodies based in Wales such as the DVLA, the drivers' licensing body, are all subject to Welsh-language schemes approved by the Welsh Language Board. The preparation of such schemes has allowed the Welsh Language Board to engage in very detailed micro-planning at the local level, all within the framework of a nationally determined long-term strategy, as set out in *A Strategy for the Welsh Language*, and medium-term strategy, as set out in 'The Welsh Language: A Vision and a Mission for 2000–2005'. Without question, this regime has ushered in greatly expanded opportunities to use the Welsh language in a wide range of settings. While it is notoriously difficult to comment on the causative relationship between any particular legal regime for minority language maintenance and actual patterns of language acquisition and use, raw census data does show a relatively significant increase between 1991 and 2001 in the numbers of people in Wales who claim the ability to speak Welsh.[75] It would, however, be difficult to claim with authority that the Welsh model has had a demonstrably less positive effect on patterns of minority language maintenance and revival than the various Canadian models.

It is, however, also important to bear in mind the relatively unique position of Welsh as compared to French in the predominantly English-speaking provinces of Canada. Unlike French in those provinces, Welsh can claim to be the language of the Welsh nation, of which even non-Welsh speaking Welsh people form a part, and this status is acknowledged as a political reality. Second, the Welsh-speaking minority in Wales is larger in absolute terms than any of the francophone minorities in the English-speaking provinces, and Welsh speakers, at roughly 21 per cent of the Welsh population, make up a much larger percentage of the population of Wales than francophones in any province but New Brunswick. A very sizeable minority of the members of the National Assembly of Wales are Welsh-speakers, and many of those who are not are actively learning the language. Thus, as minorities go, the Welsh-speaking minority is in a position of relative strength. In such circumstances, it is possible that a strongly rights-based regime is of somewhat less importance, particularly where a relatively powerful body such as the Welsh Language Board has been created to implement a form of bilingualism. Where the linguistic minority comprises a much smaller segment of the population, where it can command a less visible presence within political institutions, and where its language is not seen as necessarily being the patrimony of the whole society, the Welsh approach may offer less hope than the Canadian one.

Concepts of Bilingualism

Bilingualism is generally not a policy goal that has been articulated in Scotland or Northern Ireland with respect to Gaelic or Irish, but the concept does feature prominently in Wales and in Canada, at least at the federal level. However, the concept of bilingualism has subtle but very significant differences in meaning in Canada and in Wales. In Canada, the concept of bilingualism is most frequently associated with the policy of 'official bilingualism', which refers to the ability of the federal Parliament, the federal government and their respective institutions to accommodate and interact with the public they serve in both French and English, ensuring that both anglophones and francophones have access to those institutions through the medium of their own language. Another aspect of the concept of bilingualism is the maintenance of Canada's minority French- and English-speaking communities. This aspect is given clearest expression in section 41, in Part VII, of the Official Languages Act 1988, which provides that the Government of Canada is committed to enhancing the vitality of the English and French linguistic minority communities in Canada and supporting and assisting their development, and fostering the full recognition and use of both English and French in Canadian society. The promotion of bilingualism, in both of these senses, implies the desirability of increasing the number of Canadians who can speak both French and English. However, the achievement of societal bilingualism – the creation of a society in which everyone is able to speak both French and English – has generally not been the goal,[76] and the legislative and constitutional framework in Canada is not directed at the accomplishment of such a goal. This is clearest in respect of education, the area most closely related to language acquisition. Under the Canadian constitution, education is, as already noted, a matter for the provinces. As was also noted, section 23 of the Charter seeks to ensure that English-speaking parents in Quebec and French-speaking parents elsewhere in the country can have their children receive primary and secondary education in their own language, thereby ensuring that the linguistic majority of the province or territory cannot deny minority language education to the minority. However, the constitution says nothing about the acquisition by the linguistic majorities of the language of the minority. While the provinces tend to offer students the opportunity to learn the official minority language in schools, and, indeed, generally require all students to receive some instruction, the relatively limited exposure to the minority language through the school system does not, and likely cannot, produce fully bilingual students. Given the benefits, including employment benefits in the federal civil service, which come with bilingual skills, provinces generally want to provide students with the opportunity to acquire such skills, but they do not require the acquisition of such skills.

In Wales, there is also a commitment to bilingualism conceived of as 'official bilingualism'. This is clear, for example, in the Welsh Language Act 1993 itself, which, as discussed above, provides that every public body which is required by the Welsh Language Board to produce a language scheme must do so with a view to giving effect to the principle that in the conduct of public business and the administration of justice in Wales the English and Welsh languages should be treated on the basis of equality. Unlike Canada, however, the promotion of societal bilingualism both is a policy goal and is given expression in the legislative framework. This is most clearly reflected in the Education Reform Act 1988, which, as noted above, makes Welsh a core subject in the curriculum for *every* student in Wales, from the age of five to sixteen. The government's goal was to ensure that '*all* children should by the time they complete their compulsory schooling at sixteen and after eleven years' study of Welsh in school have acquired a substantial degree of fluency in Welsh' (emphasis added).[77] It is also implicit in the Welsh Assembly Government's vision of the position of the Welsh language in Wales; the government 'is wholly committed to revitalizing the Welsh language and creating a bilingual Wales', and explicitly shares the following vision of the Assembly's Culture and Education Committees:

> In a truly bilingual Wales both Welsh and English will flourish and will be treated as equal. A bilingual Wales means a country where people can choose to live their lives through the medium of either or both languages; a country where the presence of two national languages, and other diverse languages and cultures, is a source of pride and strength to us all.

The goal of putting people in a position to choose to live their lives through either or both Welsh and English clearly implies that all Welsh people should be equipped with the capacity to make that choice, and that implies a sufficiently strong command of both languages. This is a much different and, it is suggested, a much more thoroughgoing and radical understanding of bilingualism than that which has been accepted in Canada which, as noted, tends to limit itself to ensuring that members of the linguistic minority have some of the tools necessary to assist the transmission of their language and its use in certain domains.

Language Maintenance and Reversing Language Shift as the Primary Focus

A final way in which the Canadian federal model and the UK models – especially the Welsh model – differ is in respect of the emphasis put on legislation as a means of maintaining minority language communities and reversing the decline of such communities. The Welsh model is unambiguously directed at the revitalization of the Welsh language. As we have seen, the centrepiece of the Welsh approach is the creation of a relatively powerful language planning body, the Welsh Language Board. The Board is legislatively required to produce guidelines which will be applied by all public bodies in Wales in the preparation of Welsh-language schemes; legislation also empowers the Board to designate those public bodies which must prepare such a scheme and effectively requires Board approval of such schemes. In 1996, the Board published *A Strategy for the Welsh Language*, a document meant to guide the Board in its work in the period up to the 2001 census. The main aim of the strategy was 'to enable the Welsh language to become self-sustaining and secure as a medium of communication in Wales'. The Board identified four main challenges: increasing the number of people who are able to speak Welsh; providing opportunities to use the language; changing habits of language use, and encouraging people to take advantage of the opportunities provided; and strengthening Welsh as a community language.[78] As we have also seen, the goal of education policy and education legislation is the acquisition by all students of fluency in Welsh, and to the extent that instruction in Welsh is required, there is, in fact, an element of coercion involved. An aspect of language revitalization is therefore not simply the protection of the Welsh language in those communities in which the language is presently spoken as a community language, but the acquisition of the language by all. The major limitation on the policy tools available for the revitalization of the Welsh language is the limited ability to intervene in the private or voluntary sectors; the Welsh Language Act 1993 only contemplates the preparation of language plans by and the promotion of bilingualism through public sector institutions. The Welsh Language Board can and does work with the private and voluntary sectors in promoting the use of the language in such sectors, but it does not have any legislative powers that would allow it to demand action.

The preservation of minority linguistic communities is also an aspect of the Canadian approach at the federal level, but it is arguably not the overriding aspect, as it is in Wales. The first concern of the Canadian model seems to be linguistic equity: ensuring that speakers of either official language have access to federal institutions through the medium of their own official language, or their official language of choice. A goal of the Welsh model is certainly to promote effective choice by the public as to which language can be used in accessing public services, but given that many francophones in Canada are monolinguals, the question of minority language services is more than a matter of linguistic choice; it is a matter of linguistic necessity. The goal of language maintenance and revitalization is given explicit recognition in Part VII of the Official Languages Act 1988. As noted, section 41 commits the government of Canada to enhancing the vitality of the English and French linguistic minority communities in Canada, and by virtue of a 2005 amendment to section 41, every federal institution now has the duty to ensure that positive measures are taken for the implementation of this commitment. Section 42 requires the Minister of Canadian Heritage to encourage and promote a coordinated approach to the implementation by federal institutions of the section 41 commitments, and section 43 requires the minister to take such other measures as he or she considers appropriate to advancing the equality of status and use of English and French in Canadian society, including a number of particular measures set out in that section. However, as shall be seen below, the policy tools available to implement these commitments are limited: the federal government has very limited power to intervene in areas of exclusive provincial legislative powers—the 2005 amendment to section 41, for example, made clear that the duty imposed on federal institutions to take positive measures to enhance the vitality of the official language minorities must respect the jurisdiction and powers of the provinces–and a large number of areas relevant to language use and which are crucial to any language maintenance and revitalization strategy fall within the provincial jurisdiction. With respect to the crucial area of language acquisition, section 23 of the Charter, by creating minority language education rights, effectively erodes provincial autonomy. However, section 23, as noted, ensures only that parents who speak the minority language can ensure their children are taught that language. It provides one very important tool for maintaining linguistic identity to the linguistic minority, but it does not contemplate that persons who are not already members of the linguistic minority will be enabled to become part of that minority.

The only Canadian jurisdiction in which a policy which is unmistakably and unequivocally directed at language maintenance and revitalization is Quebec. The Charter of the French Language is predicated on the idea that the societal position of the French language must be reinforced, and that the domains in which it is used must be significantly expanded. The education system is therefore directed to the greatest extent compatible with the minority language education guarantees of section 23 of the Charter to the acquisition by all students of the French language. In this sense, the Quebec model employs an element of compulsion, and one which is even more thoroughgoing than that employed in Wales, as the means by which acquisition of French is to take place is through full French-medium education. The other important respect in which the Quebec model goes well beyond the Welsh one is that the Charter of the French Language regulates language use not only in the public sector, but also in the private and voluntary sectors. This is seen in the requirements of the Quebec legislation relating to the compulsory use of French on all public signage, and the preparation by business enterprises having more than one hundred employees of 'francization plans'; that is, plans for the use of French as the language of commerce and the workplace.

Implementation and Enforcement: 'Coercion' or 'Consensus'?

We have seen that one of the most striking differences between the Canadian approach – in particular, that taken at the federal level – and the British is the heavy reliance on 'rights' in the former and their almost complete absence in the latter. This essential difference in the structure of the regimes has important implications for the manner in which those regimes are implemented and, especially, for how they are enforced.

In addition to having a crucial role in the creation of Welsh-language schemes of public bodies in Wales, the Welsh Language Board also has a role in the enforcement of such schemes. In particular, where it appears to the Board that a public body may have failed to carry out a scheme approved by the Board, it may conduct an investigation in order to ascertain whether there has been a failure.[79] On the completion of the investigation, the Board must send a report of the results of the investigation to the public body concerned and to the National Assembly for Wales,[80] and may arrange for the broader publication of the report, where the Board considers that this would be appropriate.[81] If the Board feels that the public body has failed to carry out the scheme, it may include in its report recommendations as to the action to be taken by the public body to remedy the failure.[82] If the Board is then of the view that any of the recommendations it has made have not been acted upon, it can refer the matter to the Welsh Assembly Government.[83] At this point, things are largely left to the discretion of the Welsh Assembly Government. The legislation provides that if the Government is satisfied, after receiving representations from both the Board and the public body concerned, that the public body has failed to take any action recommended in the report, the Government 'may give such directions to the public body as [it] considers appropriate'. Where such directions are given, they shall be enforceable by the Government on an application made by it by mandamus, a public law remedy in England and Wales by which the courts would be required to order the public body to implement the direction.

While this process would be an effective remedy, it is important to note the very significant discretion that is left both to the Board and to the Welsh Assembly Government. The Board has considerable discretion in determining whether to initiate an investigation. It will do so only where it 'appears to the Board' that a public body may have failed to carry out its plan; this creates a standard that is based on the Board's subjective assessment of the situation, without reference to any objective standards. Even where the Board believes that the public body may have failed to carry out its plan, it still has discretion as to whether to begin an investigation.[84] Similarly, where the Board has found a failure, it has discretion as to whether to include recommendations, and where it is of the view that the recommendations are not being implemented, it also has discretion as to whether to refer matters to the Welsh Assembly Government. However, at no point does the Board have any independent powers of enforcement. Ultimately, enforcement of the Welsh-language schemes rests with the Welsh Assembly Government, and the Government itself has a similarly broad discretion in the matter: if it is convinced that a public body is not implementing the Board's recommendations, it is authorized to act, but is not *required* to do so.[85] Where it does act, the Government also has wide discretion as to the nature of the action it takes: it may give such directions as 'it considers appropriate'.

Under the Welsh model, the role of the user of Welsh-medium services – the people who are the ultimate beneficiaries of the Welsh-language schemes of public bodies – is limited and marginal. As we have seen, the Welsh model creates very few language 'rights', and as such, the individual Welsh-speaker has no clear legal remedy through the courts. Under the Welsh Language Act 1993, any person who claims to have been directly affected by a failure of a public body to carry out its Welsh-language scheme can make a written complaint to the Welsh Language Board.[86] If it appears to the Board that the public body has indeed failed to carry out its scheme, it may conduct an investigation of the sort described above, and the procedure described above would apply. Even on a complaint by a member of the public, though, the Board has discretion as to whether to make an investigation. Given the fairly broad discretion given to the Board with respect to this initial and subsequent decisions in the investigatory process, it is not clear that a complainant has any other legal remedies; in particular, if the Board has come to its decision in good faith, it would not appear that a complainant could successfully use any of the available administrative law remedies.[87] Under the Gaelic Language (Scotland) Act 2005, a broadly similar approach to enforcement is taken, although the powers of the statutorily created language board, Bòrd na Gàidhlig, are even weaker than those of the Welsh Language Board.

In Canada, by contrast, the individual has, as we have seen, a broad array of rights, and therefore a range of remedial options. With respect to any minority language rights that are guaranteed under the constitution, individuals whose rights have been infringed may apply directly to the courts for a remedy.[88] With respect to minority language rights protected under the Official Languages Act 1988, Part IX of that legislation creates the Office of the Commissioner of Official Languages, one of whose duties is to oversee implementation of the legislation. Subsection 58(1) of the act provides that the Commissioner *shall* investigate any complaint arising from a broad range of acts or omissions relating not merely to the Official Languages Act 1988 but also those which involve the status of an official language, or any provision of an Act of Parliament or regulation relating to the status or use of an official language. Thus, as in Wales, the legislation empowers a public body to investigate complaints; unlike the Welsh Language Board, though, the Commissioner of Official Languages has a more limited discretion as to whether to proceed with an investigation. In particular, the Official Languages Act 1988 provides that the Commission can refuse to investigate a complaint only in very limited circumstances, namely, where, in the opinion of the Commissioner: the subject matter of the complaint is trivial, the complaint is frivolous or vexatious or is not made in good faith; or, the subject matter of the complaint does not involve a contravention of the Act or does not, for some other reason, come within the authority of the Commissioner under the act.[89]

On completion of the investigation, if the Commissioner of Official Languages is of the opinion that action should be taken, the Commissioner is required to report that opinion, with reasons, to the President of the Treasury Board (a federal Cabinet member) and the deputy or administrative head of the federal institution concerned, and the Commissioner may make such recommendations as he or she sees fit. Where the investigation was made in response to a complaint from a member of the public, the Commissioner must inform the complainant of the outcome of the investigation, and where the Commissioner has made recommendations for action by the federal institution, the Commissioner may inform the complainant of those recommendations as well.[90] If, in the opinion of the Commissioner, adequate and appropriate measures have not been taken within a reasonable time in response to the Commissioner's recommendations, the Commissioner may transmit those recommendations to the federal Cabinet, and if, within a reasonable time, the Cabinet has not acted, the Commissioner may make such report to the federal Parliament as the Commissioner considers appropriate.[91]

As is the case under the Welsh Language Act 1993, then, the language enforcement body has some discretion as to how to move an investigation forward – although the extent of this discretion is more constrained – and provision is made for the involvement of politicians in the process as a final step. However, unlike Wales, things do not end here. Above and beyond the process just described, the Official Languages Act 1988 provides for court remedies.[92] In particular, any person who has made a complaint to the Commissioner of Official Languages in respect of rights or duties under various provisions of the legislation may apply to the Federal Court – Trial Division for a remedy.[93] Where the court concludes that the federal institution has failed to comply with the Official Languages Act, 1988, it may grant such remedy as it considers appropriate and just in the circumstances.[94] Finally, the Commissioner can apply to the Federal Court – Trial Division for such a remedy in relation to a complaint if the Commissioner has the consent of the person who made the complaint.[95] Thus, the complainant has considerable power in the process of enforcing rights guaranteed under the legislation; significantly, the investigatory body – the Commissioner of Official Languages – also has considerable scope for participating in litigation.

Not only are there significant differences in the formal enforcement mechanisms between Canada and the UK, there has been a marked difference in the way in which, and the frequency with which, such mechanisms have been used. In Canada, both the available complaints procedures – in particular, that provided under the Official Languages Act 1988 – and the courts have been used regularly and with considerable effect. Literally hundreds of cases have gone before the Canadian courts in respect of both the constitutionally and legislatively created minority language rights, and language rights cases have been amongst the most important and most prominent decisions of Canada's highest court, the Supreme Court of Canada. Cases such as *Ford v. Quebec (A.G.)*,[96] *Mahé v. Alberta*,[97] *R. v. Beaulac*,[98] *Arsenault-Cameron v. Prince Edward Island*,[99] *Doucet-Boudreau v. Nova Scotia*,[100] and other decisions referred to in this chapter have done much to clarify the nature and extent of language rights in Canada, but have also marked important victories for minority language communities and have forced changes in administrative practices and, in some cases, in legislation. In recognition of the fact that litigation can be expensive, a federally funded non-profit organization, the Court Challenges Programme of Canada, was created to provide financial assistance to litigants for various aspects of language rights litigation.[101] Finally, the complaints mechanism available under official languages legislation tends to be very well used. Each year, the Office of the Commissioner of Official Languages provides considerable information in the institution's annual report on the number, nature and disposition of complaints under the Official Languages Act 1988; in the 2003–4 annual report, some 1,031 complaints were made, about 74 per cent of which were found to be admissible.[102]

The contrast with the British experience, as exemplified by the most developed minority language regime, that in respect of Welsh, is sharp. The Welsh regime appears to have generated very little litigation over the years; this is not surprising, given the general absence of clear language rights in Wales. Indeed, the only provision which has generated some litigation before the Welsh courts is the predecessor to section 22 of the Welsh Language Act 1993, subsection 1(1) of the Welsh Language Act 1967, which embodied essentially the same right.[103] Significantly, the Welsh-language schemes created under the authority of the Welsh Language Act 1993, perhaps the most important mechanism for ensuring the delivery of Welsh-medium services and expanding the Welsh language into new linguistic domains, do not appear to have given rise to any litigation in the Welsh courts. While the Welsh-speaking public does make regular use of the complaints mechanism provided, the Welsh Language Board's annual report generally does not provide information on numbers or outcomes of complaints, and the Board's very extensive website does not appear to contain information about the complaints procedure.[104] Most significantly, the Board has used its investigatory powers under section 17 of the Welsh Language Act 1993 sparingly. From the creation of the Act until the summer of 2004, there have only been six formal investigations under section 17 which lead to the production of recommendations to the public body in question, and in each case, those recommendations have ultimately been accepted. As a result, a matter has never been referred to the National Assembly for Wales under section 20 in order to obtain a direction enforceable in the courts by way of mandamus.[105]

The relatively infrequent use of the full enforcement powers under the Welsh Language Act 1993 is due to a range of factors. The most important is the nature of the enforcement provisions themselves. Ultimately, the enforcement of compliance with Welsh-language schemes is dependent on action by the Welsh Assembly Government, and this can be effected only in an atmosphere of political support. It is therefore in the interests of the Board to seek to work in a manner that obviates any conflict, because of the politicization of the language which could occur. There is a deepening though still fragile consensus on the nature of Wales as a 'bilingual country', and the Board is mindful of the dangers of damaging this consensus and thereby the development of the services that it seeks to expand.[106] Also important is the dual nature of the Board. On the one hand, the Board is required to work with public bodies to design and implement Welsh-language schemes. As the schemes are to be updated from time to time, the Board is required to have an ongoing relationship with public bodies, and one which depends on trust, good faith and cooperation. On the other hand, the Board is charged, through section 17 of the Act, not only with monitoring implementation, but ultimately with policing it. The sort of investigatory and, ultimately, disciplinary functions involved sit uneasily with the cooperative relationships that the Board is otherwise trying to build with the very same public bodies. Given the foregoing considerations, it is useful to consider whether it might not be appropriate to segregate the two functions – on the one hand, planning and implementation, both of which involve technical advice and close working relationships, and, on the other, monitoring and investigation – perhaps through the creation of two separate bodies to discharge each type of task.

The Impact of Constitutional and Quasi-Constitutional Structures

One significant difference between Canada and the UK is that Canada is a federal state and the UK is unitary one, although devolution of legislative powers to the Scottish Parliament and the Northern Ireland Assembly and of administrative powers (and, since the enactment of the Government of Wales Act 2006, potentially some legislative powers as well, by virtue of Part 3 of that act) to the National Assembly for Wales has complicated the picture. These constitutional arrangements have an interesting impact on minority language policy.

In Canada, important areas of governmental policy, such as education, health care, municipal government and so forth are within the legislative jurisdiction of the provinces, meaning that the provision of minority language services in such areas, and the regulation of the private and voluntary sector, is generally within the hands of the provincial governments. The language of services provided directly by the provincial governments is also, of course, generally a matter for the provincial governments, as is the question of the language of the provincial courts. As we saw in the first part of this chapter, the Canadian constitution does limit the autonomy of the provincial governments with respect to minority language matters in a number of ways. One provincial government, New Brunswick is officially bilingual, and is required under the Charter to provide all services through the medium of French and English. In other provinces, notably Quebec and Manitoba, the Constitution Act 1867 or the legislation which brought the province into the Canadian federation imposed requirements concerning the use of both French and English in the legislature, in the records of the legislature, and in the provincial courts. And, of course, in spite of the fact that education is a matter for the provinces, section 23 of the Charter guarantees the right to primary and secondary school education to the medium of the French or English linguistic minority of provinces in which the other linguistic group forms the majority. However, very important linguistic domains, and ones in which intervention may be necessary as part of a policy of minority language maintenance and revitalization, are within the sole legislative jurisdiction of the provinces.

The extent to which the exercise of these legislative powers by the provinces in respect of matters relating to official language minorities is unfettered may not, however, be absolute. Although health care, for example, is a matter within the legislative power of the provincial governments, the Ontario Divisional Court and the Ontario Court of Appeal in the case of *Lalonde v. Ontario (Commission de restructuration des services de santé)*[107] placed some limits on the ability of the Ontario legislature substantially to reduce the services of the province's only French-speaking hospital, Hôpital Montfort, located in the Ottawa-Carleton region. Significantly, the hospital was located in an area designated bilingual under Ontario's French Language Services Act, which, as noted earlier, gives a measure of legislative protection to a wide range of French-language services throughout the province. However, both courts also accepted that, based on the ruling of the Supreme Court of Canada in *Reference re Secession of*

Quebec (Secession Reference),[108] one of the fundamental unwritten organizing principles of the Canadian constitution was the principle of the respect for and protection of minorities, and that this principle, together with other principles developed in a range of Supreme Court decisions relating to the interpretation of language rights, required that the French Language Services Act be given a broad interpretation. By enacting that Act, Ontario had committed itself to continue to provide the services at the time the hospital was designated under the Act unless it was 'reasonable and necessary' to limit them, and this the province had failed to do. This case certainly does not guarantee anything like a right to French-medium health care or other services to the French minority of Ontario. It does, however, impose some limitations on the ability of a province to reduce such services where they are already offered, particularly where those services are statutorily guaranteed by language legislation, as is the case in Ontario.

At the federal level, the Official Languages Act 1988 has, as we have seen, created a robust institution, the Office of the Commissioner of Official Languages, to oversee the implementation of that legislation and other aspects of minority language policy. However, the scope for this institution to act as an holistic language planning body and to plan intervention in many linguistic domains and contexts is limited. This is particularly true in respect of those domains that are wholly within the jurisdiction of the provincial governments. The same can be said for the federal government itself, and the minister in that government with responsibility for the official language minorities, the Minister of Canadian Heritage. For example, as has already been noted, subsection 41(1) of the Official Language Act 1988 commits the Government of Canada to enhancing the vitality of the English and French linguistic minority communities in Canada and supporting and assisting their development, and to fostering the full recognition and use of both English and French in Canadian society. Amended subsection 41(2) imposes a duty on every federal institution to ensure that positive measures are taken for the implementation of the subsection 41(1) commitments. However, subsection 41(2) also provides that this implementation shall be carried ouot while respecting the jurisdiction and powers of the provinces. Similarly, the Minister of Canadian Heritage is required, under section 42 of the Official Languages Act 1988 to 'encourage and promote a coordinated approach to the implementation of federal institutions' of the commitments imposed upon the Government of Canada under section 41. Furthermore, the minister is required, under section 43, to take such measures as he considers appropriate to advance the equality of status and use of English and French in Canadian society. However, in respect of those matters that are within the powers of the provinces, the minister's powers are once again limited, as section 43 acknowledges: paragraph (d) provides that the minister can *encourage* and *assist* provincial governments to support the development of English and French linguistic minority communities generally and, in particular, to offer provincial and municipal services in both English and French and to provide opportunities for members of those communities to be educated in their own language; paragraph (e) provides that the minister can *encourage* and *assist* provincial governments to provide opportunities for everyone to learn both French and English. Thus, the minister can 'encourage' and 'assist', but cannot require provinces to act.

In Wales, by contrast, the situation is much different. The four major pieces of legislation described above were all acts of the Westminster Parliament, and there are effectively no constitutional limits under the British constitution as to what that Parliament may do. Thus, the possibility exists for the Westminster Parliament to legislate in a much more thoroughgoing way in respect of minority language use than is possible for any Canadian government, federal or provincial. As we have seen, under the Welsh Language Act 1993, the Welsh Language Board has very broad powers with respect to language planning, and can require any public body to prepare a Welsh-language scheme; as noted, the preparation of those schemes should follow guidelines that the Board itself was required to prepare, and those schemes must generally gain the approval of the Board. The only limitation on the powers of the Board to require public bodies to prepare schemes is imposed by the definition of the term 'public body' itself, in section 6 of the Act. Section 6 lists the public bodies which may be subject to the requirement to prepare a Welsh-language scheme, and, although the list is not comprehensive, it is extensive, and has been supplemented over time. This statutory framework has allowed the Welsh Language Board to take a structured, strategic and holistic approach to minority language planning, allowing for coordinated intervention at the local and national level within Wales in a way that is generally not possible for any single body in Canada. This is particularly true of the Office of the Commissioner for Official Languages, whose role is more constrained both by the terms of the Official Languages Act 1988, which places somewhat greater emphasis on the role of the institution in enforcement of language rights than on language planning, and by the constitutional limits just discussed.

Devolution has, however, complicated matters somewhat. As a result of devolution, a number of powers and duties that were originally given to the Secretary of State for Wales under the Welsh Language Act 1993 were transferred under the Government of Wales Act 1998 to the National Assembly for Wales. However, the National Assembly was not given any powers to create or amend primary legislation. Thus, the Welsh Language Act 1993 and the other important pieces of legislation described earlier cannot be amended by the National Assembly; only the Westminster Parliament can do so. The National Assembly can promote the Welsh language through administrative rather than legislative means, and this ability may be significant. But unless and until the Westminster Parliament chooses to act, the legislative framework for the Welsh language is now fixed. This situation may change, however, under the Government of Wales Act 2006, one of the inspirations for which was the recognition of the need for the Assembly to have greater legislative powers. Under Part 3 of the 2006 legislation, the Westminster Parliament can now confer legislative competence on the National Assembly in respect of any matter set out in Schedule 5 to the 2006 legislation; one such matter is the Welsh language. Thus, while action is still required by Westminster—that Parliament must first confer authority on the Welsh Assembly—the Assembly would now at least be in a position to control the shape and content of Welsh language legislation. In 2007, in the coalition agreement published on 27 June,, the Labour Party and Plaid Cymru have agreed to seek enhanced legislative competence on the Welsh language, with a view to legislating to confirm 'official status' for both English and Welsh, to create linguistic rights in the provision of services, and to establish the post of Language Commissioner. Thus, it is possible that the Welsh model will begin to resemble more closely the Canadian federal model (see Williams, chapter 15).

In Scotland, matters are somewhat different, due to the different nature of Scottish devolution. Unlike the Welsh Assembly, the Scottish Parliament does, under the Scotland Act 1998, have a wide range of legislative powers, and can already pass primary legislation in respect of all matters except those reserved under the act to Westminster. In 2005, the Scottish Parliament passed, without a single dissenting vote, the Gaelic Language (Scotland) Act 2005. The two principal aspects of the legislation are the creation of a language board, Bòrd na Gàidhlig , the Gaelic Language Board, having powers similar to, but less extensive than the Welsh Language Board, and the empowerment of Bòrd na Gàidhlig to require public bodies in Scotland to prepare Gaelic-language plans. However, the legislation makes clear that departments and other institutions of the Westminster government and Parliament will not be subject to this requirement. The reason for this is that the Scottish Executive, which introduced the legislation, was not convinced that the Scottish Parliament could legislate to impose obligations with regard to the use of Gaelic on bodies which are solely within the legislative authority of Westminster under the Scotland Act 1998. The Gaelic Media Service, the public body which can fund the production of Gaelic-medium television and radio programming, has been campaigning for both an increase in the fund which it can distribute and the creation of a stand-alone Gaelic channel, similar to S4C. As broadcasting is a matter that is reserved to Westminster under the Scotland Act 1998, the Scottish Parliament and Executive have claimed that they are unable to deal with either issue, and the matter must be resolved at Westminster. Thus, devolution has been something of a mixed blessing for Gaelic. The language has commanded a higher political profile in Edinburgh than it ever would have had on the busy legislative docket at Westminster, and it is likely that language legislation such as the Gaelic Language (Scotland) Act 2005 would have been slower to emerge at Westminster. However, certain areas, particularly broadcasting, which are of considerable importance to the development of the language, are still within the sole legislative jurisdiction of Westminster, and this hinders the development of the sort of coordinated and holistic approach that has emerged in Wales.

The International Context

The final area of contrast is in respect of the international commitments which press upon policy and law in Canada and the UK.[109] Generally, Canada is subject to a more limited range of international commitments, and these commitments have tended to be of less importance in the development of domestic Canadian minority language policy and legislation. The UK, by contrast, has been party to a range of regional developments in Europe, particularly since about 1998, which have had an important impact on UK domestic policy and legislation, especially in respect of Gaelic and Irish, and these obligations have considerable ongoing relevance, both for these languages and for Welsh.

International law, particularly international human rights law, provides for a range of rights which protect speakers of minority languages. For example, the right to freedom of expression, guaranteed in provisions such as Article 19 of the United Nation's International Covenant on Civil and Political Rights (the ICCPR)[110], protects the rights of persons to use their languages in public and private without interference from the state. Indeed, this very provision has been used to challenge those provisions of Quebec's Charter of the French Language which sought to ban the use of all languages other than French on exterior business signage. In *Ballantyne,*

Davidson and McGregor v. Canada,[111] the Human Rights Committee, the UN body which oversees implementation of the ICCPR, found that those provisions violated Article 19. However, those international legal standards relating to measures of positive support for linguistic minorities tend to be found in relatively recent instruments relating to the protection of minorities, and as we shall see, the UK is party to a number of these but Canada generally is not.

The most important 'minorities' provision to which Canada is subject is Article 27 of the ICCPR, which provides that in those states in which ethnic, religious or linguistic minorities exist, persons belonging to such minorities shall not be denied the right, in community with the other members of their group, to enjoy their own culture, to profess and practise their own religion, or to use their own language. There have been a number of communications to the UN Human Rights Committee under Article 27 which have been brought against Canada.[112] These communications have been brought by members of Canada's aboriginal communities, and they have generally not related to language issues. Thus, Article 27 has yet to have an effect on Canada's minority language policies. Given the rather vague and limited way in which the article is formulated, it is not likely to have a dramatic effect in future. It should be noted, though, that the Human Rights Committee has made clear that the article does, in spite of its formulation in the negative, require states to take positive measures to support minority linguistic identity, although it has not clarified the nature or extent of those measures.[113] As already implied, Article 27 does apply in respect of aboriginal peoples, and communications involving aboriginal language rights may yet arise. As interesting, in a Canadian context, is the very wide approach which the Human Rights Committee appears to take to the range of minorities that are potentially covered. In particular, the committee has noted that Article 27 confers rights on persons belonging to minorities which 'exist' in a state party, and that it is therefore not relevant to determine the degree of permanence that this word connotes. As a result, the committee has concluded that migrant workers or even visitors in a state party may benefit from the protection of Article 27.[114] This article may therefore be relevant to Canada's many 'heritage' language communities. In particular, if Article 27 does, as the Human Rights Committee insists, require states to take some unspecified positive measures to support minorities, speakers of those languages may benefit; as noted above, the various minority language regimes in Canada generally do not extend to speakers of such languages.

Another United Nations convention which may yet have an impact on Canada is the 1989 Convention on the Rights of the Child (the CRC). The most obvious area in which this treaty may have an impact is in respect of minority language education. Article 28 of the CRC guarantees a right to education, and Article 29, paragraph 1(c) provides that the education of the child shall be directed 'to the development of respect for the child's . . . own cultural identity, language and values . . .' Article 30 of the CRC echoes Article 27 of the ICCPR, but also makes specific reference to aboriginal peoples.[115] Again, there is no obvious reason why the application of both of these provisions would be limited to children of only official language minorities.[116]

One other area which has not yet had significant impact on Canadian minority language policy but which may in the future is the developing international standards on the protection of indigenous peoples. The most important binding international commitment is International Labour Organisation Convention No. 169, Concerning Indigenous and Tribal Peoples in Independent Countries.[117] Canada has not yet become a party to this treaty. However, the treaty has a number of provisions relevant to languages of indigenous peoples. For example, Article 28, paragraph 1 provides that children belonging to indigenous peoples shall, wherever practicable, be taught to read and write in their own indigenous language or in the language most commonly used by the group to which they belong. Paragraph 3 of this article provides that measures shall be taken by states to preserve and promote the development and practice of the indigenous languages of the peoples concerned. Important, though non-legally binding standards are also being developed in the United Nations – in particular, the Draft United Nations Declaration on the Rights of Indigenous Peoples, which was adopted by the UN Subcommission on the Prevention of Discrimination and Protection of Minorities[118] – and these standards also contain a number of provisions with respect to the languages of indigenous peoples in education, broadcasting and so forth. Again, these standards do not yet create binding legal obligations for Canada, but they may at some point have a certain normative value, and would enhance the claims of members of Canada's aboriginal communities for positive measures of support in respect of their languages.

The UK is also subject to the provisions of the ICCPR; however, the minority standards set out in Article 27 thereof have been significantly expanded upon and clarified in a number of international treaties, the most important of which for these purposes are two treaties of the Council of Europe to which the UK is subject, the Framework Convention for the Protection of National Minorities (the 'Framework Convention') and the European Charter for Regional or Minority Languages (the 'Languages Charter').[119] Space does not permit an analysis of the provisions of either of these treaties, but the Languages Charter, in particular, can be expected to have an interesting ongoing impact on the UK. Neither treaty creates a complaints procedure that allows members of linguistic minorities to take a government to court to ensure compliance. However, both treaties creating a system of state reporting under which the UK must report at regular intervals – every five years under the Framework Convention and every three under the Language Charter – on its implementation of its international obligations under both treaties. These reports are scrutinized by a body of independent experts – the Advisory Committee under the Framework Convention and the Committee of Experts under the Languages Charter – who ultimately prepare a report on state compliance and recommendations as to measures which should be taken to enhance compliance. Significantly, non-governmental organizations are entitled to comment on the reports of the UK government, thereby ensuring that the two committees have alternative sources of information for assessing the claims that the UK itself makes. As importantly, members of the two committees will normally visit the state being monitored to meet politicians, civil servants, representatives of local and regional governments, as well as non-governmental organizations and representatives of the minority language communities themselves.

Both treaties require states parties such as the UK to take a range of measures to provide support to linguistic minorities – under the Languages Charter, only long-standing minority languages such as Welsh, Gaelic, Irish, Scots, Ulster Scots, Cornish and Manx Gaelic can benefit – and although the impact of the Languages Charter, which tends to contain the more detailed and arguably more extensive commitments with respect to languages, has been limited by the rather restrictive and unimaginative approach taken by the UK to ratification, the effects of the Languages Charter have already been felt, particularly with respect to Gaelic. The 2003 visit of the delegation from the Committee of Experts was particularly important in this, for it gave the Gaelic community an opportunity to raise a wide range of issues with an international body to which the UK authorities had to listen, and it required those same authorities to explain their policies and practices in a systematic way, and to account for their decisions and actions. Such authorities had previously generally not been required to account for their policies and practices. In its first report, the Committee of Experts made a number of points with regard to the inadequacy of current provision for Gaelic-medium broadcasting and Gaelic-medium education. Of particular note was that, under the Charter, the UK government had committed itself to encouraging and/or facilitating the creation of at least one television channel in Gaelic; the Committee of Experts pointed out the failure of the UK authorities to deliver, and this criticism has proved useful in the ongoing discussions between the Gaelic Media Service and the UK government with respect to the creation of a stand-alone Gaelic channel. The Committee of Experts also made a number of comments with respect to Welsh and Irish, as well as Scots and Ulster Scots, and the Committee of Experts revisited these in its second report, which it released in 2007.[120] Brief reference should also be made to the situation of minority languages – particularly Irish – in Northern Ireland. In many ways, the legislative framework for Irish in Northern Ireland is the least developed of all the Celtic languages in the UK. However, international obligations have been important in spurring domestic action. In addition to the various commitments imposed under the Framework Convention and the range of commitments voluntarily undertaken by the UK under the Languages Charter, the 1998 Belfast Agreement between the UK and Irish governments is also of considerable significance.[121] Language issues were dealt with in a separate section of the agreement, and these provisions drew heavily on the Languages Charter. Paragraph 3 of this section of the agreement refers to the recognition by all parties to the agreement of 'the importance of respect, understanding and tolerance in relation to linguistic diversity, including in Northern Ireland the Irish language, Ulster-Scots and the languages of various ethnic communities'. Paragraph 4 makes particular reference to Irish, and commits the UK government to taking 'resolute action to promote the language', to 'facilitate and encourage the use of the language in speech and writing in public and private life where there is appropriate demand' and to 'seek to remove, where possible, restrictions which would discourage or work against the maintenance or development of the language'. Finally, the paragraph contains further commitments with respect to Irish in Northern Ireland, such as the placing of a statutory duty on the department of education to encourage and facilitate Irish-medium education, the encouragement of financial support for Irish language film and television production in Northern Ireland, and a commitment to exploring the possibility of expanding the availability of the Irish state-sponsored Irish-medium service, *Teilifis na Gaeilge*, now TG4, in Northern Ireland. A number of steps have subsequently been taken towards implementing these commitments, particularly in the area of education.

Since November, 2004, Irish language organizations in Northern Ireland, led by the umbrella organisation representing all such organizations, POBAL, have created proposals and have been lobbying for an Irish Language Act for Northern Ireland, and in the Agreement at St Andrews, arrived at between the British and Irish Governments in late 2006 in an effort to revive the devolved institutions in Northern Ireland—they had been suspended in 2002—the

British Government committed itself to an Irish Language Act for Northern Ireland. It subsequently entered into two consultations, the second one being on 'indicative clauses'—in effect, this was a draft bill. POBAL had recommended a strongly rights-based approach, and the creation of a Canadian-style language commissioner; the 'indicative clauses' prepared by the British Government are considerably weaker, and include few rights, favouring instead an approach which is influenced more by the Welsh model and, particularly, the Scottish model for Gaelic. Now that devolved government has been re-established in Northern Ireland, the British government is taking the position that legislating on the Irish language is now a matter for the revived Northern Irish Assembly; given the power-sharing arrangements in place under devolution between nationalists and unionists, and the strong opposition of unionist politicians, particularly those in the now-dominant unionist party, the Democratic Unionist Party of Dr. Ian Paisley, who is now Northern Ireland's First Minister, the prospects of any legislation in respect of the Irish language are not promising.

Conclusions

I have sought to demonstrate that, in spite of the obvious affinities and clear similarities between Canada and the UK, the legal framework for the management of minority language issues in the two countries, and within those two countries, shows a surprising degree of variation. Perhaps the most striking difference between the general approaches which are evident in the two countries is the much greater reliance in Canada on a rights-based model. Yet, despite the relative absence of clearly defined minority language rights in Wales, a comprehensive and holistic approach to minority language maintenance and revival has been created, and it is clear that numbers of speakers have grown and that the capacity to use the language has expanded into many new linguistic domains.[122] While much research needs to be done on the actual sociolinguistic impact of the Welsh approach, there is some reason to believe that it is having some success.

The relatively unique conditions which presently exist in Wales must, however, be borne in mind. The size of the Welsh-speaking community is proportionately much larger than that of the official language minority in any Canadian jurisdiction but New Brunswick. While there is undoubtedly some hostility to the wider use of Welsh in Welsh society, it generally enjoys the status of a national language, and is considered part of the patrimony of all Welsh people, whether Welsh speaking or not; French and English, on the other hand, are official languages but neither can claim to be a 'national' language of *all* Canadians. If the Welsh-speaking community were proportionately smaller, and if the position of the Welsh language as part of the patrimony of all Welsh people are more hotly contested, the Welsh model might not be as effective, and the need for more clearly defined legal rights might be more important.

In this regard, the experience of Gaelic in Scotland will be interesting. The Gaelic Language (Scotland) Act 2005 borrows heavily on the Welsh model; unlike that model, however, no rights whatsoever have been created for Gaelic-speakers in respect of any public service. The Gaelic-speaking population is a much smaller minority in Scotland than either the French minorities in Canada or the Welsh-speaking minority in Wales, and the position of Gaelic as a 'national' language, rather than a regional language belonging to those Scots of Highland origin and being relevant to one part of the country, the Highlands and Hebrides, is contested by very many Scots. Given the much less hospitable circumstances in which the Gaelic Language (Scotland) Act 2005 must work, the Gaelic experience will provide an illuminating test of the limits of the Welsh approach.

NOTES

1 See, for example, Vernon V. Palmer, *Mixed Jurisdictions Worldwide: The Third Legal Family*, (New York, Cambridge: Cambridge University Press, 2001).

2 Quebec private law is arguably more obviously civilian than Scots private law, based as it is on the *Code Napoleon*; the complexities of

this debate are, however, beyond the competence of the author and beyond the scope of this contribution.

3 59.1 per cent claimed English and 22.9 per cent claimed French, Statistics Canada, *Profile of Languages in Canada: English, French and many* others, 2001 Census: Analysis Series, (Ottawa: Ministry of Industry, 2003), p. 26.

4 67.5 per cent claimed English and 22.0 per cent claimed French.

5 According to the 1996 census, there were some 842,105 anglophones in Quebec, representing about 13 per cent of the population of the province, Statistics Canada, *Profile of Languages in Canada: English, French and many others*, 2001 Census: Analysis Series, (Ottawa: Ministry of Industry, 2003), p. 26.

6 Statistics Canada, *Profile of Languages in Canada: English, French and many others*, 2001 Census: Analysis Series (Ottawa: Ministry of Industry, 2003), pp. 26, 27. In a few provinces, such as Alberta and British Columbia, the francophone population is growing significantly, but part of the increase is due to migration of francophones looking for work, and whether they will form self-sustaining linguistic communities is doubtful. The anglophone minority in Quebec is in no immediate danger of disappearance, and, while it has declined somewhat in both absolute and percentage terms, this is due to in considerable measure to the outward migration of anglophones to other provinces, rather than assimilation into the francophone majority; furthermore, while there is some evidence that a larger number of Quebec anglophones have become fluent in French, assimilation is rare, and subtractive bilingualism, the norm for many francophone minority communities, does not hold for the anglophone minority of Quebec.

7 Statistics Canada, *Profile of Languages in Canada: English, French and many others*, 2001 Census: Analysis Series, (Ottawa: Ministry of Industry, 2003), pp. 27, 28.

8 Statistics Canada, *Profile of Languages in Canada: English, French and many others*, 2001 Census: Analysis Series, (Ottawa: Ministry of Industry, 2003), p. 6.

9 Office of National Statistics, available at: http://www.statistics.gov.uk/census2001/profiles/rank/walskills.asp. The numbers of persons being able to speak Welsh has increased in absolute terms over the last three censuses (510,920 in 1991, and 508,207 in 1981) and in percentage terms over the last two censuses (18.7 per cent in 1991, but 18.9 per cent in 1981).

10 Released 19 December 2001. Unlike Welsh and Scottish Gaelic, a very small percentage of those reporting themselves as being able to speak Irish are native speakers, and only a minority speak the language fluently or use it regularly: a 1987 survey indicated that only 6 per cent of those claiming an ability in censuses to speak Irish did so fluently; 84 per cent of those surveyed claimed never to use Irish in the home, only 15 per cent claimed to use it occasionally and

only 1 per cent daily: see the Eurolang service of the European Bureau for Lesser-Used Languages, *http://www.eurolang.net/State/uk.htm.*

11 *Scotland's Census 2001*: The Registrar General's Report to the Scottish Parliament, 13 February, 2003, available at http://www.gro-scotland.gov.uk/grosweb/grosweb.nsf/pages/file5/$file/rg_report_parliament.pdf. In 1991, 65,978 people reported themselves to be Gaelic-speakers, representing 1.4 per cent of the population of Scotland. Like Welsh, there are no known monolingual Gaelic-speakers, but unlike Welsh, the long-term sharp decline in both numbers and percentages of Gaelic speakers has not yet been stopped.

12 See Philip Payton, 'Cornish', in Glanville Price (ed.), *Languages in Britain and Ireland* (Oxford: Blackwell, 2000), pp. 109–19, at 118.

13 The 2001 Census indicated that 1,689 people reported themselves as being able to speak Manx, and 1,689 reported themselves as being able to speak, read or write Manx; see *Isle of Man Census Report 2001*, Vol. 2, Economic Affairs Division, Isle of Man Government Treasury, March 2002, pp. 37–8, available at: *http://www.gov.im/lib/docs/treasury/economic/census/reportvolume2.pdf.*

14 It has been estimated that between a third and a half of Scotland's roughly 5 million people speak some Scots, although the problems in attempting to build a reasonable estimate are extensive, as illustrated in Caroline Macafee, 'The demography of Scots: the lessons of the census campaign', (2000), in *Scottish Language*, vol. 19, 1. The Ulster Scots Language Society has estimated the number of speakers of Ulster Scots to be 100,000 (The Ulster Scots Language Society, 'What is Ullans?', 2 *Ullans* (1994), 56. It has been noted that the language of contemporary lowland Scotland is fluid, 'marked by a wide and almost infinitely variable range of speech-styles, ranging from the full Scots of some fisher-folk and farming people in the North-East, through various intermediate 'mixtures of Scots and English', to a variety of Standard English spoken in a Scottish accent', see Mairi Robinson (ed.), *The Concise Scots Dictionary* (Aberdeen University Press: Aberdeen, 1985), xii. The same is likely to be even more true of Ulster Scots in Northern Ireland.

15 http://www.statistics.gov.uk/CCI/nugget.asp?ID=764&Pos=1&ColRank=1&Rank=176.

16 Only about two thirds of London's 850,000 school children came from homes in which English was the mother tongue, and amongst the languages spoken by large numbers of school children were Panjabi, Gujarati, Hindi/Urdu, Bengali and Sylheti, Turkish, Arabic, Cantonese and Yoruba: see Vivian Edwards, 'Community languages in the United Kingdom', in Guus Extra and Durk Gorter (eds), *The Other Languages of Europe* (Clevedon: Multilingual Matters, 2001), 243–60, at 243–7.

17 R.S.C., 1985, *c*.31 (4th supplement).

18 Part I of the *Constitution Act, 1982*, being Schedule B to the Canada Act 1982 (UK), 1982, *c*.11.

19 (UK) 30 & 31 Victoria *c*.3.

20 Subsection 17(1), the Charter.

21 Subsection 18(1), the Charter. Section 133 of the 1867 constitution provided that English and French shall be used in the records and journals of both Houses of Parliament, but made no reference to the language of statutes, nor of the status of the versions in each language.

22 Subsection 19(1), the Charter.

23 Thus, this subsection 20(1) guarantee applies in respect of all of the departments and agencies of the federal government.

24 Part I expands on Subsection 17(1), Part II expands on subsection 18(1), Part III expands on subsection 19(1), and Part IV, together with regulations thereto, expands upon and particularizes the right set out in subsection 20(1) of the Charter.

25 Section 92, Constitution Act 1867.

26 Section 27 has been referred to by the Supreme Court of Canada in the context of interpreting section 14 of the Charter, which provides that a party or witness in any proceedings who does not understand the language in which the proceedings are conducted has the right to the assistance of an interpreter. The court noted that the Charter, including section 14, had to be interpreted in a manner consistent with the preservation and enhancement of the multicultural heritage of Canadians, and that '[i]n so far as a multicultural heritage is necessarily a multilingual one, it follows that a multicultural society can only be preserved and fostered if those who speak languages other than English and French are given real and substantive access to the criminal justice system': *R. v. Tran*, [1994] 2 S. C. R. 951. Again, however, the court did not interpret section 27 as in any way embodying a free-standing right.

27 See, for example, Shin Imai, *Aboriginal Law Handbook* (Scarborough: Carswell, 1999), 2nd edn, p. 29.

28 Subsection 16(2), the Charter.

29 Subsection 17(2), the Charter.

30 Subsection 19(2), the Charter.

31 Subsection 18(2), the Charter.

32 As at the federal level, subsection 20(2) has been further particularized through the creation of the Official Languages Act 1988, which expanded upon the Official Languages Act 1969.

33 S. C. 1870, *c*.3.

34 In *Re Manitoba Language Rights*, [1985] 1 S. C. R. 721, the Supreme Court of Canada ruled that all unilingual (English only) Acts of the Legislature of Manitoba were invalid, and that the province was required to re-enact, print and publish all of its laws passed unilingually in French and English.

35 R. S. Q. c. C-11."

36 More accurately, section 23 of the Manitoba Act 1870 contained similar provisions with respect to English and French as section 133 of the Constitution Act 1867.

37 The provisions of section 133 were successfully relied upon to quash provisions of the Charter of the French Language that had sought to grant official status only to the French version of Acts and regulations of Quebec and to make French alone the language of the Courts of Quebec: see *Blaikie v. Quebec (A.G.) (No. 1)*, [1979] 2 S. C. R. 1016.

38 R.S.N. W. T. 1988, c. O-1, as amended by An Act to Amend the Official Languages Act, No. 3, S.N. W. T. 2003, *c*.23.

39 S. C. 1993, *c*.28.

40 While the statutes of 1731 and 1737 were primarily aimed at problems of intelligibility of the legal process to the lay person caused by the widespread use of legal French and Latin in the courts, they had the effect of excluding autochthonous languages from the courts, as they provided that neither Latin nor French nor 'any other tongue or language whatsoever' could be used. In the wake of this legislation, the British legal system as a whole switched from a multilingual to a monoglot ethos: Ruth Morris, 'Great mischiefs – an historical look at language legislation in Great Britain', in Douglas A. Kibbee (ed.), *Language Legislation and Linguistic Rights* (Amsterdam, 1998), pp. 32–54, at p. 32. Although the 1731 legislation was repealed by the Civil Procedure Acts Repeal Act of 1879, English remained the sole language of the courts; the 1737 legislation has not, however, apparently been repealed.

41 The core funding of S4C is statutorily guaranteed in the Broadcasting Act 1990 (section 61) and the Broadcasting Act 1996 (subsection 80(1)), and S4C is under a statutory duty to ensure that a 'substantial proportion' of the programmes it broadcasts are in Welsh and that programmes broadcast between 6.30 p.m. and 10.00 p.m. 'consist mainly of programmes in Welsh' and that such programmes maintain 'a high general standard in all respects (and, in particular, in respect of their content and quality)', and 'a wide range in their subject matter': Broadcasting Act 1990, paragraphs 57(2)(b) and (c).

42 1988, *c*.40, (the '1988 Act'). These provisions were retained in the Education Act 1996, *c*.56 (the '1996 Act').

43 Section 2, the 1988 Act, and section 353, the 1996 Act.

44 Subsection 3(7), the 1988 Act, and subsection 354(8), the 1996 Act.

45 The three specific functions are: to advise the National Assembly on matters concerning the Welsh language; to advise persons exercising public functions on the ways in which to give effect to the principle that, in the conduct of public business and the administration of justice in Wales, the English and Welsh languages should be treated on the basis of equality; and to advise those and other persons providing services to the public on the use of the Welsh language in their dealings with the public.

46 Subsection 47(1).

47 Subsection 122(1).

48 Subsection 32 (c).

49 There is nothing in the law which would otherwise have prevented the Assembly from taking such action; any action it proposes to take

is limited by the limitations placed on it under the Government of Wales Act 1998 – for example, it cannot, as we shall see below, pass primary legislation – but this is true regardless of subsection 32, which can clarify the Assembly's powers but not expand them beyond what is permitted generally under the devolution settlement.

50 The notion of two 'founding peoples' is, of course, contested, not only by the aboriginal peoples whose ancestors lived in Canada from time immemorial, but also by the descendants of non-English- and -French-speaking immigrants who were the first non-aboriginal settlers in many parts of the country.

51 The choice of a federal structure was in part a recognition of Quebec's linguistic distinctiveness and the aspirations of its French-speaking majority to maintain this distinctiveness, and the guarantees of section 133 of the Constitution Act 1867 were an attempt to accommodate both linguistic groups in the federal Parliament and courts.

52 The Irish-language community in Northern Ireland is, indeed, a highly politicized one, and language is certainly an aspect of Irish nationalism there; by this, however, I mean that language is not necessarily central to the nationalist question as it is in Quebec or, perhaps, in Wales, a point I shall explore momentarily.

53 This appears to be true even of Gaelic, spoken, as noted above, by fewer than 60,000 people in Scotland, or about 1.2 per cent of Scotland's population. Based on census data concerning ethnic minorities, no visible minority community comes close to this number, and even if one assumed that every person who declared him- or herself as, say, 'Pakistani' spoke Urdu, an unlikely eventuality, the numbers would still be considerably less than the numbers of Gaelic-speakers. Mass immigration, and with it, significant linguistic diversity, has been much more marked in certain English cities, particularly London, than in the 'Celtic fringe'.

54 See, for example, Leslie Green, 'Are language rights fundamental?', *Osgoode Hall Law Journal*, (1987) 25, 639; Leslie Green and Denise Réaume, 'Second class rights? Principles and compromise in the Charter', *Dalhousie Law Journal*, (1990) 13, 564; and Alan Patten and Will Kymlicka, 'Introduction: language rights and political theory: context, issues, and approaches', in Will Kymlicka and Alan Patten (eds), *Language Rights and Political Theory*, (Oxford: Oxford University Press, 2003), p. 1.

55 Section 22, the Official Languages Act, 1988.

56 Subsection 32(1), the Official Languages Act, 1988.

57 See, for example, *Mahé v. Alberta*, *Arseneault-Cameron v. Prince Edward Island*, and *Doucet-Boudreau v. Nova Scotia*, *infra*.

58 R. S. O. 1990, c. F.32, as amended.

59 Defined in section 1, and includes a ministry of the government of Ontario, a board, commission or corporation a majority of whose members or directors are appointed by the government, a non-profit corporation or similar body that provides services to the public, is

subsidized by public money and is designated as a public service agency by regulation, but not a municipality.

60 R. S. O. c. E.2, as amended.

61 R. S. O. 1990, c. C.43, as amended.

62 Under subsection 126(2), those hearings specified by the party must be presided over by a judge or officer who speaks both English and French; this subsection and other subsections in section 126 contain more detailed rules with regard to the use of both languages where the subsection 126(1) right is exercised.

63 The term 'public body' is defined by way of a sizeable list set out in section 6 of the act, to which the National Assembly for Wales can make additions.

64 Subsection 5(2), the Welsh Language Act 1993.

65 Subsection 9(1), the Welsh Language Act 1993.

66 Subsection 5(3), the Welsh Language Act 1993.

67 Section 13, the Welsh Language Act 1993.

68 Section 14, the Welsh Language Act 1993. If no scheme is submitted to the Board within the time it has specified, or if the Board does not approve the scheme, the Board, or in the latter case, the Board or the public body may refer the matter to the National Assembly for Wales, in which case the Assembly will decide upon the scheme.

69 Bwrdd yr Iaith Gymraeg/Welsh Language Board, *Welsh Language Schemes: Their Preparation and Approval in Accordance with the Welsh Language Act 1993* (Cardiff, March, 1996).

70 See guidelines 6 and 7.

71 Subsecdtion 47(3), the Government of Wales Act 1998.

72 Subsecdtion 122(1), the Government of Wales Act 1998.

73 Standing Order 8, from Standing Order 7 to Standing Order 8, "Rules of Debate", order 8.2.]

74 See Peter W. Hogg, *Constitutional Law of Canada* (Scarborough: Carswell, 1992), 3rd edn, p. 7.

75 The number of persons who claimed an ability to speak Welsh increased from 510,920 in 1991 to 575,640 in 2001, and Welsh-speakers as a percentage of the total Welsh population increased from 18.7 per cent to 20.5 per cent.

76 Indeed, if it were the goal, it would be hotly contested by many in Canada. While there is generally fairly high popular support for the existing regime for the protection of linguistic minorities, there is evidence of considerable variation in support for a regime that would be more extensive, to say nothing of a vision of a fully bilingual nation: see, for example, C. Michael MacMillan, *The Practice of Language Rights in Canada* (Toronto: University of Toronto Press, 1998), ch. 2, esp. pp. 58–9.

77 Welsh Office, *Welsh for Ages 5–16: Proposals of the Secretary of State for Wales* (Cardiff, 1989), p. 4.

78 See, for example, the Welsh Language Board, 'Language revitalization: the role of the Welsh Language Board', in Colin Williams (ed.),

Language Revitalization: Policy and Planning in Wales (Cardiff: University of Wales Press, 2000), pp. 83–115, at pp. 88–9.

79 Subsection 17(1), the Welsh Language Act 1993.

80 Subsection 19(1), the Welsh Language Act 1993.

81 Subsection 19(2), the Welsh Language Act 1993.

82 Subsection 19(3), the Welsh Language Act 1993.

83 Subsection 20(1), the Welsh Language Act 1993.

84 Note the use of the permissive 'may' rather than the mandatory 'shall' in subsection 17(1).

85 Note the use of the permissive 'may' rather than the mandatory 'shall' in subsection 20(2).

86 Paragraph 18(1)(a); the complaint must be made within twelve months of the complainant first knowing of the failure that he or she is alleging, and before the Board takes any action, it must be satisfied that the complainant has brought the matter to the notice of the public body in question and that the body has had a reasonable opportunity to consider the complaint and to respond: paragraphs 18(1)(b) and (c).

87 See Part IV, A. W. Bradley and K. D. Ewing, *Constitutional and Administrative Law* (London and New York: Longman, 1997), 12th edn, esp. ch. 29, at pp. 773–82.

88 With respect to Charter-protected language rights, the usual remedy is that contained in subsection 24(1) of the Charter, which provides that anyone whose rights or freedoms, as guaranteed by the Charter, have been infringed or denied may apply to a court of competent jurisdiction to obtain such remedy as the court considers appropriate and just in the circumstances. See, generally, Michel Bastarache (ed.), *Language Rights in Canada* (Cowansville, Que.: Editions Yvon Blais, 2004), 2nd edn, pp. 535–75.

89 Subsection 58(4), the Official Languages Act 1988. The Commissioner can also cease an investigation for any of these reasons or, more generally, can refuse to investigate further if it appears to the Commissioner that, having regard to all the circumstances of the case, any further investigation is unnecessary: subsection 58(3).

90 Subsections 64(1) and (2), the Official Languages Act 1988.

91 Subsections 65(2) and (3), the Official Languages Act 1988.

92 Part X, the Official Languages Act 1988.

93 Subsection 77(1), the Official Languages Act 1988. The application must be made within 60 days of the notification to the complainant by the Commissioner of the outcome of the Commissioner's investigation, or of the notification to the complainant by the Commissioner of the failure of the federal institution to implement the Commissioner's recommendations.

94 Subsection 77(4), the Official Languages Act 1988.

95 Paragraph 78(1)(a); the Commissioner can also appear in court on behalf of a complainant who has him- or herself brought a case to the Federal Court – Trial Division under section 77, and can, with leave of that court, appear as a party to such proceedings.

96 [1988] 2 S. C. R. 712.
97 [1990] 1 S. C. R. 342.
98 [1999] 1 S. C. R. 768.
99 [2000] 1 S. C. R. 3.
100 (2000) 2003 SCC 62.
101 The website of this programme is: http://www.ccppcj.ca.
102 Office of the Commissioner of Official Languages, *Annual Report 2003–2004*, (Ottawa: Department of Public Works and Government Services Canada, 2004), pp. 83–90.
103 The requirements of subsection 1(1) were generally applied rather narrowly in these cases: see Zenon Bankowski and Geoff Mungham, 'Political trials in contemporary Wales: cases, causes and methods', in Zenon Bankowski and Geoff Mungham (eds), *Essays in Law and Society*, (London, Boston: Routledge and Kegan Paul, 1980), pp. 53–70, at p. 53.
104 Even the section of the website 'Welsh and the Law' contains no clear information with respect to the possibility of making complaints about failures to implement Welsh-language schemes: see http://www.bwrdd-yr-iaith.org.uk/en. It should be noted that only the English section of the website was consulted, and that such information may be contained on the Welsh section.
105 The foregoing information was provided in response to correspondence with Mr Gethin Jones of the Language Schemes Review Unit, Strategic Operations Team, the Welsh Language Board, and the author is most grateful for the very generous assistance and insights provided.
106 The author is grateful to Mr Gethin Jones for this insight.
107 (1999), 48 O. R. (3d) 50 (Div. Ct.); (2001), 56 O. R. (3d) 505 (C.A.).
108 [1998] 2 S. C. R. 217.
109 For a more detailed consideration of international legal aspects of the protection of linguistic minorities, see Robert Dunbar, 'Minority language rights in international law', *ICLQ* (2001) 50, 90.
110 Adopted and opened for signature, ratification and accession by United Nations General Assembly resolution 2200(A) (XXI) of 16 December 1966, and entered into force on 23 March 1976. Both the UK and Canada are parties to this treaty.
111 Communication No. 359/1989, CCPR/C/47/D/359/1989, 5 May 1993.
112 See, for example, *Lovelace v. Canada*, Communication No. R 6/24, U. N. GAOR, 36th Sess., Supp. No. 40, at 166, UN Doc. A/36/40, Annex 18 (1977), and *Ominayak, Chief of the Lubicon Lake Band v. Canada*, Communication No. 167/1984, U. N. GAOR, 45th Sess. Supp. No. 40, vol. 2, at 1, UN Doc. A/45/40, Annex 9(A) (1990).
113 See General Comment No. 23: The Rights of Minorities (Art. 27), 8 April 1994, CCPR/C/21/Rev.a/Add5, especially paragraphs 6.1 and 6.2.
114 General Comment No. 23, at paragraph 5.2.
115 Article 30 provides: 'In those States in which ethnic, religious or

linguistic minorities or persons of indigenous origin exist, a child belonging to such a minority or who is indigenous shall not be denied the right, in community with other members of his or her group, to enjoy his or her own culture, to profess and practice his or her own religion, or to use his or her own language.'

116 Indeed, it is unlikely that these provisions would apply to children of the English-language 'minority' at all; as the international obligations apply to the state as a whole, a minority in a particular sub-state jurisdiction which is part of the majority of the state as a whole would be likely not to be covered by these 'minority' commitments.

117 Adopted by the General Conference of the International Labour Organisation, Geneva, 27 June 1989, and entered into force on 5 September 1991.

118 Resolution 1994/45, 26 August 1994, UN Doc. E/CN.4/1995/2, E/CN.4/Sub.2/1994/56, at 105 (1994).

119 The UK became party to the Languages Charter on 27 March 2001, and the treaty entered into force on 1 July of that year.

120 The report of the Committee of Experts in respect of the first UK state report, which was submitted on 1 July 2002, and in respect of the second UK state report, which was submitted on 1 July, 2005, are available at the following website: http://www.coe.int/T/E/Legal_Affairs/Local_and_regional_Democracy/Regional_or_Minority_languages, under 'documentation'

121 For a more complete discussion than can be provided here, see Aodan Mac Poilin, director of the ULTACH Trust/Aontaobhas ULTACH, 'The Belfast Agreement and the Irish language in Northern Ireland' (January 2000), (unpublished); see also 'The Charter and the Belfast Agreement: implications for Irish in Northern Ireland', and 'Ulster Scots – The European Charter/Belfast Agreement', 15(1) *Contact Bulletin* (November 1998) (the European Bureau for Lesser-Used Languages).

122 This holistic approach owes much to the writings and policy influence of Colin H. Williams, who, since the early 1970s, has been advocating a more syncretic, realistic approach to language policy and planning issues.

6

Rethinking Language Policies: Challenges and Opportunities

MÁIRÉAD NIC CRAITH

Within an international perspective, the concept of language planning is hardly ever associated with global languages such as English, Spanish or Chinese. Society assumes that these languages have developed naturally and organically without the benefit of state support, legislation or finance. This presumption explains the often vigorous reaction of speakers of dominant languages to state policies and funding for lesser-used languages. Speakers of minority tongues rarely refer to the intense planning process that is employed for dominant languages. Instead they focus on policies for lesser-used speech forms in different contexts. For example, advocates of Irish examine the language, not merely in the context of other Celtic languages, such as Welsh or Scots-Gaelic, and frequently draw analogies with Basque, Catalan and other non-related language minorities. Although this outward-looking approach is to be applauded, it hardly suffices as it ignores the process of planning that is employed by dominant language groups.

In this chapter, I wish to address issues of enhancement and reinforcement for linguistic minorities by recontextualizing the concept of lesser-used languages. I call for a policy transfer – not just from the experience of one 'more successful lesser-used' language to another – but also from the experience of a global tongue such as English or Spanish to a more local language such as Manx.

Linguistic Diversity in Contemporary Society

Estimates of the number of languages in the world today vary. Recent surveys by the US Summer Institute of Linguistics calculate that there are approximately 6,809 languages in existence (Grimes, 2000). Experts agree that language loss and decay are occurring at an unprecedented rate at the beginning of the twenty-first century. Krauss (1992, 1995) has predicted that half of the languages currently spoken may die within the next hundred years. In addition to this, a further 40 per cent are 'threatened' or 'endangered'.

Clearly, any assessment of this nature is fraught with difficulties. Although Chinese is commonly regarded as a single language, it has many different forms which are not necessarily mutually intelligible. Gaelic dialects spoken in the extreme south and extreme north of Ireland are regarded as a single language whereas Gaelic spoken in Scotland or the Isle of Man is conventionally classed as a separate language. Speech forms such as Piedmontese, which have many of the characteristics of language, are officially regarded as dialects and 'there is no definition of "language"' (as opposed to "dialect") which is not hopelessly mired in the politics of language' (McCloskey, 2001: 13).

Currently, the top ten spoken languages are Chinese, English, Hindi/Urdu, Spanish, Arabic, Portuguese, Russian, Bengali, Japanese and German. Each of these has more than 100 million mother-tongue speakers. Although they make up only between 0.1 and 0.15 per cent of the world's spoken languages; speakers of these languages comprise almost half of the world's population. Since they dominate indigenous languages in many contexts, they have been described by Skutnabb-Kangas (1999) as 'killer languages'.

Another 300 languages in the world are spoken by groups of more than one million. The largest of these are French and Italian with over fifty million speakers each. Although languages such as Croatian, Czech, Danish, Estonian, Finnish, Hungarian, Slovak and Swedish may appear small, they have well-established mother-tongue groups. Demographically, these 'large' and 'middle-sized' languages account for more than five billion speakers or close to 95 per cent of the world's population (Skutnabb-Kangas, 1999).

In contrast, over half of the world's languages and most of its sign languages are spoken by communities of less than 10,000 speakers. Most of these language groups are confined to single countries and are irrelevant for communication at international levels. About half of these (or a quarter of the world's oral languages) are spoken by groups numbering fewer than 1,000. Speakers of these threatened languages approximate some eight million people in total; less than 0.2 per cent of the world population. However, small, threatened languages are not the focus of this chapter. Instead I wish to concentrate on examples from the middle-sized group, which are frequently called 'minority languages'.

Linguicism

When speaking of languages in the Western world, academics and policy-makers usually organize languages in distinct categories. Dominant languages are easily identified but several categories are used to order languages from the middle-sized group, which may be classed as 'lesser-used', 'minorized', 'less-widely spoken' or even the convoluted 'less-widely taught, less-widely used' languages.

Logic hardly applies in the use of these designations. Although there are some 6,565,000 speakers of Catalan and 5,326,000 speakers of Danish (Grimes, 2000); Catalan is classed as a lesser-used language while Danish enjoys the advantages of officialdom. Moreover, such categories are contextual and the ascription of minority or majority status to a language depends entirely on specific political contexts. French is spoken as a first language by over fifty million speakers and is clearly a world language, yet in the context of Quebec, it is considered a 'minority language'. Spanish is a majority language in Spain and in many Latin American states but is a minority language in the USA.

While the distinction between majority and minority languages in the Western world usually refers to numerical size, it is more appropriate to think of it in terms of access to power (see Nelde *et al.* 1996, Skutnabb-Kangas 2000). The primary difference between dominant and minority languages pertains to rights and privileges and, perhaps, the one common factor uniting speakers of minority languages is that in specific contexts they do not have majority status in government. This applies, for example, to speakers of German in Denmark or of Frisian in the Netherlands.

Dominant languages invariably have government support and have emerged in the world scene in consequence of their political strength. Such languages are constructs of the nation-state in the first instance and have enjoyed state sponsorship over a number of centuries. They appear eminently suitable for contemporary society as the linguistic and educational processes employed in the construction of nation-states have linked them 'inexorably to modernity and progress while consigning their minority counterparts to the realms of primitivism and stasis' (May, 2001: 310).

Essentially dominant languages are given state recognition and affirmation in the public space. Society imagines that these languages are naturally advantaged rather than socially and politically constructed. In contrast, minority languages are, generally, deemed to be inherently handicapped and unworthy of state respect or planning. Official recognition is frequently withheld from such languages, which are deemed to be simply incapable of dealing with modern contexts. This is not simply a matter of non-recognition. Instead it is a process of 'mis-recognition' (Bourdieu, 1991) as it denies the inherent potential of such languages.

The negativity implied in the classification of some languages as 'lesser-used' or 'minorized' impacts on their speech communities who frequently become active themselves in the process of jettisoning or abandoning their traditional languages and cultures. 'The negative attitudes may be so entrenched that even when the authorities get around to doing something about it – introducing community projects, protective measures, or official language policies – the indigenous community may greet their effort with unenthusiasm, scepticism, or outright hostility' (Crystal, 2000: 84). They frequently consent to the 'symbolic violence' that is visited upon them and presuppose their traditional languages to be inherently inferior and incapable of dealing with the modern technological world. Grillo (1989) has called this 'the ideology of contempt'.

Linguicism is the term used to describe this categorization of languages and it has been defined as 'ideologies, structures and practices which are used to legitimate, effectuate and reproduce an unequal division of power and resources (material and immaterial) between groups which are defined on the basis of language' (Skutnabb-Kangas, 1998: 13). The process of linguicism is of significant influence in determining political and economic advantages for dominant languages. It is also used to construct some languages negatively as non-resources, even as handicaps, which may prevent children from enjoying the 'full benefits' of majority languages. It is time to reconstruct the pattern that ascribes 'majority' or 'minority' status to specific languages, which enhance the former and stigmatize the latter.

Re-evaluating Language Shift

Why have some languages become marginalized and even endangered whereas others have gained great status internationally? Is it simply the case that some languages are inherently more capable of dealing with modernity or even postmodernity whereas others are locked into a time warp? The answer to this question lies not so much in the perusal of policies of lesser-used languages but in an examination of policies of majority languages.

Many contemporary dominant languages were once in a position of low status. In the British Isles, English once had a status that was inferior to French or Latin. As a consequence of the Norman invasion of 1066, French was the language of nobility and social aspiration. The first king since 1066 to speak English as a mother tongue was Henry IV who did not assume the throne until 1399. Some two centuries later, English was still perceived as a local language. In 1598 John Florio, the compiler of an English–Italian dictionary remarked that English was 'a language that will do you good in England, but past Dover it is worth nothing' (Hale, 1993).

In contrast, some of the Celtic languages were once in a position of power in Ireland and Britain. During the Elizabethan period, there were parts of England where the original Celtic language had not yet been eradicated, particularly in Cornwall and in Cumbria. With the exception of the English colonizers, Irish was the language spoken throughout the entire island of Ireland. It was also spoken in the greater part of Scotland. While it is difficult, due to a lack of statistics to ascertain the exact numbers of Irish- and English-speakers in these islands at this time, it appears that there was no great difference in absolute terms. 'English had bigger cities and more books; Irish had a wider geographical spread' (Titley, 2000: 63). There was little reason to suppose that the fate of the two languages would alter so dramatically and yet they did. What prompted this change is a question that has hardly been analysed (but see for example Crystal, 1997a) and why did an insular language such as English arrive at a position of world power?

English is the mother tongue of more than 300 million people worldwide. A further 300 million speak it as a second language. Another 100 million speak it fluently as a foreign language. Although there are more first- and second-language speakers of Mandarin Chinese worldwide, English has a higher social and political significance in several key areas. English is used at official and semi-official levels in over sixty countries and has a significant status in another twenty. It has established a presence in all six continents and is the primary language of newspapers, books, airports and air-traffic control, science, technology and medicine. More than two-thirds of the world's scientists write in English. Some three-quarters of the world's mail is composed in English, and it is also the primary language used on the Internet. Over fifty million children learn English as an additional language while a further eighty million study it at secondary levels of education (Crystal, 1997b: 360).

Although English may appear naturally suitable for post-modern society, it is important to note that it did not derive its national and international status without intense planning. A publication on the British Council website explains that 'national' languages not existing in Europe prior to the creation of nation states, had to be constructed. Consequently, the

English language was self-consciously expanded and reconstructed to serve the purposes of a national language (Graddol 1997: 6).

By implication, lesser-used languages are not inherently inferior because they failed to achieve national status. They merely have not had the benefit of official support over a number of centuries.

> A language does not become a global language because of its intrinsic structural properties, or because of the size of its vocabulary, or because it has been a vehicle of great literature in the past, or because it was once associated with a great culture or religion. . . [Instead] a language becomes an international language for one chief reason: the political power of its people – especially their military power (Crystal, 1997a: 7).

Several factors aided the development of English as a language of state. Modern institutions of science such as the Royal Society in Britain were established and language became part of their scientific agenda. New terms and ways of writing in English were developed. 'National' systems of education throughout Britain and Ireland promoted the use of English and demoted the status of Celtic languages (see Durkacz, 1983; Withers, 1984). English was adopted as the language of government, of commerce, of law and of social status. Speakers of English were regarded as prestigious, contrasting with speakers of Celtic languages who were perceived as backward and traditional (see Nic Craith, 1993).

Emigration and colonization were significant factors in the development of English as a global language. Towards the end of the sixteenth century there were some five to seven million speakers of English, almost all of whom lived in the British Isles. Expeditions to North America in the sixteenth century established the first significant presence of English-speakers outside Britain. A penal colony was set up in Sydney towards the end of the eighteenth century and British control was established in South Africa at the beginning of the nineteenth century. English-speaking in South Asia also has its roots in Britain. The emerging international trend of English-speaking has proved irreversible and today the vast majority of people with English as their mother tongue live outside England.

Contemporary society associates English with modernity and progress but this association is not accidental and 'the development model with capitalism and English as both the means and the goal has been exported worldwide' (Skutnabb-Kangas, 1999: 194). The colonization process was a significant factor in the spread of English in the past. Substantial contemporary aid from British and American donors consolidates the dominant role of English in much of Africa and Asia.

The British Council is one of the chief agencies for the promotion of English worldwide. Visitors to the website (http://www.britishcouncil.org/)are directed to the success of this international organisation in 109 countries and territories. Stories of the work of the British Council on the world stage focus not so much on the English language itself but on the bringing together of people throughout the world as well as the establishment of cultural connections and lasting relationships. By implication the reader associates English language skills witi opportunities for networking and success.

Of notable interest in selected publications commissioned by the British Council is the lack of complacency regarding the future of English. Although English is widely regarded as the global language, readers are encouraged to query whether it will retain its pre-eminence in the twenty-first century. They are advised that the next decade will be critical for English. It would be 'foolhardy to imagine that its pre-eminent position as a world language will not be challenged in some world regions and domains of use as the economic, demographic and political shape of the world is transformed' (Graddol, 1997: 2). This note of caution may surprise speakers of lesser-used languages as it implies that advocates of the use of English work hard at maintaining its world status even when that appears unlikely to be threatened.

There is also the challenge of cultural property for speakers of English as ownership of that language is increasingly challenged. Many countries adopting English as their second language are asserting that it is '*their* language, through which they can express their own values and identities, create their own intellectual property and export goods and services to other countries' (italics original, in Graddol, 1997: 2).

When speaking of her 'multicultural English', for example, Rajendran (1999) asserts that her 'English is simply a Malaysian English. Whatever the accent I choose to use and whatever the lexical item I choose to incorporate, it is *my* English and it is Malaysian. Because I am Malaysian' (italics original).

A similar view has been expressed by several prominent Indian writers such as Salman Rushdie who has argued that the debate about the appropriateness of English in post-British India has 'meaning only for the older generation. The children of independent India seem not to think of English as being irredeemably tainted by its colonial provenance. They use it as an Indian language, as one of the tools they have to hand' (in Crystal, 1997a: 136).

This universalization of English as a language of wider communication has ensured that many countries have developed their own teaching programmes in the language. It is hardly necessary to travel to Britain or the USA to practise one's English linguistic skills. The onset of mass media ensures that one can speak, hear and write English in the local environment. If this trend were to progress, English would not necessarily be associated with Britain or the US and these countries would not necessarily reap economic benefits from their primarily monolingual use of English.

Language and Economy

Most significant is the association of English with economic progress. The current demand for English 'reflects contemporary power balances and the hope that mastery of English will lead to the prosperity and glamorous hedonism that the privileged in this world have access to and that is projected in Hollywood films, MTV videos, and ads for transnational corporations' (Phillipson, 1996: 2). A language that is spoken by people of wealth or by those in authority or in government does not die. Language death seldom, if ever, occurs in wealthy and privileged communities (Crawford, 1994). Instead it occurs among the dispossessed and disempowered.

The perception of wealth makes a language infinitely more attractive to a learner. 'A language which is spoken by rich countries is more attractive to learners than one which provides no access to personal betterment or lucrative markets' (Graddol, 1997: 28). From 1982 to 1989 the rise in numbers of students enrolling on courses for Japanese as a foreign language worldwide closely mirrored an increase in the value of the Japanese yen against the US dollar (Coulmas, 1992: 78). The implications of this are obvious. If a language is to flourish, then language policies must pay significant attention to the economic well-being of the people who speak that language. Individuals do not wish merely to survive on government grants; if they are to be persuaded to speak a language on more than a token basis, then they require the prospect of economic success in that linguistic context. This is not to imply that market forces alone can determine the future of a language, but they contribute significantly to the processes of language decline or spread.

There are some instances of wealthier communities speaking a lesser-used language. Catalan is the obvious example (see Hall, 1990; Leprêtre, 1992), but economic success is more frequently associated with national and international languages. English has become one of the major business lingua francas throughout the world, and there is a general perception that 'English is indispensable to personal material success and to the performance of a technologically advanced economy' (Grin, 1999: 175). This is a feature that may change with time. As English-language skills become more widespread, they may become less valued and it is quite feasible that an ability in languages other than English will become sought after as market forces change.

In the meantime proponents of minority languages must creatively address the development of business in their languages. Most lesser-used language regions in Europe are located in the economic periphery and have experienced uneven development in the past. Broadly speaking, economic development in lesser-used languages can be grouped into different categories (Price, Ó Torna, Wynne Jones, 1997). Brittany, Corsica, Fryslân, Galicia, Ireland, Sardinia and Valencia have all undergone a rapid process of urbanization and industrialization in the post-war period and as such are 'late developers' in peripheral regions. These contrast with peripheral areas such as the Basque Country, Wales and Scotland, which were industrialized in the nineteenth century. In that period, the economic emphasis was on heavy industries such as coal, the manufacture of steel and shipbuilding. More recently these industries have declined and the Basque Country in particular suffers from a significant degree of regional unemployment.

Some lesser-used languages in core European regions have become quite prosperous economically. Speakers of Catalan live in the most economically advanced region in Spain. Traditionally the Flemish community was comparatively underdeveloped, but its speakers appear to have 'successfully engaged in a dual process of economic modernisation and language normalisation' in a process similar to Quebec's Quiet Revolution (Price, Ó Torna, Wynne Jones, 1997: 15). The German-speaking region in Alsace and the Swedes in Finland are also economically advantaged and have developed more significantly than other core regions such as the German-speaking minority in North Schleswig or the Finnish Torne Valley in Sweden.

All of these peripheral and core regions have been influenced by factors such as migration, which can endanger the cohesion of any language. Many of them have developed a culture of dependency on externally based capital (the 'branch plant syndrome') and are lacking in indigenous leadership and entrepreneurship. Regional policy is frequently geared to attract foreign investors and the employment generated can be poorly integrated with the local economy. Moreover, it often results in a cultural division of labour which reserves the lower level positions for bilinguals or speakers of lesser-used languages. Most significantly, there is a strong perception of cost in relation to the minority language, which is not considered at all in the case of the more established language.

The Cost of Language Promotion

The promotion of any language costs money and how is this question to be addressed? Consider a Celtic language like Irish, Welsh or Breton. If one wishes to ascertain the cost to their respective states of the maintenance or promotion of these languages, it will be incredibly easy to locate these statistics. But if one endeavours to ascertain the cost of the maintenance of English or French in the same locations, the statistics may prove more difficult to compile. Why is this the case?

In the past the language of the majority, or in some instances the official language, has been construed as 'costless'. Somehow the language of the majority (usually the official language) is not considered in terms of expenditure. Instead, it is perceived as a matter pertaining to normal affairs of the state or in some instances a matter for civilization. This is directly related to the notion of civic and ethnic nationalism, which I believe is a false dichotomy (see Nic Craith, 2003). Civic nations like Britain or France do not, in theory, accord primacy to culture. This apparently is in contrast with ethnic nations like Germany who are deemed be obsessed with culture. Overall, the concept of culture is regarded as problematic – an issue to be avoided – a notion for the natives or the 'minority'. Primarily it is regarded as something that 'costs', but the language of any majority also costs and an important challenge for language policy-makers is to evaluate the cost of promotion and the marketing impetus for all languages.

Let us reconsider the cost of multilingualism. In an everyday situation who really costs the taxpayer? Is it the bilingual who can use different languages where appropriate or the monolingual who is absolutely unable to use any language other than one? Let us stop associating the concept of cost simply with minority languages and realize that all languages – not just some – are subsidized. Dunbar (2000: 70) argues very effectively that '[i]f there is a subsidised language in Scotland, it is English. Unfortunately, mention is almost never made of the 'English subsidy' which Scottish Gaels have had to bear for many long decades – of having to fund through their taxes things like English medium education in Gaelic-speaking areas'. Similarly in Brittany, the Breton people have funded the cost of French-medium schools for decades. Yet it is the cost of the Diwan, the Breton-medium schools system, rather than the cost of the French-medium school that is noted.

Bilingualism in a minority language is frequently regarded negatively rather than positively and speakers of lesser-used languages need to reverse the perspective on language skills. Tron Trosterun illustrates the growing optimism among the Sámi community with an account of a meeting attended by Sámi and Norwegian officials. 'One of the Sámi participants was asked: do you need an interpreter? No, she responded, I don't. But I will give my talk in Sámi, so it might be that you will need one' (in Crystal, 2000: 130).

How does one persuade governments and peoples that all languages – majority and minority – require funding? Language minorities have traditionally resorted to the moral principle of historical legitimacy. They premise their argument on their existence over a number of centuries – or even millennia – in a specific geographical location. Indigeneity entitles them to government protection and the right to cultural survival. Language in such arguments is considered central to ethnic identity and the loss of a specific ethnicity would inevitably follow the loss of a language.

More recently language minorities have adopted the discourse of human rights. Researchers in several fields point out that the suppression of minority languages through policies of assimilation or devaluation 'are not only degrading of human dignity and morally unacceptable, but they are also an invitation to separatism and an incitement to fragmentation into mini-states' (Smolicz, 1986: 96). Advocates of linguistic human rights argue for the right of mother-tongue maintenance in spheres such as education and/or the media (see Kontra, 1999; Skutnabb-Kangas and Phillipson, 1995). Although such arguments are intrinsically good, they rarely persuade speakers of majority languages that public funding ought to be spent on language minorities. Moreover, they can raise complex issues such as irreconcilable claims to a particular territory or the indivisibility of the state.

The justification of expenditure on minority languages must be grounded in economic arguments, but unfortunately the economics of language is a much neglected discipline (see Grin, 1990; 1993a). Most governments concur that minority languages require state sponsorship but argue against the prohibitive costs of such protection. However, the cost of any expenditure per se is meaningless. *'The real problem is never how much some commodity or project costs, but whether it is worth the expense or not'* (italics original, in Grin, 1993b: 30).

Language as a Resource

While speakers of minority languages commonly think of their language as a public resource, such languages lack many of the obvious characteristics associated with resources. Society is perfectly willing to pay for resources such as coal or food and these products are easily assigned a market value, but who pays for a language? The continued existence of a language is not an item that individuals can purchase. Does this automatically imply that language has no value? No.

Consider the example of public lighting, which is usually funded by the state. It is obviously an important amenity as it provides light for motorists, pedestrians and householders. Moreover it reduces criminal activity. Everybody benefits from street lighting – even the tourist or the traveller who has not paid public taxes. Street lighting is a case of 'non-rival consumption' in that everyone can enjoy it equally. One individual's enjoyment of street lighting does not deprive another of the same light. It is impossible to exclude anyone from the benefits of street lighting on the basis of their not having paid any tax (Grin, 1993b: 34). The impossibility of exclusion and non-rival consumption are two characteristic makers of public goods. These essential characteristics imply that they have no market value; therefore they have to be financed by the state. 'It is therefore considered normal for the government to spend money on making sure that such a valuable resource as street lighting is available' (Grin, 1993b: 34).

The case for funding languages is remarkably similar to that for environmental goods and arguments used to evaluate assets such as clean air are easily applied to languages. Although clean air has no market value; its worth is infinite since all forms of human, animal and vegetal life require it. Similarly, scenic landscapes or clean rivers have no specific market value, yet people commonly assign great value to such natural commodities and rarely object to government sponsorship of the natural environment.

A minority language has no specific market value; yet it is still a valuable public good on which public expenditure can be justified. Like other public goods, individuals cannot be prevented from enjoying the linguistic environment through price mechanisms. Visitors to Catalan regions cannot be prevented from enjoying the Catalan linguistic environment on the basis of any payment and their enjoyment of it will not reduce its availability to others. Besides, if such tourists are sufficiently interested in the language subsequently to learn it, this enhances the Catalan-language environment. For this reason, 'language is not just a public-good; it is a super-public good' (Grin, 1993b: 38).

Although lesser-used languages have no specific market value, this does not imply that they have no economic value and examples of successful initiatives in lesser-used languages are on the increase (see Ó Muircheartaigh, 1996). Gaillimh le Gaeilge (Galway with Irish) is a case in point (Grin, 1999; Nic Uidhir, 1996). This project was established in 1988 by Comhdháil Náisiúnta na Gaeilge, which is a non-governmental organization involved in the promotion of Irish. Initially Comhdháil Náisiúnta na Gaeilge commissioned an evaluation of the economic impact of government measures in Irish on Galway City and the surrounding *Gaeltacht* (Irish-speaking region). The evaluation report concluded that funding for Irish had generated an additional 13 million punts of business in Galway city or an additional 17 million for the city and the nearby *Gaeltacht* (Ó Cinnéide and Keane 1988).

This justified government spending on the language, as Irish was clearly an income-generating asset. As a result, an increasing number of retailers, hoteliers and other business people were encouraged to strengthen the visibility of Irish in the city. Bilingual signage, stationery and menus have become increasingly common and many local and international corporations have determined to become bilingual. None of these business ventures receive financial support from Comhdháil Náisiúnta na Gaeilge. Instead, it is the economic factor which is the primary motivator. Businesses wish to enjoy the financial advantages of bilingual signage and do not want to lag behind the latest monetary trend.

The most significant aspect of the Gaillimh le Gaeilge project is that its success has been determined by economic factors rather than any appeal to high moral ground. Outside intervention has harnessed market forces for the benefits of a minority language. Moreover, this success has been achieved at little cost to the authorities whose financial support is a pittance when contrasted with the financial benefits accrued from this project.

Language and Multimedia

Much has been made in recent times of the impact of globalization on languages such as Breton, Frisian or Alsace. Prophets of doom insist that satellite TV and computers will spread the use of English and eliminate other languages. There is an impression that forces of globalization specifically disadvantage minority languages. 'The Gaelic comedy show *Ran Dan* was not too far off the mark when it showed a Gaelic household waking in the small hours of the morning, putting on tea and racing downstairs in their night-clothes to see the half hour of Gaelic programming' (Dunbar, 2000: 71). Yet there are several aspects to this scenario that have not been fully explored (Nic Craith 2004).

When satellite TV channels were established initially, their primary intention was to acquire as large an audience as possible in as wide a territory as possible. Economically this required the initial use of international languages such as English and many TV industries filled the airwaves with cheap imports from America. As competition for audiences continues , satellite TV channels have introduced languages other than English and developed programmes for national or regional rather than global audiences.

Home-produced programmes are exceedingly popular in many regions. The most popular TV show in South Africa is *Generations*; a locally produced multiracial soap. *Julie Lescaut*, a French police series in France attracts very large audiences. One of the more popular programmes in Brazil is *O Clone*; a *telenovela* made by TV Globo. As globalization progresses, the demand for locally produced television programmes increases and lesser-used languages may acquire increasing visibility on the airwaves.

This is not to imply that international characters such as Disney's Mickey Mouse are not in demand. As reported in the *Economist* (Anon, 2002), this icon of American culture was recently involved in an experiment in locally tailored programming. An art show for the Disney channel was shot outside the English town of Maidstone. About three-fifths of each show in the series *Art Attack* consisted of shared footage. This section demonstrated the close-ups of the hands of a Liverpudlian artist constructing the cut-out of a bumble bee. The remainder of the programme was filmed separately in each instance and involved editing in, seamlessly, the head and shoulders of 'local' presenters speaking 'local' languages with the Liverpudlian hands. Although different presenters were flown in to complete each 'local' version of the programme, the costs of production of 'local' programmes were vastly reduced and viewers in different regions regard the programme as 'theirs'. In 2001, 216 episodes of the show were created in six different languages.

Disney is not the only American channel producing 'local' versions of its content. The pioneer in this regard has been MTV, (Music Television) which has launched many new regionally diverse channels in Europe. In 1996, MTV Europe created four distinct services including one in Ireland and the UK, MTV Central (which serves Austria, Germany, and Switzerland), MTV European (for 76 territories, including Belgium, France, Greece, Israel, and Romania), and MTV Southern (Italy). The channels profile local personalities as well as shows in regional formats. Two years later, MTV Nordic was launched for Norway, Sweden, Denmark and

Finland. In 2000 MTV Networks Europe specifically targeted French-speaking audiences in France, Switzerland, and Belgium with MTVF. This channel features French subtitles and profiles artists from the French music scene. MTV Polska was also launched that year in Poland, This channel delivers Polish-language music programming to more then 1.5 million households. (http://groups.msn.com/MTV/mtv.msnw). The regional diversification has continued unabated and there is an emphasis on subtitling in relevant languages. In the Baltic States, for example, one finds MTV Eesti (Estonia), MTV Latvija (Latvia) and MTV Lieutva (Lithuania). Trademark shows on this Baltic initiative are shown with subtitles in Estonian, Latvian and Lithuanian. Such initiatives are not confined to MTV and one can now download the CNN news in several languages including Arabic (http://arabic.cnn.com), Spanish (hppt://www.cnnexpansion.com) and Turkish (http://wwwcnnturk.com).This trend has not been generated by a desire on the part of satellite TV stations simply to cater to local needs. Instead, it is economically driven and makes good commercial sense. The advantage of such formats is that it meets both the growing need to export and the increasing demand for locally produced programmes.

Like television, the invention of computers initially appeared to facilitate the further spread of English, but this is no longer necessarily the case. Computers were largely invented in English-speaking areas. Moreover, computer hardware and software has served the needs of the English language. In the early decades, text-based communication was unable to cope with accented characters which are a feature of many lesser-used languages and it was almost impossible to communicate in languages using non-roman writing systems (Graddol, 1997: 30).

As computers become more widely used in non-English-speaking countries, it is reasonable to expect a greater range of languages on the Internet. In 1996, the Internet Society published protocols for browsers on the web facilitating the use of web pages in different languages. Provided the host contacted maintains web pages in a particular language, computer users will be able to browse the web in the language of their choice. While English appears to have accounted for

80 per cent of computer-based communication in the 1990s, Graddol (1997: 61) predicted a significant decrease within a decade.

Statistics from the Global Reach website (http://www.glreach.com/globstats/index.php3) indicate that the use of languages other than English on the Internet is already on the increase. Their calculations suggest that 35.8 per cent of people currently online are native speakers of English, 37.9 per cent are native speakers of European languages other than English, while 33.0 per cent speak an Asian language as their mother tongue. Moreover they estimate the proportion of web content in English at the time of writing to stand at 68.4 per cent, representing a considerable decline from the previous decade. It should be noted, however, that this proportion vastly exceeds that stored in any other language. Web content in Chinese, for example, is a mere 3.9 per cent and that in German is 5.8 per cent (http://global-reach.biz/globstats/refs.php3).

The scenario of language restriction has changed, and computers can be effectively used to promote languages other than English. There are Chinese versions of many of the major American programs, including the Microsoft Word processor and the Windows operating system. Computer software has rapidly become customized for lesser-used languages and children in many regions speaking a lesser-used languages use locally produced software in schools. For example, Microsoft has launched a Welsh-language version of Word (see: http://www.bwrdd-yr-iaith.org.uk). Computer software has become incredibly adaptable, and desktop publishing systems facilitate short-run printing in minority languages. The Internet ensures equality for speakers of different languages as the 'cost of a Web page is the same, whether the contributor is writing in English, Spanish, Welsh or Navajo' (Crystal, 2000: 142).

At this stage there are probably more than 500 languages with a presence on the Internet, and language providers generally speaking do not involve themselves in language repression. (Crystal (2000: 142) cites one report of the closure of message boards in Irish by AOL American OnLine). The advantage of communication on the Internet is that it has become de-territorialized. Identity is no longer necessarily linked to a specific geographical location and individuals can maintain linguistic links with friends all over the world. Although migration has traditionally impacted negatively on lesser-used languages, the Internet has provided a new and easy mode of communication that is not dependent on location. 'The close linkage that once existed between computers and English has broken down' (Graddol, 1997: 30).

Modern technology will allow languages such as the Celtic ones to develop new imagined communities abroad. In recent years a radio station like Raidió na Gaeltachta has developed an international audience. Through their computers, Irish emigrants in Britain, Brazil, Canada and the USA are listening to the Irish-language radio station. In 2001 a new Internet journal *Beo* has been established with great success (http://www.beo.ie/). This is a glossy journal, which focuses on issues of concern to Irish-speakers at home and abroad, but it does not confine itself to such topics – a mistake that occurred in other journals in the past. Each month *Beo* reviews the extent of an Irish-speaking community abroad. Thus it is gradually establishing and redefining the 'imagined community' of Irish-speakers as an international rather than a local or peripheral group.

One could argue that an international language such as English also benefits from this new technology. This is true, but such languages have always had the resources for developing international networks. Without the onset of multimedia they would have financed the international dimension in an alternative manner. This might not have applied to a language such as Irish where economic resources are scarcer. For this reason I would argue that modern technology is of even greater benefit to lesser-used languages than it is to speakers of more international languages.

Cultural and Linguistic Diversity

Proponents of international languages are encountering new challenges in the twenty-first century and an examination of the British Council's website suggests that the era of the English-speaking monolingual is rapidly in decline. There is a new respect in postmodern society for cultural and linguistic diversity. The British Council warns against any complacency regarding the future of English as the spread of an international language could be linked with social inequality.

Speaking English could be regarded as the preserve of the socially privileged and 'in many countries English has become implicated in social and economic mechanisms which structure inequality'. In the past, poverty was a matter of geography, ethnicity or social class. Now it may also depend on one's access to the lingua franca of the globally privileged (Graddol, 1997: 38). For this reason the spread of English may be regarded in a similar way as exploiting rainforests. 'It may be seen as providing a short-term economic gain for a few, but involving the destruction of the ecologies which lesser-used languages inhabit, together with consequent loss of global linguistic diversity' (Graddol 1997: 62).

These trends suggest a 'nightmare scenario' in which the world turns against the English language, associating it with 'industrialisation, the destruction of cultures, infringement of basic human rights, global cultural imperialism and widening social inequality' (Graddol, 1997: 30). In a post-colonial era it is inevitable that there is some reaction against the language of the former colonial power. In 1908, Gandhi equated knowledge of English with slavery and highlighted the anomaly in the use of English in court. As a barrister he was not permitted to speak his mother tongue in court proceedings. Instead he spoke English and a translator was employed to translate Gandhi's English into Gandhi's mother tongue.

The Kenyan author, Ngugi wa Thiong'o was similarly forceful in his book *Decolonising the Mind* (1986). He lamented the post-colonial situation in which European bourgeoisie were stealing Kenyan talents and geniuses as they had their minds. 'Europe is stealing the treasures of the mind to enrich their languages and cultures. Africa needs back its economy, its politics, its culture, its languages and all its patriotic writers' (in Crystal, 2000: 114).

The spread of English is already being associated with linguistic genocide in some quarters. Skutnabb-Kangas (1999:

191) regards the ten language groups as speaking 'real killer languages'. English is foremost among these languages 'whose speakers have allocated to themselves and to their languages more power and (material) resources than their numbers would justify at the cost of speakers of other languages'. She queries the manner in which

> mostly monolingual English-speakers are running around the world as experts on how multilingual people in other parts of the world can become still more multilingual (by learning English) when Britain and the United States are notoriously failing to teach their majorities even the first elements of another language. (Skutnabb-Kangas, 1999: 195)

Crystal (2000: 87) argues against this oversimplification of the process of language loss and makes the case that the terminology of 'domination' must disappear. In a healthy bilingual environment two languages can coexist in a complementary fashion, each fulfilling a different role. A positive attitude must be adopted for all languages.

Several ideological movements have reinforced the significance of lesser-used languages in recent decades. In 1992 the Council of Europe adopted the European Charter for Regional or Minority Languages (cf. Dunbar in this volume, Nic Craith 2003, 2006). This binding convention came into force in March 1998. At the same time the USA passed two Native American Languages Acts designed to promote the freedom of Native Americans to speak and develop their mother tongue. The Law on Languages of the Russian Federation enacted in 1991 conferred the status of a national property on all languages and placed them under the protection of the state. In 1991, the Colombian Constitution gave autochthonous languages official status in their own territories. UNESCO and the UN have also produced statements in support of linguistic and cultural diversity (Crystal, 2000: 135).

All of these initiatives have helped to enhance the status of languages worldwide and have generated a new interest in the concept of linguistic human rights. The British Council refers to the growing demand for linguistic rights within a human rights agenda, arguing that educational provision in a child's mother tongue should be regarded as a basic human right. Such arguments may be carried to the heart of the political process in countries that are experiencing demand for regional autonomy or repositioning themselves as regional centres for economic initiatives .

Conclusion

In time the monolingual may become the exception rather than the rule. Forces of globalization will ensure a continuing demand for international languages, but lesser-used languages may also command new audiences on the airwaves and on the Internet. It is important that policies of respect for any language (including an international language such as English) will be accompanied by strategies for the economic development of speakers of that language. In the past many governments focused primarily on economic improvements for speakers of majority languages, to the neglect of speakers of other languages.

In recent decades many international agreements have promoted respect for speakers of lesser-used languages. Multimedia also facilitates the development of international networks for speakers of minority tongues. In this new global context, speakers of minority languages do not constitute a minority group. Instead they represent an ever-increasing international community with well-established contacts. These international minority language groups have the potential to harness national and international state support for their languages and to persuade governments to reconsider their attitudes towards the 'cost' of linguistic diversity.

In 1992, linguists attending the International Linguistics Congress in Quebec called on UNESCO to promote and sponsor linguistic organizations to respond urgently to the situation of language loss. Since that time many organizations such as the Foundation for Endangered Languages in the UK have been established. Despite these initiatives, the current rate of language loss is unprecedented and effective language policies are urgently needed to reverse this trend. State support and economic development are crucial in the regeneration of lesser-used languages. Moreover, forces of globalization may prove an aid rather than a hindrance to the revival and regeneration of minority tongues.

REFERENCES

Anonymous (2002) 'Think Local: Cultural Imperialism Doesn't Sell', *The Economist*, 13 April, pp. 12–4.

Bourdieu, P. (1991) *Language and Symbolic Power*. Cambridge: Polity Press.

Coulmas, F. (1992) *Language and Economy*. Oxford: Blackwell.

Crawford, J. (1994) 'Endangered Native American Languages: What is to be Done and Why?' *Journal of Navajo Education* 11(3), pp. 3–11.

Crystal, D. (1997a) *English as a Global Language*. Cambridge: Cambridge University Press.

Crystal, D. (1997b) *The Cambridge Encyclopaedia of Language*. Cambridge: Cambridge University Press.

Crystal, D. (1999a) 'The Death of Language', *Prospect,* November, 56–9.

Crystal, D. (1999b) 'Death Sentence', *Guardian*, 25 October, G2, pp. 2–3.

Crystal, D. (2000) *Language Death*. Cambridge: Cambridge University Press.

Dunbar, R. (2000) 'Legal and Institutional Aspects of Gaelic Development'. In G. McCoy and M. Scott (eds), *Aithne na nGael: Gaelic Identities*. Belfast: Institute of Irish Studies, pp. 67–87.

Durkacz, V. E. (1983) *The Decline of the Celtic Languages: a Study of Linguistic and Cultural Conflict in Scotland, Wales and Ireland from the Reformation to the Twentieth Century*. Edinburgh: John Donald Publishers Ltd.

Graddol, D. (1997) *The Future of English? A Guide to Forecasting the Popularity of the English Language in the 21st Century.* London: The British Council.

Grillo, R. (1989) *Dominant Languages: Language and Hierarchy in Britain and France*. Cambridge: Cambridge University Press.

Grimes, B. (2000) *Ethnologue: Languages of the World*, Vol. 1, 14th Edition. Texas: US Summer School of Linguistics.

Grin, F. (1990) 'The Economic Approach to Minority Languages', *Journal of Multilingual and Multicultural Development*, 11, pp. 153–73.

Grin, F. (1993a) 'European Economic Integration and the Fate of Lesser Used Languages', *Language Problems and Language Planning*, 17, pp. 101–16.

Grin, F. (1993b) 'Minority Language Promotion: On the Practical Usefulness of Economic Theory' in Llinos Dafis (ed.), *Economic Development and Lesser Used Languages: Partnerships for Action.* Bangor: IAITH Cyf., pp. 24–9.

Grin, F. (1999) 'Market Forces, Language Spread and Linguistic Diversity'. In Kontra, M., Phillipson, R., Skutnabb-Kangas, T., and

Várady, T. (eds), *Language: a Right and a Resource: Approaching Linguistic Human Rights*. Budapest: Central European Press, pp. 169–86.

Hale, J. (1993) 'The Renaissance Idea of Europe'. In Soledad García (ed.), *European Identity and the Search for Legitimacy*. London and New York: Pinter, pp. 46–63.

Hall, J. (1990) *Knowledge of the Catalan Language (1975–1986)*. Barcelona: Generalitat de Catalunya.

Kontra, M., Phillipson, R., Skutnabb-Kangas, T. and Várady, T. (eds), (1999) *Language: a Right and a Resource: Approaching Linguistic Human Rights*. Budapest: Central European Press.

Krauss, M. (1992) 'The World's Languages in Crisis', *Language,* 68, pp. 4–10.

Krauss, M. (1995) 'Language Loss in Alaska, the United States and the World. Frame of Reference', *Alaska Humanities Forum,* 6(1), pp. 2–5.

Letrêtre, M. (1992) *The Catalan Language Today.* Barcelona: Generalitat de Catalunya.

May, S. (2001) *Language and Minority Rights: Ethnicity, Nationalism and the Politics of Language*. London: Longman.

McCloskey, J. (2001) *Voices Silenced: Has Irish a Future?* Dublin: Cois Life Teo.

Nelde, P., Strubell, M. and Williams, G. (1996) *Euromosaic: the Production and Reproduction of the Minority Language Groups in the European Union*. Luxembourg: Office for Official Publications of the European Communities.

Nic Craith, M. (1993) *Malartú Teanga: Meath na Gaeilge i gCorcaigh sa Naóú hAois Déag*. Bremen: European Society for Irish Studies.

Nic Craith, M. (2003) 'Facilitating or Generating Linguistic Diversity: the European Charter for Regional and Minority Languages'. In G. Hogan-Brun and S. Wolff (eds) *Minority Languages in Europe: Frameworks, Status, Prospects*. Basingstoke: Macmillan/Palgrave, pp. 56–72.

Nic Craith, M. (2004) 'Local Cultures in a Global World' in U. Kockel and M. Nic Craith (eds) *Communicating Cultures*, Műnster: LIT Verlag, pp. 279–99.

Nic Craith, M. (2006) *Europe and the Politics of Language: Citizens, Migrants and Outsiders*. Basingstoke: Macmillan/Palgrave.

Nic Uidhir, M. (1996) 'Gaillimh le Gaeilge: an Effective Bilingual Movement'. In M. Nic Craith (ed.), *Watching One's Tongue: Issues in Language Planning*. Liverpool: University Press, pp. 103–11.

Ó Cinnéide, M. and Keane, M. (1988) *Local Socio-economic Impacts Associated with the Galway Gaeltacht*. Galway: University College.

Ó Muircheartaigh, L. (1996) 'The Tipperary Irish Language Project: a Typology of Minority Language Education'. In M. Nic Craith (ed.), *Watching One's Tongue: Issues in Language Planning*. Liverpool: University Press, pp. 131–44.

Phillipson, R. 1996 *Globalizing English: Are Linguistic Human Rights an Alternative to Linguistic Imperialism*? Paper delivered to International Conference on Language Rights, the Hong Kong Polytechnic University, 22–24 June.

Price, A., Ó Torna, C. and Wynne Jones, A. (1997) *The Diversity Dividend: Language, Culture and Economy in an Integrated Europe.* Brussels: European Bureau for Lesser Used Languages.

Rajendran, C. (1999) *Performing Identity: a Stage for Multilingual English and Multicultural Englishness.* Paper delivered at *Looking Into England*, conference hosted by the British Council and the Centre for British and Comparative Cultural Studies at the University of Warwick, 12–18 December.

Skutnabb-Kangas, T. (1988) 'Multilingualism and the Education of Minority Children'. In T. Skutnabb-Kangas and Jim Cummins (eds), *Minority Education: From Shame to Struggle.* Clevedon: Multilingual Matters, pp. 9–44.

Skutnabb-Kangas, T. and Phillipson, R. (1995) *Linguistic Human Rights: Overcoming Linguistic Discrimination.* Berlin, New York: Mouton de Gruyter.

Skutnabb-Kangas, T., (1999) 'Linguistic Diversity, Human Rights and the 'Free' Market' in Kontra, M., Phillipson, R., Skutnabb-Kangas, T., and Várady, T. (eds), *Language: a Right and a Resource: Approaching Linguistic Human Rights.* Budapest: Central European Press, pp. 187–222.

Skutnabb-Kangas, T. (2000) *Linguistic Genocide in Education – or Worldwide Diversity and Human Rights?* Mahwah. NJ: Lawrence Erlbaum.

Smolitz, J. (1986) 'National Language Policy in the Phillipines'. In Bernard Spolsky (ed.), *Language and Education in Multilingual Settings.* Clevedon/Philadelphia: Multilingual Matters, pp. 96–116.

Titley, A. (2000) *A Pocket History of Gaelic Culture.* Dublin: O Brien Press.

Withers, C. (1984) *Gaelic in Scotland 1618–1981: the Geographical History of a Language.* Edinburgh: John Donald Publishers Ltd.

Part II

Comparing Legislative and Institutional Frameworks

7
Official Language Minorities in Canada: A Selected Profile

GÉRARD FINN

In order better to understand the present language planning approach practice in Canada, it is important to be somewhat familiar with the following aspects of the Canadian reality: historical context, the demographic diversity and, last but not least, the division of responsibilities (commonly called powers) amongst the various governments, all democratically elected. Obviously, in this chapter only a brief limited set of details about each aspect will be presented as they could be each, in their own right, the subject of long discussions.

It should be remembered that language issues were brought to the forefront with the arrival of the first Europeans on the North American continent. There were already a large number of native languages being spoken. Because of the societal values of the day, which persisted well into the twentieth century, little attention was paid to these languages. The French governed New France from 1604 to 1760. The treaty of Paris of 1763 confirmed politically the British victory over the French and marked the end of the Seven Years War. The treaty specified that the French inhabitants could return to France or, if they were to stay in the 'New World', they would be permitted to keep their religion. The vast majority stayed. The Act of Quebec signed by the French and British governments in 1774 confirmed the stipulations of the Treaty of Paris and stipulated that the inhabitants could keep the French legal system.

The British North America Act of 1867 created the political structure of Canada as we know it today. Canada has many levels of government within its territory. In this context, level of government does not imply a superior or inferior status, as the federal government and provincial, territorial governments have different responsibilities in different field of competence. These two levels of government are clearly identified in the Canadian Constitution. To these two levels of government, we must add the municipal or local governments, which are a creation of the provinces, as well as the school boards. We must also include regional governments in some provinces and native authorities in others.

It is important to comprehend the implementation of language-related laws fully to understand the distribution of 'legislative powers', as they are called in the Constitution, between the federal government and the provinces. The powers of the federal Parliament include: taxation, regulation of trade and commerce, postal services, census and statistics, militia, navy, naval services, defence, quarantine, banking, incorporation of banks, the issue of paper money, currency and coinage, naturalization and aliens, criminal law, etc. In parallel to the federal powers, the Constitution lists the 'Exclusive Powers of Provincial Legislatures'. These powers include: taxation, hospital (health), municipal institutions, non-renewable natural resources, education, local services, agriculture, land use etc. Although not all the powers attributed to each level of government are listed above, two major sectors of human activities have not been named: notably culture and languages. They are not left out intentionally. Both levels of governments can and have intervened in the fields of culture and languages within their legislative powers.

For a century or so following the Confederation of 1867, many language-related rights were abolished by provincial legislatures. As an example, the legislature of the province of Manitoba adopted in 1890 an Official Language Act stipulating that English was the only language of records and journals of the legislature, for the publication of statutes and in the courts. Also, over time, health services and education, which were provided mostly by religious orders in the language of the minority, were taken over by provincial authorities as stipulated in the Constitution.

Over the years, several provinces passed legislation limiting or banning the teaching in French. In 1912, the province of Ontario enacted a regulation stipulating that English was to be the sole language of instruction after grade three and the study of French was to be limited to one hour a day. In 1931, the province of Saskatchewan adopted an act stipulating that English was to be the only language of instruction in its public schools. In these cases and others, minorities had to attend private schools in order to receive instructions in their language while simultaneously supporting the public system through their taxes. During the same period, some efforts were made to improve the availability of public services to the French-speaking minority. For example, the federal government's Translation Bureau was established in 1934 in order to ensure the publication of documents in both languages. In 1959 and in 1961 simultaneous interpretation was introduced in the House of Commons and in the Senate, a practice which has been refined and used as a model for other bilingual legislatures.

The relations between the two linguistic communities, French and English, were limited and the French-speaking community living in Quebec felt that in was not in control of its own destiny. The two communities were described as 'two solitudes'. The decade of the 1960s corresponded to what has become known as the 'Quebec Quiet Revolution'. This was a period which saw the development of a strong nationalist movement in Quebec and an era during which a number of French-speaking leaders expressed frustration as they were not equal partners in the Confederation. Consequently, the federal government decided in 1963 to appoint a Royal Commission on Bilingualism and Biculturalism to

> inquire into and report upon the existing state of bilingualism and biculturalism in Canada and to recommend what steps should be taken to develop the Canadian Confederation on the basis of an equal partnership between the two founding races, taking into account the contribution made by the other ethnic groups to the cultural enrichment of Canada . . .

In 1967, the commission recommended that the government adopt an Official Languages Act to establish the equal status of English and French in Canada and recommended that the government appoint a Commissioner of Official Languages to oversee its application. The government accepted the recommendations and adopted the first Official Languages Act which came into force in 1970.

In 1982, the constant evolution of the language rights and practices in Canadian society was enshrined in the Charter of Rights and Freedoms which is an integral part of the Canadian Constitution. The most significant clauses state that:

> 16. (1) English and French are the official languages of Canada and have equality of status and equal rights and privileges as to their use in all institutions of the Parliament and government of Canada.
>
> 16. (3) Nothing in this Charter limits the authority of Parliament or a legislature to advance the equality of status or use of English and French.
>
> 17. (1) Everyone has the right to use English or French in any debates and other proceedings of Parliament.
>
> 18. (1) The statutes, record and journals of Parliament will be printed and published in English and French and both language versions are equally authoritative.
>
> 19.(1) Either English or French may be used by any person in, or in any pleading in or process issuing from, any court established by Parliament.
>
> 20. (1) Any member of the public in Canada has the right to communicate with, and to receive available services from, any head or central office of an institution of the Parliament or government of Canada in English or French, and has the same right with respect to any other office of any such institution where
>
> A) there is a significant demand for communications with and services from that office in such language; or
>
> B) due to the nature of the office, it is reasonable that communications with and services from that office be available in both English and French.

Another provision of the Charter of Rights and Freedoms which is important for our subject and consequently worth quoting is section 23 dealing with educational rights.

23. Minority Language Educational Rights

(1) Citizens of Canada

(A) whose first language learned and still understood is that of the English or French linguistic minority population of the province in which they reside, or

(B) who have received their primary school instruction in Canada in English or French and reside in a province where the language in which they received that instruction is the language of the English or French linguistic minority population of the province, have the right to have their children receive primary and secondary school instruction in that language in that province.

(2) Citizens of Canada of whom any child has received or is receiving primary or secondary school instruction in English or French in Canada, have the right to have all their children receive primary and secondary school instruction in the same language.

(3) The right of citizens of Canada under subsections (1) and (2) to have their children receive primary and secondary school instruction in the language of the English or French linguistic minority population of a province

(A) applies wherever in the province the number of children of citizens who have such a right is sufficient to warrant the provision to them out of public funds of minority language instructions; and

(B) includes, where the number of those children so warrants, the right to have them receive that instruction in minority language educational facilities provided out of public funds.

The current Official Languages policy, at the federal level in Canada, is founded on the principles found in Sections 16 to 20 of the Charter of Rights and Freedoms.

In 2001, according to the census, Canada had a population of 29.6 million people. The vast majority of these 29 million people live on a rather narrow strip of land in the most southern part of the country, north of the 49th parallel, along the US border. Of the 29.6 million population, some 17.5 million declared English as their mother tongue (first language learned and still understood); 6.8 million declared French as their mother tongue, while slightly more than 5.3 million people declared other languages as their mother tongue. Of these, more than 203,000 declared one of the fifty or so native languages as their mother tongue. Of the non-official languages, Chinese is the mother tongue of 872,000 persons, Italian, of 494,400 people, while 455,500 declared German as their mother tongue and 260,800 declared Spanish. Numerous other languages are also spoken by Canadians. An important characteristic of the population distribution is that the vast majority (5.8 million) of the people who declared French as their mother tongue live in the province of Quebec. Of the remaining one million or so, 748,700 live in the provinces of Ontario (500,000) and New Brunswick (242,000). The remaining 231,000 or so are distributed unevenly in the other provinces and territories. As for the English-speaking population, 591,400 live in Quebec, the only province with a French-speaking majority. The Table 7.1 indicates for each province and territory (the data for the Nunavut are included in the Northwest Territories) the distribution of the population, English and French mother tongue, in thousands.

Table 7.1: The distribution of English and French mother-tongue population in 2001

Provinces/Territories	English	French
Newfoundland	500.1	2.3
Prince Edward Island	125.4	5.9
Nova Scotia	834.8	35.4
New Brunswick	468.1	239.4
Quebec	591.4	5802.0
Ontario	8042.0	509.3
Manitoba	831.8	45.9
Saskatchewan	822.6	18.6
Alberta	2395.8	62.2
British Columbia	2849.2	58.9
Yukon	24.8	0.9
Northwest Territories	28.9	1.0
Nunavut	7.2	0.4

Source: Census of Canada 2001, Office of the Commissioner of Official Languages.

In 2001, 5.2 million Canadians (or 17.7 per cent of the population) considered themselves bilingual compared to 1.7 millions (or 12 per cent of the population) in 1951. More than 90 per cent of the population who declared themselves to be bilingual lived in the four provinces of Quebec, New Brunswick, Ontario and British Columbia. 67 per cent of the anglophones living in Quebec were bilingual while 84.8 per cent of the francophones living in provinces and territories other than Quebec were also bilingual.

It is instructive to compare various educational and economic indicators of the total francophone minorities living outside Quebec with those relating to the anglophones of these same provinces and territories and also compare data on the minority communities living in Ontario, New Brunswick and Quebec with the majority population of these provinces. In the sector of education, 34.8 per cent of the francophones living outside Quebec have attended high school compared with 38.4 per cent of the anglophones living in provinces and territories other than Quebec. Also, 19.5 per cent of the francophones have completed a university degree compared with a national average of 22.4 per cent.

In Ontario, 35.7 per cent of the francophones have completed high school compared with 37.8 per cent of the anglophones. In the same province 20.5 per cent of the francophone population has completed a university degree compared with 23 per cent of the anglophones. The gap is somewhat higher in New Brunswick where 35.7 per cent of the francophones have completed high school compared with 40.1 per cent of the anglophones. 16.2 per cent of the francophones have a university degree compared with 19.3 per cent of the anglophones. In Quebec, where there is a significant difference at the university level, 28.0 per cent of the anglophones went to university compared with 16.9 per cent of the francophones. As for high school attendance, the situation is closer to that which obtains in Ontario and New Brunswick, as 33.2 per cent of the anglophones attended high school while 34.7 per cent of the francophones have done so.

In terms of economic indicators, in 2001 the average annual income from employment for Canadians who declared French as their first official language spoken was $27,286 while for anglophones (first official language spoken, English) it was $30,930. In Quebec, the annual income of the anglophone minority is higher ($30,277) than the annual income of the francophone population ($26,923). Although there is still a gap on revenue between the anglophone and the francophone populations, it is significantly narrower than it was fifty years ago. The data related to the labour market participation rates follows the same pattern for francophones living in a minority situation. Of the francophones living outside Quebec, 64.3 per cent declared being active in the labour market, compared with 69.4 per cent of the anglophones. In Ontario, 64.8 per cent of the francophones participated in the labour market compared with 69.5 per cent of anglophones. We observe a similar situation in New Brunswick: 61.7 per cent for francophones compared with 64.0 per cent. In Quebec, the minority English-speaking community is also less active in the labour market at 63.1 per cent compared with 64.9 per cent for francophones. As noted in the preceding educational and economic data, the results, with one or two exceptions, are generally less favourable for communities living in a minority setting.

In the last fifty years, the Canadian population has changed significantly. From 1951 to 2001, the population more than doubled. The population of English mother tongue followed the same pattern while the francophone population increased from 4 million to 6.8 million over the same period. Another significant difference is that while the anglophones maintained their percentage share of the total population (59.1 per cent in 1951; 59.1 per cent in 2001), the francophone population decreased in percentage terms (29.0 per cent in 1951; 22.9 per cent in 2001).

In the 1990s, the Canadian government like many governments of the Western world was facing a very difficult budgetary situation with an important debt load and annual operating deficits. As a result, the government embarked upon a major expenditure reduction exercise. The cumulative effect of budgetary reductions and the sort of government transformations discussed by Cardinal below, resulted in a significant erosion of the Official Languages programme.

Recognizing the negative effects of the reduction of resources allocated to the programme in the ten previous years, the government launched in March 2003, an action plan for Official Languages entitled: The Next Act: New Momentum for Canada's Linguistic Duality. The government injected over $751 million dollars of new funds into the Official Languages programmes over a five-year period. The established priorities for the new funds are education, community development and a bilingual public service, as discussed by various contributors to this volume. It will take a few years before we will be able to observe the effect of the implementation of the government action plan.

REFERENCES

The Canadian Constitution (1982) *Canadian Charter of Rights and Freedoms*, Ottawa: Government of Canada.

Corbeil, J-P. and M. L. (2004) *Languages in Canada 2001 Census in New Canadian Perspectives*, Ottawa: Minister of Public Works and Government Services Canada, p. 161.

Government of Canada (1969) *An Act Respecting the Status of the Official Languages of Canada*, 17–18 Elizabeth II, *c*.54 (Can.), Ottawa: Government of Canada

Laurendeau, A. and Davidson Dunton, A. (1967) *Reports of the Royal Commission on Bilingualism and Biculturalism, Volume 1, The Official Languages*, Ottawa: Queen's printer.

Statistics Canada (2004) The Canadian Census of 2001, Ottawa: Statistics Canada.

The Official Languages Act (1988) *An Act Respecting the Status and Use of the Official Languages of Canada c*.38 (Can.), Ottawa: Government of Canada.

8
The Official Languages Act and the Constitutional and Legislative Recognition of Language Rights in Canada

WARREN NEWMAN[1*]

Introduction

The Official Languages Act (1988)[2] is the cornerstone of Canada's legislative and regulatory regime of language rights protections. It is intimately linked, both in its inspiration and its application, to the official language rights and related guarantees enshrined in the Constitution of Canada, including section 133 of the Constitution Act, 1867[3] and sections 16 to 23 of the Canadian Charter of Rights and Freedoms.[4] In this chapter, I shall endeavour to provide a brief analytical overview of the operation of this regime, with reference to the legal history of the provisions.

The Nature and Significance of Language Rights in Canada

The protection of minorities is, as the Supreme Court of Canada held in the *Quebec Secession Reference*, one of the basic structural principles of Canada's constitutional framework.[5] This principle is reflected in the guarantees afforded to minorities by the Charter of Rights and other provisions of the Constitution, notably those that entrench and protect rights in relation to the use of the English and French languages. Some of these provisions, such as those of section

23 of the Charter which guarantee minority-language education rights, are restricted in their application to linguistic minorities; other language rights, however, may be seen to benefit both linguistic minorities and majorities. (Newman, 2004).

'The importance of language rights', the Supreme Court stated eloquently in the *Manitoba Language Rights Reference*, (1985) 'is grounded in the essential role that language plays in human existence, development and dignity.'

> It is through language that we are able to form concepts; to structure and order the world around us. Language bridges the gap between isolation and community, allowing humans to delineate the rights and duties they hold in respect of one another, and thus to live in society. (*Reference re Manitoba Language Rights*, [1985] 1 S. C. R. 721, *per curiam*, p. 744)

Justice La Forest of the Court, writing for the majority in *Mercure's Case*, noted that 'language is profoundly anchored in the human condition'.[6] Language rights 'are a well-known species of human rights and should be approached accordingly', he emphasized.[7] 'If human rights legislation can be said to be fundamental or almost constitutional', so too could it be said of language rights legislation; which is 'rooted in a deeply sensitive reality recognized in the *Canadian Charter of Rights and Freedoms*' and which, 'among our fundamental constitutional values, sets forth that English and French are the official languages of this country'.[8] He added further:

> I realize, of course, that, as in the case of other human rights, governmental measures for the protection of language rights must be tailored to respond to practical exigencies as well as to the nature and history of the country. But when Parliament or the legislature has provided such measures, it behoves the courts to respect them. Any inroads on them should be left to the legislative branch. This is particularly so of rights regarding the English and French languages, which are basic to the continued viability of the nation.[9]

More recently, the Supreme Court has placed renewed emphasis upon the importance of language rights in Canada's constitutional and statutory framework. Justice Bastarache underlined in *Beaulac's Case* that '[l]anguage rights must *in all cases* be interpreted purposively, in a manner consistent with the preservation and development of official language communities in Canada' and must be construed 'as a fundamental tool for the preservation and protection of official language communities where they do apply'.[10]

Section 133 and Equal Access to the Laws, Legislatures and Courts

Any account of the constitutional and legislative history of language rights since Confederation must really begin with section 133 of the British North America Act. The Union Act of 1840 had made English the official language of legislative records and journals in the Legislative Council and Assembly of the province of Canada, with French relegated to a lesser status, but this arrangement had rapidly proved to be unsatisfactory.[11] Thus in 1867, when the provinces of Canada, New Brunswick and Nova Scotia were federally united (and the provinces of Quebec and Ontario thereby established in the stead of the former province of Canada) and the Dominion of Canada was established by the Constitution Act 1867, section 133 ensured that English and French would be the official languages of the Parliament and the courts of Canada and of the legislature and courts of Quebec, the only province with a French-speaking majority. The provisions of section 133 did not extend beyond the legislative and judicial spheres to the executive and administrative spheres of government, which were, at the time, rudimentary both in their state and their importance. However, when the governments of Canada and Quebec spoke through the solemn voice of parliamentary debates, legislative enactments and court proceedings, both English and French were, formally at least, on an equal footing. The text of section 133 reads as follows:

> Either the English or the French Language may be used by any Person in the Debates of the Houses of the Parliament of Canada and of the Houses of the Legislature of Quebec; and both those Languages shall be used in the respective Records and Journals of those Houses; and either of those Languages may be used by any Person or in any Pleading or Process in or issuing from any Court

> of Canada established under this Act, and in and from all or any of the Courts of Quebec.
>
> The Acts of the Parliament of Canada and of the Legislature of Quebec shall be printed and published in both those Languages.

Three years after Confederation, when the new province of Manitoba was established, virtually identical protections respecting the use of English and French were extended to the legislature and courts of that province by section 23 of the Manitoba Act 1870.[12] However, an Act of the Manitoba legislature passed in 1890 purported to abrogate the guarantees of section 23 by making English the sole official language of legislative records, journals and enactments, and of proceedings before the courts.[13] In 1979 the Supreme Court of Canada overturned the constitutionality of this statute in *Forest's Case*.[14] Six years later, in the *Manitoba Language Rights Reference*, the court struck down as invalid and unconstitutional more than nine decades of provincial laws that had been enacted and promulgated only in English, in contravention of section 23. In this seminal opinion on the rule of law and the supremacy of the Constitution, the Supreme Court held that the purpose of both section 133 of the Constitution Act 1867 and section 23 of the Manitoba Act 1870 'was to ensure full and equal access to the legislatures, the laws and the courts for francophones and anglophones alike'. The 'fundamental guarantees' of section 133 and section 23 were 'constitutionally entrenched' and 'beyond the power of the provinces of Quebec and Manitoba to amend unilaterally'. Those protections 'would be meaningless and their entrenchment a futile exercise were they not obligatory' (Manitoba Act 1870, p. 739).

In *Blaikie's Case*,[15] rendered at the same time as the decision in *Forest* in 1979, the Supreme Court had ruled *ultra vires* provisions of Quebec's Charter of the French Language (1977) that made French the sole official language of the legislature and courts of the province. An administrative translation of the Acts of the legislature enacted in French would continue to be 'printed and published', and this, it was argued by the Attorney General of Quebec, was sufficient to satisfy section 133's requirement of bilingual promulgation (if, in the event, it was beyond the power of the legislature to amend and abolish that requirement outright). The Supreme Court held that nothing less than simultaneous enactment, printing and publication of equally authoritative English and French versions of the Acts of the legislature would meet the duty imposed by section 133, and, moreover, that this duty extended to subordinate legislation as well.[16] Section 133, the court stated, 'not only provides but requires that official status be given to both French and English in respect of the printing and publication of the Statutes of the Legislature of Quebec'.[17]

> It was urged before this Court that there was no requirement of enactment in both languages, as contrasted with printing and publishing. However, if full weight is given to every word of section 133 it becomes apparent that this requirement is implicit. What is required to be printed and published in both languages is described as 'Acts' and texts do not become 'Acts' without enactment.[18]

Now, in the *Manitoba Language Rights Reference*, the full import of the Supreme Court's rulings in *Blaikie* and *Forest* was brought home to the legislature and government of Manitoba in ringing terms:

> The constitutional entrenchment of a duty on the Manitoba Legislature to enact, print and publish in both French and English in section 23 of the *Manitoba Act, 1870* confers upon the judiciary the responsibility of protecting the correlative language rights of all Manitobans including the Franco-Manitoban minority. The judiciary is the institution charged with ensuring that the government complies with the Constitution. We must protect those whose constitutional rights have been violated, whomever they may be, and whatever the reasons for the violation.
>
> The Constitution of a country is the statement of the will of the people to be governed in accordance with certain principles held as fundamental and certain prescriptions restrictive of the powers of government. It is, as section 52 of the *Constitution Act, 1982* declares, the 'supreme law' of the nation, unalterable by the normal legislative process, and unsuffering of laws inconsistent with it. The duty of the judiciary is to interpret and apply the laws of Canada and each of the provinces, and it is thus our duty to ensure that the constitutional law prevails. (Manitoba Act 1870, pp. 744–5)

The Supreme Court, faced with the question of vindicating the language rights of Manitobans and the principle of constitutionalism, whilst preserving the province from the legal chaos that might ensue should the whole corpus of the province's laws be removed in one fell swoop, invoked the principle of the rule of law to maintain Manitoba's invalid laws in force for the minimum period of time necessary for their translation into French and their re-enactment in both languages.[19]

Constitutional power over Language Rights and the principle of Advancement: The Official Languages Act of 1969

Section 133 of the Constitution Act 1867 and its counterpart, section 23 of the Manitoba Act 1870, were the only provisions of the Constitution of Canada that guaranteed rights in relation to the use of English and French, and these protections were limited to the legislative and judicial spheres of government at the federal and provincial levels (and, amongst the provinces, applicable only to Quebec and Manitoba).[20] It was not until the 1960s that the first major reform of Canada's heretofore piecemeal approach to language legislation was conceived and undertaken.

On 9 July 1969, the Parliament of Canada gave effect to one of the principal recommendations of the Royal Commission on Bilingualism and Biculturalism by enacting the first Official Languages Act.[21] Section 2 of the Act declared that English and French were the official languages of Canada 'for all purposes of the Parliament and Government of Canada'. It also recognized the 'equality of status and equal rights and privileges' of both languages, 'as to their use in all the institutions of the Parliament and Government of Canada'. By its very terms, therefore, the Act extended beyond the constitutionally guaranteed use of English and French in Parliament and federal courts to embrace federal institutions more generally, including ministries and departments of government, Crown corporations and agencies, and quasi-judicial or administrative bodies. Amongst the other institutional duties established by the statute, the Act imposed a substantive obligation upon federal institutions to ensure that members of the public might obtain services and communicate with designated offices of these institutions in both official languages.[22]

In lieu of enforcement by way of a judicial remedy, the Act was innovative in creating the position of the Commissioner of Official Languages, described by the Bilingual and Biculturalism Commission as ‘a high state official, independent of the government, with responsibility for inquiring into and reporting upon the implementation’ of the legislation. The Commissioner would play an important role as a *linguistic ombudsman*, receiving complaints and being ‘the active conscience – actually the protector – of the Canadian public where official languages are concerned’.[23] The Commissioner would also function as a *linguistic auditor*, reporting to Parliament on the implementation of the Act by federal institutions and bringing to light systemic issues and challenges. A third role, conceived not so much by the Bilingual and Bicultural Commission but evolving from the Commissioner’s broad statutory mandate to ‘take all actions and measures within his authority with a view to ensuring recognition of the status of each of the official languages’ – was that of the *promotion* of Canada’s linguistic duality, reaching beyond the black letter of the law to encourage ‘compliance with the *spirit and intent* of this Act in the administration of the affairs of the institutions of the Parliament and Government of Canada’.[24]

The Official Languages Act of 1969, whilst much broader in scope and design than section 133 of the Constitution Act 1867, and although contemplating the possibility of complementary provincial legislative or administrative action,[25] was limited in its application to the fields of legislative competence assigned to Parliament by the Constitution of Canada. Only New Brunswick, with its sizeable Acadian population, followed suit and enacted its own Official Languages Act, making English and French the official languages of the province and recognizing the equality of status of both languages in the institutions of the provincial legislature and government.

The validity of both the federal and provincial statutes was challenged in *Jones* v. *Attorney General of New Brunswick*,[26] notably on the basis that the legislation exceeded the limits imposed by section 133 of the Constitution Act 1867 and was *ultra vires*, having regard to the division of legislative powers under the Constitution. The Supreme Court of Canada upheld the constitutionality of both Official Languages Acts.

The judgment of the Supreme Court in *Jones' Case* was delivered by Chief Justice Bora Laskin, who ruled emphatically that the existence of section 133 of the Constitution Act 1867 in no ways precluded Parliament or a provincial legislature from exercising their respective legislative powers to enhance language rights in areas beyond the scope of section 133, as long as such legislation did not undermine the protections afforded by that constitutional provision itself.

> The submission as to section 133 by counsel for the appellant is that that provision is exhaustive of constitutional authority in relation to the use of English and French, and that a constitutional amendment is necessary to support any legislation which, like the *Official Languages Act*, would go beyond it. I do not accept that submission which, in my opinion, is unsupportable as a matter of such history thereof as is available, and unsupportable under the scheme of distribution of legislative power as established by the *British North America Act* and as construed by the Courts over a long period of time.[27]

Although the Report of the Royal Commission on Bilingualism and Biculturalism and certain governmental white papers had recommended, inter alia, the constitutional entrenchment of language rights going beyond section 133, 'that is hardly a support', reasoned Chief Justice Laskin, 'for the contention that there can be no advance upon section 133 without constitutional amendment'.[28]

> Certainly, what section 133 itself gives may not be diminished by the Parliament of Canada, but if its provisions are respected there is nothing in it . . . that precludes the conferring of additional rights or privileges or the imposing of additional obligations respecting the use of English and French, if done in relation to matters within the competence of the enacting Legislature.[29]

This saving principle of advancement of language rights through legislative action by Parliament and the provincial legislatures, respectively, was later captured succinctly in the express terms of subsection 16(3) of the Constitution Act 1982: 'Nothing in this Charter limits the authority of Parliament or a legislature to advance the equality of status or use of English and French.'

By now it should be evident from this account that, given the federal character of the Canadian state, legislative authority over language as a subject matter is, from a constitutional perspective, divided between Parliament and the provincial legislatures. Interestingly, despite its significance in the Canadian context, 'language' is not mentioned amongst the numerous heads of federal and provincial powers set out in sections 91 and 92 of the Constitution Act 1867. For purposes of constitutional classification, the competence of Parliament or a provincial legislature to enact language rights legislation is not a plenary power but, rather, is ancillary to exercise of jurisdiction over the institutions or activities to which the provisions of the law apply; and the validity of such legislation will be determined accordingly.

Thus, the Official Languages Act of 1969 was upheld in *Jones' Case* as legislation validly enacted by Parliament pursuant to its general (or residual) power to enact legislation for the 'Peace, Order and good Government of Canada';[30] and certain provisions in the Act dealing with the language of proceedings in criminal cases were maintained under Parliament's exclusive power to legislate in relation to the 'Criminal Law . . . including the Procedure in Criminal Matters'.[31] Similarly, certain provisions of provincial language rights legislation have been upheld as a valid exercise of provincial authority over 'Property and Civil Rights in the Province', the 'Administration of Justice in the Province . . . including Procedure in Civil Matters', or 'Generally all Matters of a merely local or private Nature in the Province'.[32] However, language legislation that oversteps the bounds of legislative competence or interferes with entrenched language guarantees will be ruled by the courts to be *ultra vires*, as we have witnessed above in *Blaikie's Case*, *Forest's Case*, and the *Manitoba Language Rights Reference*.

The view that legislative competence in regard to language is *ancillary*, rather than plenary, in nature – a view that was implicit in the Supreme Court's approach to the issue in *Jones* – was further elaborated by Professor Peter Hogg in a passage that was, in turn, expressly adopted by the Court in *Devine v. Attorney General of Quebec*.[33]

The 1973 Parliamentary resolution and the scope of the declaration of equal status

The enactment of the Official Languages Act in 1969 was a major step in the development of Canada's legislative framework of institutional bilingualism. Nonetheless, for many years it was uncertain whether, as a matter of law, the duties established by the Act extended beyond the provision of governmental instruments, communications and services to the public in both languages, to embrace the use of English and French as working languages within the internal administration of federal institutions. In 1973, the Senate and the House of Commons of Canada adopted a parliamentary resolution that recognized the equality of status of both languages as the languages of work in the federal public service, as well as the principle of the equitable participation of both language groups in federal institutions. The resolution helped to underpin the government of Canada's policy intentions and efforts in these areas, but since it was not a legislative enactment it did not have the force of law.

In *Thorson's Case* Chief Justice Laskin of the Supreme Court had characterized the Official Languages Act of 1969 as being 'both declaratory and directory in respect of the use of English and French by and in federal authorities and agencies'.[34] In later cases, the federal and superior courts appeared to be divided on the issue of the true scope and the enforceability of the declaration of equal status set out in section 2 of the Act, as the *Joyal* and the *Gens de l'Air* decisions demonstrated.[35] There was also the related question as to whether the Act would enjoy primacy in the event of a conflict with other federal legislation.

One important legislative development during this period was the enactment in 1978 by Parliament of amendments to the Criminal Code of Canada to grant to English-speaking and to French-speaking accused persons the right to a trial before a judge (or a judge and jury, as the case might be) who speak the official language that is that of the accused. These new provisions of the Criminal Code were implemented first in New Brunswick and in Ontario, and then in Manitoba. Since January 1990 they have been in force across the country.[36]

The 1982 Charter of Rights

The enactment of the Canadian Charter of Rights and Freedoms in 1982 put an end to the debate concerning the scope of the declaration of equality of official languages that first appeared in the 1969 Official Languages Act. Subsection 16(1) of the Charter constitutionally guarantees the principle of equality of English and French as to their use in the institutions of the Parliament and government of Canada. Subsections 17(1), 18(1) and 19(1) repeat and reinforce the provisions of section 133 of the Constitution Act 1867 as regards parliamentary, legislative and judicial bilingualism at the federal level. Subsection 20(1) entrenches the right of members of the public to communicate with federal institutions and to receive services in English and French. Finally, the rule of interpretation established by the Supreme Court in *Jones' Case* – the principle of advancement of language rights by statutory enhancement beyond the content of the constitutional guarantees – was added expressly to the text of the Charter. The text of *section* 16(3) bears repeating here: 'Nothing in this Charter limits the authority of Parliament or a legislature to advance the equality of status or use of English and French.'

Subsection 16(3) is not itself a source of legislative authority: the legislative competence of Parliament and the provincial legislatures, respectively, is, as we have seen, to be found in sections 91 and 92 of the Constitution Act 1867 and related provisions on the distribution of powers. Nor does subsection 16(3) create positive rights.[37] What subsection 16(3) does is preclude the sort of legislative challenge that occurred in *Jones*. For example, the validity of a statute enhancing the equality of the English and French languages could not be attacked under section 15 of the Charter on the basis that it infringed the principle of equality therein.[38]

Moreover, the constitutional rights entrenched in subsections 16(1) to 20(1) are linked to the court remedy provided in section 24 of the Charter, which states: '24(1) Anyone whose rights or freedoms, as guaranteed by this Charter, have been infringed or denied may apply to a court of competent jurisdiction to obtain such remedy as the court considers appropriate and just in the circumstances.'[39] These language rights are also protected by the supremacy clause of the Constitution. Section 52 of the Constitution Act 1982 declares: '52(1) The Constitution of Canada is the supreme law of Canada, and any law that is inconsistent with the provisions of the Constitution is, to the extent of the inconsistency, of no force or effect.'

While this is not the focus of this chapter, no discussion of the language rights entrenched by the Charter would be complete without a mention of subsections 16(2) to 20(2), which extend to the institutions of the legislature and government of New Brunswick the guarantee of equality of status of English and French as the official languages of the province, authorize the use of either language in the proceedings of the legislature and the courts, require the printing and publishing of the records, journals and Acts of the legislature in both languages, and ensure the right of any member of the public in New Brunswick to communicate with and to receive services from any office of an institution of the legislature or government of the province in either English or French. Mention must also be made of section 16.1 of the Charter, which was added by a constitutional amendment in 1993. Section 16.1 recognizes the equality of status and the equal rights and privileges of the English and the French linguistic communities of the province, notably as respect to the right to distinct educational and cultural institutions, and affirms the role of the legislature and government of New Brunswick in preserving and promoting those rights and status.[40]

The 1988 Official Languages Act

With the entrenchment of the equality of status of English and French in federal institutions and the right of the public to communicate with those institutions and to receive their services in either language, it became clear that the 1969 Official Languages Act needed to be modernized and the legislative framework for the implementation of language rights improved. The Prime Minister and the Clerk of the Privy Council established a Special Committee of Deputy Ministers comprised mainly of senior officials from the Department of Justice, the Treasury Board Secretariat and the Secretary of State Department (now the Department of Canadian Heritage) to determine how to bring the legislation, policies and programmes on official languages up to date and in conformity with the new constitutional guarantees. The committee considered, amongst others, the recommendations of the Special Joint Committee of the Senate and the House of Commons and those of the then Commissioner of Official Languages, Mr D'Iberville Fortier, and his predecessors. Broad consultations were held, notably with anglophone and francophone linguistic minority community groups.

Bill C-72, *An Act respecting the status and use of the official languages of Canada* – which was introduced in the House of Commons in June 1987 by the Minister of Justice, the Right Honourable Ray Hnatyshyn — was the centrepiece of all this intensive effort. The new Official Languages Act was enacted by Parliament in July 1988 and proclaimed in force in September of that year.[41]

Overview of the 1988 Act as a Whole

The Official Languages Act of 1988 contains a preamble comprised of ten recitals, a purpose clause, and eleven major parts. The first five parts of the Act set out *rights and duties* with respect to the equality of status of the official languages within federal institutions as well as with respect to federal government services available to the public in both languages. These initial five parts of the Act are broadly related to the rights and duties that are constitutionally entrenched by subsections 16(1), 17(1), 18(1), 19(1) and 20(1) of the Charter. The sixth and seventh parts set out *governmental commitments* regarding the full participation of English-speaking Canadians and French-speaking Canadians within federal institutions, and the advancement of English and French within Canadian society.

The eighth part of the Act deals with the powers and responsibilities of the Treasury Board with respect to the implementation by federal institutions of parts IV, V and VI. The ninth part of the Act relates to the powers, duties and functions of the Commissioner of Official Languages in ensuring compliance with the Act in the administration of the affairs of federal institutions, including their activities related to the advancement of English and French in Canadian society. The tenth part of the Act establishes a court remedy before the trial division of the Federal Court with regard to a right or duty arising mainly under parts I, II, IV and V of the Act. The third, sixth and seventh parts of the statute are not covered by the judicial remedy provisions. Finally, the eleventh part of the Act contains general provisions, including a primacy clause that embraces the first five parts of the law. (Parts XII, XIII and XIV of the original Bill contained related amendments to the Criminal Code dealing with the language of the accused, as well as other related and consequential amendments and transitional provisions. These are now an integral part of the Criminal Code itself and the other statutes that were amended through the enactment of Bill C-72.)

The Objects and Status of the 1988 Official Languages Act

As the several references to the Constitution of Canada in the opening recitals of the preamble attest, the first objective of the new Official Languages Act was to ensure that the legislative and regulatory framework for the implementation of government policy and programmes in relation to the status and use of the English and French languages was structured in accordance with the constitutional norms and precepts the Act was meant to acknowledge and embody. This, in turn, required that the Act set out and clarify the respective roles of the principal institutional actors charged with ensuring the implementation of, and compliance with, the Act's substantive provisions.

Beyond the substantive rights and correlative institutional duties established by the Act, the legislation was also meant to capture, in a solemn and permanent statement of aims, a sense of the federal government's enduring commitment to the protection and enhancement of Canada's linguistic duality and its multicultural heritage,[42] and in particular, its policy of assisting Canada's official-language minority communities. This is recorded in the preamble's recognition of the Government of Canada's commitment to 'enhancing the vitality and supporting the development of English and French linguistic minority communities, as an integral part of the two official language communities of Canada' and, indeed, to 'fostering full recognition and use of English and French in Canadian society' within a framework of federal–provincial–territorial cooperation. This undertaking is also reflected in section 2 and in part VII of the Act. Section 2 of the Act declares that the objectives of the new legislation are threefold:

> 2. The purpose of this Act is to
>
> (a) ensure respect for English and French as the official languages of Canada and ensure equality of status and equal rights and privileges as to their use in all federal institutions . . .
>
> (b) support the development of English and French linguistic minority communities and generally advance the equality of status and use of the English and French languages in Canadian society; and
>
> (c) set out the powers, duties and functions of federal institutions with respect to the official languages of Canada.

In the decision of *Lavigne* v. *Canada (Office of the Commissioner of Official Languages)*,[43] Mr Justice Charles Gonthier, writing for the nine judges of the Supreme Court of Canada, described the 1988 Official Languages Act as 'a significant legislative response to the obligation imposed by the Constitution of Canada in respect of bilingualism in Canada'. Citing the preamble of the Act's express references to the duties in the Constitution with respect to the equality of status of both languages as to their use in federal institutions, the guarantee of full and equal access in both languages to Parliament and to the laws and courts of Canada, and the right of any member of the public to use either language in communicating with and receiving services from federal institutions, he added that '[t]he fact that the *Official Languages Act* is a legislative measure taken in order to fulfil the constitutional duty in respect of bilingualism is not in doubt'.[44] Referring next to the specific aims set out in section 2 of the Act, Justice Gonthier underlined that '[t]hose objectives are extremely important, in that the promotion of both official languages is essential to Canada's development'.[45]

Moreover, the Official Languages Act is 'more than a mere statement of principles'.[46] Its provisions 'impose practical requirements on federal institutions',[47] and the principle of substantive equality that is recognized in section 16(1) of the Charter and section 2 of the Act, as Justice Bastarache had affirmed earlier in *Beaulac's Case*, 'has meaning'.

> It provides in particular that language rights that are institutionally based require government action for their implementation and therefore create obligations for the State; . . . It also means that the exercise of language rights must not be considered exceptional, or as something in the nature of a request for an accommodation.[48]

The significance of the objectives embodied in the Official Languages Act and the constitutional values underlying the legislation give the Act 'a special status in the Canadian legal framework', continued Justice Gonthier in his analysis.[49] This 'quasi-constitutional status' had been recognized by the courts. An excellent illustration of this was to be found in the eloquent words employed by the Federal Court of appeal in *Viola's Case*:

> The 1988 *Official Languages Act* is not an ordinary statute. It reflects both the Constitution of the country and the social and political compromise out of which it arose. To the extent that it is the exact reflection of the recognition of the official languages contained in subsection 16(1) and (3) of the *Canadian Charter of Rights and Freedoms*, it follows the rules of interpretation of that Charter as they have been defined by the Supreme Court of Canada. To the extent that it is an extension of the rights and

> guarantees recognized in the Charter, and by virtue of its preamble, its purpose as defined in section 2 and its taking precedence over other statutes in accordance with subsection 82(1), it belongs to that privileged category of quasi-constitutional legislation which reflects 'certain basic goals of our society' and must be so interpreted 'as to advance the broad policy considerations underlying it.[50]

Parts I to III of the Act: Equal Access to Federal Laws, Parliament and the Courts

The first three substantive parts of the Act reflect the constitutional guarantees pertaining to the use of English and French in the debates of the Senate and House of Commons, in the promulgation of the Acts of Parliament and in proceedings before the courts of Canada that are to be found in section 133 of the Constitution Act 1867, and more recently, in subsections 17(1), 18(1) and 19(1) of the Canadian Charter of Rights and Freedoms. In a trilogy[51] of cases rendered in 1986, a majority of the Supreme Court had taken a rather restrictive view of the scope of section 133 of the Act of 1867 and section 19(1) of the Charter in respect of their application to the language of court proceedings. In the course of his reasons in *MacDonald's Case*, the late Mr Justice Jean Beetz stated that section 133 had 'not introduced a comprehensive scheme or system of official bilingualism, even potentially, but a limited form of compulsory bilingualism at the legislative level, combined with an even more limited form of optional unilingualism at the option of the speaker in Parliamentary debates and at the option of the speaker, writer or issuer in judicial proceedings or processes'.[52] He added trenchantly:

> This incomplete but precise scheme is a constitutional minimum which resulted from a historical compromise arrived at by the founding people who agreed upon the terms of the federal union. The scheme is couched in a language which is capable of containing necessary implications, as was held in *Blaikie No. 1* and *Blaikie No. 2* with respect to certain forms of delegated legislation. *It is a scheme which, being a constitutional minimum, not a maximum, can be complemented by federal and provincial legislation*, as was held in the *Jones* case. And it is a scheme which can of course be

> modified by way of constitutional amendment. But it is not open to the courts, under the guise of interpretation, to improve upon, supplement or amend this historical constitutional compromise.[53]

In the companion decision rendered in the *Société des Acadiens* case, Mr. Justice Beetz affirmed that the rights protected by ss. 17 and 19 of the Charter are 'of the same nature and scope' as those guaranteed by section 133 of the Act of 1867:

> They vest in the speaker or in the writer and issuer of court processes and give the speaker or the writer the constitutionally protected power to speak or to write in the official language of his choice. And there is no language guarantee, either under section 133 of the *Constitution Act, 1867*, or section 19 of the *Charter*, any more than under section 17 of the *Charter*, that the speaker will be heard or understood, or that he has the right to be heard or understood in the language of his choice.[54]

These provisions were to be contrasted, Justice Beetz stated, with section 18 of the Charter, which requires the promulgation of law in both official languages, and with section 20, which provides expressly for a right to communicate with government institutions and to receive services in either official language at the instance of the public.[55] Sections 17 and 19 merely provide, on Beetz's reasoning, a right to use either English or French as languages of record in parliamentary and judicial proceedings. Any purported entitlement to understand and be understood would arise – at least in the context of court proceedings – as part of a broader legal right to natural justice and a fair hearing, which would apply to anyone (not only English- or French-speakers), and may be satisfied by recourse to a court-appointed interpreter, as provided under section 14 of the Charter. The role and function of legal rights (such as the right to a fair trial) and language rights should not be confused, warned Justice Beetz. The former were said to be more universal, 'seminal in nature' and 'rooted in principle'; the latter 'founded on political compromise'.[56] Additional language rights might be established through enactment, but this was the province of the legislature, not the courts. This 'attitude of judicial restraint' was, in Justice Beetz's view, 'compatible with section 16 of the *Charter*':[57]

> I think it is accurate to say that section 16 of the *Charter* does contain a principle of advancement or progress in the equality of status or use of the two official languages. I find it highly significant however that this principle of advancement is linked with the legislative process referred to in section 16(3), which is a codification of the rule in *Jones* v. *Attorney General of New Brunswick*, [1975] 2 S. C. R. 182. The legislative process, unlike the judicial one, is a political process and hence particularly suited to the advancement of rights founded on political compromise. The position of Mr. Justice Beetz and the majority of the Supreme Court to the effect that because language rights were the fruit of political compromise, the courts should pause before giving them a large and liberal interpretation, was the subject of cogent criticism both by the then-Chief Justice, the late Brian Dickson,[58] and by Madam Justice Wilson,[59] as well as by a number of academic commentators.[60] The majority position in *MacDonald's Case* and in *Societé des Acadiens* on the role of the courts in construing language rights was reversed more than a decade later by a new majority of the Supreme Court in *Beaulac's Case*, through the pen of Mr. Justice Michel Bastarache.
>
> Though constitutional language rights result from a political compromise, this is not a characteristic that uniquely applies to such rights . . . To the extent that *Société des Acadiens du Nouveau-Brunswick* . . . stands for a restrictive interpretation of language rights, it is to be rejected.[61]

When the Supreme Court's decisions in the 1986 trilogy were released, the majority's view – that the advancement of language rights beyond the constitutional minimum was primarily a matter to be left to the legislative process – provided a powerful impetus for political leaders to seize the day and to reform the Official Languages Act accordingly. The first three parts of the Act, which deal with the traditional realms of parliamentary and judicial proceedings contemplated by section 133 of the Constitution Act 1867 and sections 17, 18 and 19 of the Canadian Charter of Rights and Freedoms, reflect that political will to enhance the basic rights with additional statutory obligations and entitlements.

Part I of the Act is entitled 'Proceedings of Parliament'. It declares that English and French are the official languages of Parliament, and goes on to repeat the constitutional right of everyone to use either language in parliamentary debates that is guaranteed by subsection 17(1) of the Charter. This constitutional right is supplemented by additional statutory provisions, beyond the constitutional minimum, which ensure the availability of simultaneous interpretation and the reporting and translation of everything said in either language in the Official Reports of Parliamentary Debates, the Hansard.

Part II of the Act is entitled 'Legislative and Other Instruments'. This part deals essentially with the constitutional duty set out in subsection 18(1) of the Charter, which requires the use of both English and French in parliamentary journals and other records, in the Acts of Parliament, and in certain regulations made under those Acts.[62] This constitutional minimum is also supplemented by other statutory provisions that require bilingualism in other regulations and orders in council as well as with respect to other formal texts issued by federal institutions. Section 13, which confirms the rule of equal authenticity set out in *Blaikie's Case* and the *Manitoba Language Rights Reference* (see above), as well as in section 18 of the Charter, gives a sense of the broad compass of instruments to which the rules of part II apply:

> Any journal, record, Act of Parliament, instrument, document, rule, order, regulation, treaty, convention, agreement, notice, advertisement, or other matter referred to in this Part that is made, enacted, printed, published or tabled in both official languages shall be made, enacted, printed, published or tabled simultaneously in both languages, and both language versions are equally authoritative.

The Department of Justice of Canada pairs English-speaking and French-speaking legislative drafters together in teams so that Bills are drafted simultaneously in both languages, as opposed to being drafted in one language and translated into the other. This innovative programme of legislative co-drafting ensures that both official language versions of federal statutes are of the highest quality. The programme has generated much interest as a potential model in several other jurisdictions.[63]

Part III of the Act deals with the 'Administration of Justice'. The first provision declares English and French to be the official languages of federal courts and repeats the constitutional right set out in subsection 19(1) of the Charter, that is, the right of any person to use either language before courts established by Parliament and in any pleading or process therein. Pursuant to the expansive interpretation given to the term 'Courts' in section 133 of the Constitution Act 1867 by the Supreme Court of Canada in *Blaikie's Case*, the term 'federal court' is defined in section 3(2) of the Act to mean 'any court, tribunal or other body that carries out adjudicative functions' and that is established by or under an Act of Parliament.

The provisions of part III of the Act go beyond the constitutional minimum to add other statutory obligations, including the duty of federal courts to make available interpretation services for witnesses and parties, to ensure that presiding judges are able to hear matters in the official language or languages of the parties without resorting to the assistance of an interpreter, and to ensure the availability of judgments of the court in both official languages. As well, it is incumbent on Her Majesty's counsel to use the official language chose by the other parties (or, if no choice has been made, the official language that is reasonable in the circumstances) in any oral and written pleadings in the proceedings. Court forms must be printed in bilingual format, although they may be completed in writing in either language (in which case, a translation of the particulars is to be made upon request). These provisions have been carefully framed as institutional duties so as to preserve the constitutional rights of individual litigants, witnesses and judges.

Similar duties with respect to the language of the accused were placed upon provincial courts exercising criminal jurisdiction under the federal Criminal Code, through related amendments made under part XII of the Official Languages Act. Section 530.1 of the Criminal Code provides that, where an order has been granted that an accused be tried before a judge or judge and jury who speak the official language that is the language of the accused or in which the accused can best give testimony, the accused and his counsel have the right to use either official language during the preliminary inquiry and trial, including the use of either language in written pleadings or other documents; witnesses may testify in either language; the accused has a right to have a justice presiding over the preliminary inquiry who speaks the official language of the accused; the accused also has a right to a Crown prosecutor who speaks that language; the court shall make interpreters available to assist the accused, his counsel or any witness during the preliminary inquiry or trial; the record of proceedings shall include a transcript of everything that was said in the official language in which it was said, a transcript of any interpretation, and any documentary evidence in the language in which it was tendered; and finally, that any trial judgement issued in writing in either official language, shall be made available by the court in the official language of the accused. Subsection 841(3) of the Criminal Code was also added by the 1988 amendments to provide that pre-printed court forms shall be printed in both official languages.

The constitutional validity of the requirement under section 530.1 of the Criminal Code that the accused has a right to a prosecutor who speaks the official language that is the language of the accused, and the requirement under section 841(3) of the code that court forms be printed bilingually, was challenged by the Attorney General of Quebec on the basis that they infringed the guarantee in section 133 of the Constitution Act 1867 that either English or French 'may be used by any Person or in any Pleading or Process in or issuing from . . . all or any of the Courts of Quebec'. The Attorney General of Canada submitted that section 530.1 of the code was a valid exercise of the Parliament of Canada's legislative powers in relation to the criminal law and criminal procedure under section 91(27) of the Constitution Act 1867. Section 133 of that Act was not infringed by a provision designed to advance language rights beyond the constitutional minimum by imposing upon the state (the Crown administration in the province) the duty to assign a prosecutor whose choice of official language, under section 133, would coincide with that of the accused; in other words, a prosecutor who was ready, able and willing to exercise his own language rights in a manner that respected the language of the accused. So too, in the case of bilingual forms, the language rights under section 133 of the writer or issuer of the court process were not infringed because only the pre-printed portions of the form were bilingual and the particulars could be completed in writing in either English or French. The Court of Appeal of Quebec upheld the validity of both of the impugned provisions.[64]

Under the Government of Canada's Action Plan for Official Languages, released on 12 March 2003, the Department of Justice is devoting $45.5 million over a five-year period to improving access to justice in both official languages in cooperation with provincial and territorial governments and the legal community. An intergovernmental working group on access to justice in both languages was established following the Federal–Provincial–Territorial Meeting of Deputy Ministers responsible for Justice in June 2002. The governments of the three territories and most provinces are represented on the working group, and the federal government will continue to encourage the other provincial governments to join.[65]

Communications with Federal Institutions and the Provision of Government Services

Part IV of the Official Languages Act relates to 'Communications with and Services to the Public'. Herein section 21 *et seq*. of the Act sets out the constitutional right of members of the public to communicate with and to receive available services from federal institutions that is guaranteed by subsection 20(1) of the Charter. Part IV and the regulations made thereunder implement and complete this right by a series of correlative institutional duties that are designed to implement the right. Those offices of the institutions of the Parliament and government of Canada that are head or central offices, and federal offices and facilities in the National Capital Region of Ottawa (including its environs in Ontario and Quebec), must ensure that members of the public can communicate with them in the official language of their choice and can receive services in that language. Elsewhere in Canada, the offices and facilities of federal institutions must ensure that members of the public can communicate with them and receive services in either language where there is a significant demand in that language, or where the nature of the office is such that it is reasonable that communications with and services from that office be available in both languages.

Both part IV of the Act and the regulations thereunder on communications with and services to the public, which came into force in December 1992, give detailed guidance on the implementation of these constitutional criteria. Services to the travelling public, and services provided on behalf by third parties acting on behalf of federal institutions, are also covered by part IV. An 'active offer' is required, in order to make it known to the public that bilingual services are readily available from the designated offices.

The Use of English and French as Languages of Work in Federal Institutions

Part V of the Official Languages Act, dealing with the 'Language of Work', was drafted in a manner similar to part IV; that is, it sets out a basic right that is to be implemented with reference to a series of correlative obligations. The introductory provision of part V, section 34, declares that English and French are the languages of work in federal institutions, and that the officers and employees of those institutions have the right to use either language in accordance with the institutional duties set out in sections 35 and following. Part V can be seen to flow from subsection 16(1) of the Charter, which guarantees the equality of status of the English and French languages and equal rights and privileges 'as to their use in all institutions of the Parliament and government of Canada'.

Part V deals with one of the most difficult goals to achieve in practice: to ensure an effective environment for the use of the minority language within the internal activities of government, where the majority language tends to dominate; where it is essential that English-speaking and French-speaking colleagues continue to work together in the pursuit of common institutional objectives; and where the express constitutional right of the public to be served in either official language must take precedence.

Under part V of the Act, every federal institution has the duty to ensure that in the National Capital Region and other prescribed regions, the 'work environments' of the institution are 'conducive to the effective use of both official languages' and that the working milieu accommodates the use of either of those languages by the officers and employees of that institution. In the predominantly English-speaking or French-speaking areas outside these bilingual regions (so to speak), a rough and ready level of equality is still to be maintained: federal institutions are to ensure, in these latter areas, that 'the treatment of both official languages in the work environments of the institution in parts or regions of Canada where one official language predominates' is 'reasonably comparable' to the treatment of both languages in the work environments of the institution in those parts of the country 'where the other official language predominates'.

This legislative policy recognizes that if both English and French are to be vibrant working languages within the administration of federal institutions, it is incumbent upon those institutions to create and maintain settings in which both languages can be used freely, without internal impediments. However, for both languages truly to flourish as languages of work, there must be sufficient numbers (a 'critical mass', in the jargon of those who measure these things) of employees of both language groups; which in turn will depend, to a considerable extent, on the presence of both groups in the various regions in which these institutions operate. In other words, the official languages policy on the language of work must be progressive, but its application must take into account the sociolinguistic, demographic and geographic realities of Canada. In the National Capital Region and in the prescribed regions, federal institutions must make available in both official languages internal services that are meant to support them in the performance of their duties, work instruments, computer and informatics systems, as well as bilingual supervision and management groups responsible for the direction of the institution (such as the executive and management committees) must be able to function collectively in both languages.

Beyond these somewhat static requirements, the Act imparts some dynamism to the process by requiring federal institutions to ensure that such additional measures as can reasonably be taken to establish and maintain bilingual work environments are also implemented. The policies of the Treasury Board on the language of work help to complete this framework.

Primacy of Parts I to V of the Official Languages Act and Court Remedy

Because the first five parts of the Official Languages Act flow mainly from the language rights and duties guaranteed by subsection 16(1) to 20(1) of the Canadian Charter of Rights and Freedoms – that is, the equality of status of English and French in the debates and proceedings of Parliament, legislative and other instruments, the administration of justice before federal courts, governmental communications and services, and as languages of work in federal institutions – Parliament decided it was appropriate to recognize the special nature of these five parts by providing, in section 82 of the Act, a *primacy* clause to the effect that the provisions of parts I to V 'prevail' over 'any other Act of Parliament or regulation thereunder . . . to the extent of the inconsistency'. (The primacy clause does not apply to the Canadian Human Rights Act, another quasi-constitutional statute.)

The court remedy established by part X of the Official Languages Act is directed in its application to 'a right or duty under' part I, part II (with two exceptions), part IV and part V. The provisions respecting the administration of justice were excluded from the judicial recourse established by the Act for reasons of judicial comity. It would have been inappropriate, for example, to seize the Trial Division of the Federal Court with an alleged violation of part III by the Federal Court of Appeal or by the Supreme Court of Canada. Any such possible infringement would be better corrected by these courts themselves or through administrative law recourses, as in *Devinat's Case*.[66]

The court recourse provision, like section 24 of the Charter, authorizes the court to grant such remedy as it considers 'appropriate and just in the circumstances'. Under the scheme of the Official Languages Act, however, complainants are directed first to the Office of the Commissioner of Official Languages. This encourages the investigation and resolution of complaints through the administrative mechanisms of the Commissioner's ombudsman role, rather than judicializing the process from the outset.

The Federal Government's Commitments under Parts VI and VII of the Act

Beyond the first five parts of the Act that flow from subsections 16(1), 17(1), 18(1), 19(1) and 20(1) of the Charter, and which create rights and duties, the Official Languages Act contains two parts – parts VI and VII – which record *commitments* on the part of the federal government.

Part VI of the Act, which is entitled 'Participation of English-Speaking and French-Speaking Canadians', sets out a commitment in principle which is based partly on the parliamentary resolution of 1973 regarding the equitable participation of members of both language communities within federal institutions. Part VI is not subject to the court remedy set out in part X, nor to the primacy clause in section 82 of the Act.

The marginal note to section 39, the opening provision of part VI, speaks of a commitment to 'equal opportunities and equitable participation', and the undertaking is framed in subsection 39(1) in the following terms:

> The Government of Canada is committed to ensuring that
>
> (*a*) English-speaking Canadians and French-speaking Canadians, without regard to their ethnic origin or first language learned, have equal opportunities to obtain employment and advancement in federal institutions; and
>
> (*b*) the composition of the workforce of federal institutions tends to reflect the presence of both the official language

> communities of Canada, taking into account the characteristics of individual institutions, including their mandates, the public they serve and their location.

This twin commitment to ensuring equal opportunities for anglophone and francophone Canadians and to maintaining a federal workforce that is reflective of both official language communities is to be carried out by federal institutions whilst 'taking due account of the purposes and provisions of Parts IV and V' of the Official Languages Act dealing with communications and services to the public, and the languages of work of public servants, respectively, and 'the principle of selection of personnel according to merit' is expressly maintained. In other words, this is not a quota system, but rather, a recognition that if opportunities for appointment and advancement in the federal public service are open to members of both official language groups alike, then federal should generally resemble, over time, the make-up of the population pool from which they draw their officers and employees.

Part VII of the Act, which relates to the 'Advancement of English and French', also records a commitment in principle. By virtue of section 41:

> The Government of Canada is committed to
>
> (*a*) enhancing the vitality of the English and French linguistic minority communities in Canada and supporting and assisting their development; and
>
> (*b*) fostering the full recognition and use of both English and French in Canadian Society.

The marginal note indicates that section 41 of the Official Languages Act represents 'government policy'. The scope and tenor of that policy are in some ways analogous to the government of Canada's 'multiculturalism policy' set out in section 3 of the Canadian Multiculturalism Act, which was also enacted in July 1988, contemporaneously with the Official Languages Act. The preamble of that Act records inter alia that the 'Government of Canada [. . .] *is committed to* a policy of multiculturalism designed to preserve and enhance the multicultural heritage of Canadians . . .'

Section 41 of the Official Languages Act contains a formal statement of policy on behalf of the Government of Canada. That declared policy is to advance Canada's linguistic duality, and to enhance the vitality and support the development of English and French linguistic minority communities. This undertaking is solemn, permanent, and visible to all Canadians, because it is declared and recorded in the terms of the Act itself. Only a statute enacted by the Parliament of Canada could amend or modify the commitment of the federal government.

The Official Languages Act provides, in section 42, that it is the Minister of Canadian Heritage who is responsible, in consultation with other ministers, for coordinating the implementation by federal institutions of the commitment. Furthermore, section 43 of the Act sets out the specific mandate of the minister of Canadian Heritage to take such measures as the Minister deems appropriate 'to advance the equality of status and use of English and French in Canadian society'. This mandate, like part VII as a whole, is clearly built upon the principle of advancement of official languages that underlies subsection 16(3) of the Canadian Charter of Rights and Freedoms.

The commitments of the federal government under part VII of the Act are very broad. Their realization depends not only on establishing and managing priorities and allocating funds and other available resources, but also, to a large extent, on the cooperation of many other actors, including provincial and territorial governments, private sector enterprises, voluntary organizations and other institutions and associations, many of which are not within the legislative and regulatory control of the federal government.

It will be recalled that the policy commitments recorded in part VI and part VII of the Official Languages Act are not justiciable under the terms of the court remedy set out in part X of the Act. The Government of Canada's view at the time of the enactment of the Act in 1988 was that the oversight role in relation to the implementation of these commitments was best left to the responsible ministers (the President of the Treasury Board as regards parts IV, V and VI of the Act, and the Minister of Canadian Heritage, as regards part VII); the

Commissioner of Official Languages (an ombudsman, a 'linguistic auditor general', and an officer of Parliament); and by the committees of the Houses of Parliament designated, under section 88 of the Act, with the review, on a permanent basis, of the 'administration of this Act' and the regulations, directives and reports to Parliament made thereunder. The role of the Commissioner of Official Languages and the parliamentary committees are, one might argue, particularly suited to the examination of measures under part VII that involve broad areas of social policy, the use of the federal spending power, and 'polycentric' decision-making involving multiple actors and collaborative relationships amongst all level of government in the Canadian federation.

There have been some efforts, through challenges brought before the Federal Court[67] and private member's bills introduced in the Senate,[68] to buttress respect for the commitments in part VII of the Act by making those undertakings subject to judicial enforcement. As consideration of these issues is still before the Court and before Parliament, respectively, it would be imprudent (not to say unwise) for me to comment directly on the merits of those submissions and proposals.[69]

Nevertheless, it should be noted that in an important decision, three judges of the Federal Court of Appeal, including Chief Justice Richard and Justice Noël, unanimously rejected any claim to the effect that part VII of the Act contains justiciable duties that are enforceable by the courts. In his reasons for judgment on behalf of the Court, Justice Robert Décary wrote as follows:

> This asymmetry of the Act is easily explained when we note that it deals not only with policies and commitments but also with rights and duties. Subsection 77(1) is itself highly instructive in this regard, as it specifies that the complaints it covers are addressed not to the sections or parts of the Act in themselves, but to 'a right or duty under' particular sections or parts. So Parliament has spoken with great care, so as to ensure that only those disputes in respect of particular rights or duties may be taken before the Court. This prudence is especially warranted in that the remedial authority conferred by subsection 77(4) is exceptional in scope and it is readily understandable that Parliament did not intend to give the

> courts the power to interfere in the area of policies and commitments that is not usually within their jurisdiction.
>
> . . .
>
> In short, the respondent and the interveners are asking that the Court amend section 41 of the Act and make mandatory what, on its face, is simply a policy commitment, and that the Court add to subsection 77(1) and section 82 the words 'Part VII'. This would do violence not only to the text of the Act but also to the express and implied intention of Parliament to exclude these areas from judicial intervention.[70]

It should also be mentioned that a new Bill, the purpose of which is to enhance the enforceability of part VII of the Act and to make it subject to the court remedy set out in part X, has received three readings in the Senate and has been introduced for first reading in the House of Commons.[71]

Certainly it can be said that the focus of the recent efforts of the government of Canada to date in ensuring respect for its commitments under part VII of the Official Languages Act has been to work within the existing legislative structure to develop concrete, tangible policies and programmes, as well as additional administrative mechanisms for coordination and enforcement. Under the auspices of the Prime Minister, the President of the Queen's Privy Council for Canada and the Minister of Intergovernmental Affairs, the Honourable Stéphane Dion, chaired a group of Cabinet colleagues (including, amongst others, the Minister of Justice, the President of the Treasury Board and the Minister of Canadian Heritage) to develop the centrepiece of the government of Canada's renewed efforts to enhance the positive attributes of Canada's linguistic duality, the *Action Plan for Official Languages*.[72]

The *Action Plan for Official Languages* is a remarkable document that envisions broad policy goals whilst establishing specific objectives and allocating corresponding resources. It also contains an 'Official Languages Accountability and Coordination Framework', which sets out 'enforcement procedures' in respect of the duties under parts I to V of the Official Languages Act, the commitments under parts VI and VII, and the responsibilities of federal institutions in that regard. The accountability framework does not purport to change the formal legal framework of the Act, but rather to enhance it and to render it fully operational through effective and efficient coordination and appropriate enforcement mechanisms.

On the substantive side, the Action Plan has three main thrusts: action on official languages in the areas of education, community development and the public service as well as in the development of the 'language industries' of translation and interpretation. It is a forward-looking approach, addressing linguistic duality in a modern Canada, both as part of the heritage of Canadians, but especially as an asset for their future. By reinvesting in minority-language education and second-language instruction; by targeting key priorities of minority-language community development, such as early childhood, health care, justice, immigration and economic development; by making the official languages a core priority again for the federal public service and its organizational culture; by acting as a catalyst in the economic development, succession planning and skill enhancement of the language industries; the Government of Canada intends to assist Canadians of both language groups in realizing the potential, for themselves, their children and their country, of Canada's linguistic duality. The Government of Canada is committed to allocating more than $750 million over the next five years to attain the varied objectives in the Action Plan. This in turn, it is believed, ought to create 'a ripple effect among other governments, the private sector, communities and other partners, prompting them to initiate complementary action.[73]

> But the strength of this Plan lies not so much in the funding per se but in the entire set of measures it includes. Each one taken in isolation would not have the desired impact. But, combined within an integrated plan, with the contribution of communities, the provinces and territories and all Canadians, these measures contemplate one another and create a synergy for success.[74]

Conclusion

The legal and constitutional framework relating to official languages law and policy in Canada is draped with a complex web of federal, provincial and territorial legislative, regulatory and policy measures. This is to be expected in a modern federal state where two languages, English and French, are in common use amongst millions of Canadians every day. Language rights in Canada are shaped by history, geography and demography, as well as by deeply held conceptions of individual, group and national identity. Efforts to respect and accommodate the place of the two official language communities in Canada and the minority communities within them go to the heart of the Canadian experience and its model constructs of bilingualism and multiculturalism. The federal Official Languages Act is a key element of that framework.

REFERENCES

British North America Act, 30 & 31 Victoria, *c*.3 (U.K.) London: Westminster Parliament.

Manitoba Act (1870) *An Act to Provide that the English Language shall be the Official Language of the Province of Manitoba*, 1890, *c*.14 (Man.).

Newman, W. J. (1988) 'Language rights, the Charter and the *New Official Languages Act*' (paper presented at the First Annual Conference of the Department of Justice of Canada on Human Rights and the Charter, Ottawa, 21 November 1988), pp. 6–9 and 24–6.

Newman, W. J. (1993) 'Language difficulties facing tribunals and participants: the approach of the new *Official Languages Act*', in W. Tarnopolsky, J. Whitman and. M. Ouellette, (eds), *Discrimination in the Law and the Administration of Justice.* Canadian Institute for the Administration of Justice, Montreal: Les Éditions Thémis, pp. 178–80.

Newman, W. J. (2004) 'Understanding language rights, equality and the Charter: towards a comprehensive theory of constitutional interpretation', *National Journal of Constitutional Law*, 15, 363.

Official Languages of Canada (1988) *An Act respecting the status and use of the official languages of Canada*, 1988, *c*.38 (Can.). Ottawa: Parliament of Canada.

NOTES

1 The views expressed herein are those of the author; they do not bind the Department of Justice, Government of Canada.

2 *An Act respecting the status and use of the official languages of Canada*, 1988, *c*.38 (Can.). The author of this chapter was responsible for developing the legislative proposals leading to the

enactment of Bill C-72, the 1988 Official Languages Act and was the instructing officer on the drafting of the legislation. He also advised the Minister of Justice, the Right Hon. Ray Hnatyshyn, who was the minister responsible for carriage of the Bill through parliamentary study and passage of the legislation by the House of Commons and Senate of Canada.

3 Formerly entitled the first of the Constitution Acts 1867 to 1982, as amended.

4 The Charter is part I of the Constitution Act 1982, which in turn is Schedule B of the Canada Act 1982 (UK), 1982, *c.*11.

5 *Reference re Secession of Quebec*, [1998] 2 S. C. R. 217, *per curiam*, pp. 261–3 (paras 79 ff.). (The author discloses that he acted as co-counsel in that Reference, in the *Manitoba Language Rights Reference*, *infra*, and several other of the cases mentioned in this chapter.)

6 *R. v. Mercure*, [1988] 1 S. C. R. 234, p. 268.

7 Ibid.

8 Ibid.

9 Ibid., p. 269.

10 *R. v. Beaulac*, [1999] 1 S. C. R. 768, p. 791 (para. 25) *per* Justice Bastarache for the majority of the Court; see also *Arsenault-Cameron v. P.E.I.*, [2000] 1 S. C. R. 3, p. 25 (para. 27), *per* Justices Major and Bastarache for a unanimous Court.

11 3–4 Vict., *c.*35 (UK); s. XLI provided that all legislative instruments, records and journals shall be in the English Language only; Provided always, that this Enactment shall not be construed to prevent translated Copies of any such Documents being made, but no such Copy shall be kept among the Records of the Legislative Council or Legislative Assembly, or be deemed in any Case to have the Force of an original Record.

This limitation upon the use of French was abrogated by the Imperial Parliament in 1848.

12 33 Vict., *c.*3 (Can.); confirmed by the British North America Act 1871, 34–35 Vict., *c.*28 (UK), the latter now styled the Constitution Act 1871.

13 *An Act to Provide that the English Language shall be the Official Language of the Province of Manitoba*, 1890, *c.*14 (Man.).

14 *Attorney General of Manitoba v. Forest*, [1979] 2 S. C. R. 1032.

15 *Attorney General of Quebec v. Blaikie*, [1979] 2 S. C. R. 1016.

16 Ibid., p. 1027:

Dealing now with the question whether 'regulations' issued under the authority of acts of the Legislature of Quebec are 'Acts' within the purview of s. 133, it is apparent that it would truncate the requirement of s. 133 if account were not taken of the growth of delegated legislation. This is a case where the greater must include the lesser.

(For the detailed categories of subordinate law-making to which this obligation extends, see *Attorney General of Quebec v. Blaikie*

(No. 2), [1981] 1 S. C. R. 312. With respect to the application of s. 18(2) of the Canadian Charter of Rights and Freedoms to the Acts of the legislature of New Brunswick and the question of municipal by-laws, see *Moncton (City) v. Charlebois*, [2001] N. B. J. No. 480 (N. B. C.A.).

17 Ibid., p. 1022.

18 Ibid.

19 Ibid., p. 747 ff; 'The only appropriate resolution to this Reference is for the Court to fulfil its duty under s. 52 of the *Constitution Act, 1982* and declare all the unilingual Acts of the Legislature of Manitoba to be invalid and of no force and effect and then to take such steps as will ensure the rule of law in the Province of Manitoba.' (At p. 754.)

20 Section 110 of the former Northwest Territories Act, 1886, was, like its predecessors, s. 133 of the Constitution Act 1867 and s. 23 of the Manitoba Act 1870, a language rights provision requiring the use of English and French in territorial ordinances and authorizing the use of either language in the debates of the territorial legislature and in proceedings before territorial courts. Section 110 was later held by the Supreme Court of Canada to be still in force in the provinces of Saskatchewan and Alberta, which had been created out of parts of the Territories in 1905: see *R. v. Mercure*, [1988] 1 S. C. R. 234 (*supra*, note 9); *R. v. Paquette*, [1990] 2 S. C. R. 1103. However, as was explained by LaForest J. in *Mercure's Case*, s. 110 – unlike s. 133 and s. 23 of the Acts of 1867 and 1870, respectively – was not an entrenched provision forming part of the Constitution of Canada, and could be amended or repealed by competent federal or provincial legislation. See the Language Act, S. S. 1988–89, c. L.-6.1; the Languages Act, S. A. 1988, c. L-7.5; *Lefebvre v. R.*, (1993) 100 D. L. R. (4th) 591 (Alta. C.A.).

21 *An Act respecting the status of the official languages of Canada*, 1969, 17–18 Elizabeth II, *c.*54 (Can.).

22 Ibid., ss. 9, 10.

23 Excerpts from the *Final Report* of Royal Commission on Bilingualism and Biculturalism reproduced as Appendix I of the *First Annual Report* of the Commissioner of Official Languages, 1970–1 (Can.), pp. 99–103.

24 *Supra*, note 23, s. 25; emphasis added.

25 Ibid., s. 15(2).

26 [1975] 2 S. C. R. 182.

27 Ibid., p. 192.

28 Ibid.

29 Ibid., pp. 192–3.

30 Under the opening words of s. 91 of the Constitution Act 1867 (it being evident that only the Parliament of Canada was competent to legislate in relation to the status and use of languages in the institutions of Parliament and the government of Canada).

31 Under head 27 of section 91 of the Act of 1867.

32 Under heads 13, 14 and 16, respectively, of s. 92.

33 [1988] 2 S. C. R. 790, *per curiam*, at pp. 807–8, citing Peter W. Hogg, *Constitutional Law of Canada* (2nd edn, Toronto: Carswell, 1985), pp. 804–6. Professor Hogg wrote, inter alia, that 'a law prescribing that a particular language or languages must or may be used in certain situations will be classified for constitutional purposes not as a law in relation to language, but as a law in relation to the institutions or activities that the provision covers'. The Court added (p. 808): 'In order to be valid, provincial legislation with respect to language must be truly in relation to an institution or activity that is otherwise within provincial legislative jurisdiction.'

34 *Thorson v. Attorney General of Canada*, [1975] 1 S. C. R. 138, p. 151.

35 *Joyal v. Air Canada*, [1982] C. A. 39 (Quebec Court of Appeal); *Association des gens de l'air du Québec v. Hon. Otto Lang*, [1978] 2 F. C. 371 (Federal Court of Appeal).

36 See ss. 530 ff of the Criminal Code, R. S. C. 1985, c. C-46. These provisions were brought into force throughout Canada by related amendments made to s. 534 and s. 638 of the Criminal Code by part XII of the 1988 Official Languages Act. Substantial improvements to the language rights of the accused were also made by that Act.

37 See the decision of the Ontario Court of Appeal in *Lalonde v. Ontario (Commission de restructuration des services de santé)*, 56 O. R. (3d) 505, para. 92, which recognized that s. 16(3) 'builds on the principle established in *Jones*' and 'reflects an aspirational element of advancement toward substantive equality' that is 'not without significance when it comes to interpreting legislation'. However, s. 16(3) is 'not a rights-conferring provision'.

38 *Lalonde v. Ontario*, ibid. Section 15 of the Charter provides a general guarantee of equality rights. Subsection 15(1) states: 'Every individual is equal before and under the law and has the right to the equal protection and equal benefit of the law without discrimination and, in particular, without discrimination base on race, national or ethnic origin, colour, religion, sex, age or mental or physical disability.' For a discussion of the interplay between s. 15 and the language rights provisions of the Charter, see W. J. Newman (1988), pp. 6–9, note 5.

39 For a very significant judgment of the Supreme Court on s. 24 of the Charter, particularly in the context of the implementation and enforcement of language rights under s. 23, see *Doucet-Boudreau v. Nova Scotia (Minister of Education)*, [2003] 3 S. C. R. 3.

40 Canadian Charter of Rights and Freedoms, as amended by the Constitution Amendment, 1993 *(New Brunswick)*, SI/93–54.

41 S. C. 1988, c.38; R. S. C. 1985, *c*.31 (4th Supp.)

42 Section 27 of the Charter states: 'This Charter shall be interpreted

in a manner consistent with the preservation and enhancement of the multicultural heritage of Canadians.' The Canadian Multiculturalism Act, S. C. 1988, *c*.31, R. S. C. 1985, Fourth Supp., *c*.24, was enacted contemporaneously with the new Official Languages Act. Amongst the numerous objectives of the multiculturalism policy set out in s. 3 of the Act is the policy of the government of Canada to 'advance multiculturalism throughout Canada in harmony with the national commitment to the official languages of Canada'.

43 *Lavigne v. Canada (Office of the Commissioner of Official Languages)*, [2002] S. C. R. 773, p. 786, para. 21.

44 Ibid.

45 Ibid., p. 787, para. 22.

46 Ibid.

47 Ibid.

48 Ibid.; pp. 787–8; Justice Gonthier is citing herein (with additional emphasis), the words of Justice Bastarache in *R. v. Beaulac*, [1999] 1 S. C. R. 768, (*supra*, note 12), at para. 24.

49 Ibid., p. 788, para. 23.

50 *Canada (Attorney General) v. Viola*, [1991] 1 F. C. 373, at p. 386 (cited by Justice Gonthier in *Lavigne*, *supra*, at para. 23.)

51 *Bilodeau v. Manitoba (Attorney General)*, [1986] 1 S. C. R. 449, *MacDonald* (*infra*, note 55) and *Société des Acadiens* (*infra*, note 57).

52 *MacDonald v. City of Montreal*, [1986] 1 S. C. R. 460, p. 496.

53 Ibid., emphasis added.

54 *Société des Acadiens v. Association of Parents*, [1986] 1 S. C. R. 550, p. 574.

55 Ibid., pp. 575 and 576.

56 Ibid p. 578.

57 Ibid.

58 See the powerfully stated reasons of Chief Justice Dickson:

Linguistic duality has been a longstanding concern in our nation. Canada is a country with both English and French solidly embedded in its history. The constitutional language protections reflect continued and renewed efforts in the direction of bilingualism. In my view, we must take special care to be faithful to the spirit and purpose of the guarantee of language rights enshrined in the *Charter*. . . What good is a right to use one's language if those to whom one speaks cannot understand? . . . We speak and write to communicate to others. In the courtroom, we speak to communicate to the judge or judges. It is fundamental, therefore, to any effective and coherent guarantee of language rights in the courtroom that the judge or judges understand, either directly or through other means, the language chosen by the individual coming before the court. (At pp. 564, 566)

59 See Justice Wilson's reasons in *Société des Acadiens* at pp. 609 ff.,

and especially, her eloquent dissent in *MacDonald's Case*, *supra*, at pp. 504 ff., and at p. 540:

A purposive reading of s. 133 leads, I believe, inevitably to the conclusion that the state's obligation is not satisfied if its courts and their documents speak either French or English without regard to the language of the litigant. . . With all due respect to those who think differently, I cannot read s. 133 as merely permitting the litigant to use the language he or she understands but allowing those dealing with him or her to use the language he or she does not understand. What kind of linguistic protection would that be?

60 See Newman, 1988: 6–9 and 24–6; Newman, 1933: 178–80; Professor Leslie Green, 'Are language rights fundamental?', (1987) *Osgoode Hall L.J.*, 25 639; L. Green and Denise Réaume, 'Second class rights? Principle and compromise in the Charter' The Dulhousie Law Journal, 13 (1990) p. 566.

61 *R. v. Beaulac*, [1999] 1 S. C. R. 768 (*supra*, note 12), at paras 24 and 25. Justice Bastarache was, however (at para. 41 of his reasons), careful to preserve the conceptual distinction drawn by Justice Beetz in *MacDonald* and *Société des Acadiens*, between language rights and legal rights to a fair hearing.

The right to a fair hearing is universal and cannot be greater for members of official language communities than for persons speaking other languages. Language rights have a totally distinct origin and role. They are meant to protect official language minorities in this country and to insure the equality of status of French and English. This Court has already tried to dissipate this confusion on several occasions.

He added (at para. 45) that the ability of the accused to express himself in English 'is irrelevant because the choice of language is not meant to support the legal right to a fair trial, but to assist the accused in gaining equal access to a public service that is responsive to his linguistic and cultural identity'. See also para. 47: 'Language rights are not subsumed by the right to a fair trial. . . Language rights may no doubt enhance the quality of the legal proceedings, but their source lies elsewhere.'

62 See also *An Act to re-enact legislative instruments enacted in only one official language*, S. C. 2002, *c.*20 (assented to 13 June 2002).

63 Notable amongst these is Wales; see the official report of Winston Roddick, QC, then Counsel General to the National Assembly for Wales, on Canadian models of legislative bilingualism.

64 *Cross v. Teasdale*, [1998] R. J. Q. 2587 (Quebec C.A.; appeal to S. C. C. withdrawn, 1 September 1999); and *Noiseux v. Belval* [1999] R. J. Q. 704 (Quebec C.A.; leave to appeal to S. C. C. denied on 21 October 1999). An English version of the reasons for judgment of the Court of Appeal of Quebec in both cases may be found in the *Dominion Law Reports*: see *R. v. Cross*, (1998) 165 D. L. R. (4th) 288 and *R. v. Noiseux* (1999), 172 D. L. R. (4th) 447.

65 See the government of Canada's *Response to the Third Report of the Senate Standing Committee on Official Languages*, November 2003.

66 *Devinat v. Canada (Immigration and Status of Refugees Commission)*, [2000] 2 F. C. 212 (F.C.A.), leave to appeal to S. C. C. denied, 12 October 2000.

67 *Canada (Commissioner of Official Languages) v. Canada (Department of Justice)*, (2001) 194 F. T. R. 181 (trial level); *Le Forum des Maires de la Péninsule acadienne v. Canadian Food Inspection Agency*, 2003 FC 1048 (trial level); *Raîche v. Canada (Attorney General)*, 2004 F. C. 679 (trial level).

68 Bill S-32, *An Act to amend the Official Languages Act (fostering of English and French)*; Bill S-11, *An Act to amend the Official Languages Act (promotion of English and French)*. Senator Jean-Robert Gauthier, long an advocate for the effective protection and advancement of minority language rights, introduced Bill S-32 and its successor, Bill S-11, in 2002 and March 2003, respectively.

69 For the author's testimony on Bills S-32 and S-11 as a law officer of the Crown, see W. J. Newman, *Evidence before the Standing Committee of the Senate on Legal and Constitutional Affairs*, 6 March 2002, and *Evidence before the Standing Committee of the Senate on Official Languages*, 27 October 2003. On the legal issues, see, the testimony of Marc Tremblay, on the same dates, and of the Commissioner of Official Languages, Dyane Adam, on 21 February 2002 and 27 October 2003, respectively.

70 *The Canadian Food Inspection Agency v. Le Forum des Maires de la Péninsule acadienne*, 2004 FCA 263, judgment rendered on 22 July 2004; paras 27 and 38 of the reasons for judgment of Justice Décary. On 29 September 2004 the respondent filed an application for leave to appeal before the Supreme Court. The application for leave is still under consideration.

71 See Bill S-3, *An Act to amend the Official Languages Act (promotion of English and French)*, introduced in the Senate by Senator Gauthier for first reading on 6 October 2004 and passed by the Senate on 26 October 2004; the Bill received first reading in the House of Commons on 1 November 2004.

72 *The Next Act: New Momentum for Canada's Linguistic Duality – The Action Plan for Official Languages*, Government of Canada, ISBN 0–662–33725–5; 2003.

73 Ibid., p. 61.

74 Ibid.

9
Canada's Official Languages

DIANA MONNET

Introduction

Canada is a large country, covering an area of approximately ten million square kilometres, which makes it the world's second-largest country. It spans across six time zones and is made up of ten provinces and three territories. Canada has consisted of two major language communities for about three hundred years: English and French. Canada has a population of approximately thirty million. The official languages are English and French. About 75 per cent of Canadians are English-speaking, and 25 per cent are French-speaking. Quebec is predominantly francophone although one million anglophones live in Quebec and approximately one million francophones live outside of Quebec.

Linguistic duality and the sometimes spirited discussions between the two main language communities are as old as Canada – some might even say that they pre-date Confederation.

Speech from the Throne, 30 January 2001:

> Canada's linguistic duality is fundamental to our Canadian identity and is a key element of our vibrant society. The protection and promotion of our two official languages is a priority of the Government – from coast to coast. The Government reaffirms its commitment to support sustainable official language minority communities and a strong French culture and language. And it will mobilize its efforts to ensure that all Canadians can interact with the Government of Canada in either official language.

In this Speech from the Throne, the Government of Canada wanted to promote linguistic duality, position itself as

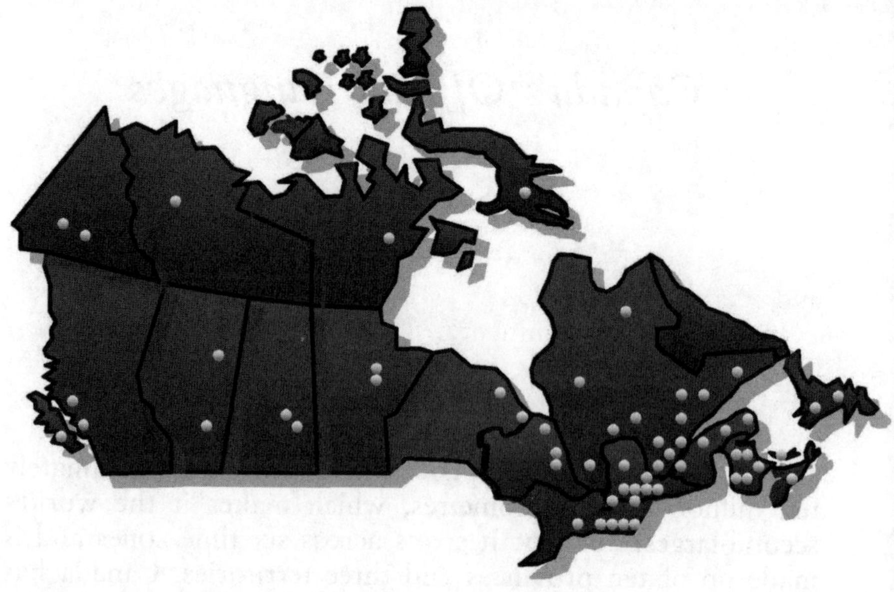

Figure 9.1: Bilingual offices and service points of the government of Canada.

an ally of the French language, demonstrate that it wanted to take into account the priority needs of official language minority communities, and strengthen the service delivery in both official languages. On 30 September 2002, in a new speech from the Throne, the government made a commitment to strengthening the Official Languages Programme. The Official Languages Action Plan, passed on 12 March 2003, was developed to meet that commitment.

Statutory Authority

The British North America Act, today called the Constitution Act, 1867, created the Canadian federation as a new dominion, 'a powerful nation, to take its place among the nations of the world', according to the design of the Fathers of Confederation. The Act set out the distribution of powers between the federal government and the governments of the four provinces of the time: Ontario, Quebec, Nova Scotia and New Brunswick. It also established the make-up and powers of the two houses of the Parliament of Canada and provided for the status of the English and French languages.

The British North America Act provided that either English or French may be used in the debates of the federal Parliament and the Quebec legislature and in written and oral proceedings before federal and Quebec courts; it also requires that the acts and documents of the federal Parliament and the Quebec legislature be printed and published in both English and French (section 133).

In 1982, the government of Canada passed a new constitution act. This new act, which integrates the 1867 British North America Act and establishes the process for amending the Constitution, stipulates that English and French are the official languages of Canada and of the province of New Brunswick (sections 16 to 22). It also guarantees education in the minority language for the children of English-speaking or French-speaking parents living in minority situations in a province if certain conditions are met. A charter of rights and freedoms is also enshrined in the Constitution Act 1982.

The Canadian Charter of Rights and Freedoms guarantees the rights and freedoms set out in it, subject only to such reasonable limits prescribed by law as can be demonstrably justified in a free and democratic society. Canadian courts ensure that the *Canadian Charter of Rights and Freedoms* is upheld.

The 1982 Canadian Charter of Rights and Freedoms affirms that English and French are the official languages of Canada and have equality of status and equal rights. Nearly a quarter of the Charter's provisions deal with official languages, and one provision stipulates that anyone whose rights or freedoms have been infringed may apply to the courts for a legal remedy. Furthermore, the Charter has precedence over the other acts.

In 1969, the Parliament of Canada passed the Official Languages Act, upholding and strengthening the status of English and French as the official languages of Canada.

In 1988, the Official Languages Act was amended to make the guarantees established in the 1982 Charter enforceable. This new version of the Act states that criteria may be applied to the delivery of service to the public in both official languages and to the language of work for federal employees. It establishes Treasury Board's responsibilities for managing the Official Languages Programme (Part VIII).

The 1988 Act addresses the judicial system, delivery of service to the public by federal institutions, the language rights of federal employees, equitable participation of both language groups in the Government of Canada, the promotion of Canadian linguistic duality, the development and vitality of official language minority communities, and the role of the Commissioner of Official Languages.

The Official Languages (Communications with and Services to the Public) Regulations were established in 1991. They define the circumstances under which offices are required to provide their services in both official languages. Services are always provided in French in Quebec and in English elsewhere in Canada. They are provided in both official languages in all offices in the National Capital Region, in the head or central offices of all federal institutions and wherever there is a significant English-speaking or French-speaking minority. The regulations establish the offices' language obligations, which are determined by their mandates and by the distribution and location of the linguistic minority population, as well as other services requirements. In enacting these regulations, the Government of Canada found a concrete solution to a complex problem.

Overview of the Official Languages Act

The Official Languages Act gives federal institutions specific instructions concerning service to the public, language of work, equitable representation of both communities, the promotion of English and French, and the development of the official language minority communities.

Part I (Proceedings of Parliament) enshrines the status of English and French as the official languages of Parliament; debates and all other proceedings may be carried out in either language. Simultaneous interpretation services must be provided, and the official reports must be published in both languages.

Part II (Legislative and Other Instruments) prescribes that parliamentary records shall be kept and legislation shall be enacted in both official languages. This requirement extends to regulations and statutory instruments of a public and general nature. All documents issued by a federal institution must exist in both official languages if tabled in Parliament. The rules of procedure of federal courts must also be published in both official languages. International treaties and some federal–provincial agreements must be concluded in both official languages.

Part III (Administration of Justice) enshrines the status of English and French as the official languages of the federal courts. It provides that everyone has the right to use either English or French in any oral or written submission or proceeding or process before a federal court. The right of 'any person' to use either English or French before federal courts also applies to the persons on trial, counsel, witnesses, judges and other officers of justice.

Part IV confirms the right of the public to communicate with and receive services from all federal institutions in either official language in the following locations:

- head or central offices of federal institutions as well as their offices located in the National Capital Region;
- offices that report directly to Parliament, such as those of the Auditor General;
- offices where there is 'significant demand' for communications and services in both official languages (the Act stipulates that, in assessing significant demand, the government may take the following into account: the population of the minority in the region served, its particular characteristics, its proportion of the total population, the volume of communications and services by an office in either official language, as well as any other relevant factors);
- offices whose 'nature' makes it reasonable that both languages be used in communications and services (the Act stipulates that the 'nature of the office' will be assessed the government, taking into account such criteria

as the health, safety and security of the public, the location or the national or international mandate of the office);
- offices providing services to the travelling public where there is significant demand.

Part V of the Act stipulates that English and French are the languages of work in federal institutions. In regions designated as bilingual and in certain circumstances, the employees of federal institutions have the right to use English or French at work (for example, in meetings, with their supervisors, regarding their work tools).

In the National Capital Region and in designated regions, federal institutions must ensure that the work environment is conducive to the effective use of both official languages and that their employees may exercise the right to use either language, subject to the obligations to serve the public and other employees.

Federal institutions located in the National Capital Region and in prescribed regions are also required to take other measures to establish work environments conducive to the effective use of both official languages. Every institution has the duty to determine what measures are possible and achievable, with due regard to the principles of equality of status of the two official languages and equal rights and privileges as to their use in federal institutions.

In areas outside the prescribed regions (sometimes called 'unilingual regions'), the language of internal communications will be English or French, depending on which language predominates in the region where the office is located. Federal institutions must ensure, however, that English and French minority languages receive comparable treatment in regions where one language predominates. For example, if a federal institution provides work instruments in English to its English-speaking employees in predominately French-speaking regions, it should provide work instruments in French to its French-speaking employees in predominately English-speaking regions.

Part VI of the Act (Equitable Representation) confirms the federal government's commitment to ensuring that English-speaking and French-speaking Canadians have equal opportunities to obtain employment and advancement in federal institutions. The government must also ensure that the composition of the workforce of federal institutions tends to reflect the presence of both language groups in the general population, bearing in mind the institution's mandate, the public served and the location of the offices. In fulfilling these commitments, federal institutions must respect the merit principle when staffing positions and must also take into account the provisions of the Act regarding service to the public and language of work.

There are no jobs set aside for each linguistic group because the government is committed to respecting the principle of non-discrimination in hiring and promoting English-speaking and French-speaking Canadians.

Furthermore, quotas or goal setting to achieve better participation of members of both official languages groups are specifically prohibited. Accordingly, rates of participation will not be the same in each institution, employment category and region

Part VII explicitly sets out the Government of Canada's commitment to enhancing the vitality of official language minority communities and to promoting English and French in Canadian society. It also stipulates that Canadian Heritage is responsible for encouraging and promoting a coordinated approach to the implementation of this commitment. Besides coordinating the implementation of this commitment by all federal institutions, the Minister of Canadian Heritage may take measures to

- enhance the vitality of official language minorities;
- encourage the learning of both English and French in Canadian society;
- assist the provinces to support official language minorities, to offer bilingual services, and to provide minority-language and secondlanguage education;
- encourage and assist the private and voluntary sectors to provide services in both official languages;

- encourage Canadian organizations and institutions to project the bilingual character of Canada both at home and abroad.

The Minister of Canadian Heritage reports annually to Parliament on the progress.

Part VIII of the Official Languages Act gives the Treasury Board responsibility for general manager of the Official Languages Programme in federal institutions. The Treasury Board is a Cabinet committee consisting of several ministers. It is therefore responsible for the implementation of the parts of the Official Languages Act governing service to the public (Part IV), language of work (Part V) and the participation of English-speaking and French-speaking Canadians in all federal institutions (Part VI).

In carrying out its responsibilities for managing the programme, the Treasury Board may establish policies to give effect to Parts IV, V and VI of the Act, recommend policies or regulations, issue directives, monitor and audit federal institutions, evaluate the effectiveness and efficiency of policies and programmes, and provide information to the public and to officers and employees of federal institutions. The President of the Treasury Board must submit an annual report to Parliament on the application of the above-mentioned parts by institutions that are subject to the Official Languages Act. The Treasury Board of Canada Secretariat's Official Languages Branch (OLB) assists the Treasury Board in fulfilling its obligations under the Act.

Part IX mandates the Commissioner of Official Languages with ensuring that the status of official languages is recognized and that federal institutions comply with the spirit and intent of the Act, including in their activities in promoting English and French in Canadian society. In addition to the Commissioner's general mandate to promote the equal status of both official languages and to create links between the two official language groups, he or she is authorized to carry out investigations of federal institutions.

Under Part X, any person who has submitted a complaint to the Commissioner of Official Languages alleging that a federal institution has not fulfilled its duties under sections 4 to 7, 10 to 13, and 91 as well as Parts IV and V of the Act may seek a remedy from the Federal Court. Application for the remedy is normally made within sixty days after the results of the investigation by the Commissioner are reported to the complainant. If the Court finds that a federal institution has failed to comply with the Act, it may grant such remedy as it considers fair and reasonable. This remedy may consist of an order of mandamus compelling compliance with the Act or an award of damages, if the facts in the case justify it.The Commissioner may take a case to the Federal Court with the consent of the complainant. The Commissioner may also appear on behalf of the complainant as a party to a case initiated by the complainant. Finally, the Commissioner may present, as evidence during court proceedings, information relating to similar complaints involving the same federal institution.

Part XI provides that in the event of any inconsistency between the rights and obligations in the Official Languages Act and the provisions of any other federal act, the Official Languages Act prevails, except in the case of the Canadian Human Rights Act and regulations, as stipulated in section 82.

Part XI also protects the legal and customary rights or privileges enjoyed by languages other than English and French. Nothing in the Act may be interpreted in a manner that is inconsistent with the preservation and enhancement of other languages.

Part XI provides that a parliamentary committee shall regularly review the implementation of the Act and of the reports submitted by the Commissioner of Official Languages, the President of the Treasury Board and the Minister of Canadian Heritage.

Part XI emphasized the need for objectivity in setting the language requirements of jobs in federal institutions for the purposes of a particular staffing action. In general terms, this provision states that no federal employer may arbitrarily set language requirements in applying the provisions relating to service to the public or language of work. These requirements must be genuinely necessary to perform the duties of the position to be filled. The Act applies to 179 institutions, including the 71 federal institutions for which the Treasury Board is the employer, the 63 Crown corporations and 45 privatized corporations.

Main Partners

Until its abolition in 2002 the Standing Joint Committee on Official Languages was the parliamentary committee made up of representatives from the House of Commons and the Senate. It was responsible for monitoring implementation of the Official Languages Act and its regulations and directives as well as the implementation and review of the reports to Parliament by the Commissioner of Official Languages, the President of the Treasury Board and the Minister of Canadian Heritage. It called ministers and deputy ministers to appear before it and answer its questions on the issue of official languages. It was replaced by two separate standing committees on official languages, one for the Senate and one for the House of Commons.

The Commissioner of Official Languages, as ombudsman for language rights in Canada, investigates complaints concerning official languages in federal institutions and conducts special studies on all aspects of the Official Languages Programme. Canadian Heritage, in consultation with the other federal departments, encourages and promotes a coordinated approach to implementation of the commitments to the official language minority communities and the equality of status of English and French in Canadian society. The Department of Justice of Canada plays a role of advisor and attorney general for all parts of the Act and is responsible for the implementation of certain sections dealing with the administration of justice.

Although this is not specifically mentioned in the Act, the Privy Council Office has been instructed by the Prime Minister to coordinate all matters relating to the official languages. Specifically, it has been given the task of developing a new framework to strengthen the Official Languages Programme. On 12 March 2003, the President of the Privy Council and Minister for Intergovernmental Affairs announced the details of the Action Plan to strengthen the Official Languages Programme. Between 2003 and 2008 more than $750 million would be spent on education, community development and public service excellence. The Public Service Commission of Canada administers the Public Service Employment Act and carries out responsibilities that are covered by the Official Languages Programme, such as staffing, recruitment and language training. It also ensures that the merit principle is applied in staffing. Other federal institutions are responsible for implementing the Official Languages Programme in their organizations.

The Ministers' Reference Group on Official Languages was formed by the President of the Privy Council shortly after he was appointed minister responsible for coordination of the official languages matters. The group discusses horizontal issues related to the official languages.

The Committee of Deputy Ministers on Official Languages (CDMOL), chaired by the Deputy Minister of Intergovernmental Affairs, is mandated to provide integrated leadership in official languages management. It provides a high-level forum for dealing with any issue considered to be of interest to a number of federal institutions. Each year it adopts priorities and an implementation plan and develops strategic objectives for institutional bilingualism, promotion of linguistic duality and development of the official language minority communities.

Since March 1998, senior public service employees have been acting as official languages champions in institutions that have language obligations under the Act. The mission of this network of champions is to make official languages more visible in their institutions and to ensure that the official languages obligations are respected in the areas of institutional bilingualism (service to the public, language of work and equitable participation of English-speaking and French-speaking Canadians) and development of the official language minority communities. There are two networks: one for departments and one for Crown corporations.

The purpose of the Departmental Advisory Committee on Official Languages (DACOL) is to provide a mechanism for consultation and communication concerning official languages among the main players. DACOL studies issues relating to the direction and implementation of the Official Languages Programme in federal organizations at an operational level. The Crown Corporations Advisory Committee on Official Languages (CCACOL) is a mechanism for consultation and communication concerning official languages between Treasury Board Secretariat (TBS) and Crown corporations and other institutions subject to the Official Languages Act for which the Treasury Board is not the employer. CCACOL studies issues related to the direction and implementation of the Official Languages Programme in those organizations.

Distribution of Bilingual Offices and Service Points

Canada's linguistic model is based on the principle of institutional and territorial bilingualism rather than individual bilingualism. It is therefore the institution's responsibility, first and foremost, to use both English and French and to provide services to the public in both official languages. Figure 9.2 gives a general picture, by province and territory, of the number of offices required to provide services to the public in both official languages.

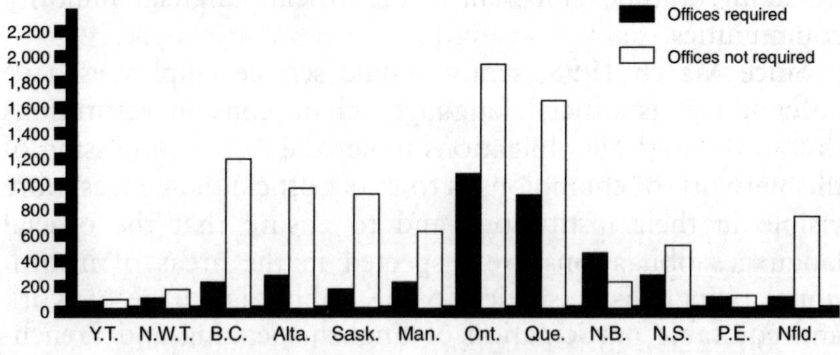

Figure 9.2: Distribution of offices and service points

Canada's language policy does not require all federal offices across the country to provide services in both official languages. Bilingual service must be provided in places in Canada where this is warranted by decennial census results and significant demand.

The Official Languages Act provides that 'significant demand' for service in either official language in a federal institution must be defined by regulation. The regulations must take the following criteria into account:

- the size of the English-speaking or French-speaking minority in the area served, the particular characteristics of that minority, and its proportion to the total population of that area; and
- the volume of communications or services between an office and its users.

Approximately two million Canadians live in official language minority communities – nearly one million anglophones in Quebec and one million francophones outside Quebec.

In accordance with its commitment under the Official Languages Act, the Government of Canada supports a network of 350 community groups that are working to improve the cultural, social and economic well-being of the English-language and French-language minority communities. For example, Canadian Heritage has reached an agreement with the official language minority community in each province and territory (multi-year funding reflecting each community's priorities).

Significant progress has been made over the past thirty years. Although the situation is not yet ideal, we can be proud of our achievements:

- 37 per cent of executives are francophone;
- 32 per cent of employees at the officer level or equivalent are francophone;
- 30 per cent of the support staff are francophone;
- the proportion of bilingual positions rose from 21 per cent to 35 per cent between 1994 and 2000; and
- work tools are available in both official languages.

Recently progress has slowed. A new, more values-based approach is required if profound and lasting changes are to be made. The resources allocated to management of the Official Languages Programme in the Public Service were considerably reduced during the 1990s (management of the Official Languages Programme was actually reduced by 50 per cent, while the average cuts across the Public Service were 20 per cent). Of course, the services provided to the official language minority communities are suffering as a result. Also, the indicators are based on skills and seldom on results, so the situation must be reviewed.

In this context, OLB will build on the successes of the past thirty years. The branch will also emphasize the importance of a values-based approach in order to make a lasting change with respect to official languages. In this regard, there is currently an initiative underway to ascertain the attitudes toward the use of both official languages in Canada's Public Service and determine what public service values embody our linguistic duality and the desire fully to embrace our two official languages. Among those values are respect for others and inclusiveness as well as the desire to put others at ease and enable them to contribute fully, according to their abilities and culture. It is through an approach based on values like respect for others and inclusiveness that a lasting culture change can be made with respect to official languages.

The current vision is to make the Public Service exemplary with respect to official languages in order for it to accurately reflect the linguistic duality of Canada's population. The expected outcomes are:

- Canadians receive services of equal quality in their preferred official language.
- The Public Service enthusiastically takes up the challenge of enabling its employees to work and be managed in their preferred official language.
- Both official language communities participate fully and equitably.
- The Public Service supports the official language minority communities.

- Official languages are linked to the fundamental values in the Public Service.
- Senior management demonstrates strong leadership and a clear commitment to language of work and language of service.
- Both languages are used and supported in the workplace in bilingual regions.

10
Quebec's Language Policy: Perceptions and Realities

GUY DUMAS

Introduction

The language situation in Quebec has no equivalent in North America. It is the product of the specific sociological, historical and geopolitical context. Francophones, who constitute the majority of the province's population, are nonetheless a minority group within Canada and in North America where English predominates. In contrast, anglophones, who make up 10.5 per cent of Qubec's population, constitute the vast majority of the population in the other nine Canadian provinces, as well as within federal institutions and throughout North America. In the latter areas, francophones represent a mere 2 per cent of the population. This characteristic has always given an especially sharp edge to Quebec's language debate.

Although not entirely unique, Quebec's geopolitical situation makes it a sort of original microcosm where issues linked to the preservation of a particular linguistic and cultural heritage can be studied as they unfold. Certainly, more recent events deserve attention here, namely those that have had a determining influence upon Quebec's linguistic history.

By the beginning of the twentieth century, Canada already stretched from the Atlantic to the Pacific oceans. Immigration also considerably expanded in scope. After the Second World War, the number of immigrants grew very rapidly indeed: in twenty years, between 1947 and 1967, three million new arrivals settled in Canada. This massive influx had an enormous impact upon the make-up of Quebec. In fact, for a majority of new Quebecers at that time working in English and sending their children to English school represented the best option, especially since English, even in Quebec, was the language of social and economic advancement, even though 80 per cent of the population was French speaking. Given the overall North American context, this is perhaps not surprising. However, from the perspective of a minority nation on the continent, the low social and economic attractiveness of the French language exacerbated a feeling of cultural insecurity and was viewed, ultimately, as a harbinger of the community's own eventual disappearance.

Then, in the early 1960s, a series of changes took place in Quebec on the political and social fronts, as well as with respect to people's mentalities. Religious and cultural nationalism diminished and was replaced by nationalism of a more political nature. The 1960s were characterized by the rise of a francophone elite, which succeeded in putting in place, at breakneck speed, the machinery of modern government, the goal of which was a fairer distribution of wealth. Convinced that the francophone population was increasingly threatened within the Canadian and North American context and believing in the will of the Quebec people to make French their common language in the public sphere, all Quebec governments that have held power since the 1970s have undertaken corrective measures in order to ensure that the people of Québec are able to live in French and flourish in their own language in Quebec.

Quebec's Current and Future Demolinguistic Profile

The overall demographic weight of francophones in Canada and in North America is, generally speaking, on the decline. Francophones make up 22.9 per cent of Canada's population, whereas fifty or so years ago they represented 29 per cent. In a publication entitled *Languages in Canada: 1996 Census* (Marmen and Corbeil, 1999) researchers from Statistics Canada stated that: 'It is hard to imagine a reasonable scenario that might reverse the downward trend as concerns the demographic weight of francophones within the country as a whole.' Quebec has 7.2 million inhabitants, and according to the 2001 census, 81.4 per cent of its people speak French as their mother tongue and 8.3 per cent English, while 10.3 per cent have another language as their mother tongue. As far as the language most often spoken at home is concerned, 83.1 per cent of Quebecers speak French most often at home, 10.5 per cent English and 6.5 per cent another language. Furthermore, an analysis of the most recent census data shows that an increasing number of anglophones and allophones have learned French, chiefly through the school system.

The linguistic profile of the Montreal area, on the other hand, is very different from the profile of the rest of the province. Indeed, the largest percentage of non-francophones (anglophones and allophones) live on Montreal Island (46.8 per cent, as opposed to 18.6 per cent in the whole of Quebec). Hence, the area has, over the years, become the main centre of anglophone and allophone influence within Quebec. All these various findings were important contributing factors leading to the development of Quebec's language policy, as well as to periodic adjustments of the policy, and, given these demographic elements, the relevance of the protective measures undertaken can be easily understood.

The Main Principles of Quebec's Language Policy

The basic premise of Quebec's language policy is that in order for French to survive – and thrive – on the North American continent it must be given the greatest possible competitive edge and protection within Quebec, the only place on the continent where French is the language of the majority. The goal is for French to be the language of public discourse and thus to become, as English is predominantly in the other provinces of Canada, the common language as well as the natural means of public communication for all Quebecers, whatever their mother tongue and family background.

A number of measures that promote both French and various other languages are included in Quebec's language policy. The most important among them can be found in the Charter of the French Language.[1] The latter are complemented by measures proposed by various ministries, most notably education and immigration, and in other areas, such as the health care and social services sector, as well as in judicial circles. This desire to live in French is being affirmed while the institutions of Quebec's English community and its native peoples continue to be respected and due consideration is given to other cultural communities. Although not designed to lead to an institutional bilingualism that would, sooner or later, be very detrimental to the French language, this policy does reflect an effort to strike a delicate balance between, on the one hand, a clear affirmation of the French character of Quebec society and, on the other, respect for the anglophone, allophone and native communities of Quebec.

The recognition of French as the official language of Quebec and the common language of all Quebecers in no way contradicts the importance of and need to learn other languages. On the contrary, according to the spirit of the language policy, studying and learning languages is a special means of reaching a better understanding among Quebecers of various cultural backgrounds speaking different languages. As concerns its minorities, Quebec's integration policy focuses on the language of public discourse; it thus respects private life and the right of people to perpetuate their various languages of origin as mother tongues, even going so far as to provide support for the teaching of these languages.

Quebec's language policy aims at creating a dynamic, hospitable and attractive French-language environment which can influence the linguistic choices and behaviour patterns of all Quebec citizens. Promoting the French language is closely linked to the general image of its language and culture that Quebec wishes to project. The will to promote and to protect the French language in Quebec is not a unique phenomenon. Other states take similar measures to protect their own cultural and linguistic specificities. This may in fact explain the current international movement to defend cultural diversity.

Where Quebec's Language Policy is Applied

More than twenty-five years ago, Quebec's National Assembly adopted the Charter of the French Language. The goal of this language legislation is to reaffirm the will of the majority of Quebecers to make French the common and customary language of work, education, communication, trade and commerce.

The Charter of the French Language stipulates that all laws must be printed, published, adopted and approved in both French and English. Legislation appears in both languages; this is the case for all regulations as well. The French and English versions of these texts have the same legal status. Furthermore, people subject to trial, lawyers, witnesses, judges and other officers of the court have the right to use French or English at their discretion whenever they speak or undertake any action whatsoever during a legal argument before a Quebec court of law.

The Ministère de l'Éducation is responsible for ensuring the application of the section of the Charter of the French Language that deals with the language of instruction. The policy of providing instruction in French for all students at the primary and secondary levels is designed to facilitate the linguistic integration of allophones into the French majority within Quebec society. On the other hand, it is important to note that the teaching of English as a second language is compulsory for all these children, starting in the third year of primary school.

For a good many years, Quebec has had a comprehensive English public education system extending from kindergarten to the university level. As opposed to most other Canadian provinces, Quebec provides educational services in its minority language everywhere, notwithstanding student numbers, when in fact it could, under the terms of the Canadian Constitution, provide services in the minority language only where the numbers of students actually justify such an approach. Furthermore, there are private, non-subsidized French- and English-language institutions that are not subject to the provisions of the Charter of the French Language dealing with the choice of language of instruction. It should be pointed out that, with regard to admissions to Quebec's schools, all citizens who have immigrated to Quebec, whatever their country of origin or mother tongue, are subject to the same rules. After having completed primary and secondary school, all Quebecers, regardless of their language, citizenship or prior schooling, have total freedom of linguistic choice at the college and university levels. Quebec has three English-speaking universities: McGill University, Concordia University and Bishop's University.

In order to ensure that French is spoken in both public and private life and that learning and speaking the language are perceived as useful as well as appealing, it is important for French to be an essential tool in the workplace in Quebec. Otherwise, the usefulness and appeal of the language will rapidly decline in favour of English, this being particularly true for newcomers to Quebec. This is why one main objective of the Charter of the French Language is to make French the customary language of the workplace and why the right of all workers to carry out their tasks in French is enshrined in the Charter. Thus, the adoption of French as the language of work constitutes one of the major goals of the Charter of the French Language, given that, without such a stipulation, it would be more difficult to ensure that all workers really are able to perform their duties in French in various workplace environments. For companies employing fifty or more people, programmes facilitating the adoption of French, designed to ensure that French is generally spoken within the company, are drafted by the business in question in collaboration with the Office québécois de la langue française (the French language bureau). These programmes are customized for each company, taking into account its particular characteristics, needs and constraints and ensuring that the deadlines and objectives of the programme are realistic.

The Charter of the French Language sets down various requirements with respect to the language of trade and commerce, the goal of these stipulations being to protect consumers and clearly to establish the French character of Quebec. The Charter of the French Language thus makes general provisions for the mandatory predominant use of French in billboard advertising, a measure whose legitimacy has been recognized by the Supreme Court of Canada. The Charter also provides for the use of French labelling on products, their containers and packaging, as well as the documents and objects included with them. However, this general rule in no way prohibits the use of another language. This legislative measure has been adjusted to include various exceptions, formulated especially so that, under certain circumstances, documents can be drawn up, and posters lettered, in a language other than French, without French being present.

Quebec's public administration plays a key part in enhancing the prestige of the French language, and it is entrusted to guarantee that the role of the language in society genuinely reflects its status as the official language of Quebec. Thus, the public administration (including, most notably, the government as well as the various ministries, government organizations, municipalities and educational and health care and social service institutions) has many obligations stemming from Quebec's Charter of the French Language so that services must be delivered in French. However, the public administration can provide services in other languages considered opportune. Moreover, the Charter of the French Language makes provisions for the legal recognition of some municipal, educational, health care and social service institutions as 'bilingual'. That recognition gives them more leeway in some situations. Thus, they can use French and another language in their name, on signs and posters, in their internal communications and they can hire personnel who do not know French.

How the Charter is Applied

Three administrative bodies have been created as a means of applying the Charter of the French Language. First of all, the Office québécois de la langue française (French language bureau) defines and implements Quebec's linguistic research and terminology policy and makes sure that French remains the language of communications, work, trade and commerce, public administration and company operations. It also ensures that the Charter is in fact respected: it may, in response to complaints or on its own initiative, carry out inspections and inquiries. Another body with administrative links to the Office, called the Commission de toponymie du Québec (geographic names board), is mainly in charge of officially approving and disseminating place names. Lastly, the Conseil supérieur de la langue française (French language council) advises the minister on all matters related to the French language in Quebec. In all, these bodies have 260 employees and an annual budget of $22.5 million.

A Few False Perceptions

All of us realize that perceptions of external sociocultural situations are often inaccurate. This is particularly true in the case of language policy initiatives. In 1999, Quebec's Secrétariat à la politique linguistique (language policy secretariat) held focus group discussions in four American cities (New York, Boston, Atlanta and Chicago) involving seventy opinion leaders from the US in order to learn more about their perceptions and knowledge of Quebec. In general, the participants knew very little about Quebec, having heard next to nothing about the province except under special circumstances (referendum, flooding, ice storm, etc.). As a result, their perceptions and opinions concerning Quebec were rarely based on reliable and objective information, reflecting instead impressions derived from rumours and hearsay. Here are a few examples of the general perceptions of participants concerning Quebec's language policy:

- The public school system is French only, and anglophones can only attend private or bilingual schools;
- as concerns the justice system, the defendant has the right to an English-speaking lawyer but not much else;
- English signs are prohibited, and offenders go to prison;
- anglophones cannot live in English in Quebec; and
- Quebec's laws come from France, and a defendant is presumed guilty until proven innocent.

However, when focus group participants learned the true nature of Quebec's language policy, a number of these false perceptions were dispelled, with participants affirming that Quebec's Charter of the French Language seemed on the whole rather balanced.

Consequently, there is a need to outline a few elements of the language policy which will help set the record straight by countering some of the more widespread negative perceptions:

- Quebec's laws are published in both English and French and have exactly the same legal status;
- in Quebec's courts, people can choose to use either French or English;
- with respect to education, the anglophone minority has the right to its own publicly funded schools and school boards, and the same applies at the post-secondary level for colleges and universities;
- in the area of health care, the law also grants all English-speaking people the right to receive health care and social services in their own language;
- the anglophone media network is very impressive indeed: it includes 17 radio stations, 3 television stations, 2 daily newspapers, 17 weeklies appearing exclusively in English, and 15 in both French and English. Among the magazines and periodicals sold in Quebec, 27.5 per cent are in French (approximately 1,100), while the rest (in the neighbourhood of 3,000) are in English, representing about 70 per cent of the total Quebec market.
- Lastly, the Quebec government funds and subsidizes libraries, theatres, films, television and cinematic productions, as well as various English-language cultural institutions in the same manner and according to the same rules as those applied to their francophone counterparts.

Another area is often the target of erroneous comments: signs and commercial advertising. In this respect, the Charter of the French Language stipulates that, in principle, French must always be present; however, there is nothing to prevent the incorporation of another language or languages, so long as the visual impact of French is more significant. This regulation, which includes various exceptions, is designed to protect francophone consumers, who constitute the majority of Quebec's population and to ensure that Quebec maintains its 'French character' as established by the Supreme Court of Canada.

This social justice measure is part of the process of 'reconquering' Montreal undertaken by the city's francophone majority who formerly had to live there as if in a 'British city that accidentally contained a few French-speaking citizens' (Levine, 1997: 32).Seen from this perspective, the measure is a way of reappropriating the public sphere where, all too often, especially in Montreal, English was the only language used on signs and in commercial advertising – until the adoption of the Charter of the French Language in 1977. The province's sign legislation is designed to ensure a form of cultural security for Quebecers.

Many media outlets (often anglophone) have spread the notion that Quebec has its very own repressive and intolerant language police. First of all, it is important to point out that there is no such thing as the language police; what does exist is an administrative body (the Office québécois de la langue française) responsible for ensuring that the law is respected and possessing very limited powers of inquiry having absolutely nothing to do with the powers of a police force. In fact, the work of the latter involves two facets. First of all, it investigates citizens' complaints concerning infringements of the law and tries to establish whether the perceptions of the offended parties are well founded. When a complaint is deemed admissible, the office then contacts the offending party, asking that it rectify the situation. Over 90 per cent of all cases are settled out of court. In cases where there is no agreement, the office may issue a formal notice demanding that the offender proceed with the necessary changes. If the latter does not respond to this demand, the office then transfers the file to Quebec's attorney general who decides whether or not to take legal action. Cases of prosecution are in fact few and far between, and nobody has ever been imprisoned for having contravened the Charter of the French Language. At the most, individuals can receive fines ranging from $250 to $700 Cdn. – that is, from £120 to £300.

All in all, like any other piece of legislation, the Charter of the French Language includes measures to ensure compliance. This is no different from what takes place in other nations and autonomous areas, including France, Belgium and Catalonia, all of which have adopted regulations of a linguistic nature. Quebec is a constitutional state that is careful to respect human rights and freedoms. Thus, whenever legislation is drafted, particular attention is paid to respecting the rights guaranteed under the Quebec Charter of Human Rights and Freedoms and the Canadian Charter of Rights and Freedoms (1982). Furthermore, the courts may be called upon at any time to verify the constitutional validity of a given law. In fact, important amendments have been made to the Charter of the French Language over the years in order to bring some of its clauses in line with decisions of the Supreme Court of Canada concerning the language of instruction as well as of trade and commerce. In other words, the Charter of the French Language has, up until now, met the requirements of the Canadian Constitution and the Charter of Rights and Freedoms.

Conclusion

Since its adoption, the Charter of the French Language has enabled French in Quebec to recover a certain degree of status and has provided francophone Quebecers with a measure of cultural security. It has restored Quebec's French character with respect to public billboards and commercial advertising, most notably in Montreal. It has enabled francophone consumers to obtain services in their own language. It has contributed to an increased use of French among workers and in everyday business life. It has led immigrant children to attend French schools and has facilitated their integration into the francophone community.

However, there is still a great deal of progress yet to be made in all sectors of activity, and the balance that has been reached remains delicate and precarious. The forces dominating the linguistic market in Canada and North America, in conjunction with a globalized economy and the powerful presence of information and communications technologies, all contribute to the widespread use of English. Furthermore, the opening up of markets and the globalization of economic activity is leading Québec's businesses and industries to have regular dealings with the outside world and to an increase in the demand for and the use of languages other than French. Lastly, we must take into account the long-term demolinguistic future of francophone society (characterized by an ageing population with a low birth rate) that depends to an ever increasing extent on immigrants for its survival. Hence, if the Charter of the French Language has made it possible, in part, to contain these forces, it has certainly not made them disappear; the pressures that are being brought to bear on the French language in Quebec remain constant. This is why the law is still, and will remain, a necessity.

REFERENCES

The British Council, (1997). *The Future of English*, London: The Glenton Press.

Charte de la langue française (1977) *Charter of the French language*, R.S.Q., c. C-11. (1977) *Québec:* Gouvernement du Québec,

Charte québécoise des droits et libertés de la personne (*Québec Charter of Human Rights and Freedoms*), R.S.Q., c. C-12. (1982) *Québec:* Gouvernement du Québec.

Commission de toponymie du Québec website at http://toponymie.gouv.qc.ca.

Conseil supérieur de la langue française website at http://cslf.gouv.qc.ca.

Fishman, J. A., (1998–1999). 'The New Linguistic Order', *Foreign Policy*, 26.

Gouvernement du Québec, (1977). *Politique québécoise de la langue française*, March, Québec: Gouvernement du Québec,

Gouvernement du Québec, (1996).*Rapport du comité interministériel sur la situation de la langue française*. Direction des communications du ministère de la Culture et des Communications, Québec: Gouvernement du Québec.

Government of Canada (1982) Charte canadienne des droits et libertés (*Canadian Charter of Rights and Freedoms,* Enacted as Schedule B to the *Canada Act 1982*, (U.K.) 1982, c.11.Ottawa: Government of Canada.

Levine, M. V., (1990). *The Reconquest of Montréal. Language Policy and Social Change in a Bilingual City*, Philadelphia: Temple University Press.

Levine, M. V., (1997). *La Reconquête de Montréal*, Montréal: VLB Éditeur.

Marmen, L. and Corbeil, J-P (1999) *Languages in Canada: 1996 Census.* Ottawa: Canadian Heritage and Statistics Canada.

Office québécois de la langue française website at http://oqlf.gouv.qc.ca.

11

One Nation – Two Voices? The Welsh Language in the Governance of Wales

WINSTON RODDICK CB QC

Introduction

In this chapter I propose to examine the legal status of the Welsh language, its role in the governance of Wales and the relevance of its legal status to the aspirations of the Welsh Assembly Government's Welsh Language policy, *Iaith Pawb* (Everyone's Language), and I shall address the central question of whether there is a need for further primary legislation to enhance the status of the language and its use in the governance of Wales.

My first involvement in the field of language and governance began in 1989 when I was invited by the Minister of State at the Welsh Office, Lord Roberts of Conwy (as he now is), to join a small group to examine the arguments which had been advanced in support of a new Welsh Language Act and to advise him as to whether there was a sound case for one or not. The background was that there had been a sustained campaign over a number of years which enjoyed widespread support for an Act which made provision with regard to the status and use of the Welsh language in Wales. There were serious concerns as to the viability of the language. The group recommended that there should be established a non-statutory Welsh language board to collect and consider the evidence and arguments for a new Act and, in the light of the evidence and arguments, to make recommendations as to what provisions the legislation should make. The government accepted the recommendations and immediately established a

Welsh Language Board as a non-statutory body under the chairmanship of Mr John Elfed Jones CBE. It had nine members of whom I was one. I chaired the board's legislation committee and I was the author of the report which the board adopted as its findings and recommendations to the government in February 1991 for a new Welsh Language Act (Welsh Language Board, 1991).

The second phase of my involvement with the Welsh language in the governance of Wales began in November 1998, when I was appointed Counsel General to the National Assembly for Wales (the Assembly) for a term of five years. The Assembly was established by the Government of Wales Act 1998. It devolved to the Assembly executive responsibility in a number of fields including extensive powers to make secondary legislation in its fields of responsibilities. It made a number of limited provisions with regard to the status of the Welsh language and its use in the conduct of Assembly business. The most significant of these was that, save in the limited circumstances described in the Act, the Assembly's subordinate legislation should be made bilingually and that the English and Welsh versions of that legislation should be of equal standing. As the Counsel General, I was responsible for the preparation of that legislation.

There was no precedent in the United Kingdom for drafting bilingual legislation and what bilingualism there was in the governance of Wales was largely permissive and very limited. It was necessary therefore to look to other jurisdictions for experience of bilingual governance and bilingual government generally and of making bilingual legislation in particular. I chose as my models Canada and Ireland. In both those countries the English language was not only one of the national or official languages of the nation but it was the predominant language. In fact it was of such dominance as to threaten the existence of their minority languages. Other highly relevant factors in my decision to chose those countries as my models was that both had been governed in recent times from Westminster and had been subject to laws made there and to the sovereignty of the Westminster Parliament. At the invitation of the governments and the judiciary of Ireland and Canada I visited both countries on a number of occasions and had the opportunity to observe at first hand a constitution and a system of government, law-making and justice that treats two official languages on a basis of equality. It provided me with a real insight into and an understanding of bilingualism in the governance of nations. That, briefly, is my own background in the field of language and governance.

'The Principle of Equality' and Like Expressions

In the course of writing this chapter I realized that the expressions 'the principle of equality', 'the basis of equality' and 'equal validity' are not only confusingly similar but are often used interchangeably in the numerous reports and other contributions to the debates about the standing of the Welsh language. The expression 'basis of equality' appears in two recent statutes dealing with the Welsh language. There also appeared to be uncertainty as to what exactly is meant by a status equal to that of English and as to the difference between that concept of equal status and 'official' status. It might be helpful, therefore, if I were to explain my understanding of these expressions.

In the context of languages, 'the principle of equality' means that the citizen shall have the same or similar right to do through the medium of the minority language what that citizen can do there through the medium of English and that the act, writing or other thing done in pursuance of that right shall be to the same legal effect as if it had been done in English. It is a right which attaches to the citizen and is a part of the basic and much wider right to be treated equally. It was a declaration to this effect that the Hughes Parry Committee (1965) and the Welsh Language Board (1991) recommended to the government in their respective reports of October 1965 and February 1991. The two expressions, 'principle of equality', and 'basis of equality' were used interchangeably by the Secretary of State, David Hunt (as he then was), during the debates on the government's Welsh Language Bill of 1993 (which became the Welsh Language Act 1993) (Hansard, 1993). We can take it, therefore, that they mean one and the same thing and that the purpose of the language schemes made under section 5 of the Welsh Language Act 1993, which introduced the expression 'basis of equality' to the statute book for the first time, is to explain how public bodies which transact business in Wales propose to give effect to the principle of equality in the provision of their services.

'Equal validity', in the sense in which it was used in the Hughes Parry Report (1965) and in the 1991 report of the Welsh Language Board, means that any act, writing or other thing done in Welsh shall be to the same or similar effect as if it were done in English. A statutory provision giving effect to this principle would not of itself create any legal right to do the act, writing or other thing in Welsh. On the other hand, a general declaration that the status of the Welsh language in Wales shall be equal in all respects to that of English would, unless the Act expressly limited its effect, create such a right and, as a consequence, would confer legal validity on any act, writing, or other thing done in Welsh in pursuance of that right. In other words, equal validity is a product of an equal status. I believe that to be the point made in paragraph 171 of the Hughes Parry report.

In its application to languages, 'status' is that condition which attaches to them by law. It is the measure of the rights, duties, capacity and incapacity of the citizens in their choice of language in dealing with the state. It is that condition which confers or effects or limits the rights of those who provide public services in their choice of the language in which they will provide those services. The status of a language determines its relationship to the state and its relationship to other languages.

What is the test of status and equality? A language has legal status and enjoys equality of status if

- it is declared by statute to be or has become established through long usage as the national or one of the national languages of the nation;
- the citizens of that nation can insist as of right on being dealt with in that language or, if there is more than one national language, the language of their choice when they deal with all or any aspect of public administration including the administration of justice; and

- the citizens can insist as of right on being dealt with in the one language in circumstances in which they could insist on being dealt with in the other.

'Status' in this sense should not be confused with 'official'. A language might at the same time be official in its use and permissive in its status. The test of whether its use is permissive or as of right is not whether the Welsh language is used officially but whether it is so used as of right. In the course of the second reading debate on the government's Welsh Language Bill in the House of Commons on the 26 May 1993, it was said on behalf of the government:

> The Government believes that Welsh already has [official] status. Anyone who doubts that statement has only to look at how public business is conducted in Wales today and, indeed, has been conducted for many years. Welsh plays a prominent part in our public administration and special provision has been made for it in Acts passed by this Parliament. By establishing the principle of equality the Bill reaffirms that official status.

There is no doubting the correctness of that statement as far as it goes, but 'official status' in the sense it was there being used means no more than that the language is used in the transaction of public business; it does not say anything about the extent of its use as such or whether the use is simply permissive or as of right.

What flows from status? If Welsh were declared to be a national language of Wales and equal in its status to that of English, the state would be bound to do everything within its sphere of activity to establish and maintain it in its status as one of the national languages of Wales and to give effect to the rights of the citizens of Wales to use it in all aspects of public business in Wales in which English may be use (*O'Foghludhe v. Mc Clean*, 1934). If the status of a minority language is declared by statute to be equal to that of the majority language and its use is reinforced by legal rights, its survival is more assured even in nations which do not have written constitutions. A minority language which depends on the whim and the priorities of government and of the executive and on concessions rather than on rights for its status enjoys only a permissive status. In consequence, it is subject to the frailties and vulnerabilities of all such minority languages which suffer that incapacity.

Although the European Charter on Minority Languages does not have the force of law, it is aspirational and the UK is a signatory to it. The relevant part provides:

> considering that the right to use a regional or minority language in private and public life is an inalienable right conforming to the principles embodied in the United Nations International Covenant on civil and political rights, and according to the spirit of the Council of Europe Convention for the protection of human rights and fundamental freedoms . . . *the parties undertake to eliminate, if they have not yet done so, any unjustified distinction, exclusion, restriction, or preference relating to the use of a regional or minority language and intended to discourage or endanger the maintenance or development of a regional or minority language. The adoption of special measures in favour of regional or minority languages aimed at promoting equality between the users of these languages and the rest of the population or which take due account of their specific conditions is not considered to be an act of discrimination against the users of more widely used languages.*

What then is the status of the Welsh language today and what is its role in the governance of Wales? In seeking to answer those questions it is necessary to look at the subject historically and to bear in mind the limiting effect of the following five factors:

- Wales is but a part of the unitary state of the United Kingdom.
- The Welsh language does not have any status, legal or practical, in the UK or in the governance of the UK, only in a territorial part of it.
- As Wales is but a part of the nation state of the United Kingdom, the Welsh language does not enjoy any legal or practical status in the governance of Europe.
- Primary legislation emanating from the UK Parliament is enacted only in English. Not even the legislation the territorial jurisdiction of which is limited to Wales is enacted bilingually in Welsh and English or subsequently translated into Welsh.

- Although some executive responsibility for the governance of Wales now rests with the Assembly, much of the responsibility for the governance of Wales rests outside Wales.

The Historical Development of the Status of the Welsh Language in the Governance of Wales

The Destruction

Between the reign of Henry VIII and 1830, crucial changes were effected in government, law and the courts in Wales. Parliament emasculated Wales and its language of their legal and official status. Two Acts, popularly known as the Acts of Union, namely 27 Hen. 8 C26 (the 1536 Act) and 34 and 35 Hen. 5. C26 (the 1542 Act), incorporated Wales fully into England, divided the country into shires and made English law and administration uniform throughout and declared English to be the language of the law and governance throughout England and Wales. The following provisions of the 1536 Act demonstrate Parliament's intention vividly.

> Wales is and ever hath been incorporated, annexed, united and subject to and under the imperial Crown of this realm as a verrye member . . .
>
> (the people of Wales) do daily use a speche nothing like . . . The naturall mother tonge used in this Realm . . .
>
> all Justices . . . and all other officers and ministers of the lawe shall proclayme and kepe the sessions . . . and all other courtes . . . in the Englisshe Tonge . and all othes . . .affidavithes verdictes and wagers of lawe to be given . . . In the Englisshe Tonge.
>
> frome hensforth no personnes that use the Welsshe speche or langage shall have or enjoy any maner office or fees within the Realme of Englonde Wales or other the Kinges dominions . . . onles he or they use and exercise the speche or langage of Englisshe.

A number of statutes between 1730 and 1733 declared that all proceedings in the courts of justice in England and Wales should be in the English language. In 1747, by section 3 of the Wales and Berwick Act of that year, it was declared that wherever the term 'England' was used in any Act of Parliament it should be deemed to include Wales. The one major Welsh institution left over from the Acts of Union, the Court of Great Sessions, was abolished in 1830. The incorporation of legal Wales into England was then complete. These Acts tore the heart out of Wales. One direct consequence of them was that the Welsh language ceased to be a language of record in Wales – a status that it has not fully recovered. In the eyes of the law, the cumulative effect of these statutes was that the 'Welsh were English'.

The Reconstruction

From that brief summary of the historical background it will be seen that the Welsh language lost its legal and official status not through neglect or misuse (it continued to be spoken by a sizeable proportion of the population) but by Acts of Parliament. It was unabashed cultural cleansing. Since only Parliament can restore what Parliament takes away, the answer to the question of whether the legal and official status of the language has since been restored lies, therefore, not in the policies and practices of public bodies or Crown bodies but in the Acts of Parliament passed after 1830. It is with that fact in mind that I come to an examination of the legislation. If the conclusion were that the status of the Welsh language has been restored there would be no need for further legislation simply to declare its legal and official status. On the other hand, if it has not been restored, the question arises of whether it is necessary or not that it be restored and, if it is said to be necessary, why it is considered to be so.

Since 1942, four principal Acts concerned with the use of the Welsh language in public administration including the administration of justice have come to the statute book. They are the Welsh Courts Act 1942, the Welsh Language Act 1967, the Welsh Language Act 1993 and the Government of Wales Act 1998. It is the 1993 and 1998 Acts which provide the present statutory framework for the use of the Welsh language in the governance of Wales today.

The Welsh Courts Act 1942

This Act, like every other Act of Parliament dealing with the use of Welsh that followed it, came to be made as a result of strong protest from the Welsh-speaking community. It had the very limited purpose of removing doubts as to whether the notorious section 17 of the 1536 Act which prohibited the use of Welsh in legal proceedings remained in effect or not. It enacted that the Welsh language may be used in any court in Wales by any party or witness who considered he would otherwise be at a disadvantage by reason of his natural language of communication being Welsh, that the language of record of the proceedings in courts in Wales should continue to be kept in English and it made provision to facilitate the making of rules for taking of oaths and affirmations in Welsh.

It did not enhance the status of the Welsh language save in its recognition of its existence as a language which it would be permissible to use in court proceedings if the witness would be disadvantaged if he were required to use English. In that concession to the Welsh language it simply equated those who wished to use it in court proceedings with all other persons who because of inadequate command of English wished to use some other language in which to give their evidence. Its effect is best summarised in a demeaning passage from the judgment of Mr. Justice Widgery in the case of *R v. Merthyr Tydfil Justices, Ex parte Jenkins* [1967] 1 All ER 636 at p. 638:

> the language difficulties which arise in [courts] in Wales can be dealt with by discretionary arrangements from an interpreter precisely in the same way as language difficulties at the Central Criminal Court are dealt with where the accused is a Pole.

It is difficult to imagine that those remarks were made as recently as 1967.

The Report of the Council of Wales on the Welsh Language

Following an objective survey in 1960 of the use of the Welsh language in various spheres of Welsh life, the council urged the government to grant 'official status' to the Welsh language comprising the 'rights' to use the language in courts of law, in public inquiries and tribunals in Wales, in local authority meetings, in meetings with administrative officials and in correspondence with government departments and local authorities, that there be a right to keep minutes of local authority meetings in Welsh, that official documents relating to Wales should be prepared in Welsh and English, that road signs should be in both English and Welsh and that there be a right to issue rate demands and other local authority documents in Welsh. Most of these practices were already in use and although the report called for rights what the council was actually calling for were discretionary arrangements which regularized the practices and afforded them official recognition (Hughes Parry, 1965)

The Hughes Parry Report

In July 1963, the Minister for Welsh Affairs, Sir Keith Joseph, set up the Hughes Parry Committee under the chairmanship of Sir David Hughes Parry QC, LLD, DCL. Its terms of reference were 'to clarify the legal status of the Welsh language and to consider whether any changes in the law ought to be made'. Its report was presented to Parliament in October 1965. It analysed how the status of the Welsh language had been rendered inferior to English by the statutes to which I have already made reference and it concluded that an Act of Parliament declaring the status of the Welsh language in Wales to be equal to that of English was essential for clarifying and raising the status of the language. That was its central recommendation.

The Welsh Language Act 1967

Following the report and recommendations of the Hughes Parry Committee, the government introduced the Welsh Language Act 1967. Subject to provisions about giving notice, it gave any party or witness the right to use the Welsh language in legal proceedings in Wales. It was unnecessary to demonstrate disadvantage in not being able to give evidence through the medium of Welsh. It also undid the effect of section 3 of the Wales and Berwick Act 1746. 'England' now meant England and not England and Wales. It made provision in section 3(1) for Welsh versions of statutory forms. It declared that anything done in Welsh in a version of a form authorized by that subsection shall have the like effect as if done in English. To a very limited extent, this was an application of the principle of equal validity but in the very next subsection it provided that any power to prescribe a Welsh version of a form shall include the power to provide that in the case of conflict between one version of the form and the other, the English version shall prevail, in effect entrenching the inequality of the Welsh language (Welsh Language Act, 1967, section 3(2). That latter power was used on many occasions thereby rendering the Act's application of the principle of equal validity illusory.

It is probably the case that 1967 marks the beginning of the administrative policy of treating the Welsh language as an official language in Wales (Deacon, 2002) and the point at which the Welsh language began to play a practical role in the governance of Wales. It would not be correct to say that this change was a direct effect of the 1967 Act. That Act did enhance the status of the Welsh language in that it created a legal right to its use in court proceedings, it undid the effect of section 3 of the Wales and Berwick Act and it applied the principle of equal validity to the Welsh language version of forms made under section 3 but it did not give effect to the principal recommendation of the Hughes Parry report which was that the government should introduce legislation declaring the status of Welsh to be equal in all respects to that of English in Wales. The claims that the 1967 Act gave effect to that recommendation are not sustainable. Save for the limited changes which I have just described, it left the status of the language more or less as the Hughes Parry Committee had found it.

The Background to the Welsh Language Act 1993

In 1989, in response to the recommendation of the group which the Minister of State for Wales, Lord Roberts of Conwy (as he now is) had appointed to advise him on whether a language board should be set up or not, the minister established the non-statutory Welsh Language Board under the chairmanship of John Elfed Jones CBE. Its terms of reference were to promote and develop the Welsh language and to advise on matters requiring legislation. In its report of February 1991, the board found that the 1967 Act had neither halted nor retarded the marked decline in the use of the Welsh language. It said that it was left in no doubt about the Act's inadequacies. It identified three particular weaknesses:

- its failure to declare that in Wales the Welsh language shall be equal in status to the English language;
- its failure to make effective provision for greater use of the Welsh language in the public sector;
- Section 3(2) entrenched the inferiority of the Welsh language.

With regard to the use of Welsh in the administration of justice, the board found that despite the recommendations of the Council of Wales in 1960 and the changes introduced by the 1967 Act with regard to the use of the Welsh language in legal proceedings in Wales, the opportunities for its use were too limited. On the question of whether the status of the Welsh language should be declared by statute or not, the board acknowledged that the language could not be sustained by legislation alone but it argued that certain changes which only Parliament could make were essential if the language was to enjoy realistic prospects of survival. It asked itself the question: 'Why legislate at all. Why not stick with a voluntary approach?' The answer which it gave to that question is a significant piece of the background to the Welsh Language Act 1993 and highly relevant to the assessment of the effectiveness of the approach adopted in that Act towards Crown bodies. The answer it gave was:

> in our view it is necessary to introduce primary legislation dealing with the use of the language in the public sector. It is necessary from two points of view. There is the question of basic human rights and there is a need to take effective steps to help safeguard the future of the language. We accept that legislation alone cannot secure this latter objective. Much depends on a number of other things of

> which tolerance; goodwill and popular support are probably the most important. The support of the public sector, the private sector, the people of Wales generally and that of the political parties are all essential. But of central importance is legislation which gives status to the language, provides for a wider use of the language in the public sector and establishes a [Language Board] to care for the language. *These are the three essential pillars for any effective strategy for the Welsh language. The common law will provide the fourth pillar.* (emphasis is mine) (Welsh Language Board, 1991, para. 58)

That reference to the common law was to the usual public law remedies that would be available in support of the rights which would follow from the declaration of equality of status. In that same part of the report, the board expressed the view that

> Without being reinforced by statute, a bilingual policy would constantly be vulnerable to changes of priorities by government ministers, Departmental heads and others who have responsibility for formulating policy . . . In our view, the situation in which the language finds itself is too critical to be left to the will of the executive. A voluntary policy is too ambulatory an instrument to sustain the Welsh language.

The 'four pillars' argument and the arguments set out in that last passage were seen by the board as central to the case for a declaration of the equal status of the Welsh language. They are certainly critical to an understanding of the effect of the Welsh Language Act 1993 and the permissive nature of the status of the Welsh language today.

The Welsh Language Act 1993

I come then to the provisions of this Act. There are four tests of its effectiveness:

1. Did it restore the status of the Welsh language?
2. Did it make provision for securing wider use of the Welsh language in the public sector?
3. Either of itself or with other legislation still extant, did it create an effective statutory infrastructure for sustaining the language?

4. Either by itself or with other extant legislation, can it make a real contribution towards securing a 'truly bilingual Wales', which is the main objective of the Welsh Assembly Government's Welsh-language policy, *Iaith Pawb*?.

The relevance of the Act to that policy is that, together with the Government of Wales Act 1998, it determines the scope of the policy. It established the Welsh Language Board as a statutory body with the functions of promoting and facilitating the use of the Welsh language in the conduct of public business in Wales and it made provision for the preparation by public bodies of schemes giving effect to the principle of equality in the conduct of their business. It advanced the principle of equal validity by a small step and it repealed certain spent enactments including the 'Act of Union'. The Secretary of State was given power to impose schemes on recalcitrant public bodies. The Welsh Language Board was empowered to investigate any public body failing or refusing to work according to its scheme and to 'name and shame' it in its report and the Secretary of State was empowered to issue directions to comply. None of these coercive powers have hitherto been exercised. The Assembly has succeeded to the powers of the Secretary of State and in 2004 the Assembly subsumed the Welsh Language Board.

The Act has a number of serious weaknesses. It did not implement the recommendation to give equal status to the Welsh language, the class of public bodies to which the obligation so called to make schemes under section 5 is small, the sanctions for failure to make a scheme or to work according to a scheme are modest and impracticable (which may explain why they have never been applied), the limited obligations to make schemes were significantly diluted by the inherently limiting qualification 'so far as is appropriate' and it excludes Crown bodies altogether from any kind of obligation to apply the principle of equality. The government gave an undertaking that Crown bodies would make schemes voluntarily in accordance with the Board's guidelines even though they were exempt from all obligations to do so. That undertaking has proved to be less than effective.

Why did the government not make the declaration for which an unanswerable case had been made in two consecutive reports to it by committees appointed for the purpose by the government itself? The government was not opposed in principle to acknowledging the equal status of the Welsh language (Welsh Language Board, 1991, paras 41 and 42) There was no more committed supporter of the Welsh language at that time than the minister of state himself; many of the reforms of the period can be attributed to him. The answer lies in the enforceability of language rights. In its 1991 report to the minister, the board advised that a declaration of equal status and the creation of obligations on public bodies, including Crown bodies, to give effect to the principle of equality in the provision of their services would create rights enforceable at the suit of individuals who felt aggrieved by failures by those bodies to treat the Welsh language on the basis of equality with English. That is what the board meant when it said that the common law would provide the fourth pillar of support for an effective language strategy. Without some measure of enforceability, a statement of equality would be illusory and the declaring statute would be impotent. With a view to increasing the threshold of liability and thereby reducing the scope for legal challenges, the board recommended that public bodies should not be obliged to comply with a request to give effect to the principle of equality if in the particular circumstances the request to do so was unreasonable or compliance with it was impracticable (Welsh Language Board, 1991, Annexe 1 clause 2(1)). It would have been for the courts to construe that limitation and in doing so they would have given effect to the underlying purpose of the Act which was to give real effect to the principle of equality. With the courts acting as a check on public bodies in their application of the limitation, it could not be used to justify unreasonable failure to apply the principle of equality in the provision of services through the Welsh language. Without some limitation on the obligation, the duty would have appeared absolute and would have placed public bodies including Crown bodies at the mercy of zealots and perfectionists.

Despite the limitation recommended by the Welsh Language Board, the government remained concerned that the attendant right of enforcement would be damaging to the interests of the Welsh language. The minister of state explained the government's view (Hansard, 1993: col. 1012)

> It would not further the cause of the language to turn it into a legal battlefield. I, for one, do not want to see our language murdered with legal niceties by sharp faced lawyers . . . That would do nothing to promote an environment where language has the support of all parts of the community. It would be one way in which the good will that currently exists towards the language could easily be dissipated. The . . . problem with statutory rights is that they depend on the courts for their enforcement.

Countless Acts of Parliament have created rights in countless fields without turning them into battlefields. The Welsh Language Act 1967 created real rights in the field of administration of justice in Wales without that being turned into a battlefield. As it happened, Welsh Office officials did not communicate the minister's concerns to the Welsh Language Board at the time and consequently the opportunity to give further consideration to the issue of how the declaration of equality and the attendant rights of enforcement might be better balanced in the public interest was lost. Here, in the failure to achieve an acceptable balance between rights and remedies, the explanation is to be found as to why the 1993 Act did not make the recommended declaration of equality and why, six hundred years after it was taken away, the status of the Welsh language, save for the limited enhancement which I have already described, was not restored. It is also the root cause of the Act's major weaknesses.

The government's concerns about enforceability also explain the exclusion of Crown bodies from the limited obligations to make language schemes. In support of their exclusion, it was argued that giving the Secretary of State for Wales's authority to enforce against another secretary of state or other minister would be inconsistent with the indivisible character of the Crown and, therefore, could not be done. Some scepticism about that argument was expressed by Mr John Morris MP, as he then was, during the debate on the second reading of the Bill

(Hansard, 1993: col. 1009) but whether the argument was sound or not would have been nowhere to the point had the responsibility for policing the obligations been vested in an independent language commissioner, as was suggested at the time by Lord Prys Davies and Mr Dafydd Wigley, rather than in the Secretary of State. In the light of experience, it is to be regretted that the Welsh Language Board did not adopt those suggestions in its 1991 report.

As the Canadian legislation in the field of official languages demonstrates, having a language commissioner independent of government avoids altogether the kind of objections advanced in 1993 to the creation of language rights and to making Crown bodies amenable to the obligations to apply the principle of equality in the provision of services to the public in Wales. It is the Language Commissioner's duty and responsibility to regulate public bodies (including departments of the federal government) in their application of the principle of equality and for the enforcement of language rights in the first instance. He is an effective limitation on the enforceability of language rights through the courts but this limitation takes nothing away from the fullness of the declaration of equality or from the effectiveness of the rights which such a declaration creates.

As to the second test of the 1993 Act's effectiveness, it is now almost fifteen years since it came into force. There is no doubt that the Welsh Language Board in exercise of its functions under the Act has succeeded in making the language more visible in the governance of Wales at many levels and in enhancing its use amongst the public bodies to which the Act applies. It has also had a measure of success with some Crown bodies. In these respects, the Act is fulfilling its purpose though it is not solely responsible for the advances. Other significant contributors were the Government of Wales Act 1998, the Assembly, Welsh-language broadcasting and the availability of Welsh-medium education at every level.

The Welsh Language Board is in a good position to judge the effectiveness of the Act. Its evidence in 2003 to the Richard Commission (2004) described its experience of dealing with Crown bodies as one of disappointment. It had found that some of those bodies did not accept that they needed to prepare schemes. First drafts of their schemes showed inadequate regard for the board's guidelines. They tended to be selective and subjective in drawing up schemes. They applied convenience as the criteria rather than the board's guidelines. They took significantly longer to prepare adequate schemes than other public bodies. The Home Office, the Criminal Records Bureau (an agency of the Home Office), the Driving Standards Agency, the Passport Office and the Charity Commissioners were singled out for criticism. The Charity Commissioners, who deal with a large number of voluntary bodies in Wales, took seven years to submit an acceptable language scheme. Other Crown bodies had also been guilty of long delays and of creating long, drawn-out disputes with the Board. The Criminal Records Bureau (CRB) refused to provide bilingual registration forms. Letters from the Board and from the Assembly minister were disregarded. The continued refusal to make the forms available bilingually resulted in a public campaign aimed at persuading the Home Office of the injustice of its treatment of those who desired a Welsh-language service. The First Minister felt constrained to write to the Home Secretary and it was not until this high level intervention did the CRB express its preparedness to publish the forms bilingually.The Board's experience of Crown bodies in their implementation of schemes was no better. It acknowledged that some took their responsibilities seriously but found that some dragged their heels. By way of examples, some ignored their own schemes when introducing or reorganizing services. Welsh versions of publications were issued much later than the English versions, Welsh-language versions of helplines were not provided when English-language ones were. It found that the unequal treatment of the Welsh language was sometimes deliberate and often the result of a lack of awareness and understanding of the need to treat the languages on the basis of equality. It found that the difference between the treatment of the language by Crown bodies, on the one hand and the public bodies amenable to the obligations of the Act, on the other, was that the quality and efficiency of the service from the latter was much better. The board expressed its serious concerns about the adequacy of the Act in its treatment of Crown bodies and of the practical value of the concordat between the Assembly and Whitehall. It was a forthright condemnation of the voluntary approach adopted towards Crown bodies.

Mrs Jenny Randerson, when she was Minister for Culture, Welsh language and Sport, also expressed concerns in the course of her evidence to the Commission and she recognized the need for primary legislation to address the Act's shortcomings. Alun Pugh AM, Mrs Randerson's successor to the culture portfolio, in his evidence expressed the view that if the Assembly Government wished Crown bodies to deliver an acceptable Welsh-language service there would need to be further primary legislation. Rhodri Glyn Thomas, AM, chairman of the Assembly's Culture, Welsh Language and Sport Committee in his Forward to the committee's 2002 *Policy Review of the Welsh Language* stated that 'it was clear from the outset that the situation where only 18 per cent of the population of Wales speaks Welsh is unsustainable'. My understanding of that statement is that Mr Thomas did not then consider that the statutory framework and policies provided sufficient support to sustain the language.

The experience of the last ten years as described by the Welsh Language Board and the ministers in their evidence to the Richard Commission in 2003 confirms the soundness of the reasons why the Welsh Language Board in its report of February 1991 advised against the voluntary approach (Welsh Language Board, 1991: para. 58). Crown bodies, situated in and out of Wales, play a prominent and highly significant role in the governance of Wales. Together, they probably deal with all the people of Wales at one time or another. They have establishments in Wales. They are large employers of people in Wales. Their exclusion from any obligation to make language schemes is a significant obstacle to equality and to the development of bilingualism in the public sector in Wales. Their failures and refusals to make and implement schemes voluntarily demean Welsh speaking people. Without a different and more effective statutory framework for regulating the conduct of Crown bodies in their application of the principle of equality, the main aspiration of the Welsh Assembly Government's otherwise excellent policy, *Iaith Pawb*, is not likely to be achieved.

The Government of Wales Act 1998

The next Act to have a discernible effect on the role of the Welsh language in the governance of Wales was the Government of Wales Act 1998 which established the National Assembly for Wales and by which was devolved to the Assembly the executive government of Wales in the fields of responsibilities transferred to it by the various Transfer of Function Orders and subsequent Acts. The Assembly is a single corporate body but functions along the lines of a parliament in that it has cabinet government and a legislature. It has secondary law-making powers but no primary law-making powers. For primary legislation, therefore, Wales continues to rely on the UK Parliament. The Act has been drafted on the basis that functions in any field of responsibility can be devolved to the Assembly. Its present areas of responsibilities include agriculture, health, education, economic development, local government, transport and culture. It has sixty members, one-third of whom are elected by proportional representation. The three sections of the 1998 Act which directly affect the use of the Welsh language in the governance of Wales are sections 47(1), 66(4) and 122(1). Only the latter makes provision as to the status of the language.

Section 47(1) provides: 'The Assembly shall in the conduct of its business give effect, so far as is both appropriate in the circumstances and reasonably practicable, to the principle that the English and Welsh languages should be treated on a basis of equality.' Section 66(4) provides:

> The subordinate legislation procedures must include provision for securing that a draft of the statutory instrument containing any Assembly general subordinate legislation may be approved by the Assembly only if the draft is in both English and Welsh unless in the particular circumstances it is inappropriate or not reasonably practicable for the draft to be in both languages.

Section 122(1) provides: The English and Welsh texts of any subordinate legislation made by the Assembly which is in both English and Welsh when made shall be treated for all purposes as being of equal standing.'

The immediate effects of these provisions on the conduct of the Assembly's business were bilingual standing orders, bilingual debates, a bilingual daily record and that some of its legislation is made bilingually. It is also a public body for the purposes of section 5 of the Welsh Language Act 1993 and has published a Welsh-language scheme in accordance with that section setting out how in its conduct of its business, including its business with the public, it proposes to give effect to the principle of equality.

Devolution more generally has acted as a catalyst for wider changes in the use of the Welsh language in the governance of Wales in fields of responsibilities not devolved to the Assembly. Of these, the best example, probably, is the administration of justice in Wales. Since 1998, the Mercantile Court was established in Cardiff followed shortly thereafter by the Administrative Court of Wales. The Court of Appeal, Civil and Criminal Divisions, sit occasionally in Cardiff, the Employment Appeals Tribunal now sits in Wales in all cases arising from Wales and the Lord Chancellor appointed a High Court judge whose fluency in the Welsh language enables him to hear and determine cases bilingually or entirely in Welsh, according to the wishes of the parties, without translation. When opening the Mercantile Court in Cardiff in 2000, Lord Bingham using the full title of his office, Lord Chief Justice of England and Wales, said:

> This court represents the long overdue recognition of the need for the Principality of Wales to have its own indigenous institutions operating locally and meeting the needs of its citizens here. This court is another step towards recognising Wales as a proud, distinctive and successful nation.

In 2000 and 2001, a small group, comprising judges, officials of the Office of the Counsel General and myself was invited to Canada as guests of its federal government and the provincial government of New Brunswick to observe at first hand a constitution and a system of government, law-making and justice that treats two official languages on a basis of equality. Following each visit, we published a report of our findings and made recommendations. I believe both reports are having a significant effect on the use of the Welsh language in the administration of justice in Wales. Two committees, each chaired by a judge, have produced reports and recommendations dealing respectively with the training and education of the judiciary in the use of the Welsh language and the use of the Welsh language throughout the whole criminal justice process from the moment the suspect is questioned to the moment he is sentenced by the court. These developments enjoy the support of all relevant public bodies in Wales. The Lord Chancellor established a standing committee under the chairmanship of a High Court judge to be responsible for the use of the Welsh language in the administration of justice in Wales.

The 1998 Act, directly and indirectly, has, therefore, had a positive effect in enhancing and facilitating the use of the Welsh language in the governance of Wales and in making that role a more visible one. Additionally, section 122(1) of the Act was a positive step in the direction of equal validity. However, save in relation to the standing of the Welsh version of the Assembly's bilingual legislation, the Act did not advance the legal status of the language and it shares two very significant weakness in particular with the 1993 Act.

There are three key provisions which are highly relevant to the consideration of the effectiveness of the 1993 and 1998 Acts in providing infrastructure for the continued development of the Welsh language generally and its role in the governance of Wales and as support for *Iaith Pawb* in particular (see the third and fourth tests mentioned earlier in relation to the 1993 Act). They are section 5(2) (which reads into section 21) of the 1993 Act, which I have already summarized and commented on, and sections 47(1) and 66 (4) of the 1998 Act which I set out earlier. What they have in common is that the obligations they create are limited by the words 'appropriate in the circumstances'. Those words are 'inherently limiting' in their effect (Hansard: vol. 305, col. 11). They weaken very significantly the obligations to which they attach. There is a view amongst officials in the Assembly that the limitation was 'deliberately constructed to reflect the reality that the Welsh language is a minority language and to avoid political difficulties'. I would agree that they reflect the inferior status of the Welsh language and I would also agree that it is highly arguable that that was the intention of including them in this and the 1993 Act. If those three important statutory provisions are interpreted in that narrow sense, their potential for enhancing the standing and use of the language in the governance of Wales is very limited. The limitation is a serious obstacle to equality and it could frustrate the Welsh Assembly Government's Welsh-language policy, *Iaith Pawb*, in its central objective of creating a 'truly bilingual Wales'.

Another serious weakness in the 1998 Act is the absence of any means of enforcing the Assembly's obligations under sections 47 and 64 to apply the principle of equality and for challenging its decision not to apply it in any particular case by reference to some independent arbiter such as a language commissioner. It means that the interpretation of those key provisions is entirely a matter for officials and ministers, the very people to whom the obligations apply. A similar weakness affects the making of language schemes under section 5 of the 1993 Act. There is no check. Their interpretation by ministers and officials is more likely to be influenced by resources and priorities than by other and more relevant considerations. Resources and priorities are not without relevance to the proper application of statutory obligations but they carry much less weight in law than officials and ministers are likely to attach to them if free of any legal constraints. The effectiveness of both Acts is weakened by the absence of any real independent check on the decision not to apply the principle of equality in any particular case. The point about the interpretation of the obligations being left entirely to those to whom the obligations apply was well made by the Welsh Language Board in its evidence to the Richard Commission as to its experience of dealing with Crown Bodies. Since the Welsh Language Board was subsumed into the Assembly in 2004, its regulatory role has been weakened yet further. Governments cannot be both the regulator and the regulated, hence the case for an independent language commissioner as argued by Colin Williams in chapter 15 below.

The Future

Two facts are likely to have a significant influence on the future status of the Welsh language and its role in the governance of Wales. One is that the UK government is the government of Wales. The other is that the National Assembly for Wales is but the executive arm of the UK government and is so for some only of the UK government's fields of responsibilities in Wales. Furthermore, if, as in my opinion it does, the principle of equality is as concerned with the status of the citizens of Wales as it is with the status of their two official languages, it is arguable (I put it no higher) that the status of the Welsh language should remain with the UK Parliament as a reserved matter even if the Assembly were to be given primary legislative powers in that field of responsibility. For these reasons, amongst others, the policy of the UK government towards the Welsh language is no less relevant to the future development of the status of the Welsh language and its role in the governance of Wales than are the policies of the Welsh Assembly Government. For example, the UK government is responsible for UK passports and, if they come into being, with UK identity cards and it will be for the UK government, not the Assembly government, to decide whether these will be in bilingual form or not. It is difficult to imagine two official documents which have more to do with the status of the citizen than those two documents. What this boils down to is that neither the status of the Welsh language nor its role in the governance of Wales can develop to any significant extent without legislative support from Westminster and policy support from Whitehall. Without that support, the lofty objective of the Assembly Government's Welsh language policy, *Iaith Pawb*, of creating a 'truly bilingual Wales' is not achievable. It follows, in my view, that the assumption made in the Assembly's Culture Committee's *Policy Review of the Welsh Language* that 'responsibility for the future of the language lies with the Government of Wales' can be no more than partly accurate.

The UK government's policy with regard to the status of the Welsh language and its role in the governance of Wales is that a limited class of public bodies but excluding Crown bodies shall treat it on the basis of equality in so far as it is appropriate in the circumstances to treat it as such. Those limiting words constitute a condition precedent to the application of the principle. The test of whether it is satisfied or not is a subjective one and there is no independent check on whether the limitation is being used to evade the duty to apply the principle. It is the explanation for why several Crown bodies have been reluctant to apply the principle of equality in the provision of their services to the public in Wales and it circumscribes the powers of the National Assembly to develop policies towards the use of the language in the governance of Wales. This anaemic policy was carried forward into sections 47(1) and 66(4) of the Government of Wales Act 1998, thereby setting similar limits on the obligations of the National Assembly to apply the principle of equality in the conduct of its business and in making Assembly legislation. Nothing demonstrates this more starkly than the fact that, of the many statutory instruments and other orders made by the National Assembly since 1998, it was considered inappropriate or not reasonably practicable to make more than a minority of them bilingually. This is not a criticism of the Welsh Assembly Government. On the contrary, it is a recognition that it has performed according to the powers and obligations given to it by the 1998 Act. There can be no criticism of a public body which works to the limits of its obligations. If more is to be expected of a public body than that which the creating statute requires of it, the solution is to change the limits of its powers. This is precisely the point which the Welsh Language Board made in its submissions to the Richard Commission about Crown bodies and the Concordat. It is precisely the point made by Mrs Randerson and Mr Pugh in their evidence to the Richard Commission. If more is to be required from public bodies and Crown bodies, more authority to that end is required. The position then is that the status of the Welsh language cannot be restored unless the UK government changes its policy and introduces primary legislation which carries into effect the recommendations of the Hughes Parry Report and those of the Welsh Language Board in its report of February 1991.

In May 2001, which was barely two years after the Assembly was established, I was consulted in my capacity as the Counsel General by the Assembly's Culture Committee. The question on which my opinion was sought was whether the Assembly had sufficient legislative powers to create a bilingual Wales or would need further legislative powers from Westminster. My opinion was published by the committee in its report *Our Language: Its Future*. The view I expressed was that the '1993 (and the 1998) . . .Acts were 'engines for change' and if properly used in the public sector . . . could assist in creating a bilingual society'. I used the word 'assist' simply to acknowledge the fact that the Assembly's powers of themselves were not sufficient to achieve the objective. I also advised that before I could express a more definite opinion on the question of what further legislation might be required to enable the Assembly to create a truly bilingual Wales, the potential of the 1993 and 1998 Acts should be tried and tested. I also considered it necessary to wait and see how the Assembly would interpret and apply the qualifying words in sections 47 and 66 of the 1998 Act. In the four and more years since I expressed that view, cogent evidence has been produced which demonstrates the limits of the 1993 Act and which points strongly to the need for further statutory provision if the Welsh Assembly Government is to be able to fulfil its objective of creating a truly bilingual Wales. That evidence includes the statement of the Chair of the Assembly's Culture Committee in his Forward to its report of February 2002, *Our Language: Its Future*. It includes the cogent evidence of the Welsh Language Board to the Richard Commission. It includes the evidence of successive culture ministers to the Richard Commission and it includes the developing realization in the Office of the Counsel General that the limitations on the obligations to conduct business bilingually and to make legislation bilingually are inherently limited.

For the first time in centuries, Wales has a democratically elected Assembly which transacts its business bilingually. For the first time in its history, bilingual legislation is being made in Wales and each version of that legislation is equal in its status to that of the other. The administration of justice is gradually repatriating to Wales. There are early signs that Wales is developing as a legal jurisdiction. The Welsh language is playing a much more conspicuous role in the governance of Wales. This post-devolution period is one of great challenges and opportunities. Opportunities to develop new skills such as the drafting of bilingual legislation and putting the Welsh language to a use to which it has not been put for centuries, namely, as a language of the law. It is an opportunity for the language to become relevant to the business and professional as well as the cultural needs of this modernizing nation. It is a challenge to make the case for modernizing Wales's language legislation and to restore the status of the Welsh language to one of equality with English.

Devolution was a part of a much wider process of change in the relationship between Westminster and each of the other nations of the UK, between the state and the citizen and between citizen and citizen. Other fundamental and far-reaching changes enacted at the turn of the twentieth century were the Human Rights Act 1998 by which the European Convention on Human Rights became incorporated into the domestic law of the UK; the Freedom of Information Act 2000, which aims to make government more open; the reform of the House of Lords, which aims to reduce the number of hereditary peers as members of the second chamber; and the reforms in our system of voting which have been introduced for elections to some of our democratic institutions such as the Assemblies and the European Parliament. Parliament's more liberal and tolerant attitude towards the differences which characterize each of the nations of the United Kingdom is demonstrated by the devolution statutes. Its respect for the individual is demonstrated by its introduction of the Human Rights Act, the Freedom of Information Act, the Data Protection Act and the Race Relations (Amendment) Act. Its recognition of the importance of the Welsh language in the development of post-devolution Wales is demonstrated by the three specific provisions of the Government of Wales Act 1998, to which I referred earlier, and by its signature to the European Charter for Minority Languages. Together, these constitute colossal changes to a constitution that had hardly changed in over a hundred years.

That one of Wales's official and national languages continues to have a largely permissive status is out of keeping with the spirit of these changes.

It is true that language rights can enhance the use of languages and can strengthen them but their primary purpose is to secure equality as between the citizens of the nation. This is recognized in the constitutions of Canada, Belgium, South Africa and Ireland. If there is inequality between the statuses of Wales's two official languages there is inequality of status between its citizens. In deciding not to make a declaration of the equal status of the Welsh language in the 1976 and 1993 Acts, Parliament failed to attach sufficient weight to this argument. In consequence, the 1993 Act was based on promoting the use of Welsh in the public sector through what are essentially voluntary schemes. It is based not on rights or obligations but on the ability of the Welsh Language Board to persuade the public bodies to which the Act applies to provide their services in Welsh as well as in English and upon the willingness of Crown bodies voluntarily to provide services in the Welsh language.

There is an abundance of evidence to support the conclusion that in bilingual nations where the proportion of the population that speaks one of the languages is small in comparison to the proportion that speaks the other there is a real danger of the minority language being overwhelmed. This danger is increased where inward migration is significant and enlarges the proportion of the total population that speaks the majority language. This is the position in which the Welsh language finds itself today. In those circumstances, is it possible to safeguard it and how is that to be done? The position is not peculiar to Wales and there are precedents as to how other nations sought to answer those fundamental questions. It is argued that in Wales it is unnecessary to emulate those examples for the 1993 and 1998 Acts and the Assembly Government's Welsh-language policy, *Iaith Pawb*, provide the infrastructure which will safeguard the language, enhance its use and turn Wales in due course into a '*truly bilingual*' nation in which its '*people can chose to live their lives through the medium of both Welsh and English*' (emphasis is mine). Those are the words of the Welsh-language policy itself. It is the policy's definition of the expression 'truly bilingual Wales'. Choice is an empty privilege if there is not a right to exercise it. There is no doubt that those statutes and the policy are capable of enhancing the use of the language and its role in the governance of Wales but it is doubtful whether they will be as effective in those respects and in reducing the risk of extinction as effectively as they might if they were supported by the kind of legislation recommended by the Hughes Parry Committee and the Welsh Language Board in their reports of 1961 and 1991 respectively. It is for the people of Wales to decide whether the risk is an acceptable one or not. The history and linguistic make-up of a nation provides the case for (and against) protective measures. My own view is that the lesson to be drawn from the history of Wales, its linguistic make-up and the attitude of UK government departments is that a legally declared status is an essential ally of any policy the object of which is the enhancement and the survival of the Welsh language.

If the Welsh language is to develop as a language of government, legislation and the law, it must do so as one which is equal in its legal status to that of English rather than as a language the status of which is permissive. The recent case of *Cowell v. Williams* (2000) is particularly memorable for the inspirational judgement of Lord Justice Igor Judge. Commenting on the Act of 1536, the Lord Justice said:

> In other words, Welsh people appearing in courts in Wales, litigating over problems in their own country were prohibited from using their own language . . . For hundreds of years what we now regard as elementary principles were deliberately disapplied in Wales. This prolonged suppression presumably contributed to the continuing disability of many Welsh men and women to converse fluently in the Welsh language . . . The infamous Act of 1536 is indeed being rolled back. Perhaps it may be said not yet far enough but at an ever-increasing pace. (p. 199)

That last sentence summarizes the central argument. The effects of the infamous Act of 1536 will not be finally rolled back until Parliament declares the Welsh language in Wales to be equal in its status to that of English. Until then, its role in the governance of Wales will remain permissive.

REFERENCES

Davies, J. (1990) *Hanes Cymru/A History of Wales*. London: Penguin.

Deacon, R. M. (2002) *The Governance of Wales: The Welsh Office and Policy Process 1964–99*. Cardiff: Welsh Academic Press.

Hansard HC (1993), 26 May, cols. 956, 957, 1012. London: House of Commons

Hughes Parry Report (1965) *Legal Status of the Welsh Language*. Cmd. 2785. October. Lonodn: HMSO.

O'Foghludhe v. Mc Clean (1934) IR 469 *per* Chief Justice Kennedy. London: High Court.

Richard Commission Report (2004) *Commission on the Powers and Electoral Arrangements of the National Assembly for Wales*. Cardiff: National Assembly for Wales.

Welsh Language Board. (1991) *Recommendations for a new Welsh Language Act*. February. Cardiff: Welsh Language Board.

Welsh Office (1969) *Housing standards and costs of accommodation specially designed for old people*. Circular 82/69 to Local Authorities in Wales. London: HMSO.

Welsh Office (1997) *Health Services in Wales*. Circular WHSC (15) 117.Cardiff: Welsh Office.

Welsh Office [2000] 1 WLR 187, CA .Cardiff: Welsh Office.

12
Language, Law and Governance: An Irish Perspective

LEACHLAIN S. Ó CATHÁIN

Introduction

Many users of minority languages in the European Union look to Ireland as an example of a state which has protected preserved, promoted and given full legal status to the traditional language of its country, and, further, full legal protection for the users of that traditional language. Our fellow Celtic nations, particularly, sometimes envy the apparently privileged position of the Irish-language speaker in Ireland. When these same friends of ours come to visit us, they express puzzlement that they do not hear our language spoken all around them except in some small areas of our country; that they do not often see our language written on stores, shops, banks and other institutions serving the public. They even express surprise that our public announcements at airports, railway stations and transport termini are always given in the English language, sometimes with German and French, but rarely, if ever, in our native language. They do, however, see our road signs and street signs and various other directional signs and do indeed see our language written on these signs but again they ask the question why in lower-case lettering, rather than the capital lettering used in the English-language versions. Consequently, this chapter will clarify the circumstances surrounding the legal and administrative system and the Irish language, and provide a sketch of the background from which the present situation has emerged.

The legal basis of the governance of Ireland is comprised of three elements. First, a written constitution passed by plebiscite in 1937 which can only be amended by plebiscite; secondly, Acts of law passed by the legislature subject to constitution; thirdly, decisions of the courts in the material cases affecting any question, that is, the precedent and legal principles as enunciated by the courts or 'case law' as it is called.

Article 8 of the Irish Constitution declares that:

1. The Irish language as the national language is the first official language.
2. The English language is recognised as a second official language.
3. Provision may, however, be made by law for the exclusive use of either of the said languages for any one or more official purposes, either throughout the state or in any part thereof.

The primacy of the status conferred on the Irish language in the Irish Constitution under Article 8.1 is confirmed by Article 25.4.6 where it is stated: 'In case of conflict between the texts of a law enrolled under this Section in both the official languages, the text in the national language shall prevail.' In fact, a more accurate translation of Article 8.1 is 'As the Irish language is the national language, it is the primary official language' rather than the *first* official language.

I start from this point to emphasize the fact of the legal status granted to the Irish language under the Irish Constitution and to the recognition of the Irish language as the national language, although it is in fact a language in common daily usage by a minority of the Irish population. I will return to these matters of recognition, definition and status.

The Irish language is among the oldest of European languages and was the vernacular of the whole island of Ireland for almost two thousand years. The beginnings of its oral tradition are lost in antiquity. The Irish language was dominant by the fifth century and its written literature is predated only by literature in Greek and Latin. The Irish language was still spoken by all classes of society throughout Ireland at the beginning of the sixteenth century. English-speaking groups were marginal and concentrated in urban areas and fortified towns. From the sixteenth century onwards, however, the attack on the Irish language, begun in 1366, was strengthened considerably and the English administration tightened its grip. The Irish language became deprived of the legal, political and social order, which had maintained it for centuries. New acts were passed forbidding the use of the Irish language by anyone wishing to enjoy the rights of the subjects of the king of the conquering nation. Lands were confiscated and many English-speaking settlers were attracted and given lands, with the result that, although the masses of the people throughout most of the seventeenth and eighteenth centuries still spoke the Irish language, its status was inexorably reduced to that of a peasant language without legal, administrative or political function.

Towards the end of the eighteenth century, the English language became more desirable as the language of an aspiring class, of higher education and of political and social advancement. The native Irish-speaking aristocracy had either yielded or fled the land. The first seminary founded in Ireland, Maynooth College, was founded by the English administration and went with the tide of the English language. Prior to this period, the Irish priests were fluent in European languages, in the Classics and in the Irish language. They were trained in European seminaries such as Salamanca in Spain and the Irish colleges in Paris, Rome and Louvain.

By the eighteenth century, formal education in Ireland had been reduced to what is described as 'hedge schools' run by itinerant teachers. The Irish language was forbidden in the new national schools and thus the first half of the nineteenth century witnessed a rapid decline in the language, accelerated in part by the nationalist independence movement which was promoted and promulgated through English. Then, of course, the great Famine of the 1840s decimated the Irish population, reducing it through death and emigration from eight million to about four million. It was from the Irish-speaking districts that the greatest emigration occurred then and continued in the subsequent decades. By the census of 1891 only 0.08 per cent of the Irish population were monolingual Irish-language speakers. The census of Ireland of that year also revealed that approximately 14.5 per cent were able to speak both Irish and English but that for the first time in over a thousand years fully 85.5 per cent of the Irish population were unable to speak Irish. Ireland was colonized and its ancient language associated only with peasantry and poverty. In 1893, a language revival movement, self-styled in English as the Gaelic League, was started and from this grew the revolutionary movement culminating in the Irish Free State in 1922. Although the Irish language was in daily usage by probably less than 15 per cent of the population when the new state was born in 1922, the founding fathers of the state, many of whom had learnt the Irish language as adults, realized its importance to the new nation.

Revival of the Irish Language

With the foundation of Saorstát Eireann or The Irish Free State in 1922, the Irish language acquired an official status as the national language for the first time (Constitution Act, 1922). This first constitution was not passed by plebiscite but by an Irish free parliament resulting from the signing of a treaty with Great Britain in 1922. Article 4 states as follows: 'The National Language of the Irish Free Sate (Saorstát Eireann) is the Irish Language, but the English Language shall be equally recognised as an official language.'

The idea of revival of the Irish language had been a central concept in the evolution of the new nationalism and in a sense its proclamation as the official language of the new state marked the final act of national freedom. This legal status was granted to the Irish language despite the fact that the actual preponderance of the English language throughout the country compelled the acceptance of English as a second official language.

The policy of the restoration of the Irish language was adopted in its totality. In the legislative and administrative area, provision was made for all official documentation to be produced in both the Irish language and the English language and a translation department was set up to be of service to the houses of government and to assist the government departments. Translation Staff is now under the Commission for Provision of Services to the Houses of the Oireachtas and not under any government department.

Arrangements were put in place that the Irish language would be an essential subject for any position in the civil service and proficiency in spoken Irish was required as well as a written examination. Arrangements were also made for the introduction of the use of the Irish language into the army, the police force and the law courts. A nationwide programme was introduced within the school's system and also for adults, with much emphasis being placed on the training of teachers. However, when speaking of a legislative framework, it is now necessary to make a distinction. Very many of these efforts to promote the Irish language in the first fifteen years of self-government were by way of implementation of government policy in the ordinary day-to-day running of the country, by way of internal administrative regulation and/or departmental directive and not by act of law and were accepted by a substantial majority of the population. Possibly, because of this almost universal acceptance of the policies of the day, it was not seen to be necessary that the implementation of many of these policies should have been supported by legislative action or Acts of the Parliament of the country. This was a time of new nationalistic fervour and enthusiasm and it was probably not foreseen that this atmosphere could and would change. In fact, in many ways, the revival of the Irish language was left under the auspices of the new Department of Education and its training programmes.

There was no official languages act in Ireland until 2003. Besides the statement of the relevant status of the English language as a second official language, there was no reference to a right to use the English language other than an occasional reference to the fact that either language might be used in legal notices to comply with the requirements of a particular act or where descriptions in either language were involved such as, how a judge should be addressed or a minister of government or his department described. Similarly the naming of state and semi-state agencies was generally bilingual although the emphasis in recent years has passed from the Irish language to the English language in primacy of usage.

Out of the many hundreds of Acts enacted by the Irish Parliament since 1922, there are few enough that make specific reference to the Irish language. In terms of the operation of law, those enacted in the earlier years of the state were of more importance, up until very recently, when speaking of a legislative and administrative framework. A number of acts passed in 1924, gave some legislative standing to the Irish language. A directive was issued directing all second level schools to teach two languages including English or Irish in that year also. Irish was included for the first time. Many schools taught only English and Irish. Ten years later, by 1934, it was a Department of Education requirement, but not an act of law, that the Irish language should become an essential examination subject. Failure to achieve a certificate in the Irish language nullified the whole examination. This caused much genuine distress in later years and was removed in the 1970s.

In 1924 a Police Act was passed, requiring that policemen stationed in areas where the Irish language was the normal language of the people were 'insofar as they were capable', obliged to use the Irish language in the fulfilment of their duties (Garda Siochana Act 1924). An Act was passed with regard to the Local Courts in 1924 which placed a similar obligation, again, only in so far as it was possible under all the circumstances, that the local judge should be fluent in the use of the Irish language (Courts of Justice Act 1924). Also in 1924, a Railways Act made provision for the commencement of the replacement of railway station names, tickets etc. to include the Irish language (Railways Act 1924).

In 1929 two pieces of legislation were passed which made reference to the Irish language. The University College Galway Act 1929 created a duty to make appointments to the staff of the university of people competent to discharge their duties through the medium of the Irish language 'provided a person so competent be also suitable in all other respects' could be found (University College Galway Act 1929). This clause is often misconstrued as being an obligation on the governing body of the university to provide courses through

Irish. This was the intention of the legislators but again in its final form, as with the Police Act and the Courts Act, it did not impose any absolute obligation. The Vocational Education Act 1930 made special provisions for vocational education in the Irish-speaking areas dependent on the view of the relevant minister. The University College Dublin Act 1934 made provision for a special grant to University College Dublin for the specific purposes of the Modern Irish Language and Literature Department.

The Irish Language and the Legal System

The next two Acts of importance that make reference to the Irish language are the Legal Practitioners (Qualification) Act 1929 and The Insurance Act 1936 (still in force) which made a simple and absolute statement. This is that whenever a proposal for a policy of insurance is filled in wholly in the Irish language, every policy of insurance or other document issued in relation to that policy of insurance shall, if the proposer so requires, be issued in the Irish language. Peculiarly, this is the only instance in the whole corpus of Irish enactments where an absolute obligation is placed on a commercial institution to provide a service through the Irish language for the citizen of the state.

The Legal Practitioners (Qualification) Act 1929 saw the introduction of an obligation on lawyers in the country to be competent to conduct their affairs through the Irish language and was generally opposed by both branches of the legal profession. The Act *inter alia* provides that all barristers and solicitors shall be sufficiently fluent in the Irish language to conduct all aspects of their affairs on behalf of the citizens of the state through that language. This was a fine protection for the users of the minority language in all their legal dealings with the legislative functions of the state.

Prior to the passing of this Act, however, there was much political activity and serious opposition by many members of the judiciary, the barristers and particularly by the solicitors. There was opposition also among senior civil servants to the proposed law. This was the first major clash between the linguistic policy as enunciated by the new state and the operators of the administrative and legal systems within the country. Such tensions remain a basic problem to this day within the legislative and administrative systems in Ireland with regard to the use of the lesser-used language.

The Irish legal system, inherited from Great Britain, forms part of the common law system comprised of two branches of the legal profession, solicitors or attorneys at law, who deal with the individual citizen and conduct affairs on his or her behalf and the barrister at law who is employed in the courts as an advocate on behalf of the citizen.

This distinction is relevant to the issue in hand. When the barristers realized that the government of the new state as proceeding to bring in the new law in spite of the opposition, the Bar Council agreed to the proposed Irish-language requirement, with the modification that they themselves would introduce an Irish-language learning course to suit the requirements of court advocacy and that the competency of each candidate would be determined by an interview with the Chief Justice of the country on an annual basis. This is possibly one of the first examples of what we now jocosely call an Irish solution to an Irish problem. In fact, the majority of the barristers of Ireland were and are unable to conduct legal cases through the medium of the first legal official language. Equally, few of the judges were or are sufficiently competent in the Irish language fully to hear and comprehend a complicated legal case through the Irish language. The implementation of this particular Act was never seriously pursued and within the civil service itself the administration of all court documentation etc. continued, together with daily practice, through the English language.

Solicitors, who numbered some hundreds throughout the country, were in the majority opposed to the new legislation and the council of their organization resisted all overtures in favour of the use of Irish. Government reacted by creating an examination system for all solicitors to be monitored by the Department of Education. In the initial years this examination was of a relatively high standard and those solicitors who qualified did acquire a limited competency in the use of the Irish language. Unfortunately, a great antipathy to the

Irish language was also caused by this compulsion on the student of law. Solicitors and barristers of this period, although Irish born, were mainly part of the established relatively colonized and comfortable class that would not have been in total sympathy with the ideals and aims of the language revival movement.

The failure of the 1929 Act or rather its circumvention by barristers, solicitors and civil servants, was a major blow to the language revival movement as the legal administrative system and the courts never became available to the Irish-speaking Irish citizen as a practical reality.

The legislators were totally *bona fide* in their aspiration and in their intent. But the colonial civil service was almost totally re-employed and although many genuine attempts were made, with some success, the language, manner and systems of administration remained that of the colonizer. Similar genuine attempts with limited success to use Irish in the Parliament and daily administration of affairs were never completely implemented. No legislation was ever enacted in the same terms as the Legal Practitioners (Qualification) Act 1929 to impose an obligation on civil servants or parliamentarians to be sufficiently fluent in the Irish language to conduct their daily affairs through that language.

However, fluency and knowledge of the Irish language was an essential requirement within the civil service, strictly implemented as policy, and applied through an internal examination system. Up to the 1960s this policy did indeed produce a substantial number of civil servants who were articulate and fluent in Irish and competent to administer the system on a daily basis through the Irish language. In very many cases however, the ministers of government in charge of the various departments were unable to communicate with their senior civil servants through the medium of the Irish language. Through lack of use, lack of government support and lack of political will, many of these estimable idealistic people became disillusioned. An official policy of bilingualism emerged in the 1960s and the early 1970s. The Irish-language requirement for an Irish Civil Servant was removed, again by internal governmental regulation and not by Act of Parliament which would, of course, have been a more difficult and more public process. Had the will and intent of the legislators been put into effect, as intended by the Legal Practitioners Act, the effect on the subsequent revival of the Irish language in Ireland would have been profound and widespread.

The next reference to a specific obligation to use the Irish language by law was in the Transport Acts of 1944 and 1950, which state that all permanent public notices and signs maintained by the national transport system must be in the Irish language and may be in the English language also. This clause was included at the insistence of a minister of government and can be seen as the last legislative expression of the ideal of a fully Irish-speaking state. In 1945 it was felt necessary to introduce a Legal Terms Act. This Act set up a committee to determine legal terminology specifically. No such act exists in the English language and in most jurisdictions legal terminology evolves through the enactments as they are enacted and not by specific order. This Act in itself was an indication of the non-use of the Irish language in the legal and administrative operation of the state.

Other legislation which makes reference to Irish includes the Defence Act of 1954 where provision is made for the learning and use of the Irish language in the giving of orders and directions in the defence forces. The Solicitors Act of 1954 provided another Irish solution to an Irish problem in that the obligations of the Legal Practitioners Act 1929 were repeated but the monitoring of the Act and the setting of standards was left to the Council of the Incorporated Law Society of Ireland. The net result of this change has been that the standards of the statutory examinations have fallen abysmally low and could not in any way be deemed to be sufficient to fulfil the requirements of the Act, thus bringing the Irish language and the law itself into disrepute.

In 1956, a special Act was passed, setting up a ministry of government to take responsibility for the remaining Irish-speaking areas. Its purpose was 'to promote the cultural, social and economic welfare of these areas, to encourage the preservation and extension of the use of Irish as a vernacular language and to such extent as may be necessary or appropriate to consult and advise with other departments of state' in respective services, etc. (the Ministers and Secretaries

(Amendment) Act 1956). This department of government still survives today, generally as a minor part of another ministry but with a small staff and a small budget.

The Higher Education Authority Act 1971 imposed a general obligation on the Higher Education Authority to keep in mind the national aims of the revival of the Irish language and the development of Irish culture and heritage. A glance at signposting in Ireland reveals that virtually all of the English-language versions of place-names are meaningless gibberish comprised of mistranslations and anglicizations of the original place-names. These versions were first recorded in the British Ordinance Survey of the nineteenth century (An Comisiún Logainmneacha, 1992) . In 1946 the Placenames Commission was established by the Minister for Finance to advise on the investigation of the place-names of Ireland and to conduct research in order to determine the correct original Irish forms of these names insofar as they could be established and to prepare lists in their Irish forms for publication and official use (An Comisiún Logainmneacha, 1992 and website www.logainm.ie).

A number of Broadcasting Acts have been introduced with regard to radio and television broadcasting but the extent of the linguistic obligation stated extends merely to 'have special regard for the elements which distinguish that culture and in particular for the Irish language' (Broadcasting (Amendment) Act 1976).

Possibly the most important Act that was passed prior to the Official Languages Act (2003), was An tAcht Um Bord na Gaeilge, (1978), which translates as the Board of the Irish Language Act 1978. This Act, which was up to then the only Act passed by the Parliament solely in the Irish language, established a state board to foster and promote the Irish language. Despite underfunding, lack of staffing and general governmental apathy, this state board has, through its support of all the voluntary institutions, its leadership in the formulation of plans, policies, publications, the conducting of surveys and the modernization of approaches and techniques, done very much to undo the reverses since the 1960s and 1970s. An authority for the Irish-speaking areas was set up in 1979 (An tAcht um Udarás na Gaeltachta 1979) primarily for the industrial development of the areas. However, there is an obligation under this Act to preserve and promote the Irish language as the principal means of communication within these areas and to ensure that the Irish language is to be used as much as possible in the operation of its affairs.

For the past quarter of a century or so for a confluence of reasons there is an increased awareness of the precarious plight of Irish. Possibly as a result of the removal of the requirements on state employees and on the school examination system, the Irish language was not seen as a threat any more and as a consequence antipathy has lessened considerably. Simultaneously, civil rights and language rights have come to the fore in Ireland as in other jurisdictions and the consequent demands were raised. It became apparent that virtually the whole machinery of civil service had converted to the second official language and was de facto unable to deal with the Irish-speaking members of the public at any level of proficiency when its senior members retired. This created a situation where citizens resorted to the High Court to have their constitutional rights vindicated and clarified. These cases were mainly fought on the basis of equality of citizenship and choice of official language. As a result it has been determined by the courts that an Irish citizen has full right to choose the Irish language when appearing before any court or tribunal or official investigation in the country. An interpreter must be provided by the court or tribunal if necessary. Similarly, with regard to the furnishing of official documentation, it has been established that all such documentation must be made available to the public in the Irish language at the citizen's choice and be of an equal standard of quality and design. (Ó Tuathail, 2002). The constitutional right of the citizen to choose the language of his/her choice in all official dealings with the state is now accepted, albeit reluctantly, as a result of these decisions. Although widespread at one stage throughout the education system, the use of Irish was never underpinned by statute and regulation of schools, it was done by departmental circular or ministerial directive. There are references in the Foundation Acts of the University of Limerick, the Dublin Institute of Technology (Dublin Institute of Technology Act 1992) and the Regional

Technical Colleges Act (1992), to the governance of the institutions having due regard to the preservation, promotion and use of the Irish language and to the preservation and development of the national culture with specific reference to the teaching of the Irish language in the case of the University of Limerick (University of Limerick Act 1989; University Of Limerick (Dissolution Of Thomond College) Act 1991; Universities Act 1997).

However, it was not until 1998 that an Education Act of substance was enacted. This delay was primarily due to the Church's dominance of the education system within the state. However, in the Education Act of 1998 there were a number of interesting and positive provisions in relation to the Irish language. The Act established a National Council for Curriculum and Assessment and also has provision for the establishment of a Council for Irish Medium Education. The Act provides for greater partnership and involvement of parents.

There has been a change of emphasis in some recent legislation with provision being made for services through the Irish language by various bodies rather than a blanket requirement of knowledge of the language on all employees. This can be seen in the Heritage Act (1995), National Cultural Institutions Act (1997) and the Universities Act 1997. The Court ServiceAct (1998) effectively repeated the requirements laid down by the superior courts and all court services must now be available in both languages at the choice of the citizen.

Official Languages Act

There had long been a demand for an Official Languages Act in Ireland with many references being made to Canada and Wales and the success of the legislation in those jurisdictions. In March 2000 the then responsible minister sought permission to prepare an Official Languages Equality Bill which inter alia would:

1. Specify the language rights of the citizen;

2. Specify the obligations of departments of state;
3. Place statutory obligation on departments of state to deliver 'An Agreed Quantum' of services through the medium of Irish;
4. Assign general responsibility to the minister to enforce the Act and to establish an Official Languages Commissioner.

An Official Languages (Equality) Bill 2002 was initiated. While this purported to confer equal rights on the citizens in respect of both official languages it fell substantially short of that ideal. The Bill was generally welcomed by language promotion groups but many were critical of the fact that the Bill was not rights based and in fact, if anything, proposed to modify some of the existing rights of the Irish-Language speakers. However, when the Bill was presented for an enactment it had a different title, Official Languages Bill, and a number of modifications were made. The Act was passed in the summer of 2003 by a unanimous vote of Parliament without too much debate and presumably on the basis that it was deemed to be worthy. This Official Languages Act is an amalgam of the Canadian and Welsh approach discussed elswhere in this volume. The appointment of the Commissioner is made by the President on the advice of the government following a resolution passed by Dáil Eireann and by Seanad Eireann recommending the appointment of the person. The thrust of the Act is towards the Welsh model, that is, the use of agreed schemes for promotion rather than the conferring of language rights or the recognition of constitutional rights. However, with a committed minister, the Act is of great benefit as are schemes. A regrettable feature is that there are no real sanctions for failure to comply with the provisions of the Act other than citation in Parliament, although the minister has powers to bring in sanctions in the course of the implementation of the Act. The Act has been implemented and despite some unworthy criticism as to cost, it has generally been accepted.

An interesting provision was introduced into the Planning and Development Act 2000 which includes a section stating that a development plan shall include objectives for inter alia the protection of the linguistic and cultural heritage of the

Gaeltacht, including the promotion of Irish as the community language where there is a Gaeltacht (Irish-speaking) area in the area of the development plan. Judicial review proceedings were brought against the Galway County Council by Áine Ní Chonaighle and others (5 July 2002). The High Court decision was that the Planning Authority failed in their duty in that a language impact study had not been carried out. There are a number of housing developments in Irish-speaking areas in dispute at present specifically on this question of what is in effect rapid urbanization in a language-contact situation. Apropos these Irish-speaking areas, the responsible minister has, by way of statutory instrument pursuant to the Official Languages Act, declared that only the Irish-language versions of the place-names in these areas may have legal status (Placenames (Ceantair Gaeltachta) Order 2004).

At the time of Ireland's accession to the then European Economic Community in 1972, a golden opportunity was missed by our statesmen to enhance the status and use of the Irish language. The offer of full official language status was not taken up by our government of the day. The government decision at the time was probably *ultra vires*, in the context of the Irish Constitution but was unwittingly validated by the people in the plebiscite because of the general wording of the text voted on. It has, however, some official status accorded to it and is one of the languages that can be used in the proceedings of the Court of Justice. In practice, it has never been invoked as a language in the court by the Irish government in any case.

As a result of a very well-organized public debate and well orchestrated public demand, the Irish government has successfully applied for full working status for the Irish language within the European Union (EU) some thirty-three years after this was first on offer. But there may be more difficulty now than heretofore in using Irish within the EU as a result of enlargement and the linguistic implications thereof.

Uniquely possibly in western Europe, the majority of Irish-language speakers, to a greater or lesser degree, have acquired it as a second language and are not mother-tongue speakers. In the 2002 census, 1,570,894 persons identified themselves as able to speak Irish. However, that the revival and survival of the Irish language was left largely in the hands of the Department of Education is reflected in the fact that the highest level ability figure in Irish is in the 10–19-year-old age group, which stands as 67.5 per cent. There is a decline in this ability level to approximately 38 per cent at the age of 45, 34 per cent at the age of 60 and 31.2 per cent at the age of 65 and over. Interestingly, the census shows substantial levels of Irish knowledge in the urban, eastern and southern areas. Some 340,000 persons claimed that they spoke Irish on a daily basis. Again, probably about 50 per cent of this number would be mother-tongue speakers, mainly along the west coast, yet significantly more children are being reared with Irish as a mother tongue outside of the Irish-speaking areas.

Another indicator is the very encouraging growth in Irish-medium education, particularly at primary school level. From eleven primary schools and five post-primary schools in 1972, there are now approximately one hundred and thirty nine primary level schools and approximately thirty-nine post-primary level schools. Additional provision exists within the 143 primary schools and twenty largely Irish-medium schools in the Gaeltacht. While within Northern Ireland there are thirty-two primary and three post-primary Irish-medium schools.

This growth has come from local demand and voluntary local committees, which would not have been actively encouraged, although official policy is in place in respect of extra grants for Irish-language-medium schools. A further difficulty remains the inability of many teachers to teach through the medium of Irish. The low standards demanded at examination level are no longer sufficient to provide any but the better pupils with anything more than a rudimentary knowledge of the language.

Another indicator is the impact of TG4, a primarily Irish-language television service which, although underfunded, has succeeded in producing nineteen hours of television per day, seven days a week, averaging six hours a day of Irish-language programmes. Television Audience Measurement (TAM) ratings show that over 700,000 people watch this channel daily. This station receives approximately

€20–25 m a year from the government for producing Irish-language programming. It also receives 365 hours, that is, one hour a day, of programming from Radio Teilifis Eireann (RTE), the main station, free of charge, which costs RTE something in the order of €6–8 m. Its advertising and other revenue bring in somewhat less than €2m. A comparison is the Welsh-language channel, S4C, which receives abut £100m a year from the British government, together with 550 hours of programming a year from the BBC free of charge, together with the pick of the full Channel 4 schedule, also free of charge. A further comparison is a total of some £5m spent in a combination of free hours and direct programming for Gallic-language speakers in Scotland. Were it not for the personal dedication of one minister in a previous administration, it is likely that this Irish-language television station might still be awaited.

With government aid from Bord na Leabhar Gaeilge, the Irish Language Books Board, approximately one hundred and fifty books are published each year in the Irish language, covering all aspects of Irish life. These are produced by private enterprise publishers, although much good work has also been done by the government publication agency, An Gúm. Again, were it not for the existence of the grant aid available through the Books Board Scheme, these private publishers would not survive.

Since the Official Languages Act 2003, ministerial directives have been issued to the public service with regard to correspondence etc., to comply with the requirements of the citizen's right to choose the language of communication. The Commissioner for Languages has made a significant impact and both these reforms have resulted in creating a positive environment where recognition of language choice within the public service and acceptance of citizens' rights have overturned the previous thirty-year habit of neglect.

The Belfast Good Friday Agreement of 10 April 1998, the highpoint of the Anglo-Irish peace process in respect of Northern Ireland, specifically states that all participants recognize the importance of respect, understanding and tolerance in relation to linguistic diversity. In Northern Ireland this includes the Irish language, the Ulster Scots and the languages of the various ethnic communities, all of which are part of the cultural wealth of the island of Ireland. The agreement provided for north–south implementation bodies, jointly appointed by both governments, for the implementation of common policy on joint issues. One body dealing with language, has two sections: Foras na Gaeilgc, which deals with the Irish language, and Tha Boord O Ulster-Scotch. The Irish-language body has an obligation to promote the Irish language in speech and writing, in public and in private in the south, and in the context of Part III of the European Charter for regional or minority languages in Northern Ireland, where there is appropriate demand; advising both administrations, public bodies and other groups in the private and voluntary sectors; supporting and grant-aiding bodies and groups; research, promotional campaigns etc.; developing terminology; supporting Irish-medium education and the teaching of Irish. With regard to Ulster-Scots, the aim is the promotion of greater awareness and use of Ulster-Scots cultural issues both within Northern Ireland and throughout the island (Ó Catháin, 2003).

The British Irish Agreement Act 1999 pursuant to the Good Friday Agreement of 10 of April 1998 was passed into law on 22 of March 1999. Among the new bodies created was the North/South Language Body. The Bord na Gaeilge Act of 1978 was revoked and all the functions were taken over by the Irish Language Section of the new body. Additional functions were transferred from other departments such as the Department of Education, in, for example, the publication of Irish textbooks, dictionaries, developing terminology etc. There is also an obligation to support the use of the Irish language in the context of Part III of the European Charter for regional or minority languages in Northern Ireland where there is appropriate demand.

Conclusion

Since the foundation of the Irish state, the Irish-language obligations on the public service have been bedevilled by what I describe as the 'comh fada agus is féidir' syndrome.

This, depending on the Act that is read, will read, 'insofar as is practicable', 'insofar as is conveniently possible', 'circumstances permitting' and so forth. This provision has invariably provided an escape route for the official, even in the totally Irish-speaking areas. Minor bureaucrats have invariably implemented their own policy of linguistic convenience at every opportunity, such as indexing names in the English language, initials etc. Many administrative demands are made by the citizens on the state with regard to services through Irish and it is now generally accepted as a matter of public policy that these demands should be met, if all too frequently with some ill will, if not bad manners.

The assumptions of the Irish-speaker with regard to the legislative framework have changed totally. From an assumption that all services would be provided and promoted by the administrative and legal system of the state in the early years, the recent position has been that the Irish-language speakers were resorting to the courts to assert equal rights, at least, with the English-speaking citizen. This course of action is now largely redundant with the introduction of the Official Languages Act 2003. However, time may expose limitations which may have to be resolved in the courts.

As in each individual experience, there are lessons to be learnt from the experience of the Irish people in their attempts to preserve and maintain their native language. Our experience has not been all positive, but much has been achieved both at home in Ireland and in our international support, both official and unofficial, on all occasions, for other lesser-used languages.

It is clear that there has always been recognition of the constitutional status of the Irish language, albeit somewhat reluctant in the general area of governance and administration. However, it has always been tacitly accepted that the Irish language is an actual part of the national identity and this has been reflected, not always with sufficient vigour, in the various enactments. This sociolinguistic problem remains and doubtless with an increasingly multicultural population further problems will develop. However, I look forward to a time when, even without the necessity for a more comprehensive Official Language Act, an atmosphere will prevail that will enable what is, de facto, the minority language to prosper in all official areas of life and will, as set out in the Constitution, enable the citizen at the citizen's choice, to choose his/her language when dealing with officialdom at any and all levels.

REFERENCES

Acht na dTeangacha Oifigiúla, (2003) Acht na dTeangacha Oifigiúla – Official Languages Act, 2003 Dublin : Dáil Eireann.

An Comisiún Logainmneacha (1992) The Placenames of Ireland in the Third Millenium, 1st edn, Dublin: An Comisiún Logainmneacha.

An tAcht um Bord na Gaeilge, (1978) An tAcht Um Bord na Gaeilge, 1978, (now repealed). Dublin: Dáil Eireann.

An tAcht um Udarás na Gaeltachta, (1979) S. 8 An tAcht um Udarás na Gaeltachta 1979, Dublin : Dáil Eireann.

British Irish Agreement Act, (1999) Part VI British Irish Agreement Act, 1999, Dublin: Dáil Eireann.

Broadcasting (Amendment) Act, (1976) Broadcasting (Amendment) Act, (1976) Dublin: Dáil Eireann.

Constitution Act (1922) Constitution Act of the Irish Free State (Saorstát Eireann) Act 1922 Dublin:Dáíl Eireann .

Courts of Justice Act, (1924) Ss. 10, 44, 71, 88 Courts of Justice Act, 1924, Dublin: Dáil Eireann.

Courts Services Act, (1998) S. 7(2(d)) The Court Service Act, 1998, Dublin: Dáil Eireann.

Defence Act, (1954) S. 28(2) Defence Act 1954, Dublin : Dáil Eireann.

Dublin Institute of Technology Act, (1992) S. 7(4) Dublin Institute of Technology Act 1992 Dublin : Dáil Eireann.

Education Act, (1998) The Education Act, 1998, Dublin: Dáil Eireann.

Garda Síochána Act (1924) S. 6(2) Garda Siochana Act 1924, Dublin: Dáil Eireann.

Heritage Act, (1995) Ss. 18(1) and 22(1) Heritage Act, 1995, Dublin : Dáil Eireann.

Higher Education Authority Act, (1971) An tAcht um Udarás um Ard-Oideachas S. 4 The Higher Education Act, 1971, Dublin : Dáil Eireann.

Insurance Act (1936) S. 108 The Insurance Act, 1936, Dublin: Dáil Eireann.

Irish Language Commissioner (2004) Inaugural Report of Language Commissioner 2004, Dublin: Office of Irish Language Commissioner.

Irish Legal Terms Act, (1945) Irish Legal Terms Act, 1945, Dublin: Dáil Eireann.

Legal Practitioners (Qualification) Act, (1929) S. 3 The Legal Practitioners (Qualification) Act, 1929, Dublin: Dáil Eireann.

Ministers and Secretaries (Amendment) Act, (1956) Ministers & Secretaries (Amendment) Act 1956, Dublin : Dáil Eireann.
Ó Catháin, L. (2003) Róil agus Freagrachta Fhoras na Gaeilge agus na hÁisíneachta um Albainnis Uladh faoi Chomhaontú Bhéal Feirste, in D. O. Riagain, (ed.), 'Language and Law in Northern Ireland' Belfast: Belfast Studies in Language, Culture and Politics, 9
Ó Tuathail, S. (2002) Gaeilge agus Bunreacht Dublin:Coiscéim
Placenames (Ceantair Gaeltachta) Order (2004) SI 872 of 2004 The Placenames (Ceantair Ghaeltachta) Order 2004 Dublin: Dáil Eireann
Planning and Development Act, (2000) Planning and Development Act, 2000, Dublin: Dáil Eireann.
Railways Act, (1924) S. 68 Railways Act, 1924, Dublin: Dáil Eireann.
Regional Technical Colleges Act, (1992) S. 7(4) Regional Technical Colleges Act 1992; Dublin : Dáil Eireann.
Solicitors Act, (1954) S. *40(3), 88(1) The Solicitors Act 1954*, Dublin: Dáil Eireann.
Transport Act (1944) S. 60 Transport Act, 1944, Dublin: Dáil Eireann
Transport Act (1950) S. 57 Transport Act, 1950, Dublin: Dáil Eireann.
Universities Act, (1997) Universities *Act, 1997,* Dublin: Dáil Eireann.
University College Dublin Act (1934) S. 1(2) The University College Dublin Act, 1934, Dublin: Dáil Eireann
University College Galway Act, (1929) S. 3 University College Galway Act, 1929, Dublin: Dáil Eireann.
University of Limerick Act, (1991) University of Limerick (Dissolution of Thomond College) Act, (1991) Dublin: Dáil Eireann.
Unreported; 5 July 2002 before Ó Caoimh See also 'Pleanáil sa Gaeltacht' Eoin Ó hIci, FEASTA (Volume 58 No. 2 ISSSN 0014–8946)
Vocational Education Act (1930) S. 103 The Vocational Education Act, 1930, Dublin: Dáil Eireann.

Part III

Assessing Policies and Programmes

13

The Canadian Heritage Approach to the Promotion of Official Languages

NORMAN MOYER

Introduction and Background

This chapter provides a background to the official-languages developmental and promotional programmes of the Department of Canadian Heritage and describes the evolution of these programmes. It outlines the approach that Canadian Heritage and its predecessor (the Department of the Secretary of State of Canada) have utilized over the years in the effort to meet its official-languages objectives. The evidence draws on the annual reports submitted to the Parliament by the Secretary of State (Canadian Heritage) as required from 1988–9 onwards (Canadian Heritage. and Canada. Department of the Secretary of State, www.pch.gc.ca).

After a brief discussion of the historical antecedents to the formalization of an official-languages promotional role for the department, the chapter will discuss two key periods of its evolution. Phase I, which covers the period between the first Official Languages Act in 1969 and the adoption of the revised Official Languages Act in 1988, can be described as the beginning of an activist model for government.

The second period, from 1988 to the present, is marked by a widening of the scope and the formal solicitation of a broader range of partners, both within the federal government through the interdepartmental coordination role and extending outward to encompass provincial/territorial governments as well as other sectors of society. This period is also marked by fiscal and administrative challenges for the

Government of Canada, which necessarily had an impact on the department's programmes.

Historical, Geographical and Demographic Dimensions of Official Languages in Canada

The linguistic landscape in Canada has been deeply influenced by the interplay between its history, geography and demography. Since Canada became a nation in 1867, it has evolved from a situation of relative duality in which the vast majority of Canadians (91.6 per cent) had ethnic roots in the British Isles or France. There was also a fairly clear-cut duality in language and religion as the vast majority of those from France were French-speaking Catholics and most of those from the British Isles were English-speaking and Protestant. This analysis by the Department of Canadian Heritage, based on data from *Census of Canada, 1971*, vol. I, part 3, table 1 (Catalogue 92–723. Statistics Canada, 2003) also notes the presence of considerable numbers of Irish Catholic immigrants which added an element of religious diversity to this mix. Of the 'other Europeans' mentioned in Table 13.1, the vast majority (nearly 85 per cent) were of German descent.

Table 13.1: Ethnic origins of Canadians at Confederation, 1867

Ethnic Origin	No.	%
British	2,110,502	60.5
French	1,082,940	31.1
Other European	239,873	6.9
Aboriginal	23,037	0.7
Other	29,409	0.8
Total	3,485,761	100.0

The notion of two founding peoples and linguistic duality in ethnic terms has expanded to include a national identity based on respect for the aboriginal peoples and for the growing importance of the contribution of Canadians from diverse ethnic roots and religious backgrounds. The increase in diversity in its population is an increasingly important dimension to Canada as the proportion of foreign-born in 2001 (5.4 million Canadians or 18.4 per cent of the population) was the highest in seventy years. The proportion of visible minorities has nearly tripled in twenty years and close to four million Canadians are counted in that segment of the population, up from 1.1 million in 1981 (Statistics Canada, 2002).

Nonetheless, the vast majority (98.5 per cent) of Canadians speak English or French. To date, it is generally true that within two to three generations most immigrants adopt English or French as their regular language at home. With the rise in immigration and the overwhelming concentration of new immigrants in a few major urban centres (Toronto, Vancouver and Montreal), it will be interesting to see whether this pattern changes. For the present, substantially more Canadians reported one of the official languages as their mother tongue than all other mother tongues combined. In 2001, English (59.7 per cent) and French (23.2 per cent) were each more common responses than all other languages (18.5 per cent).

The distinguishing characteristic of Quebec's circumstance as the only province whose majority is francophone remains a fact, and a factor, in Canadian public life. Using the mother-tongue definition, with multiple responses distributed equally, francophones comprise 81.4 per cent of the population of Quebec. The presence of official-language minority communities across the country, intermingled with their majority-language counterparts, creates a complexity that mitigates against the reductive logic of a purely territorial approach to language policy.

Canada has more language questions on its national census than any country in the world. As of 2001, there are four census questions dealing with mother tongue, home language, knowledge of official languages and language of work. A fifth linguistic concept 'first official language spoken' is derived from census respondent's answers to the questions on knowledge of official languages, mother tongue and home language. Given that English and French are recognized as official languages under the constitution and legislation of Canada and that the legal rights are constructed to protect the interests of the 'minority', it follows that speakers of English in Quebec and speakers of French outside Quebec are considered to be members of Canada's official-language minority communities. The definition is not an ethnic one but rather based on language use, which is not static across generations.

From the beginning our linguistic diversity was a defining feature of the new country, as Georges-Étienne Cartier stated in the confederation debates, 'British and French Canadians alike can appreciate and understand their position relative to each other . . .It is a benefit rather than otherwise to have a diversity of races.' Cartier realized that the agreement on which confederation was based would need to be adjusted from time to time, but hoped that these changes would remain faithful to the original spirit of Confederation. He noted: 'I hope that if (this grand project of Confederation) must be amended . . . it will not be to narrow the principles of fairness on which it is founded, but rather to enlarge them even more.'

In 1867, when four founding provinces (Upper Canada, Lower Canada, New Brunswick and Nova Scotia) came together to found Canada, it was already evident that the religious, linguistic and ethnic diversity as well as the substantial distances between these colonies made a centrist, unitary state an unworkable concept. Accordingly, Canada was created on a federal model, with a division of powers and responsibilities between the federal, central government and the provincial governments. This pattern continued with the later addition of six provinces and three territories. Jurisdiction is shared between the two levels of government.

Demographic Distribution

In 2001, nearly two million (1,906,610) Canadians lived as members of official-language minority communities. As Figures 13.1 and 13.2 illustrate, the actual size and relative weight of official-language minority communities (OLMC) vary substantially from jurisdiction to jurisdiction. On a provincial/territorial basis, there are three large official-language minority communities (New Brunswick, Quebec and Ontario), each with over 200,000 OLMC citizens. There are a number of other jurisdictions for which the OLMC could be described as medium in size with 35,000 to 60,000 members. This group would include Nova Scotia, Manitoba, Alberta and British Columbia. A third group in terms of size would include those jurisdictions with fewer than 20,000 OLMC members (Newfoundland and Labrador, Prince Edward Island, Saskatchewan and the three territories: Yukon, Northwest Territories and Nunavut).

This portrait changes somewhat when we consider the issue of relative weight or proportion of the official-language minority communities within the general population. By this measure, New Brunswick Acadian/francophones are in a class of their own, forming one-third of the provincial population. Only Quebec anglophones join New Brunswick francophones as OLMCs above the national share of 5.3 per cent, although francophones in Prince Edward Island, Nova Scotia, Ontario, Manitoba, at 4 per cent or above, are close to the national average.

As Figure 13.3 reveals, the nearly two million Canadians who live as official-language minority community members are widely distributed across the landmass of Canada.

Milestones in the Recognition of Canada's Two Official Languages

Confederation, 1867

The British North America Act 1867 provided for the use of either English or French in the debates of Parliament and the legislature of Quebec and required the use of both languages in the statutes, records and journals of those houses. The Act also guaranteed the right of any person to use English or French in all federal and Quebec courts. The Act was silent on linguistic obligations on many aspects of government–

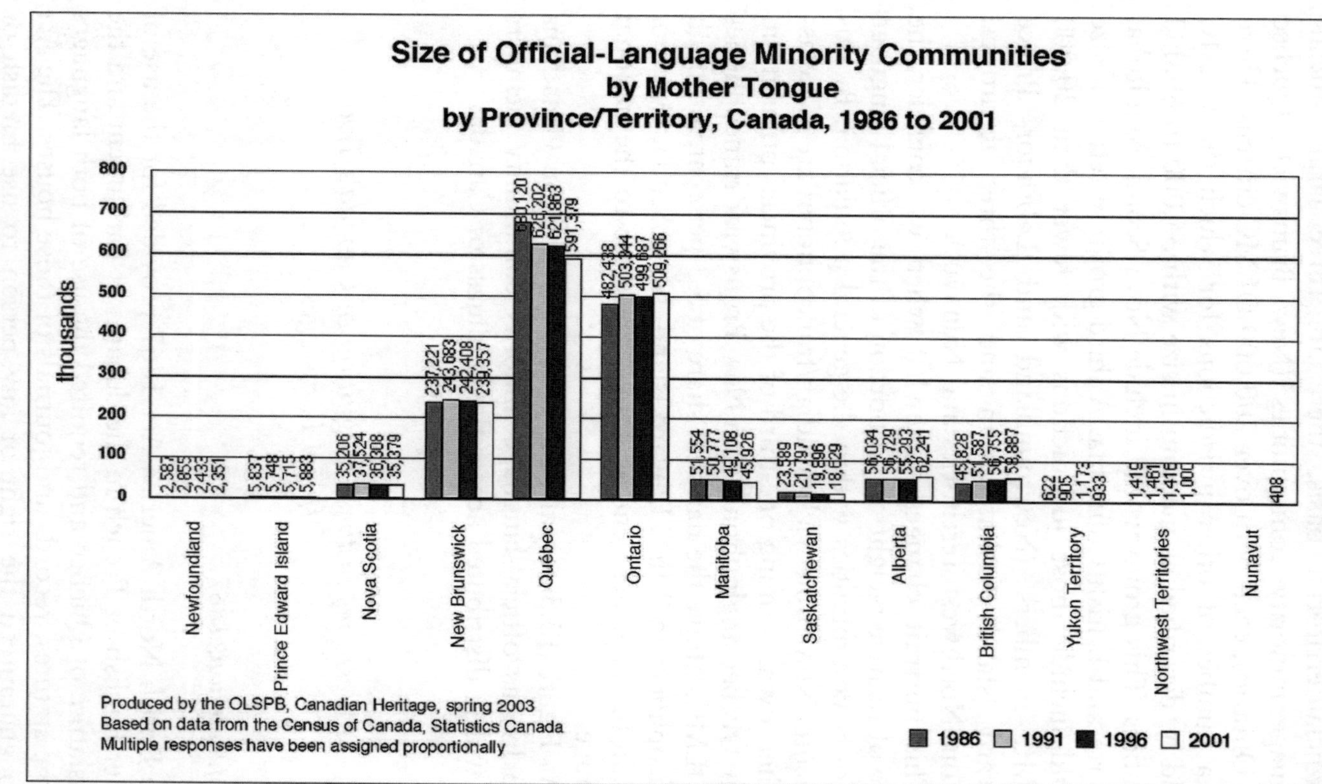

Figure 13.1: Size of official-language minority communities by mother tongue, by province/territory, Canada, 1986 to 2001

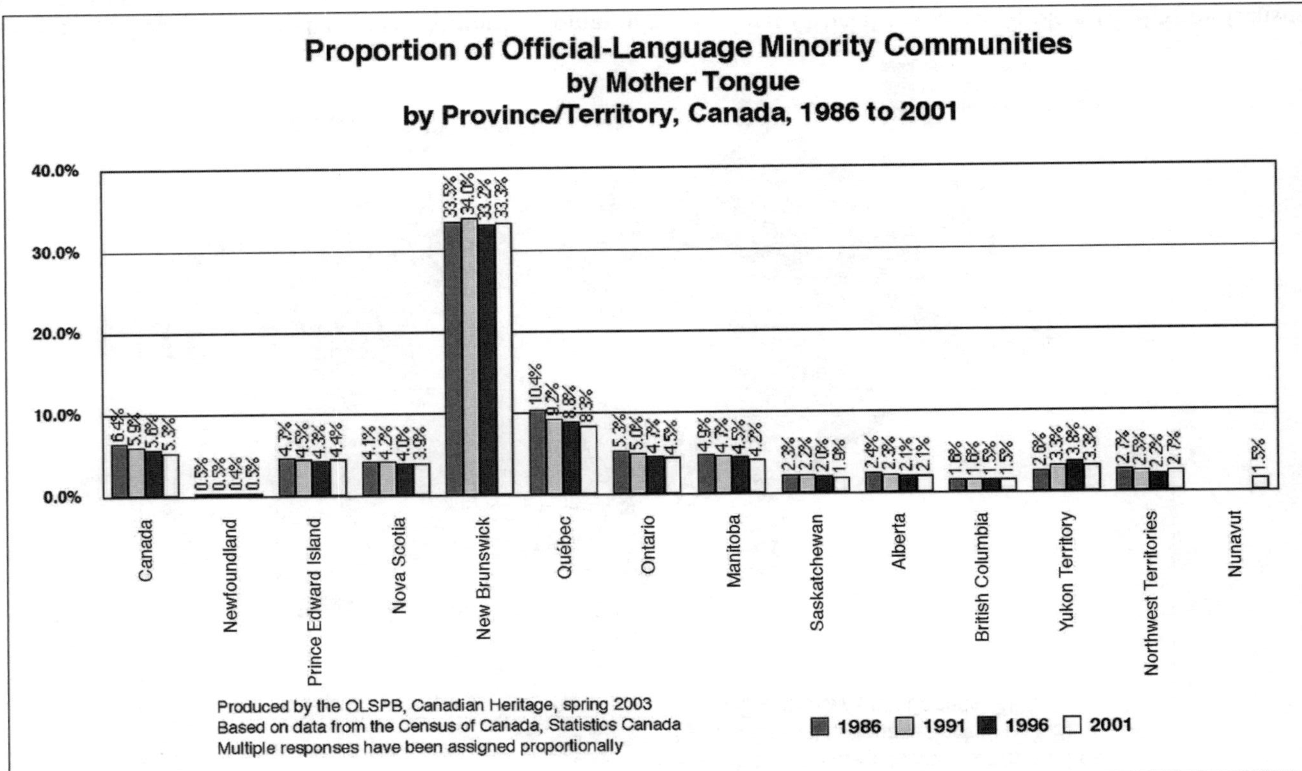

Figure 13.2: Proportion of official-language minority communities by mother tongue by province/territory, Canada, 1986 to 2001

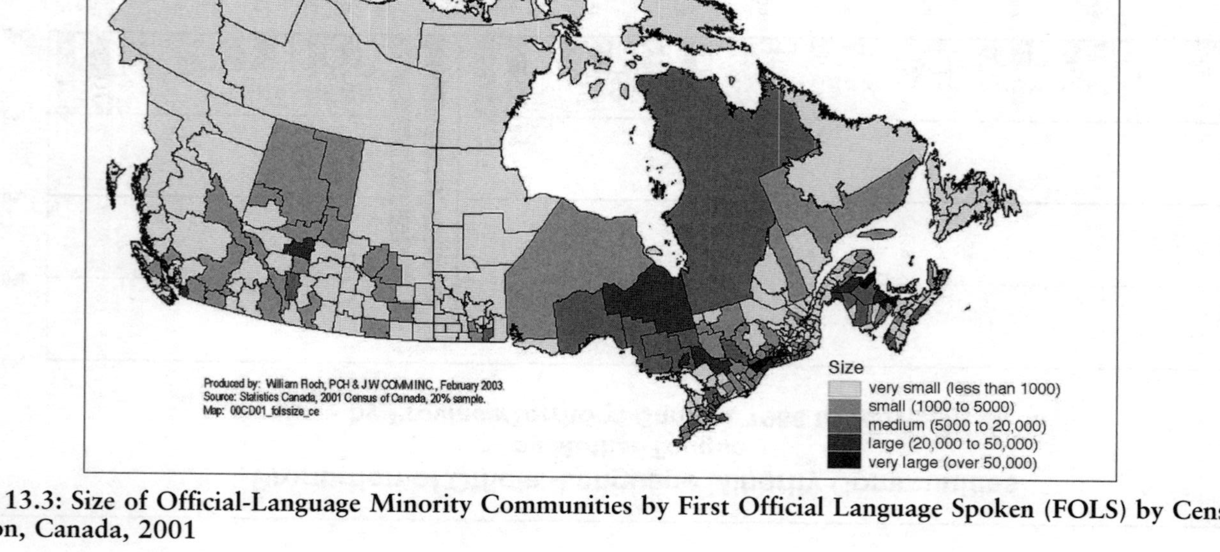

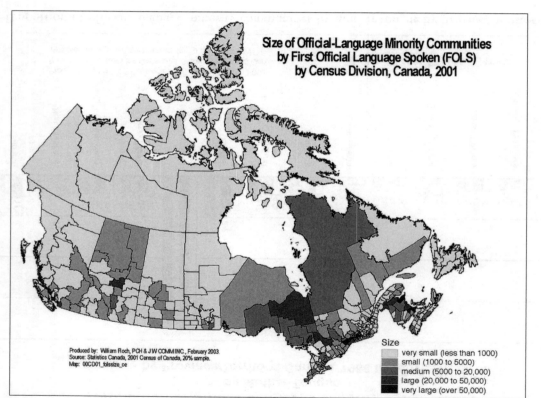

Figure 13.3: Size of Official-Language Minority Communities by First Official Language Spoken (FOLS) by Census Division, Canada, 2001

citizen relations that seem crucial in the contemporary context, but it should be remembered that the role and reach of government was much less substantial in the middle of the nineteenth century than it is today. Many of the educational, health and social needs of the population were met by church-based organizations.

Under section 93, the British North America Act did provide guarantees for the existing religious rights of Roman Catholics in Ontario and Protestants in Quebec including the right to operate tax-supported schools. This resulted in the de facto protection of English as a language of instruction in elementary and secondary schools of Protestant school boards in Montreal and Quebec City, and in the later extension of French as a language of instruction in some Catholic schools in Ontario.

Linguistic duality is therefore not a new phenomenon in this country. Indeed, it has been an integral part of Canada from the beginning and has been in the fore throughout the nation's history, gradually becoming one of the most distinctive characteristics of our federal institutions. The last forty five years (1963–2008) have witnessed a series of major constitutional, legislative, policy and societal changes which have completely transformed the language map in Canada and its provinces.

It should be noted that even before this recent period of Canadian history, various measures contributed to the recognition of the country's two official languages, although some of them appear modest in hindsight. In 1927, for example, bilingual postage stamps were issued for the first time, and in 1936 bilingual bank notes were printed. In 1934, the Translation Bureau was established to ensure that federal institutions produced Canada's official documents in both languages. In 1936, the government created a public broadcasting company with an English-language and a French-language network: The Canadian Broadcasting Corporation and Radio-Canada. The latter would play a vital role in efforts to promote the French language across the country. The National Film Board was established in 1939 and became a wellspring of outstanding artistic productions in both official languages. Simultaneous translation services were introduced in the House of Commons in 1959 and to the Senate in 1961, which contributed to a significant increase in the use of both official languages in Parliament. This period also saw the establishment of the Language Bureau, which began offering language training to federal public servants.

Despite these positive steps in the first half of the twentieth century towards recognition of linguistic duality, it cannot be forgotten that there were serious reversals in the evolution of the language landscape since confederation. The Manitoba Schools question in the 1890s and the adoption of Regulation by the Ontario government in 1917 are two major examples of the withdrawal of recognition for minority education rights which in turn provoked national political crises.

The Quiet Revolution and the Royal Commission on Bilingualism and Biculturalism

The decade of the1960s brought with it a ferment in the civic and political life of Quebec in a movement that became known as the Quiet Revolution (*la révolution tranquille*). Unquestionably, the Quiet Revolution was one of the major thrusts toward institutional recognition of both languages in Canada, which reflected the determination of Quebecers to modernize their social, political and economic institutions, and which gave rise to fundamental questions about the place of Quebec and the French language within Canada. These questions in turn led to an examination of our underlying conceptions of Canada, of the status of francophone minorities living outside Quebec and of the status that languages other than English and French should be given in Canadian society.

It was in this context that the Government of Canada created the Royal Commission on Bilingualism and Biculturalism in 1963. The commissioners were given a mandate to

> inquire into and report upon the existing state of bilingualism and biculturalism in Canada and to recommend what steps should be taken to develop the Canadian Confederation on the basis of an equal partnership between the two founding races, taking into account the contributions made by the other ethnic groups to the

cultural enrichment of Canada and the measures that should be taken to safeguard that contribution. (Churchill, 1998)

This notion of 'founding races' proved problematic in both contemporary and subsequent terms. Canadians of non-British and non-French origins felt excluded by this and many, particularly from Western Canada, mounted a campaign for recognition which resulted in the 1971 Multiculturalism Act. Similarly, Canada's aboriginal peoples object strenuously to this version of history, criticizing it as Eurocentric.

In 1965, following public hearings, the Bilingualism and Biculturalism Commission tabled a preliminary report. A few years later, after extensive research into various aspects of Canadian life, the commission tabled its findings and recommendations in six volumes, including one concerning the official languages (1967) and another concerning education (1968). The recommendations of this voluminous report evoked an ambitious response from the Government of Canada, which acted upon many of them through legislation, policies and programmes. The government's approach focused on three important aspects of the language question: first, the need, in the government's view, for the country's francophone population to identify more closely with the federal government; second, the importance of ensuring the preservation of linguistic minority communities in all parts of Canada; and, third, the need to foster greater recognition and acceptance of the official languages and promote their use, in federal institutions, but also in Canadian society as a whole, and at the same time to recognize its cultural diversity.

From Legislation to Activism (1969–88)

The 1969 Official Languages Act (OLA) was the government's main response to the complex situation that the Bilingualism and Biculturalism Commission had been asked to examine. The commission had recommended that the government take the essential step of recognizing both English and French as the official languages of Canada.

Parliament's passage in 1969 of the OLA fulfilled this recommendation, recognizing English and French as official languages for all purposes of the Parliament and the Government of Canada. The Act conferred equality of status and equal rights and privileges as to their use in all parliamentary and federal government institutions. Under the Act, federal departments and agencies had the right to provide services in English and French at their head or central offices, in the National Capital Region and in 'bilingual districts'. These 'bilingual districts' proved more difficult to implement than originally envisaged and were later replaced with more flexible concepts of 'nature of the office' and 'significant demand' which continue to be the object of discussion to the present. For an independent assessment see Cartwright and Williams (1982).

The Act also established the office of the Commissioner of Official Languages, who was charged with monitoring and reporting to Parliament on the application of the Act in federal institutions.

While the adoption of the OLA represented a major step forward in the recognition of language rights in Canada, there were certainly mixed reactions among English-speaking Canadians. On the one hand, there was a vocal segment who expressed their resentment for 'French being forced down their throats' and for being forced to see French on their cereal boxes in the morning. On the other hand, as later events proved, hundreds of thousands, indeed millions, embraced the opportunity to become bilingual through second-language learning and French immersion.

Beyond the 1969 Act itself, the government also brought forward a series of measures designed to ensure implementation of the legislation and address other issues of interest highlighted by the Bilingualism and Biculturalism Commission. The precursor to Canadian Heritage, the Department of the Secretary of State, was assigned a major role in coordinating these measures.

In 1993, the former Department of the Secretary of State of Canada was merged with the Department of Communications and the Department of Multiculturalism and Citizenship and was renamed the Department of Canadian Heritage. Under the Department of Canadian Heritage Act 1995, section 4(2)(*g*), the Department of Canadian Heritage was assigned responsibility for the advancement of the equality of status and use of English and French and the enhancement and development of the English and French linguistic minority communities in Canada. The Act goes on in section (47) to instruct that

> Every reference made to the Department of Communications, the Department of Multiculturalism and Citizenship or the Department of Canadian Heritage of Canada, in relation to any matter to which the powers, duties and functions of the Minister of Canadian Heritage extend by virtue of this Act, in any other Act of Parliament or in any order, regulation or other instrument made under any Act of Parliament shall, unless the context otherwise requires, be read as a reference to the Department of Canadian Heritage.

For the purpose of this article, and in the interests of clarity, the convention will be to replace references to 'the Department of Secretary of State of Canada' with 'the Department of the Secretary of State (Canadian Heritage)' until 1995 when the department's name was formally changed. From that point forward, the reference to Secretary of State will be dropped. (Parliament of Canada, Canadian Heritage Act (http://laws.justice.gc.ca/en/C-17.3/text.html), 1995).

Subsequent to the passage of the OLA in 1969, the Department of the Secretary of State (Canadian Heritage) was charged with establishing and administering the initiatives taken by the federal government in the area of official languages. These initiatives were brought together under a general programme known as the Bilingualism Development Programme. The programme had the broad objective of ensuring the equal status of the two official languages within federal government and encouraging their use and continued development in Canadian society as a whole. It focused on three areas:

1. the promotion of bilingualism and the coordination of programmes within the federal public service;

2. language programmes, including a federal–provincial relations division and a private-sector relations division;
3. sociocultural activities designed to support the development of minority official-language communities.

Just a couple of years after the adoption of the Official Languages Act, in 1972, Treasury Board was given responsibility for overseeing application of official-languages policy *within* the federal government; the Department of the Secretary of State (Canadian Heritage) was henceforth to concentrate on the ongoing essential dimension of promoting official languages *outside* federal institutions, and on working with the various sectors of Canadian society, including minority communities, provincial and territorial governments, and the private and voluntary sectors.

The Department of the Secretary of State (Canadian Heritage) Programmes

Since 1972, the department has essentially carried out this basic mandate through two programmes that were first assigned to it in 1969–70. The names and administrative structures of the programmes have changed over the years but the main components have remained the same: a federal–provincial programme dealing with official languages in education; and a programme to promote the official languages through the development of the official-language minority communities and through cooperation with the private and voluntary sectors and the provinces in areas other than education.

The following section provides a brief overview of the evolution of these programmes, which have been instrumental in delivering the mandate of the Department of the Secretary of State (Canadian Heritage) outside the federal government.

Official Languages in Education – Establishment of Programmes

Education has long been recognized as a crucial tool for ensuring the vitality of communities and promoting the use of languages. In Book II (Education) of the Bilingualism and Biculturalism Commission, it was recommended that provincial and territorial governments expand the curricula offered in the language of their minority official-language communities at the primary, secondary and post-secondary levels. It further recommended that the federal government accept responsibility in principle for the additional costs incurred by provincial governments in providing education in the language of the minority. The commission also recommended improving second-language instruction as a means of promoting linguistic duality and expressed its hopes for greater harmony between the country's anglophone and francophone communities.

In November 1969, the government decided to accept the commission's recommendations and indicated its willingness to cooperate financially with the provincial/territorial governments in order to implement the principles set out by the commission. In September 1970, after a year of talks with the provinces, the federal government announced the establishment of a programme of contributions to provincial governments. This programme, initially called the Bilingualism in Education (later the Official Languages in Education programme) had two objectives: to give minority-language Canadians the opportunity to be educated in or to have their children educated in their own language anywhere in the country and to make it possible for Canadians to learn their second official language, be it English or French.

These arrangements respected the provincial/territorial jurisdiction over education as set out in the 1867 Constitution Act and were intended to enable the federal government to combine its efforts with those of the provinces and territories towards common objectives in the area of official languages. Between 1970 and 1987, the federal government allocated $2.5 billion to the provinces and territories in support of the two main objectives in official-languages education.

Other early programmes, which persist to this day, include the Summer Language Bursary Programme (established in 1970–1) and the Official-Languages Monitor Programme (established in 1973–4). The Summer Language Bursary Programme enables students throughout Canada to take five-to-six-week immersion courses in English or French in accredited institutions. Most bursary recipients are majority-language students (French-speakers in Quebec and English-speakers throughout the rest of the country) although a certain number of bursaries have been awarded to francophones outside Quebec to enrol in special French-language courses aimed at improving their skills in their mother tongue.

The Official-Languages Monitor Programme promotes the instruction and use of official languages by making the services of language monitors available to teachers in Canadian educational institutions. Language monitors help students improve speaking skills and gain an appreciation of the vitality of the language being studied and of the culture associated with it.

Another longstanding programme, the Language Acquisition Development Programme (established in 1972) provides voluntary and professional organizations and Canadian universities with direct funding to compile and disseminate information related to the official languages in education and to develop and improve teaching techniques in minority-language and second-language settings.

Over this period, the mechanisms to give effect to this intergovernmental cooperation underwent substantial evolution. During the 1970s, a series of bilateral, multi-year agreements with provinces were negotiated. For the early years of the 1980s, a series of interim, single-year agreements were entered into.

In 1983, the department entered into a protocol agreement with the Council of Ministers of Education, Canada (the CMEC). The protocol can be understood as an umbrella agreement that sets the parameters for federal–provincial/territorial agreement by describing the objectives, funding arrangements and the undertakings of the two levels of government. For much of the period covered by the protocol, federal funding could be used for infrastructure support, programme expansion and development, teacher training and development and student support.

The original 1983 protocol was to cover three years but was extended mid-way for a further two years. Protocols for the 1987–92 and 1993–8 periods were subsequently signed, although interim or provisional measures were generally required, given the complexity of multi-party negotiations.

Major Accomplishments of the OLE Programme, 1969–1988

In nearly two decades of federal–provincial/territorial cooperation in the area of official languages in education, the Government of Canada, through the Department of the Secretary of State (Canadian Heritage) allocated more than $2.5 billion to the provinces and territories. This investment, which was generally matched by the other level of government, permitted enormous advancements in the offer and quality of minority-language education across the country and supported a boom in second-language learning opportunities for majority-language Canadians.

The intergovernmental cooperation provided provinces and territories with the necessary support to move forward in the areas of minority-language education and second-language instruction. As the following listing illustrates, provinces developed administrative and policy structures which were a prerequisite to sustainable progress for official languages in education. Examples include:

- Manitoba's establishment of the French-language Education office, headed by an assistant deputy minister, to handle all matters relating to the education of Franco-Manitobans and to French-language instruction for English-speaking students;
- the creation by Ontario of the position of assistant deputy minister responsible for elementary and secondary French education;
- the creation by New Brunswick of a separate school network for its francophone/Acadian community with a deputy minister responsible for French-language education;
- the opening by Saskatchewan of its Official-Language

Minority Office with the objective of promoting French-language education and the teaching of French as a second language.

Since 1970, the proportion of minority-language attending school in their language has steadily increased. While the actual numbers may have fluctuated, or dropped, in some jurisdictions, this can be attributed to such factors as low birth rates and the overall aging of the population or to general demographic challenges faced by official-language minority communities (principally language transfer or assimilation for young francophones and exodus from Quebec for young anglophones).

The increase in the number of elementary- and secondary-level education institutions has been accompanied by activities in several different areas aimed at improving teaching methods and developing teaching materials and curricula. These areas include teacher training, distance teacher training, specialized services for children with special needs, continuing education for adults and the upgrading of book collections and audio-visual materials.

The development of school-community centres has been one of the most innovative initiatives in the context of the growing minority-language education network. These centres serve both as schools and as meeting places/resource centres and are designed to promote a sense of cultural identity. School-community centres encompass a range of community services including media outlets, theatres, banks and sociocultural centres. Over the years, the Official Languages Support Programme Branch (OLSPB) at the Department of Canadian Heritage has provided financial assistance to more than seventy community and cultural centres in most regions of the country, of which about twenty are attached to minority education institutions. Such investments were building on the tenet that community-based institutions constitute a focal point whose ripple effect positively impacts the development of official-language minority communities. The initial support for such centres dates from the first phase (1969–88) but development has continued apace in the later period.

Another important area of development supported by the OLE programme in the 1969–88 phase was that of the post-secondary education milieu. Universities in various provinces, including Quebec (Bishop's, Concordia and McGill), Manitoba (Collège universitaire Saint-Boniface), New Brunswick (Moncton), Nova Scotia (Université Sainte-Anne), Ontario (Ottawa, Laurentian, Glendon) and Alberta (Faculté Saint-Jean of the University of Alberta) received federal–provincial support to permit the establishment and/or development of programmes as well as assistance for capital construction projects.

The establishment of French-language programmes and institutions across the country created a need for teacher training programmes. In response, the various post-secondary institutions serving minority-language students as well as some majority-language institutions have either instituted teacher-training programmes or expanded existing programmes.

Second-Language Instruction

This initial phase of the official-languages promotion role of the federal government saw the implementation of programmes by both the federal and provincial/territorial levels of government to help young Canadians to learn their other official language. The departments of education have promoted the learning of English and French as second languages in many ways. Beginning in the late 1970s, there has been an unprecedented proliferation of French-language immersion programmes (see Figure 13.4) across the country as a result of federal–provincial/territorial cooperation and the active involvement of a national non-profit association Canadian Parents for French, which has many thousands of members and volunteers across Canada. The major growth period was the decade from 1981–2 to 1990–1 when immersion enrolment mushroomed from under 50,000 to nearly 300,000 in the space of a decade. Through the 1980s, several colleges and universities received federal government assistance to set up French-language courses for graduates of French immersion programmes. Universities such as the University of Prince

Edward Island, the University of New Brunswick, the University of Regina and the University of Saskatchewan have upgraded their programmes in French as a second language.

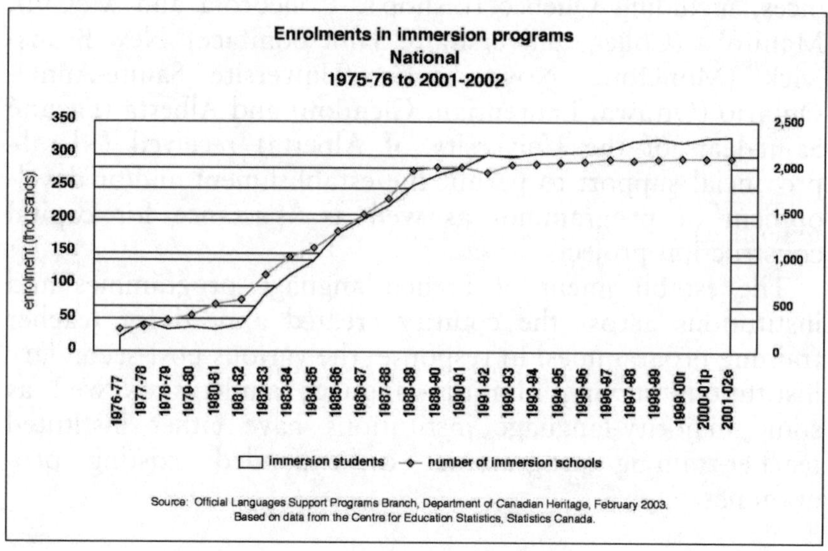

Figure 13.4: Enrolments in immersion programmes. National 1975–1976 to 2001–2002.

Promotion of Official Languages

Support to Official-Language Communities

In addition to working to expand opportunities for members of the Official-Language Minority Communities to be educated in their own language, the Department of the Secretary of State (Canadian Heritage) set up a programme in 1969 to help those communities to develop the infrastructures and tools they needed to ensure their growth and vitality. The Social Action Branch, as it was first called, helped many organizations to establish themselves or expand their activities so as to be positive forces for cultural renewal and for supporting the most isolated minority communities.

The programme emphasized social and community involvement and the establishment of representative associations in communities where there were none. It also sought to promote greater harmony between Canada's two language groups and to support programmes aimed at encouraging understanding and cooperation. By 1973, the Social Action Programme was renamed the Official-Language Minority Groups Programme but the programme retained its basic objective to promote community development.

The Fédération des francophones hors Québec (FFHQ) was founded in 1975 to give francophones living in a minority situation a common voice in their dealings with the federal government. The establishment of the FFHQ also aided the various provincial associations to establish common objectives and coordinate their projects. Other community-based organizations working in sectors such as culture, youth and economic development were recognized as worthy of support by the programme in its early years. Like the programmes described in this chapter, many of these organizations continue to serve the interests of the official-language minority communities.

A major pan-Canadian project of the FFHQ in its early years was a series of publications describing the situation and challenges of the various provincial/territorial minority communities and setting out a plan of action to advance their interests. Published in 1977, this series, *Les héritiers de Lord Durham*, remains interesting reading today.

The Social Action Programme/Official-Language Minority Groups Programme also provided early support to organizations in the Eastern Townships and Gaspé regions of Quebec. The election of the nationalist Parti Québécois government in Quebec in 1976 heightened the interest of Quebec's anglophone communities in the Department of the Secretary of State (Canadian Heritage) programmes and support was provided for a number of regional and sector-based organizations including a provincial umbrella organization known as Alliance Quebec.

By the early 1980s, the programme was actively dealing with more than four hundred organizations. Emphasis was placed on social concerns, culture, education, economic development, political and legal matters and communications issues which were considered vital to the survival and future development of these communities. Efforts were made to initiate or maintain programmes and services in these key areas.

In 1983, the community support programme was renewed under yet another name: the Official Language Communities Programme. At the same time, it was combined administratively with the Promotion of Official Languages programme (described below) in an effort to ensure a comprehensive approach in the objectives and activities of the department. Under this renewal, the programme objectives focused on key strategies such as lobbying for rights and for various institutional services in the minority language; institutional development and the provision of services by association networks where minority-language services were not otherwise available. The goal was to ensure an integrated and cooperative approach to community development.

Looking back at the 1969–88 period, it can be seen that, flowing from the findings of the Bilingualism and Biculturalism Commission, the federal government attached great importance to helping official-language minority communities survive and flourish in their language to the greatest extent possible. A major thrust in pursuit of this overall objective was support for community action and community development, through a host of volunteer-based representative organizations.

These organizations played an important role in the 1969–88 period by gathering together individuals, activists, leaders, groups and organizations effectively to speak for the interests of the various minority communities at all levels and represent their interests. Furthermore, these organizations and networks established infrastructures to facilitate coordination and representation at the local, regional, provincial and national levels through special interest groups working to ensure public awareness and promote development in such areas as culture, economics, communications, youth and the status of women.

Cooperation with the Various Elements of Canadian Society

Voluntary and Private Sectors

The department established in 1970 a private and voluntary sector support programme aimed at promoting the recognition and use of both official languages in society. This enabled the department to work towards its official-languages objectives in collaboration with some of the major players outside federal institutions, including provincial/territorial governments, voluntary associations, international organizations and businesses interested in providing services in both languages.

Under the programme, voluntary associations received financial assistance and technical advice in translation and interpretation while the private sector was eligible for technical (non-financial) assistance in language training and translation. Hundreds, if not thousands, of Canadian organizations have benefited from this programme to provide or improve services in the two official languages. In turn, thousands of Canadians who are not English–French bilingual have been able to participate in conferences, conventions and forums at the national level and to benefit from services in organizations which had previously operated in one language only.

In 1976, a variation of the programme provided voluntary associations with the opportunity to receive support in their efforts to develop a more permanent capacity for providing services in both languages through an approach which allowed funding in support of longer-term bilingualism development plans. Jointly with the Canadian Chamber of Commerce, the department published and distributed more than 70,000 copies of a brochure entitled *Thirty-six Ways to Put Bilingualism to Work for You*, promoting the use of both official languages in the private sector.

Cooperation with Provincial/Territorial Governments

During the 1970s, the department offered funding to provincial/territorial governments for development of minority-language services in areas other than education, which was already covered by the formal Official Languages in Education. While these early intergovernmental cooperation initiatives were somewhat ad hoc in nature, many provinces worked with the federal government to offer language training to government employees (Prince Edward Island, Ontario and Manitoba). Similarly, the governments of New Brunswick and Ontario received financial support for the translation of statutes. In the early 1980s, more than half of the provinces were benefiting from federal support to facilitate the use of French in the courts and in the general practice of law.

The Charter and Language Rights

The implementation of many of the key recommendations of the Bilingualism and Biculturalism Commission was complemented by the political process in Quebec which housed the majority of francophones in Canada and was the only jurisdiction with a francophone majority. In the mid-1970s, successive Quebec governments passed legislation which affirmed French as the official language of Quebec. The election of the nationalist Parti Québécois government in 1976 and the sovereignty–association referendum campaign of 1979–80 all kept the constitutional/legislative focus on Quebec-Canada relations and on official-languages policy.

It was in this evolving context that official languages provisions were enshrined in the 1982 Canadian Charter of Rights and Freedoms, and these provisions were in turn the inspiration for a renewed Official Languages Act. The Charter recognizes English and French as the official languages of Canada and affirms the equality of status and use of these languages in all institutions of the Parliament and Government of Canada (section 16). Under section 20, the Charter provided Constitutional entrenchment of the right of Canadians, under certain circumstances, to communicate with, and receive services from federal institutions in the official language of their choice.

The Charter also provides for 'the authority of Parliament or a legislature to advance the equality of status or use of English and French' (section 16.3), which provides leeway for governments to advance linguistic duality. One can thus speak of a broad and flexible application of the various rights set out in the legislation, permitting dynamic evolution rather than static application. This broad concept of promotion, as will be seen in the subsequent sections, is especially important to the efforts of the Department of the Secretary of State (Canadian Heritage) to promote the official languages.

Finally, the Charter added another major dimension: the right to elementary and secondary schooling in one's own language, throughout Canada. Section 23 provides for the right of parents of the official-language minority group in each province/territory (francophones outside Quebec and anglophones in Quebec) to have their children receive their elementary- and secondary-level education in publicly funded minority-language institutions, where the number of children so warrants. Joint federal–provincial initiatives in the area of official languages in education throughout the 1970s helped to create a climate conducive to the inclusion of such a section in the Charter. This right remains an essential condition for the maintenance and development of our official-language communities.

Court Challenges Programme

Although it has perhaps received less public attention than the direct support programmes developed and delivered by Secretary of State (Canadian Heritage), the Court Challenges Programme (CCP) has played a crucial behind-the-scenes role in the full recognition of language rights in Canada. Valuable information is available from the programme evaluation, *Summative Evaluation of the Court Challenges Programme* (2003), and from the website of the programme *About Court Challenges* (2002). At its inception in 1978, the CPP was delivered by the Department of the Secretary of State of Canada. Its original objective was to provide funding to citizens and groups in order to assist them in bringing important linguistic challenges to the attention of the courts. As the Supreme Court of Canada once noted, these court challenges combine 'legal and constitutional questions of the utmost subtlety and complexity with political questions of great sensitivity' ('Re Manitoba Language Rights [1985] 1 R. C. S. 721' (Supreme Court of Canada, 1985)).

Over time, the mandate and scope of the CCP has grown from its original exclusive focus on language rights, extending to equality rights guaranteed under section 15 of the Canadian Charter of Rights and Freedoms. The governance of the CCP has evolved considerably over the years. From 1978–85 it was delivered as a government programme with an exclusive focus on language rights. From 1985 to the present time (except for the 1992–4 period when it briefly ceased operations due to the withdrawal of government funding), the CCP has been delivered by a series of third-party entities (Canadian Council for Social Development, Human Rights Research and Education Centre of the University of Ottawa and, finally, a non-profit entity, the Court Challenges Programme of Canada).

Since 1978 in the case of languages rights and since 1985 in the cause of equality rights, the CCP has worked toward the clarification of certain constitutional rights-related provisions. Now operated by an arm's-length, non-profit corporation, the Court Challenges Programme of Canada, the programme nonetheless continues to receive funding from Canadian Heritage via a five-year contribution agreement. For the period from 1998–9 to 2002–3, the annual contribution was up to $2.75m with $525,000 of this amount earmarked for language rights.

Over the years, the Court Challenges Programme has assisted official-language minority communities to clarify their language rights. The CCP can fund test-case development, test-case litigation, and support the negotiation of alternate dispute resolution and studies of the impact of court decisions. In the area of language rights, the CCP has funded court challenges in thematic areas such as the unwritten constitutional principle of protection of minorities, minority-language educational rights, language of work, communications, and services, freedom of expression, judicial rights and legislative bilingualism.

Conclusions – Phase I (1969–1988)

Through their respective mandates and activities, the Official Languages in Education and the Promotion of Official Languages programmes did much to implement the major commitments that the Bilingualism and Bicultural Commission made to the federal government in the 1960s. The measures launched by the federal government had a profound effect on the evolution of language issues in Canada. For the official languages in education programme area, it can be seen that the 1969–88 period was extremely fruitful in terms of federal–provincial cooperation. Second-language education programmes witnessed unprecedented expansion and educational opportunities for official-language minority communities improved considerably.

Formal intergovernmental agreements in the area of official languages in education, direct funding to community-based organizations, ad hoc agreements or joint initiatives with provincial governments, the establishment of the court challenges programme to provide minority communities with the resources to seek clarification of legal rights all represent substantial evidence of a more activist federal government in the area of official languages promotion and community development. As this initial period of federal activity drew to a close with the passage of the renewed Official Languages Act, the federal government and its provincial/territorial partners would face a new challenge from minority-language parents who were prepared to use the courts to deliver the right to control and manage the schools systems which they perceived as being promised by the Charter of Rights and Freedoms and which, from their perspective, was being blocked by many of the provincial and territorial governments. A looming fiscal crisis in Canadian public life, continued soul-searching on constitutional arrangements with

Quebec, and the evolving relationship between government and the entities that it funds were to feature prominently in challenges for the next phase, which begins with great optimism with the adoption of a revised Official Languages Act and the announcement of renewed official languages support programmes under the aegis of Secretary of State (Canadian Heritage).

The New Act and Official Languages Policy Renewal (1988–2003)

In July 1988, Parliament passed an 'Act respecting the status and use of the official languages in Canada', the new Official Languages Act, thus bringing to fruition three years of intensive revision. In addition to bring the 1969 Act into line with the Canadian Charter of Rights and Freedoms, which itself was entrenched in the Constitution in 1982, this major revision was paralleled by a review and renewal of federal government policies and action in the area of official languages, the results of which were announced in 1987, at the time the Bill was tabled.

The 1987–8 period represents a progressive combination of constitutional renewal, legislative renewal and reinforcement of government action. Since the Bilingualism and Biculturalism Commission, a mix of events and official measures had contributed to an important evolution in questions and perceptions relating to official languages in Canada. For example, a 1973 parliamentary resolution reaffirmed the principles of the 1969 Act and set out the conditions in which the right of federal public servants to work in the official language of their choice could be exercised. In 1974, the Consumer Packaging and Labelling Act came into force, along with a regulation specifying the means of its application in the bilingual labelling of consumer products.

The provisions of the Official Languages Act dealing with federal institutions, coupled with the efforts of the Department of the Secretary of State (Canadian Heritage) to foster the recognition of linguistic duality outside the government, helped alter dynamically the official languages landscape. The recognition of the equal status of the two official languages led to major changes in the federal public service, which gradually became apparent in the different regions of the country. Over time, too, the various segments of Canadian society became more sensitive as well to the presence of linguistic minorities and to their own linguistic aspirations. For their part, the minority communities became adept, with the help of various types of support, at promoting their own cause. Representatives of the private and voluntary sectors also played a positive role in the general evolution. Increasingly, Canadians came to support the process of recognizing the nation's linguistic duality.

In English-speaking Canada, this attitude was evidenced by the fact that a larger number of anglophone parents wanted their children to learn French. This attitude is illustrated in particular by the enthusiasm for French immersion schooling in the 1980s: enrolment in French immersion programmes grew beyond all expectations. Moreover, according to surveys conducted in 1985, Canadians increasingly viewed linguistic duality as setting Canada apart from the United States. The 1985 surveys also found that a large proportion of English-speaking Canadians were in favour of government, education and hospital services being made available to the minority communities in their own language.

Subsequent to consultations in 1987, a new Official Languages Act received royal assent on 28 July 1988 and came into force on 15 September 1988. The new Act had a double purpose:

1. to modernize, improve and advance federal official languages policy within the government of Canada itself and in the government's dealings with the Canadian public;
2. to guide government policy and pursue efforts to promote the official languages in Canadian society as a whole.

It is this second purpose which distinguishes the new Official Languages Act from the original 1969 Act and which sets the overall thrusts of Canadian language policy into the next century. Rather than the somewhat ad hoc arrangements in Phase 1, the intent here was to go much further in promoting linguistic duality and supporting development of official-language minority communities. These major objectives are clearly declared in the preamble, which helps to give meaning to the revised Act and explains its main parts.

To understand the role of the Department of the Secretary of State (Canadian Heritage) in this new era, it is important to note that the revised Official Languages Act goes beyond the strictly governmental sphere. In conjunction with the related initiatives announced by the Department of the Secretary of State (Canadian Heritage) when the Bill was introduced, the Act breaks new ground by setting out for the first time in a federal statute the federal government's policy and objectives for the promotion and advancement of the official languages in Canadian society as a whole, as follows:

- to support Canada's English and French linguistic minority communities and to assist them in their development;
- to foster full recognition and use of both official languages in Canadian society;
- to promote full access for the linguistic minority communities to education in their own language, and to encourage Canadians to learn English and French;
- to encourage and assist the provincial governments, the private and voluntary sectors, the business community and labour organizations in promoting and using the two official languages, thus facilitating full participation of both language groups in all aspects of Canadian life;
- to promote Canada's bilingual nature internationally.

The Act gave the Department of the Secretary of State (Canadian Heritage) the role of coordinating these different commitments.

Concomitant with the tabling of the Bill for the new Act in Parliament in 1987, the Department of the Secretary of State (Canadian Heritage) announced a set of measures to give effect to the government's twofold commitment, namely, enhancing the vitality of the official-language minority communities and promoting the two official languages in Canadian society. A key commitment in Part VII of the new Act was the future involvement of a panoply of federal departments and institutions in the support of official-language minorities. Under the previous arrangement, the

Secretary of State (Canadian Heritage) had been called upon to 'be all things to all minority communities'. The new Act would call upon other departments and agencies of the Government of Canada to play an official languages role beyond service delivery in both official languages. The Secretary of State (Canadian Heritage) was assigned the role of coordinating these various federal efforts.

Another departure in the new Act was the explicit commitment for Canadian Heritage to seek opportunities to cooperate with other levels of government to advance its official-languages objectives. Combined with the minority-language education guarantees contained in the 1982 Canadian Charter of Rights and Freedoms, there was a substantial legislative/policy commitment towards ambitious outreach to further linguistic duality and to support sustainable community development.

1988 Programme Renewal

In June 1988, the government announced the renewal of the Official Languages in Education and Promotion of Official Languages programmes with an allocation of $1.4 billion over the next five years. For the first time, these programmes were renewed on a permanent basis in order to reflect their new legislative foundation and the government's commitment to official-language minority communities and the promotion of official languages. In order to pursue this commitment, increased emphasis was placed on strengthening various forms of collaboration and cooperation with the communities themselves, provincial and territorial governments, the private and voluntary sectors and other federal departments and agencies. The following pages will deal in detail with the intergovernmental partnership and interdepartmental cooperation areas which were spelled out in the new legislation.

Intergovernmental Cooperation

In contrast with the previous Act, the revised Official Languages Act explicitly calls on the federal government to work with provincial governments. The new Act committed the federal government to 'encourage and assist provincial governments to support the development of English and French linguistic minority communities generally and, in particular, to offer provincial and municipal services in both English and French and to provide opportunities for members of English and French linguistic minority communities to be educated in their own language' and to 'encourage and assist provincial governments to provide opportunities for everyone in Canada to learn both English and French' (Official Languages Act 1990).[1]

As discussed above, the 1969–88 period had witnessed some ad hoc federal–provincial cooperation in areas other than education. The explicit commitment to seek cooperation set out in the 1988 Act underlines the federal government's desire to support the development of services in other areas of daily life in the official-language communities such as health, social services, justice and culture. The introduction of these new areas of cooperation represents an important new advance in federal–provincial relations. Previously, cooperation in such fields had been on a case-by-case basis; now, there was a major thrust aimed at ensuring more coordinated and more effective development of services for the minority linguistic communities in their own languages.

To give effect to this commitment, the Secretary of State (Canadian Heritage) established an intergovernmental cooperation programme with a specific budget and the development of general agreements on promotion of the official languages that set out guidelines for, and the obligations of, the parties involved. Under these agreements, which generally run for five years, the two levels of government set objectives and define the activities covered by the agreement. The objective of the programme component was to help provincial and territorial governments foster the development of official-language minority communities (anglophones in Quebec and francophones outside Quebec) by providing these communities with services in English and French, in areas other than education. Under the programme, the department encourages the provinces and territories to implement new services or improve existing services related to the day-to-day life of official-language minority communities for example, in health, economics, justice, culture and social services), and to promote the recognition and use of the two official languages. Costs were usually shared on a 50/50 basis by the department and the provincial government involved.

Beginning in 1988–9, a series of agreements were negotiated with provincial and territorial governments. The sectors covered by these agreements varied from jurisdiction to jurisdiction, reflecting the different minority circumstances and provincial/territorial readiness to enter into such agreements and promotional/developmental activities. The jurisdictional authority of the provincial/territorial governments was a matter of great importance to the negotiators of these agreements and the federal role was that of supporter rather than direct actor. As the agreements evolved, many jurisdictions adopted administrative and even legislative frameworks to plan and develop programmes to further their official languages objectives. Intergovernmental cooperation support was frequently oriented to provinces/territories who were expanding the scope of their services to public, either through legislative commitments or through policy orientations.

These agreements contributed to the creation of a network of government officials responsible for francophone affairs and the holding of annual conferences of ministers responsible for francophone affairs. Provincial and territorial governments are increasingly involved in supporting their francophone or Acadian population, and intergovernmental cooperation agreements with the Department of the Secretary of State (Canadian Heritage) help stimulate this involvement. A major symbol of the progressive evolution of this network was its adoption in the autumn of 2002 of a joint statement of principles underlying provincial/territorial leadership with respect to francophone communities, which is reproduced below.

Principles of government leadership with respect to the Canadian Francophonie

Firmly believing that Francophones and Acadians should individually and collectively be able to live and develop in French throughout Canada, the provincial and territorial members of the Ministerial Conference on Francophone Affairs hereby acknowledge:

- The importance of government commitment and leadership in the sphere of francophone affairs;
- The importance of promoting greater use and visibility of the French language throughout Canada;
- The value of the French-speaking communities' contribution to the social fabric of Canada;
- The essential role played by dialogue and cooperation between each government and its francophone or Acadian community in the development of that community;
- The need for flexibility and practical alternatives in the planning and delivery of French-language services, given the different realities of their provinces and territories;
- The necessity of encouraging intergovernmental cooperation in order to facilitate progress in francophone affairs;
- The importance of assuming an individual and collective catalyzing role with respect to the evolution of francophone affairs;

The importance of their efforts and support for ensuring the active offer of quality services in French and the development of Canada's francophone and Acadian communities. (St John's, Newfoundland and Labrador 2002)

The statement of principles was signed by the ministers responsible for French-language services in every province and territory. Quebec also expressed its support, declaring that 'it will continue to support, together with the provincial and territorial governments of Canada, the development and enhancement of Canada's francophone and Acadian communities (and) . . . therefore joins in this declaration of principles' *(*http://www.scics.gc.ca/cinfo02/860452004_a.html).

Needless to say, this declaration sends a powerful message to francophone and Acadian minority communities and is indicative of enormous progress and change of attitudes across Canada. Recent poll results indicate that this message is being received in the minority communities. Fully 91 per cent of minority-language respondents supported the concept of federal–provincial/territorial cooperation to improve minority-language services and 63 per cent agreed that such agreements had resulted in improved services over the previous five years (GPC International, 2003).

Interdepartmental Coordination

Another major departure from the previous legislative commitment was the explicit mention of French and English linguistic minority communities. Section 41 of the Official Language Act states:

> 'The Government of Canada is committed to a) enhancing the vitality of the English and French linguistic minority communities in Canada and supporting and assisting their development; and b) fostering the full recognition and use of both English and French in Canadian society.'

Section 42 of the Official Languages Act states:

> 'The Minister of Canadian Heritage, in consultation with other Ministers of the Crown, shall encourage and promote a coordinated approach to the implementation by federal institutions of the commitments set out in section 41.'

From 1988–94, Canadian Heritage officials worked with official-language minority communities and with officials in numerous federal departments and agencies to build a better understanding of this additional commitment and to encourage the development of a policy approach across government which was more sensitive to the needs of the minority communities. Despite these efforts, there was growing frustration with the lack of tangible results from the legislative commitment toward community development across government.

Key Federal Departments/Institutions Targeted under s. 41 of the Official Languages Act

The following departments and institutions are targeted by the Official Languages Act:

Agriculture and Agri-Food Canada
Atlantic Canada Opportunities Agency
Business Development Bank of Canada
Canadian Centre for Management Development
Canada Council for the Arts
Canada Economic Development for Quebec Regions

Canada Post Corporation
Canadian Broadcasting Corporation
Canadian [Heritage]
Canadian International Development Agency
Canadian Tourism Commission
Citizenship and Immigration Canada
Department of Justice
Department of Foreign Affairs and International Trade
Health [Canada]
Human Resources Development Canada
Industry [Canada]
International Development Research Centre
National Arts Centre
National Capital Commission
National Film Board
Parks [Canada]
Public Works and Government Services Canada
Social Sciences and Humanities Research Council of Canada
Statistics [Canada]
Status of Women Canada
Telefilm [Canada]
Treasury Board of Canada
Western Economic Diversification Canada

Source: Official Languages Support Programmes Department of Canadian Heritage, Interdepartmental Coordination Directorate, *List of Key Institutions* (http://www.pch.gc.ca/progs/lo-ol/ci-ic/mofc-kfi_e.cfm, 2002 [cited]).

Accountability Framework for ss. 41–42

In August 1994, the Government of Canada approved the establishment of an accountability framework for the implementation of sections 41 and 42 of the Official Languages Act. This commitment ensures not only that official-language minority communities have access to services in their language, but also that all federal institutions actively contribute to the development and vitality of these communities. The accountability framework includes the following provisions:

- Initially, measures will target a certain number of key institutions in areas of intervention which are vital to the minority-language communities and have the greatest impact. The key federal institutions are primarily those involved in the areas of economic, human resources and cultural development.
- Each key institution develops an action plan for the implementation of section 41 which takes into account the specific needs of the official-language minority communities.
- The action plans are developed in consultation with official-language minority communities in order to identify community needs and allow institutions to take these into account in their activities.
- Ministers responsible for key institutions transmit these plans and report on the results attained once a year to the Minister of Canadian Heritage.
- The Minister of Canadian Heritage will report to Parliament via his Annual Report on Official Languages on the implementation of this governmental commitment. The Annual Report will highlight the action plan of each key federal institution and the results attained during the previous year.

Further to the 1994 framework, and in response to a critical report from the Standing Joint Committee on Official Languages a memorandum of understanding was signed between the Department of Canadian Heritage and Treasury Board Secretariat to provide central agency support for the Canadian Heritage role as coordinator of the implementation of section 41 of the Official Languages Act.

To give added impetus to the interdepartmental coordination efforts, in February 1999, the Department of Canadian Heritage announced a new initiative entitled Interdepartmental Partnership with the Official-Language Communities

(IPOLC). With a budget of $5.5 million over a period of years, the Interdepartmental Partnership provides matching funding to encourage the federal departments and agencies to support the official-language minority communities by setting up new partnerships. This initiative was launched in fiscal year 2000–1 and a small group of departments/institutions were targeted in a first round for IPOLC activity. The first group includes Health Canada, Agriculture and Agri-food Canada, Justice Canada, Industry Canada, Western Economic Diversification, the Atlantic Canada Opportunities Agency, Canada Economic Development for Quebec Regions, FedNor, the Canada Council for the Arts, and Citizenship and Immigration. The attached graphic demonstrates the value-added approach and the scope of departmental/agency support for the community development mandate set out in section 41. It is important to note that, through the involvement of community networks, the Interdepartmental Partnership offers more than simply a funding mechanism as it provides for sustained contact between communities and departments.

Another important sign of progress since the mid-1990s was the development of a series of structured relationships between key departments and official-language minority communities. Examples include departments such as Human Resource Development Canada, Health Canada, Citizenship and Immigration Canada and a series of federal partners in the multi-party agreement on Francophone arts and culture. Other indications of progress would include the development by Industry Canada, Health Canada and Human Resource Development Canada for policy/programme units within their organizations with the key responsibility for developing and delivering programmes as well as increasing access to existing departmental programmes.

Table 13.2: 2001–2002 Joint Investments under the Interdepartmental Partnership with Official Language Communities (IPOLC)

Departments/Agencies	Funds transferred from Canadian Heritage to Departments/Agencies $	Investments from federal partners $
Canada Economic Development for Quebec Regions	100000	100000
Agriculture and Agri-Food Canada	141500	141500
Atlantic Canada Opportunities Agency	743000	1481000
Department of Citizenship and Immigration	15250	15250
Canada Council for the Arts – Francophones	900000	900000
Canada Council for the Arts – Anglophones	300000	300000
Human Resources Development Canada	261550	395374
Western Economic Diversification Canada	80200	80200
Industry Canada	349528	390003
Fisheries and Oceans Canada	255000	280000
Health Canada	1775729	1983877
Canadian Broadcasting Corporation/Société Radio-Canada	140000	135000
Telefilm Canada	264500	264500
Total	**5326257**	**6466704**

Successes and Challenges in the Promotion of Official Languages

As Dr Stacy Churchill eloquently states it, the period immediately prior to the development and launching of the Department of the Secretary of State (Canadian Heritage) official languages promotion programmes was a grim one indeed. Referring to the challenge to national unity, Churchill (1998) comments that

> It was inconceivable that Canada would long survive if the conditions described by the Royal Commission on Bilingualism and Biculturalism were to continue – lack of services in French from federal offices in most of the country and even in Quebec itself, under-representation of French speakers at all levels of jobs in the federal public service, non-recognition of the French language even in the lettering carved on the doors of the Parliament buildings, obligatory use of English in most government agencies – in fact, an almost unending list of failures to recognize the French language and treat French-speaking citizens equitably in the delivery of services by federal institutions or in staffing them. In the mid-1960s, schooling opportunities in French were weak or nonexistent in most provinces, the illiteracy rates among French speakers were double the national average, and their incomes were significantly lower than those of non-French citizens. (§2:4)

Against this rather daunting indictment, we can now see tremendous strides forward in the recognition of French in Canadian society and an undeniable improvement in the educational and economic profile of Canada's francophone citizens, both inside and outside Quebec. Churchill goes on to observe that in the years

> since the Royal Commission on Bilingualism and Biculturalism delivered the first volume of its report in 1966, the linguistic landscape of Canada has been totally transformed. This period has been one of sustained progress and expansion in objectives set by the Department of the Secretary of State (Canadian Heritage). In spite of the controversies that sometimes arose, the objectives of public policies on official languages have met with broad public support – broader than the public itself is sometimes willing to believe.

This final section of the chapter will focus on some of the successes of the Canadian Heritage approach to official languages promotion and will also discuss some of the challenges for the next era.

Governance, Community Networks and Institutional Development

As described in the previous section, federal–provincial cooperation in the 1970s supported important development in the coverage and quality of minority-language education across Canada, and the coming into effect of the 1982 Canadian Charter of Rights and Freedoms provided constitutional guarantees for minority-language education rights. With the assistance of the federally–funded Court Challenges programme, Francophone minority communities mounted a series of legal challenges which aimed at securing the full implementation of their Charter rights which extended to the control and management. Three of these cases found their way to the Supreme Court of Canada, namely *Mahé* 1990, *Beaulac* 1999 and *Arsénault-Cameron* 2000. Taken together, these landmark judgments confirm the rights of the minority to control and manage school institutions, providing essential opportunities for governance as instanced by the case of the 'Commission nationale des parents francophones', *Résumé De La Jurisprudence Sous L'article 23 De La Charte, Comprenant Les Trois Jugements De La Cour Suprême Du Canada* (http://www.cnpf.ca, 2002. [cited July 2003]).

The work of the Court Challenges Programme continues to be relevant to the constitutional/legal situation of official-language minority communities, some thirty years after its creation. A telling example of the support from the Court Challenges Programme will illustrate this conviction.

French-speaking parents in Summerside, Prince Edward Island, and the organization representing them – the Fédération des parents francophones de l'Île-du-Prince-Édouard – had for several years been demanding that a French-language school be set up in their community. In January 1997, the Prince Edward Island Supreme Court sided with the parents, saying they had a right to a French-language school. The government appealed the decision and won.

> 'In 1998, the Fédération des parents de l'Île-du-Prince-Édouard were granted programme funding to take the case before the Supreme Court of Canada. Funding was also granted to Prince Edward Island's French Language Board, the Société Saint-Thomas

d'Aquin and the Commission nationale des parents francophones to intervene on behalf of the parents.

The Supreme Court's decision of January 2000 quashed the decision of the Prince Edward Island Supreme Court, Appeal Division. The Supreme Court of Canada reiterated yet again that section 23 must be interpreted according to its true purpose. The following is an excerpt of this decision pertaining to this issue:

'A purposive interpretation of section 23, rights is based on the true purpose of redressing past injustices and providing the official language minority with equal access to high quality education in its own language, in circumstances where community development will be enhanced.' (Paragraph 27)

By reiterating the true purpose of section 23 the Supreme Court fully recognized the vital role schools play in helping official language minority communities flourish. Thus, this decision was an important victory not only for the parents of Summerside, but for all official language minority communities. (*1999–2000 Annual Report of the Court Challenges Programme of Canada, http://www.ccppcj.ca/documents/annrep9900.html*)

Angéline Martel, a co-appellant in the *Mahé* case, agrees that important progress has been made, noting that 'Since 1990, nearly all of the provinces and territories have institutionalized a school governance structure for the French-speaking minorities (provincial or regional school board) and the confirmation of their rights has given new assurance to the French-speaking communities.'

The constitutional recognition of minority education rights, the operation of funding programmes which supported the activities of community-based organizations (notably the Commission nationale des parents francophones with respect to education rights), and financed crucial court challenges, and a readiness on the part of Canadian Heritage to provide financial support for the provinces as they implemented minority-language school governance functioned together to support key developments in francophone minority-language education.

The development of community-based organizations at local, regional, provincial and national levels as well as organizations serving the sectoral needs of minority communities has also provided a community infrastructure capable of providing services or lobbying the appropriate party to develop or extend services in the minority language. A recent survey of official-language minority communities revealed a high level of satisfaction regarding the scope of services across jurisdictions. The GPC survey, which was undertaken to support the programme evaluations of Canadian Heritage, also revealed a high level of personal commitment to sustaining the minority language and culture among respondents. As can be seen in Figure 13.5, fully 94 per cent of OLMC respondents agreed that the future of the minority community was important to them while 72 per cent expressed confidence that the community had the capacity to remain strong in the future, while 61 per cent expressed confidence in community leadership.

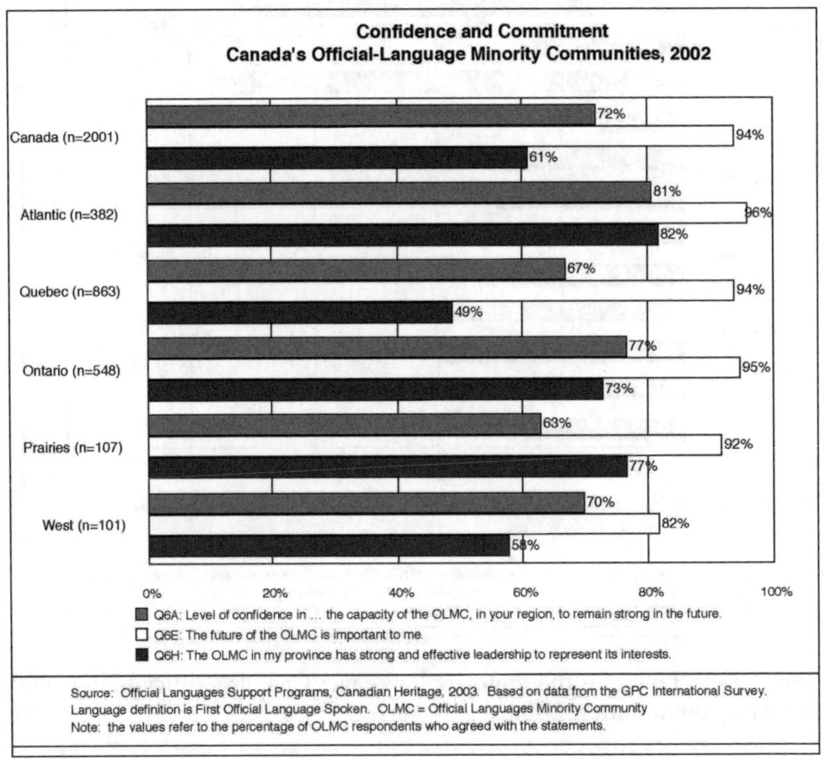

Figure 13.5: Confidence and commitment: Canada's official-language minority communities, 2002

Living in the Minority Language

More than two-thirds (73 per cent) of the members of Canada's official-language minority communities reported that they were able to live in their language in their region. This is somewhat less than the 83 per cent who responded that it would be important to do so, which indicates a deficit of 10 per cent between aspirations and reality. More troubling still is the nearly one-third (29 per cent) who expect that it will be more difficult to live in their minority language five years hence.

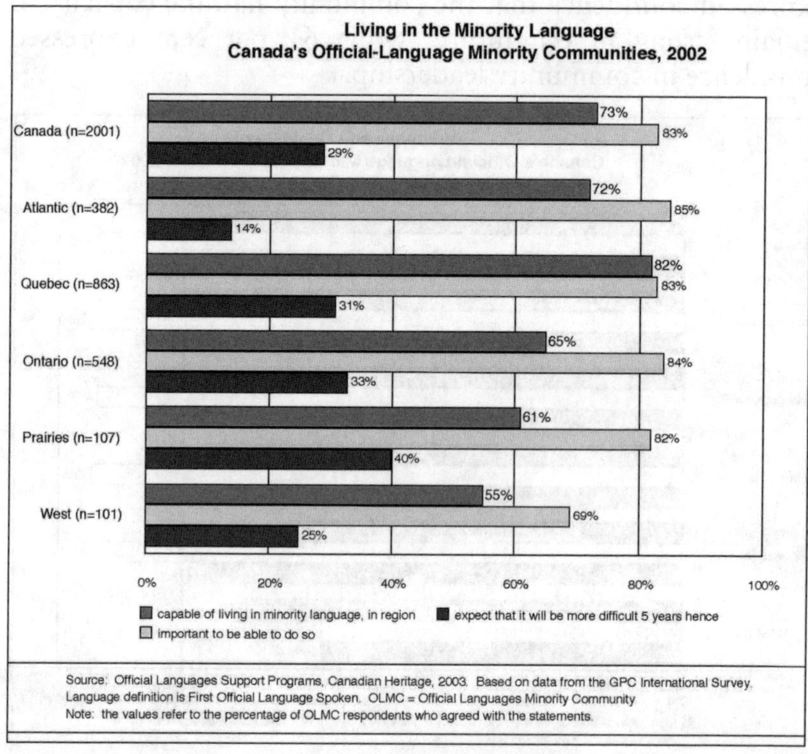

Figure 13.6: Living in the minority language: Canada's official-language minority communities, 2002.

Education/Economic Performance of the OLMCs

Analysis of the 2001 census shows clearly that the educational/ economic gap that afflicted francophones in the era of the

Bilingualism and Biculturalism Commission has been pretty much eradicated. The younger half of the working generation of minority-language francophones (those living outside Quebec, aged under 45) are somewhat more likely than their anglophone counterparts to have completed a post-secondary degree, diploma or certificate. This stands in stark contrast to their elders (aged 45 and over in 2001) whose record of educational attainment at higher levels showed a marked deficit relative to their anglophone neighbours.

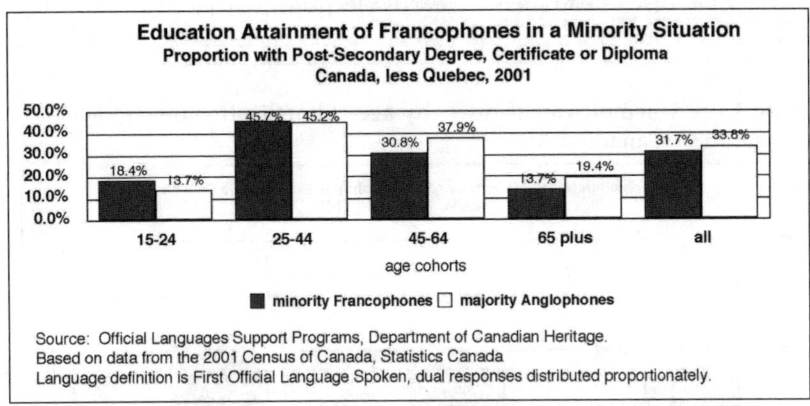

Figure 13.7: Education attainment of francophones in a minority situation

On the employment side we see that both minority-anglophone and minority-francophone communities experience higher levels of unemployment than do their majority counterparts.

In terms of employment in the public service, it is clear that francophones occupy an important place in Canada's public sector. According to the latest figures from the federal employer, Treasury Board Secretariat, francophones occupy 31 per cent of federal public service positions, compared to their 23 per cent share of the population. Previous deficits in the area of senior management positions have also disappeared in recent years as can be seen in Figure 13.9.

The catalyst role of the Department of the Secretary of State (Canadian Heritage) to support the development/promotion of official languages dates from the end of the

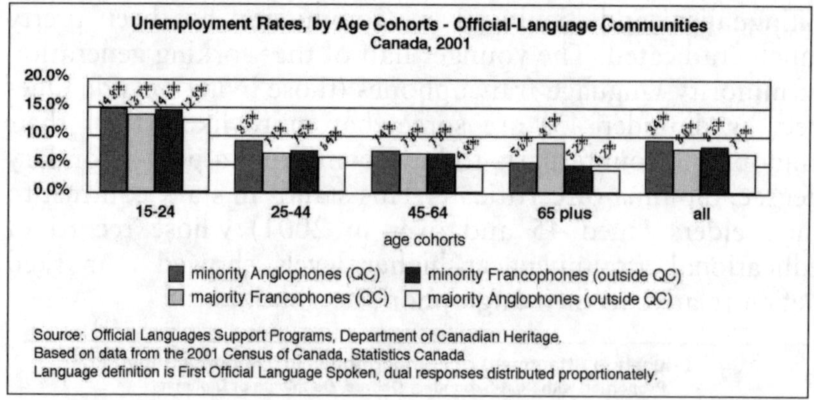

Figure 13.8: Unemployment rates, by age cohorts: official-language communities, Canada 2001

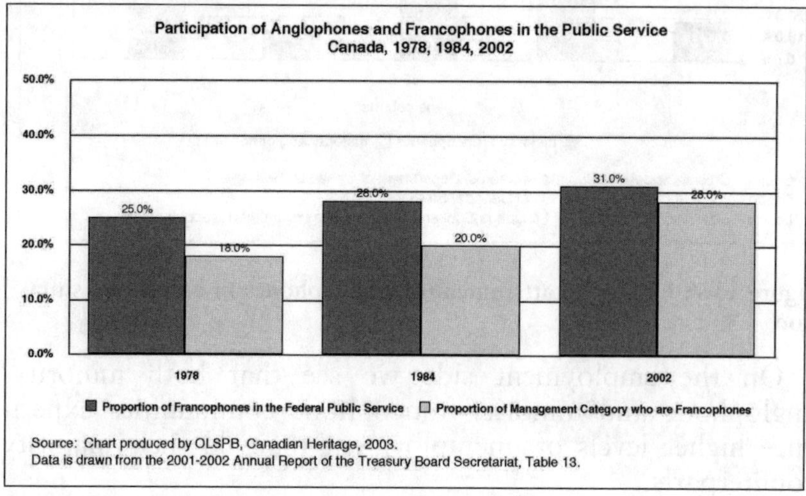

Figure 13.9: Participation of anglophones and francophones in the public service, Canada, 1987, 1984, 2002

1960s and was imbued with some of the ideals of empowerment and progress expressed by that period in Western history. The initial community support programme was named the 'Social Action Programme' and was clearly oriented towards the empowering of citizens to facilitate their organizational effectiveness. Through the 1970s and 1980s, the groups funded under the programme conceived of a variety of approaches and platforms to make their needs known and to bring about change on various fronts, including administrative, policy, legislative and even constitutional. In addition to their own energy and the financial support of the Department of the Secretary of State (Canadian Heritage's) official languages support programmes, these groups and networks also made use of the Court Challenges programme instituted by the federal government in the late 1970s to provide citizens and communities with the financial resources to seek the legal and technical services required to test and push the limits of language legislation as well as the guarantees provided under the 1982 Canadian Charter of Rights and Freedoms.

Advances in the area of official languages were by no means confined to minority community rights and developments, as the next section will show.

Second-Language Learning

As can be seen in Figure 13.10, there has been a steady and substantial increase in both the numbers and proportion of Canadians reporting on the census that they are able to speak both English and French. The number of Canadians able to speak both English and French has tripled over the past fifty years while the English–French bilingual share has risen from 12.3 per cent in 1951 to its current 17.7 per cent.

Within this overall 'good news' scenario, there are some worrisome aspects. According to Statistics Canada analysis, the proportion of young anglophone Canadians outside Quebec able to speak French dropped between 1996 and 2001. According to Statistics Canada,

> bilingualism lost some ground among anglophones aged 15 to 19 outside Quebec. In 2001, 14.7% of anglophones in this age group outside Quebec were bilingual. While this was twice the proportion for the anglophone population as a whole (7.1%), it was lower than the proportion of 16.3% among anglophones aged 15 to 19 in 1996. (Statistics Canada, 2002)

The number of English-speaking youth enrolled in French immersion and 'core' French classes reached a plateau in the last decade after rapid growth in the immersion stream in the 1980s. Additionally, a recent study by Canadian Parents for French suggests a looming shortage in teachers of French as a second language. Given that Canada faces an important demographic shift as those in the post-Second World War baby-boom generation near the end of their working careers, it is not obvious that Canada's record for excellence in this field can be easily maintained.

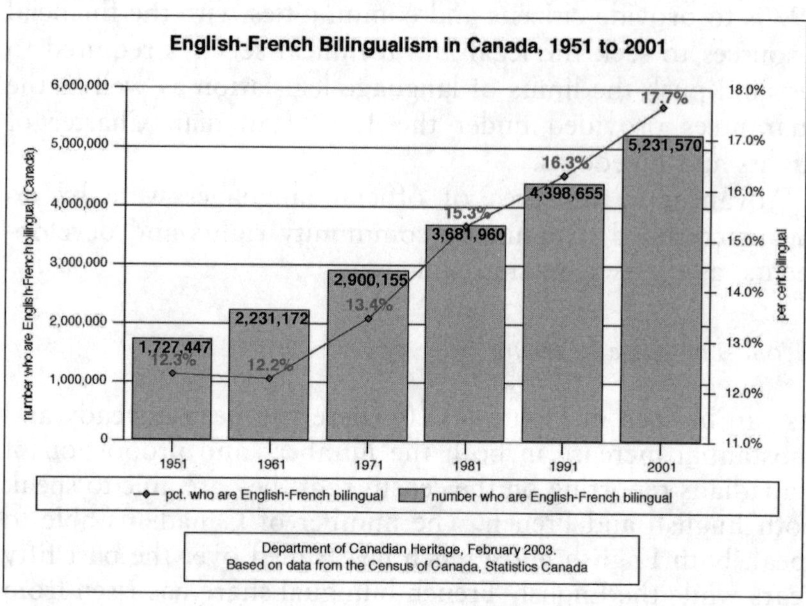

Figure 13.10: English–French bilingualism in Canada, 1951 to 2001

Effectiveness of Second-Language Learning Opportunities

As Figure 13.11 illustrates, younger Canadians (those aged 18 to 34 in 2002, who would normally have graduated from high school between 1985 and 2001) were much more likely than their older cohorts to express the view that their elementary/secondary education had provided a good opportunity to learn their second official language. It can also be noted that minority-language respondents were more likely than their majority-language counterparts to hold this view although the minority-majority gap has closed considerably over the generations. Coupled with the rising level of English–

French bilingualism noted in the census of the population, these findings support the view that important progress has been made.

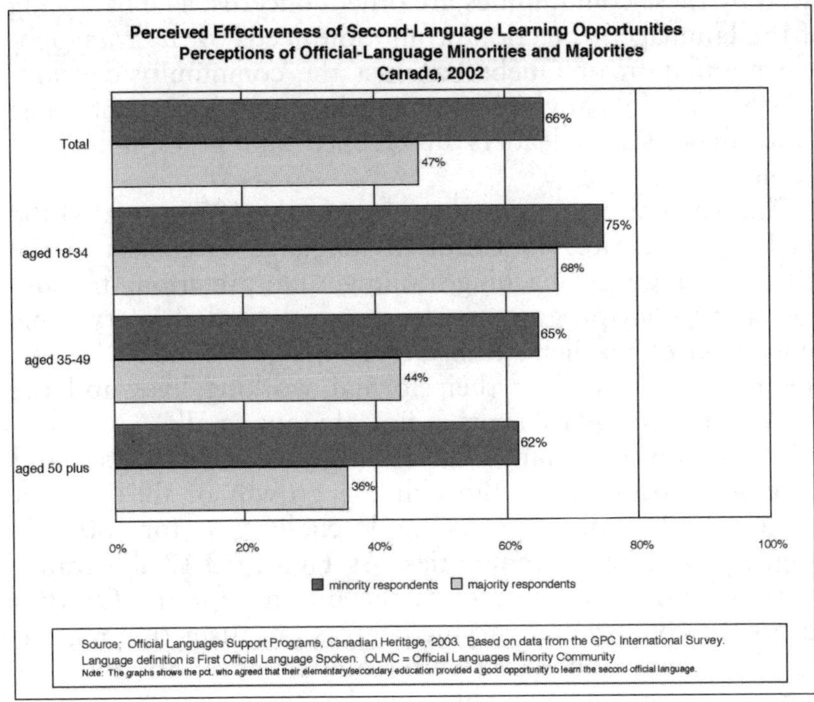

Figure 13.11: Perceived effectiveness of second-language learning opportunities

Despite the substantial successes described here, important challenges remain with respect to official languages in Canada. Although the number of francophones living in a minority situation has never been higher than it is today, it remains true that there is a continuing trend toward the adoption of English as the main language used at home and the higher than normal rate of ageing among francophone minorities may indicate some mid-term decline in numbers unless offset by interprovincial in-migration and international immigration. There are still significant gaps in education and employment levels in some regional francophone communities although the overall portrait is much more positive than it was forty years ago.

The continued decline in the numbers and proportion of members of Quebec anglophone communities as well as its higher tendency toward ageing and the employment deficit faced by these communities are other concerns. The balancing of the language protection/promotion needs of the francophone population of Quebec against the community development needs of its anglophone minority continues to challenge policy-makers and leaders in Quebec and in Canada as a whole.

The wave of promotional activity in the 1970s created the need for an entire workforce of language specialists in the areas of language teaching/training, interpretation, translation and policy/programme development and delivery. This generation of teachers, translators and government officials are nearing the end of their formal working lives and the stock of ready replacements is not obvious to all.

The enormous change in information technologies and societal transformation through the growth of the Internet creates both opportunities and challenges for official-language minority communities. As Figure 13.12 illustrates, there is both uneven access to the Internet for the OLMCs across the country and varying degrees of satisfaction regarding the extent and quality of regional information in the minority language available on the Internet. Along with Industry Canada, Canadian Heritage works with official-language minority communities to increase access and content on the Internet to minimize the information technology gap.

Demographic Diversity

There is an increasingly important discussion and debate within francophone minority communities regarding the need to embrace ethnic and national diversity and welcome, indeed encourage immigration from other francophone cultures as a way of assuring a demographic future for francophone minority communities.

As Figure 13.13 illustrates, francophone minorities are much more homogenous than their majority anglophone neighbours. Using minority–majority indices, it is clear that minority francophones are less than half as likely as their

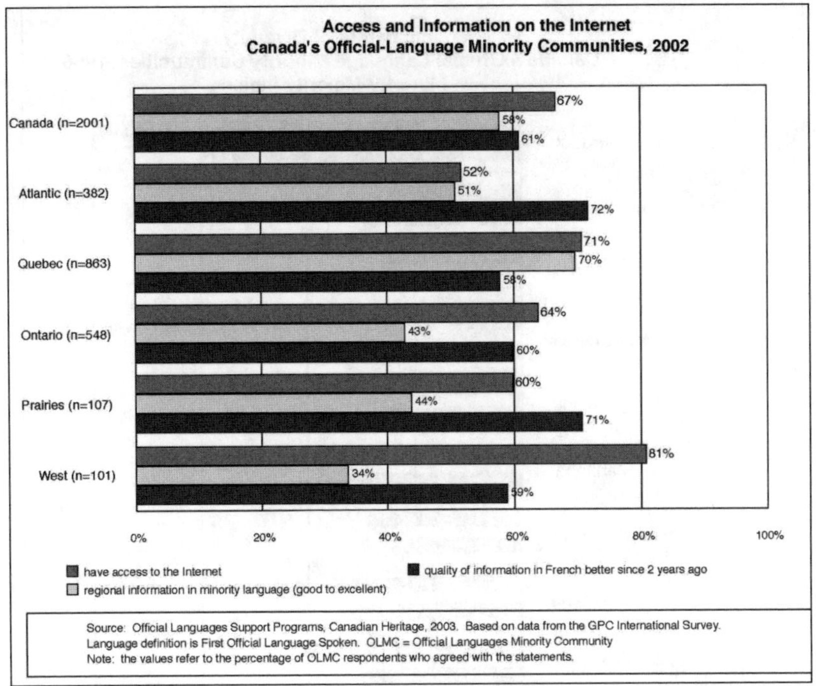

Figure 13.12: Access and information on the Internet: Canada's official-language minority communities, 2002.

anglophone counterparts to be members of visible minorities, to report aboriginal roots or to be immigrants to Canada. Given that immigration is expected to play a major role in the demographic evolution of Canada in the next few decades, given the low birth rate found in Canada and the tendency toward ageing, it will be important for minority francophone communities to attract and retain immigrants from other francophone cultures if they wish to maintain their share of the population.

Conclusions

From the adoption of the first federal languages legislation in 1969, through the enshrining of language rights in the Canadian Charter of Rights and Freedoms (1982) and the second federal languages Act in 1988 to the present day,

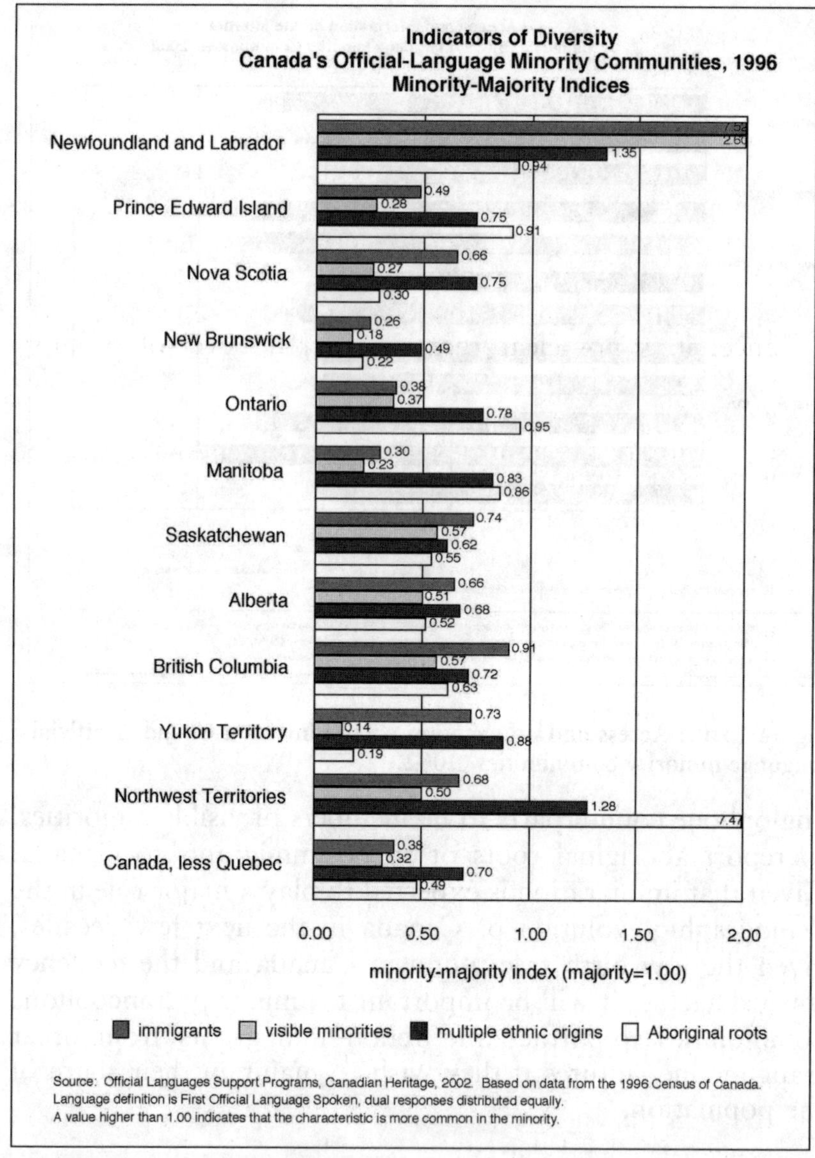

Figure 13.13: Indicators of Diversity: Canada's Official-Language Minority Communities, 1996.

the evolving programme commitments of Secretary of State (Canadian Heritage) have expressed the vision of the Government of Canada in the promotion of official languages. This evolution can be understood as:

- a **progressive expansion of scope** from simply policies and rights *within* government seeking institutional bilingualism to policies and programmes designed to effect change *outside* government and across society as a whole, with a broad involvement of various segments of civic society;
- **support for clarification of constitutional and linguistic rights** – the Court Challenges programme has permitted OLMCs to clarify and expand their rights through court action since 1978; in the crucial case of school governance, it is not clear that the current level of progress would have been possible without the support of the Court Challenges Programme;
- **expansion of the nature of intergovernmental cooperation** beyond the education sector into other sectors crucial to the interests of official-language minorities – the pursuit of intergovernmental agreements in other sectors has underlined the importance of a comprehensive approach and the joint declaration of principles;
- **empowering of official-language minority communities** – the creation of the 'social action programme' in 1969 and its continuation through to the Official Languages Communities Support programmes of today has provided nearly thirty-five years of annual funding to more than three hundred and fifty community-based organizations; the Canada-Community Agreement approach challenges community leaders to develop a longer-term vision for community development, including the articulation of priority developmental areas;
- **broadening of the base for federal government-wide response to the challenges** of supporting OLMC development and recognition of the benefits of linguistic duality through the encouragement and coordination of a broad range of federal departments and agencies in contrast to the pre-1988 period when virtually all community development aspirations were laid at the door of Secretary of State (Canadian Heritage), an expectation that was neither commensurate with its resource capacity nor with its jurisdictional scope.

The commitments of the Government of Canada to linguistic duality lie at the very heart of Canada's history. From their inception, the promotional programmes of the Department of the Secretary of State (Canadian Heritage) were delivered on the basis of cooperation and partnership with various levels of government and sectors of society.

Essentially, the type of activity that the Department of the Secretary of State (Canadian Heritage) encourages in the area of linguistic duality reflects fundamental democratic values held by Canadians: promoting community spirit and dialogue, encouraging discussion and the exchange of views, relying on the consultative process, cooperation and good will, and seeking partnership on various levels. For as long as Europeans speaking English and French have coexisted on the North American continent, the language issue has produced some tensions. These cannot be ignored but nonetheless are addressed in the spirit of openness and tolerance that has long constituted the best measure of progress in this country.

Although there has been progress, it is undoubtedly true that the presence of vital, dynamic minority communities will always require recognition and support from the state. Minority linguistic existence can be likened to swimming upstream, which requires a constant energy to ensure that the mainstream does not submerge the minority stream. Federal constitutional/legislative protections and the various programme efforts have been oriented over the years to support the efforts of official-language minorities. When the status of English and French is considered over the thirty-five-year time span of Canadian Heritage programmes, it is difficult to deny important progress. Similarly, the situation of francophone minority communities has been dramatically altered over this time period.

14
Determining Language Policy: A Decision-Maker's Perspective?

RHODRI GLYN THOMAS

My aim is to present an assessment of the relationship between language and governance in Wales from the perspective of a practising politician. I was elected chair of the National Assembly for Wales, Culture Committee when it was set up in October 2000. National Assembly committees have a cross-party membership and their role is to develop policy and scrutinize the Welsh government's policies in respect of each ministerial portfolio.

One of the first tasks we were asked to undertake was a comprehensive review of the Welsh language. In my view the challenge was to put in place a strategy for saving a minority language within the context of so many other European languages' having disappeared during the modern period. At the time the 1991 census figures told us that 508,549 (approximately 18.7 per cent) of the people of Wales could speak Welsh. There was an expectation that the 2001 census figures would show a slight increase in that figure, mainly due to Welsh-medium education, but at the point of undertaking the review there was no reliable indication of the actual percentage rise. As it turned out, the 2001 census figure of 21 per cent of the population able to speak Welsh was higher than expected, but a great deal of critical examination of the results needs to take place before we can lend any great credence to that particular statistic. As we began our review the Welsh language was in a relatively weak position following a century and more of rapid decline and only two decades of stabilization. In short, its position was unsustainable.

If the National Assembly for Wales was serious about its vision of a bilingual Wales then it needed to put forward a comprehensive package of proposals to transform the position of the Welsh language. The challenge facing the committee was to produce a package which could then be developed into government policy. A number of outside organizations, and indeed some members of the committee, felt that battles could be won and lost within the review process itself. However, my view from the outset was that unless our recommendations were transformed into government policy then there was no real value to them. Recommendations which were confined to our report, however radical, would have no affect on the situation of the Welsh language unless they were incorporated in the government of Wales's policy programme. Whilst there was every reason for us to challenge the government to act decisively there was no point calling upon it to do the impossible or the impractical. Colin Williams (in chapter 15) has presented an analytical assessment of what has been achieved by the National Assembly for Wales in terms of the Welsh language together with an earlier critique of the government of Wales's policy document *Iaith Pawb* (Williams 2004). I have no quarrel with his analysis or the conclusions he draws.

However, in this chapter I have been asked to provide an insider's perspective on governance. Thus I approach the whole process, faced by the committee, from the purely subjective position of being the chair with a responsibility for steering the project through to the presentation of the final report and beyond that into the development of government policy. That was always the challenge facing the committee, although not everyone on the committee and nor certainly those commenting from the outside realized that basic fact of political life. Later in this chapter I will consider the question of what implications does the report and the publication of the government's policy document *Iaith Pawb* have for the protest movement, for bodies who promote the Welsh language and the political parties in Wales. First of all I want to examine the process of putting together the report and the government's response.

It was never going to be an easy task. However, there was one specific area which needed detailed attention. Increasing the number of Welsh-speakers can only happen through greater access to Welsh-medium education. As a committee we decided to ask the Education and Lifelong Learning Committee of the National Assembly for Wales to use its expertise to study the statutory provision of education and appoint its own special adviser. This meant that the Culture Committee could concentrate on the wider political and socio-economic aspects of linguistic growth. It also meant that we did not need a special advisor from a purely educational background. The successful candidate as the special adviser to the Culture Committee, following the interview process, was Euryn Ogwen Williams. He offered an invaluable fount of experience and knowledge due to his membership of the original Welsh Language Board and his work with S4C and Acen, which began in 1989 as a project within S4C to teach Welsh to adults through the *Now You're Talking* series, and which is now an independent company specialising in language software and teaching methods. Euryn Ogwen Williams understood the way in which the Welsh-language institutions worked. The cross-party Culture Committee of the National Assembly also decided that it would look at nursery education and adult second-language learning, as they were not part of the statutory education provision.

Although these decisions offered a clear structure for our review we still faced a number of problems. How could we deal with the thorny issue of vested interests? How could the committee come up with proposals that would receive universal support when so many organizations in Wales had long-held, often conflicting and apparently dogmatic theories about the survival of the Welsh language? Could we really expect them to say – 'we have always demanded this but we now accept that you have come forward with some valuable recommendations, which we will endorse and support'?

The two main protagonists on the protest front were those who believed that safeguarding the heartlands was the priority and those who were campaigning for a new parliamentary act focusing on the language and the private sector. Both these views had merit and deserved and received a great deal of consideration. The leading voice promoting the importance of the Welsh-speaking heartlands was a newly formed organization called Cymuned (Community). Cymuned argued that without areas with a critical mass of Welsh-speakers actively using the language on a day-to-day basis Welsh could not survive as a living language. It was impossible and it would have been irresponsible to challenge that basic premise. No language can survive without a critical mass of natural speakers using it in every aspect of their lives. However, the problem was that the practical issues of addressing inward and outward migration and restricting access to housing and jobs to locals represented real difficulties for any government in terms of implementation.

The substantive issue of retaining a critical mass of Welsh-speakers who were both able and willing to use the language on a day-to-day basis in the traditional Welsh-speaking heartlands remained a major factor in the committee's deliberations throughout the review process. What percentage represented a critical mass? Was it 70 per cent as assumed by some commentators or could a reduced percentage hovering somewhere above 50 per cent constitute a critical mass? Should it be calculated on an area basis or a community basis? These questions were raised time and time again. There was a clear need to facilitate access for indigenous people to good-standard housing and well-paid employment in order to allow them to remain within their local communities. But there was also a real fear that such actions could be judged to be discriminatory. The committee also identified at an early stage the need to educate people who were moving into areas that were traditionally Welsh speaking that they were making a cultural as well as a geographical decision. But once again the question arose – how could this be done in a sensitive and productive way?

Cymdeithas yr Iaith Gymraeg (the Welsh Language Society) had gained wide-ranging support from numerous organisations and institutions in Wales for its demand for a new language act. The main argument in favour of such a move was that there were a number of utilities offering services to the public which were not covered by the 1993

Welsh Language Act and therefore had no statutory obligation to offer a comprehensive bilingual service. A number of these utilities had previously been in the public sector but having followed the path of privatization did not need to provide a Welsh-language scheme and were not accountable to the Welsh Language Board for their actions. This situation was clearly unacceptable, but once again the committee was faced with the question: would a new language act transform the fortunes of the Welsh language, strengthening its position and thus increasing its potential for survival?

There is little doubt that the 1993 Act needs to be reformed, if only in light of the 1998 Government of Wales Act, but the view of the committee was that a new act was not an immediate priority. There were areas where the 1993 Act could be developed through secondary legislation in the National Assembly in order to include a number of utilities and other private companies offering services to the public. There was also the consideration that recommendations by the committee, if government adopted them, could create a need for a substantially different Act and therefore the formulation of that Act at this time may be somewhat premature. If this scenario was to emerge then by the time we came to the point of developing a new act the primary legislative powers could well be in the hands of National Assembly for Wales. If a new act was needed then it was surely desirable that members elected from Wales to the National Assembly should consider it.

There were also difficulties in terms of the positions taken by the political parties in Wales. The minister, Jenny Randerson, and her party, the Welsh Liberal Democrats, appeared to come to the issue with an open mind and were prepared to look at the evidence objectively but with a commitment to do everything practical to foster and promote the Welsh language. It was a little more difficult for the other parties. The Welsh Conservatives were from the outset aware and rightly proud of the contribution made by recent Conservative governments in Westminster to the promotion of the Welsh language, primarily through the work of Wyn Roberts when he has under-secretary of state at the Welsh Office between 1979 and 1997. This included setting up a Welsh-language television channel, S4C, promoting Welsh-medium education and creating a new Welsh Language Act, which also established the Welsh Language Board in its current statutory role. While they were enthusiastic in their support for the language they were tied into the past and felt that any future support system must be based on the Wyn Roberts model of encouragement and gentle persuasion. Consequently, they were very suspicious of any proposals which were perceived as carrying an element of enforcement.

However, the parties bringing most, if very different, baggage to the table were the Welsh Labour Party and Plaid Cymru – The Party of Wales. Both had real problems in divesting themselves of past interests and addressing the issue at hand. There has been a tradition of, at the best, disinterest and at times open animosity towards the language within the ranks of the Welsh Labour Party. This has certainly changed but the awareness of that history made this a difficult issue for the party. While the vast majority of Labour Assembly Members would be described as being pro-Welsh, very few of them would be seen as actively promoting the language. It appeared at times that Delyth Evans, a Labour Culture Committee member, was fighting a lone battle although it was a highly effective one. There were some voices of dissent which were vociferous and ironically some of the most enthusiastic opponents of the language were members of the Culture and Education Committees. It was clear that leading figures in the Welsh Labour Party in the Assembly, although they themselves were amenable to the concept of promoting the language, would not countenance any measures that would inflame internal tensions.

Plaid Cymru – The Party of Wales was tied to a very different past. Many of the members, including the chair of the Culture Committee, had been active members of Cymdeithas yr Iaith Gymraeg and part of the protest movement. There was also the small matter of the party policy calling for a new language act. If the Welsh Labour Party had difficulty with some members claiming it was going too far along the route of support for the language, Plaid Cymru had the opposite problem of members' complaining that the recommendations were not strong enough. Following the first elections to the newly established Assembly, Plaid Cymru had suddenly found itself in May 1999 as the main opposition party in Wales with seventeen of the sixty Assembly Members. Being in such a powerful position in the mainstream political life of Wales proved difficult to cope with for the party. Understanding that this necessarily meant a new relationship with the protest movement was perhaps something that the party had not grasped. It was certainly true during the review and led to some rather theatrical grandstanding towards the end of the process which had no real relevance to the review process or the main recommendations of the report. However, Dafydd Wigley AM, an elder statesman within Plaid Cymru, fought a rearguard action to change dramatically the nature of the report and its main recommendations, which was more to do with keeping the troops happy in Gwynedd than any expectation that his calls would substantially change our findings.

This leads us to other problem areas faced by the committee. Wales has a weak indigenous printed news media; for example, the country lacks a national broadsheet, and this results in difficulty in stimulating a reasoned debate on the future of the language. It is not a subject that naturally lends itself to headlines and two-minute interviews. This meant that the reporting of the review continually centred on comments by individuals within and outside the two committees which had no real substance or relevance but were sensational enough to capture the imagination of the print and broadcast media. A prime example of this was the disgraceful response by some Assembly Members to the contributions of Professors Harold Carter (a human geographer) and Dafydd Glyn Jones (a linguist). These eminent academics who had spent a lifetime studying aspects of the Welsh language offered substantive, if challenging, evidence to both committees. This lead to personal attacks, which can only be described as attempted character assassinations, by individuals who clearly did not have the intellectual capacity or the basic understanding of the process of review to deal with any submissions which challenged their own preconceived positions. Fortunately, the vast majority of members on both committees showed political maturity by ignoring these childish antics.

Although the committee spent over a year ploughing through hundreds of written and oral contributions it is difficult to avoid the conclusion that much of the evidence was superficial and failed to address the issue of linguistic growth. Far too many organizations, such as Mudiad Ysgolion Meithrin (the Welsh Nursery School Movement), Rhieni Dros Addysg Gymraeg (Parents for Welsh-medium Education) and Yr Urdd (The Welsh League of Youth), saw the review as an opportunity to inform the National Assembly for Wales that they were doing a very important job of work for the language and deserved more funding. Very few organizations addressed the issue of the threat to the future of the Welsh language and how they could extend or change their activities in order to contribute towards strengthening that position. Some institutions gave the impression that they had some God-given right to exist and expect state funding and did not feel they needed to justify existing funding let alone make a case for increased support. Such complacency revealed a frightening lack of awareness of the plight of the Welsh language and the need for urgent action if it was to survive as a living language.

A number of organizations and individuals did offer a clear way forward in terms of holistic language planning (see Williams, 2007a) Once this concept had been accepted there was a need for political consensus. If the committee was going to challenge the government of Wales to commit itself to linguistic growth and a truly bilingual Wales there would have to be cross-party support for our recommendations. There were limited examples of the committee's having to take a decision on specific issues, such as the inclusion of a recommendation supporting the call for a new Welsh Language Act. But, by and large, members were asked to concentrate on the bigger picture of developing recommendations which the government of Wales could adopt to increase the number of Welsh-speakers by offering opportunities for acquiring and using the language.

Some commentators saw this process of creating a political consensus as a sign of weakness and presumed it would lead to the watering down of the recommendations. However, my view was that without the consensus there was little hope of achieving the ultimate aim of linguistic shift and while the politicians argued and organizations and individuals rehearsed their well-worn arguments the Welsh language would slide towards oblivion. Political consensus must be seen as strength in the process of saving the language. Without all-party support and a committed government that process can never take place. Protest groups will always take the easy hits but those of us who have taken the constitutional path must look to the way in which we put in place legislative processes. This in essence is the constructive approach to contemporary governance whereby the resultant policy can be implemented with a fair degree of unanimity and consequently influence the behaviour of organizations and individuals alike.

Some of the main themes of our report were recognized at an early stage. The future of the language could not be secured without an increase in the number of speakers and they in turn would need opportunities to use it in all aspects of their lives. The increase in numbers could only be achieved through Welsh-medium education. Surveys showed that, given the option, a majority of parents would choose Welsh-medium education. Parents should have access to Welsh-language nursery education in all parts of Wales. This would need a massive investment in both human and financial resources. As the numbers increased there would need to be both a continuum and a progression of Welsh-medium provision through the primary and secondary sectors and on to higher and further education. Again, the initial investment would need to be substantial. However, in the long term, this transformation of education provision could become cost neutral from the savings on the massive amounts of money spent on second-language teaching without any equivalent outcomes. Indeed, there may even be total cost savings.

What is now clear is that a major battle was lost in the Education and Lifelong Learning Committee through the failure to convince the Minister of Education, Jane Davidson, of the need for a national strategy for the provision of Welsh-medium education and the corresponding financial investment. In *Iaith Pawb* (NAfW, 2003) the government's policy document in response to the review, the glaring gaps in the section on Welsh-medium education provision appear time and time again. This without doubt is the weakest part of the government's strategy for linguistic growth. The minister's statements referring to her role as responding to initiatives by local authorities to increase Welsh-medium provision show a lack of vision and commitment on her behalf. Indeed, her response to moves by the councils of Carmarthenshire and Caerphilly to extend their Welsh-language provision showed an inclination to block rather than to promote the opportunities in this area. If the government is serious about linguistic growth then access to Welsh-language education has to be increased substantially through a comprehensive national strategy backed by a substantial financial commitment. Unless the Minister for Education would be prepared to guarantee this basic requirement, any claim by the Welsh Assembly Government to support the growth of the Welsh language (see chapter 2) is both meaningless and worthless. It just will not happen.

This takes us on to another central theme of the report. The Welsh language would have to be 'mainstreamed' and become cross-cutting in the government's policy making. A unit would need to be established in the civil service to ensure that this was coordinated and facilitated.

More than anything, there was a need for political clout within the civil service and the Cabinet that would transform the culture and mindset of government in terms of the Welsh language. The resultant Language Unit was established in 2003 and has been increasing the awareness within all departments of the need to mainstream the Welsh language. The remit letters to all ASPBs (Assembly Sponsored Public Bodies) was amended to include the call to mainstream the Welsh language. However, the unit is short of human resources and is not accountable to the Permanent Secretary in a way which would give it real political clout and allow it to function at a level that would make a real difference.

The one thing which would give the Welsh Assembly Government's commitment to linguistic growth real credibility would be a wholehearted endorsement by the First Minister. If Rhodri Morgan were to take personal responsibility for mainstreaming the Welsh language and making it a cross-cutting issue then we could look forward to real changes in terms of culture, mindset and policy. But in my view, the First Minister has been strangely silent and detached from the process of review and, indeed, the launch of the government's policy document, *Iaith Pawb*. Whether this is a sign of lack of enthusiasm, disinterest or animosity to the concept of linguistic growth is difficult to gauge. However, what is clear is without his wholehearted support and personal intervention this process has little hope of success. The ball is very much in his court.

Through its policy statement, *Iaith Pawb* (2003) the government of Wales has made a commitment to linguistic growth and this is without doubt a historic statement (Williams, 2004). This is the first time a government has pledged to promote the growth of the Welsh language. Indeed, historically the Welsh language has, from the Act of Union in 1536, been threatened by the Westminster government's actions. It would be ironic if the Government of Wales Act were to prove to be a turning point in the government's attitude towards the Welsh language. The Welsh government's target of a 5 per cent increase in Welsh-speakers by the 2011 census is ambitious and at the moment apparently unachievable. However, the target remains and it is the job of backbench members to ensure that the government makes a serious attempt at achieving its goal. The same is true of the cross-cutting element with every subject committee having an opportunity to question the relevant minister on what progress has been made to mainstream the Welsh language.

It has been suggested to me that the lack of action by the government of Wales, in terms of putting in place the structures which will allow it to achieve its aim of linguistic growth, means the whole review process was a failure and a waste of time. Far from it, for the action plan, which was developed during the review, process has been incorporated into the government's policy paper, *Iaith Pawb*. The real challenge which faces political parties and the protest movements now is to ensure that the coalition government delivers on its revised policy commitments. This is a new situation for everyone; the war has been won but the battles continue.

In terms of the language protest movements, these recent Assembly-driven events represent a major culture change. Cymdeithas yr Iaith Gymraeg, which is the main language movement in Wales of forty years standing, needs to face up to the challenge of placing pressure on the government to deliver on its own policies rather than calling for new initiatives. There is little political opening for a new language act at this particular time. Cymdeithas can arrange all the protests it wants and even a comprehensive campaign of civil disobedience without any hope of success, or it can put pressure on the Minister for Culture to speed up the process of bringing the utilities under the 1993 Act and also other companies offering a public service, such as mobile phones and IT providers. The latter is an achievable aim and Cymdeithas must ask itself the question of whether it wants to create real outcomes or carry on campaigning with no hope of success. Extending the 1993 Act in this way would create a sea change in the way in which the language is used as a means of conducting essential day-to-day business in terms of the individual consumer and commercial companies. This is an essential step forward in terms of the status of the language that could be dramatically speeded up through a major campaign by Cymdeithas yr Iaith Gymraeg. Cymdeithas is an effective and successful campaigning machine and this is an opportunity for it to embark on a campaign with the hope of real outcomes in terms of policy initiatives from the government but also the opportunity of reinvigorating the membership itself.

In the same way, Cymuned, a comparative newcomer to the language protest movement, has a major role to play in highlighting the need to ensure access to good-quality housing and jobs for people in their own communities. There is no prospect of any government of Wales restricting access into certain parts of the country because of linguistic or cultural issues. There is, however, a great deal which can be done to promote opportunities for young people to remain in their own communities if they so desire and much that can be done to ensure that those who choose to move into what has traditionally been known as the Welsh-speaking heartlands do not change the nature of those communities. This is a vital area if we are to retain communities where the critical mass of the population is able and willing to use the Welsh language in all aspects of their lives. Again, it is a matter of concentrating on the achievable and real outcomes rather than arguing about a linguistic policy that will never be adopted by government. Cymuned has the resolve and the intellectual capacity to use the present situation to ensure the government does make those commitments to our rural communities. An opportunity has already arisen with the Environment, Planning and Rural Affairs Committee's *Report into Affordable Housing in Rural Areas* (2003). Was there ever a more appropriate time for a major campaign on this issue?

The organizations promoting the language, and there are a plethora of them, must learn to work together in a coordinated way based on holistic language planning (Williams 2007b). As chair of the committee, I was able to take an overview position of the interface between government and linguistic organizations. It became obvious that major problems characterized the evidence sessions of the review process. The first was the number of organizations that promote the language. Many came along to tell us what a wonderful job they were doing and that they should be getting more money. These organizations must understand that there cannot be any additional funding without clear gains in terms of outcomes. Duplication was also evident and real savings could be made by organizations' working together and sharing resources. But, unfortunately, these tend to be highly individualistic bodies which are fiercely territorial. Someone has to 'bang heads together' and ensure that they see their own specific project as being secondary to the major project of linguistic growth.

The Assembly Government's Fforwm Iaith (Language Forum) initiative was seen as an umbrella organization which would allow all the major players promoting the language to meet in order to coordinate their activities under the banner of holistic language planning. The benefits were clear; the question was who would oversee this process. There were two options. The bottom-up approach with the Mentrau Iaith as the lead player or the top-down approach with the Welsh Language Board directing the activities. I still believe that eventually we will have to adopt the bottom-up approach in order to ensure local ownership and the enthusiastic engagement of local people. However, it was decided that Mentrau Iaith was a relatively new body without an established national structure and therefore was not in a position at the time to take up this responsibility. Bwrdd Yr Iaith Gymraeg, on the other hand, was a statutory body set up by the 1993 Language Act, which had the resources, experience and structures to enable it to be the empowerer of such a process. There is a conflict of interest when a statutory body is both the promoter and regulator of language planning. But the government may have now be moving on beyond the creation of the office of Dyfarnydd and the merger of Bwrdd yr Iaith Gymraeg with the Assembly Government, which Colin Williams analyses below. There is merit in the Canadian model where the equivalent body has a clear regulatory role even in terms of government activities. In the short term there was no real option other than to give the responsibility to Bwrdd Yr Iaith Gymraeg. But the future may well be very different. The Fforwn Iaith held its first meeting in October 2005. and even by its second meeting in May 2006 it was still unclear what its remit and impact will be. All the players, including Mentrau Iaith and Bwrdd yr Iaith, should be calling upon the Assembly Government's Culture Minister to strengthen the Fforwm Iaith. It is in all their interests to move from individualistic projects to contribute towards the holistic plan. The biggest winner of all would be the Welsh language.

This leaves us with the political parties. The Labour Party and the government of Wales, specifically, must take up the challenge of being the champion of linguistic growth in Wales. The First Minister must make a clear statement of intent about the process of promoting the Welsh language. Plaid Cymru – the Party of Wales needs to redefine its relationship both with its new coalition partner in government and with the protest movement.

All is left to play for. If the protest movement, the bodies promoting the language and all the political parties take on board the opportunities offered by this new situation for the Welsh language we can still hope to achieve the targets of the review and the *Iaith Pawb* policy document.

The Welsh language has depended on institutions to support and promote it. Over the past century this was done by the Nonconformist chapels in the years up to and just beyond the Second World War, then by Welsh-medium schools in the 1960s and further by S4C (the Welsh-medium television channel) in the 1980s and onwards. It is now the turn of the Welsh Assembly, primarily through government, but also with the active involvement of the opposition parties and other players. The opportunity is there, the preparatory work has been done. The challenge to deliver and achieve remains.[1]

REFERENCES

Jones, M. P. (2003) 'Gwaith Bwrdd yr Iaith Gymraeg ym Maes Addysg Gymraeg', in Roberts, G. and Williams, C. (eds), *Addysg Gymraeg, Addysg Gymreig*, Bangor: University of Wales, Bangor, pp. 116–128.

National Assembly for Wales (2002) *Our Language: its Future. The Policy Review of the Welsh Language by the Culture Committee and the Education and Lifelong Learning Committee*, Cardiff: National Assembly for Wales.

National Assembly for Wales (2003) *Iaith Pawb*. Cardiff: National Assembly for Wales.

Office of National Statistics (2003) *Welsh Language Statistics,* London: Office of National Statistics, http://www.statistics.gov.uk

Welsh Assembly Government (2001) *The Learning Country – A Comprehensive Education and Lifelong Learning Programme to 2010*, Cardiff: Welsh Assembly Government.

Welsh Assembly Government (2003a) *Iaith Pawb: A National Action Plan for a Bilingual Wales/Iaith Pawb: Cynllun Gweithredu Cenedlaethol ar gyfer Cymru Ddwyieithog*, Cardiff: Welsh Assembly Government.

Welsh Assembly Government (2003b) *Wales: A Better Country/ Cymru: Gwlad Well*, Cardiff: Welsh Assembly Government.

Williams. C. H. (2000a) 'Restoring the language', in Jenkins, G. (ed.), *'Let's Do Our Best for the Ancient Tongue': The Welsh Language in the Twentieth Century*, Cardiff: University of Wales Press, pp. 657–83.

Williams, C. H. (ed.), (2000b) *Language Revitalization: Policy and Planning in Wales*, Cardiff: University of Wales Press.

Williams, C. H. (2002) *Adfywiad yr Iaith Gymraeg: Cynllunio, Economi a Thiriogaeth/ The Revival of the Welsh Language: Planning, Economy and Territory*, Cardiff: Plaid Cymru.

Williams, C. H. (2004) 'Iaith Pawb: The Doctrine of Plenary Inclusion.' *Contemporary Wales,* Vol. 17. pp. 1–25.

Williams, C. H. (2007a) 'Deddfwriaeth Newydd a'r Gymraeg', *Contemporary Wales,* Vol. 19. pp. 217–33.

Williams, C. H. (2007b) *Linguistic Minorities in Democractic Context*, Basingstoke: Palgrave.

NOTES

[1] Editor's note. This chapter was completed prior to the author's appointment as Heritage Minister, Welsh Assembly Government.

15

Articulating the Horizons of Welsh

COLIN H. WILLIAMS

'Few things are more mischievous to good government and to 'domestic tranquillity' than splendid rhetoric that doesn't pay off.' (Alastair Cooke, 1973: 385)

Introduction

This chapter will analyse what effect successive changes in the British/Welsh political context have had on Welsh-language planning agencies and institutions as they seek to deliver largely pragmatic solutions to questions concerning the promotion of Welsh within the development of a bilingual society. Language policy has been determined mainly by an agency of the state which has operated at arm's length from the daily pressures of national government. This 'arm's-length' principal, a function of the quango governance inheritance, has now been abandoned by the government of Wales as it has integrated formerly 'independent' agencies such as the Welsh Development Agency and the Wales Tourist Board into the routine departments of state. The integration of the Welsh Language Board which was scheduled for April 2007 was suspended temporarily in the summer of 2006, but it remains government policy and thus is to be considered as a medium-term goal.

Having established itself as an innovative, influential agency during the period 1993–2007, the Welsh Language Board now finds its future under review and its post-integration remit is unclear. Thus there will be a significant transitional period occasioning a debate on a range of issues concerning language and governance. These include: How language policy is to be determined in the medium-term future? Which agencies will undertake language planning and consider strategic language policy issues? What is the relationship between central, national and local government with such para-public agencies? How is this likely to change and with what effect both in terms of increasing the effectiveness of language policy and in integrating and/or mainstreaming language considerations into all aspects of governance in Wales? How will the coalition government manage the issue of constructing a bilingual society?

The Welsh Office and Language Policy 1988–1998

The Welsh Office governmental system, was more concerned with implementing its statutory provision on Welsh, rather than with language planning and the creation of a new vision for bilingualism in Wales. It discharged its remit primarily through the Welsh Language Board, a quango, established by the UK Conservative government in 1989 to act as a sounding board for the development of Welsh-medium services. By 1999, the Welsh Language Board had established itself as the principal agency for the promotion of Welsh in public life. However, throughout the period, independent commentators had questioned the original settlement of the Welsh Language Act 1993 and had concluded that in vesting public institutions with language obligations, whilst eliding the issue of individual language rights, the 1993 Act had fallen far short of establishing Welsh as a co-equal language (Williams, 1998; 2000).

During the late 1980s incremental reforms in education, public administration, the legal system and local government increased the opportunities to learn and to use Welsh in society. However, these were regarded as piecemeal, insufficient and rudimentary. Nevertheless, they have had an impact on subsequent events, none more so than the Education Reform Act 1988, which granted a core-subject status for Welsh in all schools within the statutory education age range of 5 to 16. Now all children had an opportunity to develop bilingual skills and, for a substantial minority, to develop real fluency in Welsh. The challenge of the 1990s was to realize a fully functional bi/multilingual society through creating new opportunities for language choice within the public, voluntary and private sector of the economy.

The Welsh Language Act 1993 provided a statutory framework for the treatment of English and Welsh on the basis of equality. Its chief policy instrument was the refashioned and strengthened Welsh Language Board, established on 21 December 1993, as a non-departmental statutory organization. It was funded by a grant from the Welsh Office, which, for example, in the year ending 31 March 1998, prior to devolution, totalled £5,756,000. It had three main duties:

1. Advising organizations which were preparing language schemes on the mechanism of operating the central principle of the Act, that the Welsh and English languages should be treated on a basis of equality.
2. Advising those who provide services to the public in Wales on issues relevant to the Welsh language.
3. Advising central government on issues relating to the Welsh language.

The board's primary goal is to enable the language to become self-sustaining and secure as a medium of communication in Wales. It has set itself four priorities:

1. to increase the numbers of Welsh-speakers;
2. to provide more opportunities to use the language;
3. to change the habits of language use and encourage people to take advantage of the opportunities provided;
4. to strengthen Welsh as a community language.

The eleven board members were appointed by the Secretary of State for Wales and they devoted two days a month to the activities of this quango. The day-to-day work of the board was undertaken by thirty staff members divided into seven areas of responsibility, namely, policy; public and voluntary sector; grants and private sector; education and training; marketing and communication; finance; and administration.

The 1993 Act details key steps to be taken by the Welsh Language Board and by public sector bodies in the preparation of Welsh-language schemes, which are designed to implement the central principle of the Act, that is to treat Welsh and English on the basis of equality. However, as chapters 5, 11 and 14 of this volume make clear, this obligation is not absolute; public bodies need only implement the principle 'so far as is both appropriate in the circumstances and reasonably practicable'. The Act provides that the board must issue guidelines as to the form and content of schemes, to which each public body must have regard in preparing their scheme, that the public body must carry out consultations in the preparation of the scheme, and the scheme must be submitted to the board for approval. The guidelines require details on how the body's scheme will deal with the Welsh-speaking public, in terms of correspondence, telephone communication, the conduct of meetings, together with the organization's identity, iconography, signage, publishing and printing material, official notices, press notices, publicity and advertising.

Between 1995 and 1999, sixty-seven language schemes had been approved including all twenty-two local authorities. On the eve of devolution notices had been issued to a further fifty-nine bodies to prepare schemes. Under the spirit of the 1993 Act, the board had also developed partnerships with the twenty-two unitary authorities through Rhwydiaith (Language Network), with the Welsh Consumer Council, the Welsh Council for Voluntary Action and with a range of private sector organizations. During the financial year 1997–8 grants totalling £2,254,792 were distributed under the board's main grants scheme to organizations as varied as the National Eisteddfod, the Welsh Books Council and Shelter Cymru (Welsh Language Board, 1998).

The board also had the right to extend its remit in other sectors covered by the Act, and had given priority to education and training. By June 1998 the Welsh education schemes of two local authorities had been approved and a further fifteen were being developed (Welsh Language Board, 1998). Further and higher education colleges, together with Welsh-medium pre-school provision have also received attention.

Since 1998 Education Learning Wales (ELWa), with input from the board, had coordinated a national strategy for Welsh for adults, and this sector has benefited from a more robust and systematic provision of service, accreditation of adult tutors, resource development and strategic intervention related to skills acquisition in key areas of the economy, such as insurance and banking, retails sales and the legal profession. In total grants of £2,027,000 were distributed in the year 1997–8 to local authorities to promote Welsh-language education.

The National Assembly and Language Policy, 1999–2007

On devolution many of the functions previously entrusted to the Welsh Office were transferred to the National Assembly. Rawlings (2003: 140) describes this transfer as involving both more governance and a greater role for legal considerations and instruments in the conduct of government. The National Assembly was established and functions as a bilingual institution. This puts into operative effect the reality of two official languages for governance as acknowledged in the Welsh Language Act of 1993. A key question was whether or not the Assembly would have the authority to grant to the Welsh Language Board the right and the duty to monitor Assembly deliberations and actions with regard to the Welsh language. The Assembly has three types of functions under the current statutory arrangements: a) functions relating to the establishment of the regulatory framework (sections 8, 9, 10, 11); b) adjudicative functions (between the board and public bodies) in preparing and revising language schemes (sections 14, 15, 16); c) functions relating to the enforcement of the terms of language schemes (section 20). The board became answerable to the Minister for Culture, the Welsh Language and Sport and received an annual remit letter which detailed its priorities for the short term. In most cases such letters reflected the advice and problem areas identified by the board as indicated to the minister in the previous year.

The publication of the 2001 census results on the Welsh language in March 2003 revealed that there were 576,000

Welsh-speakers aged 3 and over (21 per cent of the population), which represented a 2 per cent increase since 1991. The proportion of people who could speak, read and write Welsh increased from 13.6 per cent to 16.3 per cent (1991–2001). A further 138, 000 (5 per cent) said they understood Welsh but did not speak it (Higgs, Williams and Dorling, 2004). Figure 15.1 reveals that the overall patterns from previous dates, 1981 and 1991, are retained with only Anglesey, Gwynedd, Ceredigion and Carmarthenshire having over 50 per cent of their populations who can speak Welsh. As seen from Table 15.1, however, the relationship with percentage of population born in Wales is a weak, but important one and a number of factors, such as in- and out-migration patterns and the registration of university students at their college not home domicile in 2001, make inter-censal comparisons difficult at the aggregate level.

A priority for the Assembly's first term was a thorough review of the condition of Welsh carried out by both the Culture and the Education Committees. Its recommendations fed into a new government strategy, as enunciated in *Iaith Pawb* (2003), which aimed to establish a bilingual society. It is argued that critical decisions on language policy are now being taken by involved and informed politicians. There is a belief that interest groups, local government representatives and officers, specialist agencies, individuals and social movements are somehow 'empowered' by devolution and are thus participants in the process of formulating and implementing language-related policies. All this has resulted in an additional focus, resources, energies and improved harmonization of language-related policies. Partners in Wales are far more self-consciously concerned with an approach we may label 'holistic language planning'.

In *Iaith Pawb* the Wales Assembly Government (WAG) committed itself to achieving these five goals:

1. By 2011 to increase the proportion of Welsh-speakers by 5 percentage points from the 2001 census baseline.
2. To arrest the decline in heartland communities, especially those with close to 70 per cent+ Welsh-speakers.

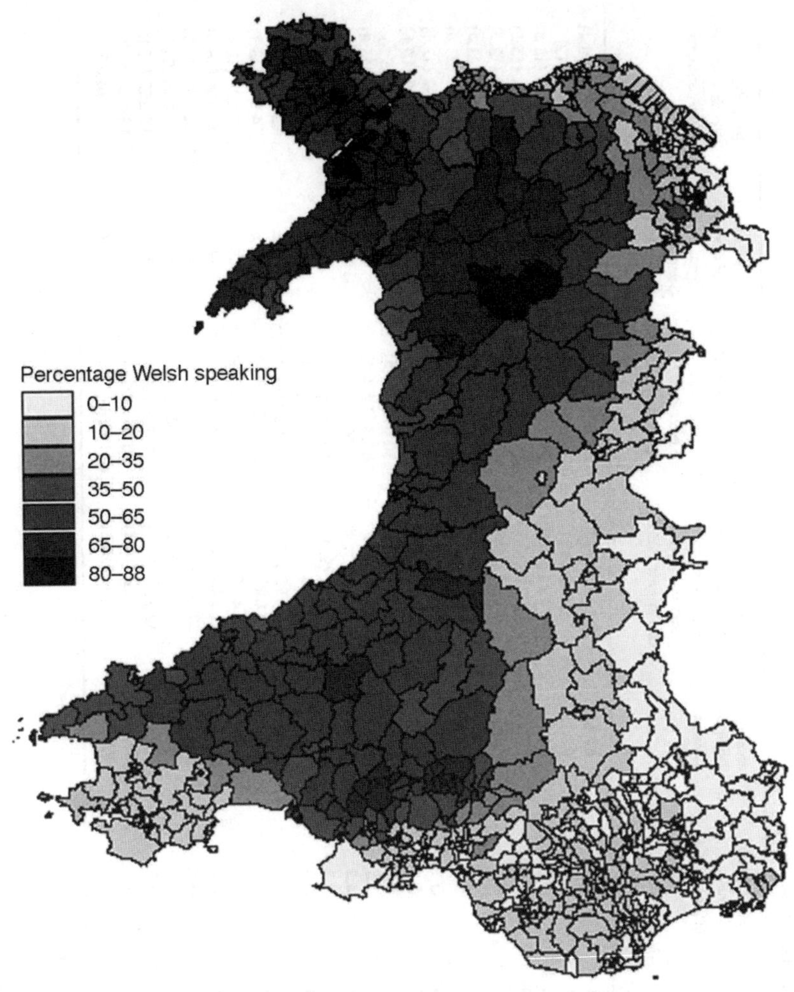

Source: Office for National Statistics (2003). Reproduced with permission from Higgs, Williams and Dorling 2004: 194.

Figure 15.1: Percentage Welsh-speakers for electoral divisions (2001 census)

3. To increase the proportion of children in pre-school Welsh education.
4. To increase the proportion of families where Welsh is the principal language.
5. To increase the provision of Welsh-medium services in the public, private and voluntary sector.

Table 1 **Results from 2001 census (by unitary authority)**

Unitary authority	2001 Population	Population change (1991–2001) %	Percentage born in Wales	Number and proportion of people aged 3 and over who can speak Welsh	1 or more skills in Welsh language (numbers/ percentages)	Percentage of people aged 3 and over with no knowledge of Welsh	Identified self as Welsh (numbers/ percentages)
Anglesey	66 829	−2.9	67.6	38 678 (59.8)	45 534 (70.4)	29.6	12 975 (19.4)
Blaenau Gwent	70 064	−1.8	92.1	6169 (9.1)	9026 (13.3)	86.7	8417 (12)
Bridgend	128 645	0.7	84.7	13 174 (10.6)	24 763 (19.9)	80.1	20 275 (15.8)
Caerphilly	169 519	1.5	89.9	17 799 (10.9)	27 228 (16.7)	83.3	26 276 (15.5)
Cardiff	305 353	8.0	74.9	32 069 (10.9)	47 998 (16.3)	83.7	40 220 (13.2)
Carmarthen	172 842	2.9	80.1	83 854 (50.1)	106 440 (63.6)	36.4	40 471 (23.4)
Ceredigion	74 941	19.8	58.6	37 754 (51.8)	44 635 (61.2)	38.8	16 307 (21.8)
Conwy	109 596	3.7	53.9	31 044 (29.2)	42 174 (39.7)	60.3	13 289 (12.1)
Denbighshire	93 065	5.1	57.9	23 512 (26.1)	32 469 (36)	63.9	9829 (10.6)
Flintshire	148 594	5.5	51.1	20 217 (14.1)	30 660 (21.4)	78.6	8662 (5.8)
Gwynedd	116 843	3.5	69.8	77 494 (68.7)	85 847 (76.1)	23.9	31 356 (26.8)
Merthyr Tydfil	55 981	−4.2	91.9	5412 (10.0)	9602 (17.7)	82.3	9065 (16.2)
Monmouthshire	84 885	5.3	61.3	7412 (9.0)	10 590 (12.9)	87.1	5871 (6.9)
Neath Port Talbot	134 468	−0.8	89.5	23 194 (17.8)	37 551 (28.8)	71.2	22 872 (17)
Newport	137 011	3.2	81.1	12 655 (9.6)	17 622 (13.4)	86.6	12 326 (9)
Pembrokeshire	114 131	2.4	68.7	23 689 (21.5)	32 340 (29.4)	70.6	14 912 (13.1)
Powys	126 354	6.5	55.6	25 474 (20.8)	36 847 (30.1)	69.9	15 927 (12.6)
Rhondda Cynon Taff	231 946	0.5	89.9	27 543 (12.3)	47 213 (21.1)	78.9	38 384 (16.5)
Swansea	223 301	0.1	82.1	28 542 (13.2)	48 582 (22.5)	77.5	34 135 (15.3)
Torfaen	90 949	1.6	85.5	9423 (10.7)	12 742 (14.5)	85.5	8934 (9.8)
Vale of Glamorgan	119 292	2.1	75.7	12 778 (11.1)	19 453 (16.9)	83.1	15 252 (12.8)
Wrexham	128 476	5.6	71.9	17 859 (14.4)	28 401 (22.9)	77.1	12 065 (9.4)
Total	2 903 085		75.4	575 744 (20.5)	661 526 (23.6)	71.6	14.39

Source: Office for National Statistics (2003)

Table 15.1: Results from 2001 census (by unitary authority)

The measures set out in the Action Plan are to be assessed against a number of key targets while the principal policy options for achieving these aims are:

1. The NAfW's Welsh Language Unit.
2. Mainstreaming Welsh-language considerations into all policy development.
3. Developing national language planning through the Welsh Language Board/ Bwrdd yr Iaith.
4. Developing the government's research and analysis capacity.
5. Creating evidence-based policies in the field of language revitalization.

Iaith Pawb is a significant declaration and represents a genuine, historical commitment by government. The strategy *has* adopted many of the recommendations put to the Assembly's Education and Culture reviews during 2002. The most notable of which are:

- The operation of the principle of language equality.
- Devising an effective in-house bilingual culture.
- Deciding how Welsh will be a cross-cutting issue in all aspects of policy.
- Producing bilingual legislation.
- Developing a professional bilingual legislative drafting team of jurilinguists as in Canada.
- Developing innovative IT translation procedures.
- Prioritizing the NAfW's translation needs.
- Finessing WAG's relationship with Welsh Language Board and its many partners.
- Relating its bilingual practices to other levels of government, institutions and to civil society.

A critical area is language transmission both within the family and within the education system. Thus a campaign has been launched to boost language acquisition, principally through the statutory 5 to 16 age education provision, lifelong learning and latecomer centres. In an increasingly mixed language of the marriage context, a successful pilot project on Twf – the Family Language Transfer – programme has been extended to other sites in Wales. There is a commitment to boosting the bilingual services of NHS Wales, of *Iaith Gwaith,* the Welsh in the workplace programme. Finally, in order to access such increased choice, government has recognized the need to invest in language tools and the sociocultural infrastructure as detailed below.

The strategy has come under some scrutiny from critical commentators, government partners and from those within the civil service charged with delivering this programme of reform. Williams (2004) has argued that, while *Iaith Pawb* contains fine rhetoric which legitimizes policy, it is also replete with ill-defined mechanisms and says next to nothing on monitoring the effects of policies. The discussion on education in particular is a major weakness, and this lacuna should addressed by a seasonal mid-term review. Of prime concern is the insufficient detail on developing Welsh within the statutory sector. There is also far too little on L2 (second language) learners, and no attention at all to the rates of language attrition between primary, secondary and tertiary levels. Compounding this, of course, is that insufficient resources are available to deliver even what is promised in the strategy. Thus the mid-term review will be a challenge as so much of the success of *Iaith Pawb* is dependent on the educational opportunities for acquiring fluency in Welsh at many entry points. The key weaknesses of the policy as it stands may be summarized as follows:

- Fine rhetoric which legitimizes policy.
- But ill-defined mechanisms, with little on the monitoring effects of policies
- Insufficient resources.
- Lacklustre political will to implement the total strategy as a coherent package.
- Discussion on education is a major weakness.
- Poor detail on developing Welsh in the statutory sector.
- Far too little on L2 learners.
- No attention to the rates of language attrition between primary, secondary and tertiary levels.
- Community regeneration promised, but partial or deficient remedies offered.

- Measures to safeguard the 'heartland' are marginalized within the proposals.
- No focused priority, thus the overall policy lacks political conviction.
- No proposed consideration of a stronger Welsh Language Act.
- The treatment of the private sector is minimal and cursory at best.
- The strategy needs far more professional attention to policy to make it convincing to economic interest groups.
- National planning policy needs specific guidance on how to treat the Welsh language as a material issue.
- Technical Advice Note 20 provides an outline on Welsh-language considerations but it is rarely invoked and it is in need of complete reform.
- Housing development guidance is weak.
- Linguistic impact assessments (LIAs) are identified and commissioned research on LIA (by 13 local authorities, two National Parks, WLB and academics) is to be sent for public consultation and then reviewed in the short term.
- The Wales Spatial Plan is referenced but there are too few details on how language and socio-spatial context are interrelated.

Realistically, *Iaith Pawb* should be treated as a signal of good intent by a government which has yet to work out exactly how to operationalize its wish list. It is best regarded as a template, a framework for action, rather than a prescriptive set of promises. The Welsh Language Board (WLB) has been designated as the principal instrument by which this policy is to be realized and has been given significant additional resources so as to recruit more specialist staff, extend its remit and open new offices in locations in west and north Wales. In many ways the principal strengths of the *Iaith Pawb* strategy reflect the considerable input by the Welsh Language Board to the consultative process and to the formal and informal dialogue which is constantly undertaken between the minister, the WAG Language Unit and the WLB. It should be recalled that the WLB has both an advisory and a monitoring role in terms of the WAG's own Language Plan.

Over and above this, the WAG has to determine how it will handle a number of pressing internal issues, viz. the operation of the principle of language equality, devising effective in-house bilingualism; deciding how Welsh will be a cross-cutting issue influencing all policy; the production of bilingual legislation; the development of a professional bilingual legislative drafting team of jurilinguists as in Canada. Among its medium-term challenges are: the need to extend its innovative IT translation procedures; prioritizing its translation needs; finessing its relationship with Welsh Language Board and its many partners; relating its bilingual practices to other levels of government, institutions and to civil society.

Even if government were to attend to the above there would remain significant structural weaknesses in terms of the implementation of language planning in Wales. Thus even the agreed WAG Language Schemes can remain symbols of good intent rather than genuine services at the point of local demand. This not only bespeaks an inefficient delivery of service but also suggests an absence of genuine participatory democracy. Secondly, there is a critical need to monitor the aims and impact of all the language schemes, whether at national or local government and within the public institutions, for many such schemes are now being renegotiated and are in their third phase. The board is able to exercise a great deal of discretion; a) as to whether to begin an investigation; b) as to whether to include recommendations in cases of failure; and c) as to whether to refer non-compliance matters to the National Assembly. As Dunbar argues in chapter 6, the board does not have any independent powers of enforcement. Ultimately, enforcement of the Welsh-language schemes rests with the National Assembly, which is authorized to act to remedy the situation, but is not *required* to do so.

The crunch question is just how much value has been added to public administration and bilingual service delivery by the adoption of such schemes? Has language-related behaviour changed? The devolution processes promise of empowerment, ownership, participation and partnership needs to be rooted in a national infrastructure and not conceived as 'add-ons' to an already over-worked, if not overwhelmed, public service.

Beyond the realms of public administration there remains the pressing need to promote Welsh elsewhere, particularly within the private sector. This would include greater political and legal encouragement, with sanctions where necessary, the adoption of holistic perspectives rather than a fragmented and sectoral mindset; the development of appropriate terminology and sharing of best practice; a Language Standardization Centre; the highlighting of the economic benefits of bilingualism; encouraging a professional discussion regarding the role of Welsh in the economy; developing role models among the SMEs (small and medium-sized enterprises) and larger companies; influencing key decision-makers who are often based outside Wales. Whether a single new Welsh Language Act can deliver such a diverse range of responses is problematic, but there can be no doubt that the absence of binding legislation affecting the bilingual delivery of goods and services from whatever source is the greatest impediment to the realization of a fully functional bilingual society.

Williams (2004b; 2006) has argued that if a revised strategy is to succeed it must tackle the following issues:

- The creation of a National Data Centre for the analysis, evaluation and monitoring of all types of statistics reflecting socio-economic trends.
- The establishment of a National Language Planning and Resource Centre.
- A review of the way in which Welsh is taught and used as a medium for other subjects within the statutory education sector.
- A comprehensive review of teacher training for Welsh-medium and bilingual schools.
- Priority action in the designated 'Fro Gymraeg' districts.
- More concerted action by the expanded government departments and agencies (having absorbed the WDA, WTB and ELWa) to implement the integrated planning and policy proposals agreed within the Language and Economy Discussion Group.
- Urgent consideration to the need to expand the bilingual education and training opportunities afforded by the Welsh University and Further education sector.

- Extension of the Welsh Language Act, and other legislative measures, both to strengthen the status of Welsh within a revised political landscape and to take account of the rights of consumers and workers within designated parts of the private sector.
- The establishment of a Language Commissioner for Wales.

If the Assembly Government were to adopt these recommendations, then the strategy enunciated in *Iaith Pawb* would be in a far stronger position to deliver what it currently promises.

Uncertainties and Prevarications

Despite all the advances in the execution of language-related policy, both the political process and Welsh civil society has yet to determine the answer to several key questions which will influence our expectations as to what is appropriate action in the construction of a bilingual society. Prior to devolution in 1998 I asked to what extent, and in what ways, will/should the Assembly take over the role of the Welsh Language Board? How could its functions be better realized in a possibly different, more democratic, organizational format? Would we need a dedicated, specialist body to continue to achieve this, or could it be done by a committee of the Assembly working directly with the civil service? Should the Assembly include a language planning centre in addition to a language standardization centre? Should the Assembly consider the need to establish the office of a language ombudsman to oversee/audit the operation of the Welsh Language Act, à la Canada? (Williams 1998).

I also argued that the neglect of individual language rights needed to be addressed.Thus we may ask: in whom are basic language rights vested? Are they to be predominantly individual or institutional in character? Do individual citizens, regardless of where they live in Wales, have specific rights? Or are we satisfied with restricting our statutory obligations to the public institutions charged with implementing an equal opportunities policy? What rights, if any, do communities have in this process? What does it mean, in law and in practice to consider communities as being the bearers of rights? How are they to be defined, maintained and challenged in law? If community rights are accepted should they be formalized within a designated Fro Gymraeg, making the Welsh Heartland region the bearer of differentiated language rights? Or is this notion counterproductive to national planning and damaging to the rights of those who live outwith a notional Fro Gymraeg? Who will champion individual rights? A 'Dyfarnydd' or a Language Commissioner? Should a Language Commissioner deal only with issues and complaints relating to Welsh, thus becoming Comisiynydd y Gymraeg? Or, as both Welsh and English are co-equal languages, should the office holder also deal with the increasing numbers of complaints made by citizens who believe that their English-language usage is somehow threatened in the new dispensation? Are we prepared to follow the Canadian example and allow critical legal judgments to influence the course of our language policy? Hitherto the British legal system has not been overly involved in these debates, not surprisingly since language rights have neither been specified nor tested. But this will surely come. How will international law, particularly the various European Conventions impact on this settlement and who will deal with issue of monitoring and restitution?

A second set of issues is whether we maintain a public sector or adopt a plural domain approach to language policy. The initial language schemes were targeted at the public sector, education and the legal domains. But language policy should seek to influence behaviour in most if not all socio-economic contexts. Despite the tension between idealists and pragmatists, there is a determination by language planning agencies to promote bilingual work practices and to champion Welsh-language skills within the economy. Clearly there is the danger that such initiatives are driven from above only and that the heralded 'partnership' conception of sociolinguistic intervention can appear hollow. Thus a critical question is: how can the various partnerships between central and local agencies, community initiatives, the voluntary sector and the world of work continue to mobilize society's energy to reinforce the central thrust of language promotion and implementation of language rights? Is there a role for language issues to be better integrated within both the equal opportunities agenda and any proposed well-being legislation, along the lines of improving the environmental health of communities and considerations of sustainable development?

Accountability and Control

Reflecting on British public administration generally, David Marquand has documented 'the war against institutions' carried out by successive government who are increasingly preoccupied by market mimicry and central control (Marquand, 2004: 114). When New Labour's populism replaced the Thatcherite version, the same maxim applied for 'populist politics are inescapably centralist' (p. 114). However, the target of the new attack were the intermediate institutions, the professions and, in the devolved territories, local government and quangos. Despite talk of 'new localisms' and inclusive, open, transparent government, the public had correctly judged that executive control was the name of the game and were consequently disenchanted with government and the electoral process. Yet interest in politics, in decision-making and in solving problems did not decline. Committed individuals shifted their ground from the all-inclusive party machines and their spin doctors to the pressing issues of the day in more direct action and intuitive engagement. But the plethora of single issue campaigns threatened the public domain as a collective responsibility. This is why the promise of governance rather than just government was so beguiling, for it left open the possibility of strengthening civil society.

In Labour-controlled Wales many signs pointed to the erosion of governance and the re-establishment of government as the sole maxim. The Labour administration within the National Assembly had gone a long way in implementing its pledge to abolish the former quangos. On 14 July 2004, it announced that the three largest quangos, the Welsh Development Agency (WDA), the Wales Tourist Board and

ELWa (a post-16 educational agency) were to be abolished and incorporated directly into government departments. A later statement by Rhodri Morgan, First Minister of Wales, on 30 November 2004 specified the absorption of the Welsh Language Board into the Welsh Assembly Government by April 2007.

The abolition of the quangos was a logical step in the establishment of sound government in Wales, or so it was trumpeted. Kevin Morgan, the most vociferous critic, avers that

> the manner in which the decision was made was not a good advert for open and consultative government. The conspicuous absence of consultation with any of its partners exposes the government to the charge that partnership, the principle which it commends to others on a daily basis, and the principle which ostensibly informs everything it does, can be unilaterally jettisoned when the occasion demands. (Morgan, 2004: 20–3).

A pressing factor was the deteriorating relationship between the Welsh government and the WDA, its flagship quango. The government's justification was that within the new structure the incorporation of the quangos will render their functions more accountable. But, Morgan asks, accountable to whom? To Cabinet ministers? To the Assembly? Or to Welsh civil society? Given that such distinctions are rarely, if ever, made, Morgan is of the opinion that the wider public and civic dimensions of accountability have 'shrivelled into a narrow and desiccated form of political accountability' (Morgan, 2004: 21).

Unlike the former Welsh Office system, which exercised a form of 'democratic deficit' (Morgan and Roberts, 1993; Williams 1993), Morgan reminds us that in post-devolution Wales the democratically elected minister holds his or her quango to account in multiple ways:

> by controlling the purse strings, by appointing the chair, by selecting the board, by setting the strategic targets and, ultimately, by sacking the chair and the board if the targets are not met. On top of all these political control mechanisms, the quango is also subject to internal and external auditors and, most visibly, to the public scrutiny of the relevant subject committee of the Assembly. (Morgan, 2004: 22).

The politicians' view of accountability is a very focused, narrow view which essentially concerns day-to-day control. Morgan makes a case for the wider perspective whereby agencies are made accountable to the public forums of civil society – to the boards of specialized professionals, to the glare of the media spotlight and to open and transparent public debate.The Welsh Language Board (WLB) meets these criteria. There is a real sense that its activities, pronouncements and public meetings are considered to be part of the mainstream considerations of Welsh-speaking circles.This is because of the relevance of its remit, and also because its operating style ensures that regular open meetings are held in various venues throughout Wales. These two-day sessions (held every six weeks) include formal presentations by the WLB and its partners together with local authority representatives. The best meetings encourage question-and-answer sessions, the formation of a dialogue and the strengthening of trust so essential to the implementation of language plans. The distinctive feature here is that both WLB board members and responsible officers together answer questions from civil society. Thus the participants are identified, known, invite recommendations and construct dialogues with interested parties and agencies. This is a rare occurrence within the conventional civil-service style of operation and one which allows the WLB to claim that it is part of both the delivery of service and the discussions within civil society.

The Legal Implications

Specialists have argued that there are no legal problems in the Assembly's transferring all the WLB's function to the Assembly. Under section 28(1) of the 1998 Act the Assembly by subordinate legislative order can transfer to itself either all of the functions of the board, including regulatory work and then abolish the board; or it can transfer some of its functions, for example, leaving the board with its regulatory functions. New primary legislation to affect this transfer would not be necessary. Neither would there be any need to enact new legislation to restructure the board's membership, for the Assembly has this power under section 28(5) of the 1998 Act. Thus in principle it is possible for the Assembly, using powers of section 28 of the Government of Wales Act 1998, either to transfer all the board's functions to the Assembly and to repeal the provisions of Schedule 1 to the Welsh Language Act 1993 relating to the constitution of the board and its staff or, if the Assembly so decides, to transfer some of the board's functions to the Assembly and amend the constitution of the board. There are only limited powers in section 28 of the 1998 enabling the Assembly to amend or repeal the board's statutory functions. Generally, the purpose of section 28 is to enable the Assembly by order to transfer, not abolish, some or all of the functions of a specified body.

Legal specialists have observed that limited exception is in section 28(2) where if the functions of the body were taken over by the Assembly (or another body) it would not be possible for the Assembly or other body to perform certain functions, for example, the requirement in section 9(2) of the 1993 Act for the board to draft guidelines and to send them to the Assembly for approval. In such case, the Assembly has power to repeal section 9(2). It should also be noted that the Assembly has powers under section 28(3) of the 1998 Act to repeal the requirements in the 1993 Act for there to be a board if the Assembly transfers all the board's functions to the Assembly.

Currently the 1993 Act charges the WLB to undertake the general function of supporting and promoting the Welsh language (section 3), including advising the Assembly and public bodies. Secondly, it discharges responsibility for functions in relation to monitoring and regulating language schemes (sections 5–21). This includes functions relating to notifying public bodies (section 7); the preparation, approval and revision of schemes (sections 12–16); publishing and approving statutory guidance (sections 9–11); and undertaking investigations and dealing with complaints (sections 17–19). What is more problematic is the notion that a transfer of responsibilities for language schemes, especially the WAG's own language scheme, from the WLB to the National Assembly, would not engender confusion. This relates to instances, under sections 10(2) and 10(3) of the

Welsh Language Act 1993 where the Assembly would be preparing for its own purposes drafts of statutory regulations and then either recommending or amending them prior to laying them before Parliament. In addition, under certain circumstances, the Assembly would adjudicate in instances wherein it was itself a named party. For example, under section 14 of the Welsh Language Act, where neither the WLB nor other public bodies can agree on the contents of language schemes, the Assembly can resolve the issue and determine the outcome. Should the Assembly incorporate the responsibilities of the WLB then it would be implicated directly within its own determining cases.

Where to Locate the Welsh Language Board?

The relationship between the Welsh Language Board and the National Assembly is still under discussion. In public debates the chief line of defence is that keeping the WLB at arm's length from the Assembly helps in defusing the language question either as a party political matter or as a conflict-generating issue. The consensus-building and 'de-politicization' argument, so beloved of establishment figures in Wales, does have considerable merit at a functional/administrative level, but does not mask the cleavages which characterize Welsh-language politics. A second plank of the argument is that, in order to develop a bilingual society in accordance with the 'the doctrine of plenary inclusion' (Williams, 2004b) an impartial agency, which can be guaranteed its relative independence of action, regardless of which political party/parties, rule in Cardiff Bay, is required. Clearly, the board would continue to operate within the broad strategy agreed by the Cabinet, the responsible minister and senior management of the board. However, by invoking a certain impartiality there is a sense in which the board could claim to be 'owned' and to be 'responsive' to a wide array of partners, clients and the general public, and not be too overly identified with the ideology and practical policy deliberations of particular parties. Finally, there is the management consideration that transferring the responsibilities and staff of the WLB into the machinery of government is one step, fully integrating its resultant activities, including its statutory duty to liaise with all public bodies, including the Assembly and the civil service, through the medium of Welsh, is quite a different step. Were it to happen it would be the most effective test to date of the ability of the civil service to operationalize its commitment to mainstream Welsh within its ranks.

The long-standing proposal was to integrate the Welsh Language Board into its sponsoring Department of Culture, Welsh Language and Sport. If the Welsh language is seen primarily as a 'cultural resource' then clearly such a move has an inescapable logic. However, if Welsh is to be seen as a coequal language, a normal means of education and of communication within a bilingual society, and if the socio-economic condition of Welsh-speaking communities is a factor, then such a move limits the capacity of government to mainstream the language. Far better to adopt a more empowering stance whereby the successor entity to the Welsh Language Board would be placed within a more advantageous position. It could, for example, be located within the Office of the First Minister to the NAfW, in line with current Basque and Catalan conventions. This would guarantee it visibility, enhanced status and power and the ability to diffuse throughout the whole edifice of government administration.

The Range of Legislative Options

Johnson has noted that 'outcomes are not infrequently shaped by the way in which they are sought and this is as true of the current wave of constitutional reform in Britain as on the pursuit of political objectives in many other spheres' (Johnson, 2004: 284). If we see constitutional revision and language reform in terms of typically British piecemeal change then there are grounds for arguing that we may see some improvement in the legislative context surrounding Welsh and in the specification of Welsh-language rights. But Marquand has cautioned that 'the trouble with piecemeal change, however, is that the expected later steps sometimes fail to follow the earlier ones, and even when they do, the underlying logic and overarching purpose of the whole exercise are not always clear' (Marquand, 2004: 148).

I believe that Welsh should be designated an official language in Wales, coequal with English. This would be an action to ensure status rather than directly to stimulate use. However, this symbolic statement regarding the Welsh language would be a means of emphasizing the government's objectives for Welsh. Other reasons for supporting additional legislation in relation to the language are:

1. It is needed – it is time that elements of Welsh linguistic rights be put on a statutory footing.
2. The Welsh language is part of the 'equality agenda' and language rights need to be developed in line with existing rights in policy areas such as anti-racism, sexual equality and disability.
3. Several European trends are leading towards more comprehensive definitions of our civil, social and economic rights. This is in response to a number of various trends, for example, globalization and the evolution of the responsive nation-state concerned with social market doctrine.
4. The abolition/integration of the Welsh Language Board within the Assembly creates a statutory vacuum relating to the question of which body will approve and monitor statutory language schemes, including in particular the Assembly's own language scheme.
5. Regardless of whether a Language Adjudicator or a Commissioner will investigate how government departments are adhering to their statutory language schemes, it is appropriate to press for legislation which will enable Welsh-speakers to use their language in the widest possible set of situations. Primary legislation will be required to establish the new regulator, and current reforms based on the logic of the White Paper, *Better Government for Wales* (2005), have proposed new ways of introducing such legislation. This is likely to be a key step forward, not only in the history of the language, but also in terms of society's democratic maturity.
6. Aspects of the existing act need refining and additional

measures need to be developed regarding linguistic rights, the development of bilingual administration within public bodies, and the instiutionalization of the use of Welsh. It follows that the National Assembly should be responsible for most aspects of legislation concerned with the Welsh language (Williams 2005b).

Key Questions

1. What kind of legislation? One comprehensive act or a number of strategic measures in line with the evolving transfer or powers to the Assembly?
2. How will the relationship between Westminster legislation and Assembly legislation impact on this unique sphere of policy?
3. How will legislation and new patterns of working together cause a change in our linguistic behaviour as citizens, customers and employees? Clearly opportunity and habit are interconnected here.

Of late there has been much activity in this area. Critical interventions include *Deddf Iaith Newydd: Dyma'r Cyfle* (Cymdeithas yr Iaith, (2005), the proposed Parliamentary Bill prepared by Hywel Williams, MP; the Assembly Special Committee which discussed evidence regarding the document 'Better Government for Wales' in 2005; the writings of legal experts, such as David Lambert and Marie Navarro of Cardiff University;, the exchanges between the Welsh Language Board and the government, and, most significantly the enhanced powers of the Assembly as summarized below.

At the international level the UK is subject to the provisions of the International Covenant on Civil and Political Rights; however, the minority standards set out in article 27 thereof have been significantly expanded upon and clarified in a number of international treaties, the most important of which are two treaties of the Council of Europe to which the UK is subject, the Framework Convention for the Protection of National Minorities (the 'Framework Convention') and the European Charter for Regional or Minority Languages (the 'Languages Charter').

Although this is an important discussion at European level regarding language policy in Wales, neither treaty creates a complaints procedure that allows members of linguistic minorities to take government to court to ensure compliance. However, both treaties create a system under which the UK must report at regular intervals – every five years under the Framework Convention and every three under the Language Charter – on its implementation of its international obligations under both treaties. These reports are scrutinized by a body of independent experts – the Advisory Committee under the Framework Convention and the Committee of Experts under the Languages Charter – who ultimately prepare a report on state compliance and recommendations as to measures which should be taken to enhance compliance. Significantly, non-governmental organizations are entitled to comment on the reports of the UK government, thereby ensuring that the two committees have alternative sources of information for assessing the claims that the UK itself makes. Members of the two committees will normally visit the state being monitored to meet politicians, civil servants, representatives of local and regional governments, as well as non-governmental organizations and representatives of the minority-language communities themselves. In the spring of 2005 the government submitted evidence to the Council of Europe on its implementation of the Charter, and the Committee of Experts received evidence from various groups and bodies during its visit to the UK in December 2005. Several public meetings were held in Wales to stimulate the role of civil society in the process, and updated information was produced which the Committee of Experts took account of in its second report, which it released in 2007

Linguistic Rights

The Human Rights Act 1998 has developed our understanding of the concept of individuals' basic rights, and the equality agenda, of which the Welsh language is a part, has developed steadily. After a decade of implementing language schemes, the stage is set to take the next steps in establishing specific linguistic rights for individuals and making the Welsh language part of the anti-discrimination legislative agenda. The Welsh Language Act (1993) places a duty on public bodies to treat Welsh and English on an equal basis when providing public services. This is done on the basis of the contents of language schemes agreed by the Welsh Language Board. However, the implementation of language schemes is inconsistent, and it is not clear to the public what they can expect to receive in terms of Welsh-language services. Indeed, as Dunbar has shown (in chapter 5), it is hard to specify just exactly what the rights of Welsh-speakers are at present. The closest any recent legislation relating to the Welsh language comes to creating a clearly expressed right is subsection 22(1) of the Welsh Language Act 1993, relating to the use of Welsh in the courts, and even that provision does not refer explicitly to a 'right', but uses permissive language to express the entitlement; it provides that 'in any legal proceedings in Wales the Welsh language may be spoken by any party, witness or other person who desires to use it', subject to such prior notice as may be necessary.

I believe it is important to mirror the duty to provide a service with the right to receive it. This principle is the basis of linguistic planning in a number of countries – but is almost completely absent in Wales. The exception is the right to a hearing through the medium of Welsh in a court of law. The legislation makes it clear that courts have a duty to provide the service – and that individuals have the right to receive it.

It also seems opportune to establish other legislative rights for Welsh-speakers, such as the right to receive Welsh-medium education, the right to use Welsh in a number of cases in dealing with the health system, or in the workplace, the right to correspond in Welsh with bodies which come within the scope of the Act, and to receive correspondence or information from them through the medium of Welsh.

The fundamental weakness is that language rights pertain to institutions and not to individuals. The current system is particularly good at fostering the capacity to prepare language schemes, but it is not as effective in terms of supervising and ensuring implementation of the schemes. One area where the legislation could be strengthened is by placing a duty on bodies to provide information as requested by the Welsh Language Board as part of any statutory investigation under section 17 of the Act into the lack of implementation of a language scheme. Bodies have exploited this and have refused to cooperate and provide the board with basic information.

The 1993 Act's hold on Crown bodies, such as UK government departments (including the Assembly Government) and a number of its agencies, also reflects the weakness of existing legislation. The board's powers to require bodies to prepare, and then to approve, language schemes do not apply to Crown bodies. We see similar failings in respect of the board's ability to review the content of schemes and, in the case of the government, the power to enforce the implementation of schemes. Instead, the goodwill of Crown bodies must be relied upon. Crown bodies, on average, take twice as long as other bodies to prepare language schemes. Crown bodies have also refused to implement the content of their language schemes – and political intervention at the highest level was necessary to rectify the situation.

This is neither acceptable nor reasonable. Consistency and clarity are needed, and the same expectations and standards should be placed on Crown bodies as on other public bodies. The Assembly Government provided evidence to the Richard Commission setting out how it is possible to bring Crown bodies entirely within the scope of the 1993 Act. It is important that the government seeks to rectify this unacceptable situation before considering the transfer of any powers to a new regulator.

Under Section 10 of the 1993 Act, the Assembly is required to obtain Westminster's approval for any amendments to the board's statutory guidance on the preparation of Language Schemes. Now I believe it would be appropriate and timely for the Assembly to have the power to approve any change to statutory guidance on the preparation of language schemes.

The 1993 Act also establishes the principle that the Welsh and English languages should be treated on a basis of equality, as far as is both appropriate in the circumstances and reasonably practical. An obvious tension exists between these two clauses and at a practical level, a body's language scheme is the means to resolving this tension. However, bodies often use the phrase relating to appropriateness and reasonableness in an arbitrary fashion, in order to avoid responsibility and acting in a way which treats both languages equally. It is time to dispense with the clause relating to appropriateness and reasonableness.

Existing legislation does not encompass the internal administrative use of Welsh. Measures to support Welsh in the workplace are core to the development of first-class public services in Wales. Practical implementation of such measures could be part of bodies' language schemes, aimed at ensuring an increase in the linguistic capacity of workforces over time.

I support Cymdeithas yr Iaith's campaign which argues that the rights to use Welsh or English should be predicated on the basis of the nature of the goods, facilities or services offered in the marketplace, rather than on the basis of the provider's status. The interpenetration of different economic sectors now makes it very difficult to define the boundaries of a particular service, which is becoming increasingly complex with the increase in the mixed market and telecommunications, and as individual rather than mass or community behaviour increasingly becomes the norm. So it is appropriate to take a more thematic rather than a sectoral view, and to consider the nature of the services provided to the public. The government has already adopted this policy by bringing water companies under the remit of the existing Act. It would be appropriate now to consider extending legislation to other sectors, such as banks and insurance companies. But extending legislation presupposes the establishment of a robust system of regulation and enforcement of language rights and obligations.

Language Regulator or Language Commissioner?

On the eve of devolution, I doubted whether the Assembly had the authority under clauses 28, 29 and 33 of the Act to establish the Office of a Language Ombudsman. I argued that this was clearly a significant omission from the 1993 Welsh Language Act as the very fact of agreed language schemes begs the question of assuring compliance (Williams, 1998;

2000b). I advised that once a recognizable system for dealing with language schemes was put in place we should return to consider the establishment of a Language Ombudsman (Williams, 1998). That time has now come.

Two alternative models have been under discussion. Until May 2007 the Welsh Assembly Government favoured the establishment of a *Dyfarnydd,* literally a regulator or adjudicator; I among others favour the establishment of a Language Commissioner (Williams, 2005a; 2005b). The First Minister noted the following in his statement on 30 November 2004:

> An office of the Dyfarnydd will be established to undertake the Board's regulatory functions. The office will oversee the Welsh language schemes of public sector bodies, including the Assembly's Welsh Language Scheme. The office will be established initially in an advisory capacity, and will be placed on a statutory footing when the opportunity for legislation arises . . . The post will be undertaken by an individual who will be entrusted with undertaking the regulatory functions which cannot or should not be undertaken by the Language Board once it is incorporated, as this would mean that we [the Government] would regulate ourselves. It will be necessary to regulate the Assembly and other public bodies, and it is better that this is done independently, and independence in this respect is protected . . . The regulatory part (of the Welsh Language Board's remit) is quasi-judicial, and it must be independent, and this is why there will be an independent office of the Rheoleiddiwr or Dyfarnydd.

The government's proposals for the merger of the board's functions assumed a two-stage process. First, the Assembly Government proposed to merge the majority of the board's functions by April 2007, keeping a residual body to deal with specific aspects of the regulatory framework. Secondly, the government proposed to establish a statutory regulator, the Dyfarnydd, under the legislative arrangements proposed within the Government of Wales Bill.

The WAG (2006) consultation paper did not discuss the residual body at any length. But this is a key part of the process and such transitional arrangements could last for a significant period. No precise timetable was proposed for the establishment of the Dyfarnydd since the government could not warrant that it would be in a position to establish the

Dyfarnydd. The proposal presupposed the enactment of the Government of Wales Bill, and a request for powers to establish the Dyfarnydd under the legislative arrangements set out in the Bill.

Legal specialists have suggested that there are two ways in which the Assembly Government, using powers which it currently holds, could establish a regulatory framework which would reflect the principles of the 1993 Act. The board could retain its existing regulatory functions and the Assembly retain its existing appellate functions under the 1993 Act, even if all the other functions of the board were transferred to the Assembly. Alternatively, the Assembly could transfer all the board's functions to itself, including its regulatory functions and its current appellate functions could be discharged by a committee of AMs which could consider representations made under section 8(8) or 14(2) of the 1993 Act. There is a precedent for this in the standing orders of the Assembly in relation to independent planning appeal committees comprising AMs whose decisions bind the Assembly.

However, it is accepted that the government would assume responsibility for the preparation and revision of language schemes guidelines and for the preparation of circulars on the implementation of Welsh-language schemes. It follows that government would undertake the role of agreeing, monitoring and revising language schemes. If, instead, the Dyfarnydd undertook these responsibilities, that would necessitate direct involvement in policy development. Board officials have long argued that there is a need for keeping together the functions of agreeing and monitoring the implementation of schemes.

What of complaints and compensation regarding the failure to implement agreed language schemes? It is possible to argue that the Dyfarnydd could handle complaints as part of the 'regulatory cycle', as happens currently in some bilingual jurisdictions within the Commonwealth. This arrangement would also reveal how well bodies were implementing their language schemes. Board officials recognise that if these functions were separated, performance would be considered separately from the agreement on the content, and thus the Dyfarnydd would consider only the content of a language scheme and the complaint in question.

It would be possible to strengthen the Dyfarnydd's remit by adding powers to conduct investigations where appropriate. Alongside this, consideration would need to be given as to whether the government could also have the power to conduct investigations; since the government's developmental work might draw attention to examples of non-compliance. An extension of this is the nature of the Dyfarnydd's adjudicative role in relation to a dispute between the board and a public body, both in terms of the preparation of language schemes and in terms of their enforcement. A major weakness of the current system is that the Welsh Language Board has little real direct power to enforce compliance. Clearly, it has recourse to normal procedures but when non-compliance is an obstacle to the implementation of the Act the only indirect avenue for the board is to ask the political authorities, particularly its sponsoring minister, to intervene.

What would happen if the Dyfarnydd were given the responsibility of adjudicating in any dispute between the Assembly Government itself and a public body regarding the content of a body's language scheme? Is this an essential function for the Dyfarnydd? Would there need to be reference to a further completely impartial body to determine the contours of language scheme enforcement? If not how would the Assembly Government seek to handle cases where it itself was a claimant, an adjudicator and an ultimate arbiter for action?

A key issue was whether the Dyfarnydd should also be given a general advocacy role in relation to the language. This would be critical in relation to the implementation of the Assembly Government's language scheme and the Assembly Government's leadership of this particular policy area. Without this advocacy role, the Welsh language would be the only equality area lacking an advocate independent from government. There are obvious dangers for the language in this respect. Section 3 of the current Act would enable the Dyfarnydd to undertake this role, but the boundary between the Dyfarnydd's functions and those of the government would not be clear. New legislation could provide more clarity on this matter, conferring on the Dyfarnydd the right, and duty, to operate independently within a defined mandate.

I have raised additional questions which cast doubts on the *Dyfarnydd* option (Williams 2005b). Should the appointment of a Dyfarnydd be a ministerial appointment, or rather an appointment that is confirmed by the Assembly? Should the Dyfarnydd be an administrator or a public figure? Government thinking about the role of the Dyfarnydd begged a number of questions. For example, there was little specification as to how members of the public might be able to complain directly to a Dyfarnydd, who may or may not be a publicly recognizable figure with a well-understood remit. Neither was it clear how the Dyfarnydd would enforce the implementation of language schemes. Current arrangements do not require public bodies to provide information on request during an investigation, neither is there much evidence that individual bodies share their experience with other public bodies in dealing with such complaints. A stronger interventionist role for the Dyfarnydd could lead to a more consistent handling and resolution of complaints.

Presumably the Dyfarnydd would have the right to ask a court of law for an order to enforce the recommendations. This, in essence, would be the opportunity to appeal against the Dyfarnydd's judgments. This power would essentially mirror what is already included in the 1993 Act. A second issue would be whether or not bodies could be fined for language scheme non-compliance, and this would be related to the implementation of recommendations made by the Dyfarnydd. As a minimum it seemed logical to revise current legislation so that the Dyfarnydd could consider the use of Welsh within public bodies, and within Crown bodies. It would also be possible to give specific powers to the government to change the administrative language of its own offices, and those of other public bodies. A similar power had been established in Ireland under the Official Languages Act 2003. Current legislation does not give the board a statutory remit in relation to Crown bodies. The government will inherit this problem if it assumes responsibility for agreeing and monitoring language schemes. Placing the language schemes of Crown bodies on a statutory basis would strengthen and simplify the regulatory system.

There is a risk that the Dyfarnydd would concentrate only on the essential matters under the current legislation, namely the implementation of language schemes, and that other parts of the work of actuating and promoting Welsh would be lost within the office of the Assembly's Administrative Ombudsman. But as the Assembly Government has established independent commissioners for children and the elderly, the same independence, strategic overview and same status should be secured for the proposed regulator for the Welsh language.

Therefore it is vital that any proposed regulator be an independent voice for the implementation of the Act. This appointment should be for a fixed term, and should be made by the National Assembly rather than the Assembly Government. This would follow the pattern mooted in *Better Government for Wales*, for the Public Services Ombudsman and the Auditor General. It should be ensured that the proposed regulator has the appropriate powers and resources to undertake his/her duties in a timely and effective fashion and has the defined role of supervising and implementing the linguistic legislation, in exactly same way as the other responsibilities provided, such as race and disability. In time one could imagine a network of Language Commissioners from Canada, Ireland, Wales, Northern Ireland, Finland and other parts of the world sharing their experience with commissioners in areas such as administration, children, the elderly, health and welfare.

The following considerations were uppermost in the WLB's response to the government's consultation paper (WAG, 2006) concerning the integration of the Language Board:

- It is difficult to predict what effect the change will have on the position of the Welsh language. It could strengthen the position of the Welsh language, but it is quite possible that it will weaken it.
- The independent regulator suggested is not strong enough in terms of practical functions or arrangements. The independent regulator should be responsible for agreeing and monitoring the implementation of language schemes, and should be accountable to the National Assembly.
- The proposed regulatory structure has been complicated

rather the simplified, with a risk that public services will decline and resources will be duplicated.

- There is a lack of clarity with regard to the arrangements for the interim period and when the Dyfarnydd will be established. Given this, would it not be more appropriate to establish the Dyfarnydd on a statutory basis before any powers are transferred. In making this proposal, it is not our intention to introduce any unnecessary delay into the process, but to ensure that the process and regulatory framework are both cogent and consistent, and build on the 1993 Act.
- The statutory function of promoting the Welsh language should be transferred to the Government or become the responsibility of the Government and the independent regulator.
- It will be necessary to maintain the flexible working methods and regional structure of the Board.
- The staff's right to work through the medium of Welsh must be protected and the staff must be maintained as a single entity.
- Success and progress should be measured on the basis of *Iaith Pawb* targets, the implementation of the Government's Welsh language Scheme and a strong statistical foundation. (Welsh Language Board, 2006)

Establishing the role of Dyfarnydd would have been an improvement upon current arrangements, but it appeared to be the soft option, an administrative tidying up exercise which fell far short of what was required.

The Case for a Language Commissioner

The establishment of an Office of Official Language Commissioner presupposes two things. First that there are identifiable Welsh and English language rights which are in need of protection. Second that the pronouncements and activities of such an office will have a clear impact on the governance of Wales. Thus to whom should appeals for establishing the office of a Language Commissioner be made? Welsh-speakers, civil society, the National Assembly and the UK Parliament. Each of these targets will be persuaded by a different set of considerations. For Welsh-speakers appeals to natural justice and to live a bilingual life would predispose some to favour an independent advocate, a champion on language matters. For civil society appeals to a more complete equality agenda and to democratic accountability are likely to be convincing. For the National Assembly, an independent arbiter and advocate investigating complaints regarding the delivery of bilingual services and language rights is likely to be a major asset. This is especially true if it serves to depoliticize a party-political cleavage concerning the extent to which public services and possibly commercial activities are regulated. For the UK Parliament there is the attraction of extending the devolutionary arrangements. As Rawlings (2003: 377) notes,

> with the ambition of an accountable and responsive public administration, independent complaint machinery is an integral part of the devolutionary scheme. This refers not only to 'fire-fighting' – redress of grievance – but also to the classic ombudsman role of 'fire-watching' – identifying deficiencies with a view to promoting improvements, and further to the especially important legitimising function in the case of the Assembly of buttressing public confidence.

The changing face of public sector service delivery is reflected in the establishment of a Welsh Administration Ombudsman (WAO), with the promise of a revamped Wales Public Services Ombudsman, the Office of a Local Commissioner for Wales and Health Service Commissioner in Wales (HSCW) while the Children's Commissioner is to be supplemented by a Commissioner for Older People. None of the established posts have been over burdened with complaints from the public, partly, according to Rawlings, as a result of the lack of interface between public administration and civil society.

Such considerations appear to favour a Dyfarnydd rather than a Language Commissioner. The ombudsman model for local government would be read across to the language arena so that adverse publicity and political embarrassment would act as the principal instruments for compensation and restitution. Soft law, speedy internal processes of dealing with complaints, accurate feedback into policy and performance would all give the impression of responsive, open government. By integrating the Dyfarnydd into an enlarged office comprising the WAO, the HSCW and others, systematic, routine procedures for dealing with complaints could be finessed with the minimum of disruption to the machinery of administration and good government.

Why then hold out for a Language Commissioner? There are two overwhelming reasons. The first is that the Welsh language struggle is far greater than an issue of administrative convenience and routine. The second is that by insisting on a Language Commissioner, attention will have to be paid to the range of language-related rights, for the principal considerations of Canadian, Irish and other language regimes is the establishment of minimal rights and expectations which citizens may enjoy in respect of official language provision and services. In Wales, it is difficult to be precise as to what exactly citizens may expect from government in respect of access to, for example, Welsh-medium education or bilingual services. The 1993 Act places a duty on public bodies to treat both languages on a basis of equality in the provision of services to the public. These language schemes are unevenly and partially implemented and, consequently, it is hard to generalize or predict the exact nature of the service being offered. Extending the range of language rights would fit into a pattern of explicating the nature of fundamental human rights. Welsh is part of the equalities agenda but does not figure prominently in comparison with discussions based upon discrimination on the basis of race, gender, sexual orientation or disability. The absence of such measures slows the growth of the use of the Welsh-language in public bodies, and inhibits the development and provision of Welsh language public services. The second major weakness is the absence of an official advocate for bilingualism, independent of government, but obliged by statute to take government and others to task if they fail to implement their own language schemes.

What type of new legislation is now needed? The two pressing issues are the establishment of basic rights for individual speakers of Welsh and a new system whereby complaints may be investigated. It is essential that the Language Commissioner is an independent office charged with holding an overview of Welsh-language legislation, dealing with complaints and undertaking investigations into the implementation of language schemes. It may or may not be advisable to ask such an ombudsman to also act as a legal champion for the language, investigating issues regardless of whether or not an official complaint has been entertained. But should English and Welsh be deemed national languages in the near future then we could have the unusual spectacle of a Language Commissioner defending the rights of individual English speakers against the collective rights of Welsh speakers in communities within Gwynedd or in terms of education policy in large parts of Wales. That would give a real political and legislative edge to the role of the Commissioner over and above what language campaigners currently envisage. The National Assembly is the obvious forum for the enactment of legislation focusing specifically on the Welsh language to ensure that it can execute its policy responsibilities appropriately and fully.

A systematic examination of language rights would conclude that it is in dealing with services to the public where the greatest discrimination appears. In an interesting synthesis both Cymdeithas yr Iaith Gymraeg (2005) and the Welsh Language Board have acknowledged that the origin of a service, whether it be offered by the public, private and voluntary sectors, is no longer as pertinent as the character of the service under discussion. Similarly, the board notes that since the Welsh Language Act was passed in 1993, many parts of what was the public sector, such as the utilities, are now in private ownership. Sectoral boundaries are now fluid and it is increasingly common to see private or voluntary bodies providing services on behalf of the public sector.

What Kind of Rights Would the New Legislation Offer?

A key priority would be to establish statutorily that individuals have a right to receive Welsh-medium education, the right to use Welsh in a number of cases in dealing with the health system, or in the workplace, the right to correspond in Welsh, which come within the scope of the Act, and to receive correspondence or information through the medium of Welsh.

Secondly the application of such rights should not be differentiated legislatively on the basis of geographic region. I argue this because spatial differentiation weakens the concept of full language co-equality within the nation and, secondly, because in comparable cases in Ireland, Belgium, Finland and South Africa the pressure to alter the boundaries (that is; to shrink them, not to extend them) about every ten years, diminishes the success of any activity to strengthen the community. Therefore, although I support programmes targeted on the Welsh-speaking heartland, I do not favour a statutory definition of the Welsh-speaking heartland, a là the Gaeltacht – whether for reasons of linguistic rights or economic services.

Thirdly, both the Assembly Government and Cymdeithas yr Iaith propose a democratic forum, a 'Council for the Welsh language' to discuss policy issues related to Welsh. I recognize that such a council or forum has an essential role in offering evidence, and giving a voice to those who would otherwise be excluded from mainstream politics and the policy community. But should it seek to achieve more than that? What would be the council's exact function and responsibilities? Would it be a new expanded Welsh Language Board without the civil servants? The real need is to translate rhetoric into action and thus attention needs to be focused on the trigger factors which allow civil society to influence the policy process. This might take the form of reporting to a strong committee of experts who would convert sound ideas into practical proposals which politicians could implement.

New Opportunities for 'Better Government for Wales'

The White Paper on Devolution, *Better Government for Wales*, published in mid-June 2005, presented proposals for amending the Government of Wales Act and is the government's response to the Richard Commission. It set out how the Assembly's powers could be increased, giving it more freedom from Westminster legislation, how its structure could be reformed, separating the legislative aspect from the Welsh Assembly Government, and how its electoral arrangements could be changed. The White Paper's proposals offered the opportunity to transfer further responsibilities to the Assembly in future to legislate in specific areas.

An obvious and unique area where these new powers would be an advantage is in the formulation of language and education policy in Wales. Of course, everything depends upon how the London and Cardiff governments would interpret their new relationship. The 'Orders in Council' are the key to this. They are measures and not acts as such and it is wholly possible to identify the specific issues for which the Assembly would have statutory responsibility in ruling, say on linguistic matters, or education. Only those elements reserved either to Parliament or to the Secretary of State would be exempted from Assembly control.

I believe the Assembly Government should make the transfer of powers pertaining to the Welsh language a priority in this respect. The creation of a bilingual Wales is a long-term project and it will be necessary to amend the relevant legislation on a regular basis. Bearing in mind that the Assembly has executive functions pertaining to the Welsh language, it makes sense for the Assembly to have the power to change the legislation rather than having to compete for legislative time in Westminster. Any transfer of legislative powers should be broad enough to deal with a range of situations and policy areas pertaining to the Welsh language. What are the necessary steps in the proposed legislative devolution?

1. The Assembly Government and the Assembly submit an 'Order' to the Secretary of State.

2. The Secretary of State lays the Order before Parliament.
3. House of Commons and House of Lords committees investigate the evidence and justification.
4. Debates of up to ninety minutes in both chambers.
5. Approval from the Queen and Privy Council.
6. The Orders are subject to affirmative resolution but not to Assembly legislation.
7. The Orders include enablement conditions to allow the Assembly to prepare legislation.

In practice, this means that the Assembly can act as an informal Parliament, developing its powers in appropriate areas without having to go back and forth to Westminster. It is possible for the Assembly to claim that it has the responsibility and expertise to act on behalf of the language and, therefore, under this interpretation of the White Paper, the Assembly could request a near monopoly of power on developing its policies on bilingualism.

The relevant clause for such an Order in Council would be 'to protect and promote the Welsh language'. This would accord with clause 32 of the Government of Wales Act, 1998. But in order for the Assembly to convince the Secretary of State, the Assembly is required to rely on Welsh civil society, prior to, during and following such legislation. In this respect, we would have a more comprehensive and constructive democracy than a number of other European countries, as henceforth the Assembly would be completely reliant on the public. A further implication would be to increase the legislative work load of Assembly Members, but recall that all pieces of legislation would have to be bilingual. But I would add a note of caution in terms of both the Assembly's lack of legislative experience and its tolerance for bilingual working practices. Rawlings has reminded us that

> the scope for mismatch between the enabling statutes and subordinate legislation is bound to be increased by the disaggregation of the traditional central government model of doing business, and so call for even more careful policing in Wales . . . As one would expect, the situations for 'adverse reporting' set out in standing orders closely echo the Westminster ones, for instance:
>
> - doubt whether the legislation is within the Assembly's powers

- the legislation appears to make unusual or unexpected use of the powers
- the form or meaning needs further explanation
- the drafting appears to be defective.

The chief addition, naturally, is the bilingual element. The (Legislation) committee thus reports 'if there appear to be inconsistencies between the English and Welsh texts' which translates as seeking to ensure there are not. (Rawlings, 2003: 250)

Speaking generally of legislative matters he warns of the need for vigilance against boredom and complacency for

> while there is an occasional nugget, so much of the committee's business is tedious in the extreme: an ambiguity here, a mistranslation there, and so on. It is worthy and necessary work, but from the view point of the political animal it represents the short straw. Against the backdrop, not only of subordinate legislation, but also of laws often driven from elsewhere, this is part of the grim realities of the life of the Assembly as a legislature. (Ibid.)

Naturally, all this raises fundamental questions regarding devolution. The implications of the full devolution of powers to legislate on the Welsh language for United Kingdom bodies which provide services in Wales would have to be considered. The Assembly should be responsible for setting the direction and determining the content of policies pertaining to the Welsh language. Given the appropriate powers so to do, legislative devolution of this kind would exemplify Rawlings's 'deepening' and 'widening' of Assembly responsibilities. For, as he has observed,

> items such as 'culture, recreation and the Welsh language' speak for themselves. Fingered in an earlier age by the Kilbrandon Commission, it is inconceivable that a scheme of legislative devolution for Wales would not include them. If the Assembly cannot be trusted with full legislative responsibilities for such matters, which bear so directly on the 'particularity' or national identity of Wales, what sensibly can it do? (Rawlings, 2003: 521)

The logic of legislative devolution would require a restructuring of the campaign for new Welsh-language legislation through the 'Orders in Council', which would require Westminster's seal of approval, but which would in turn transform the development and implementation of language policy made in Wales. Therefore, let me conclude by presenting a possible agenda for action in the firm belief that political innovation, especially when it involves reshaping the British Constitution, hardly ever follows purely logical lines. We need to work towards:

1. new language legislation through the mechanism of 'Order in Council';
2. mainstreaming the Welsh language as a consideration and as a constitutional language in the preparation of the Assembly's secondary legislation and as part of Westminster's general legislative programme;
3. establishing the office of Welsh Language Commissioner;
4. strengthening the Assembly's powers, especially in relation to legislation;
5. democratizing the contribution of civil society by providing a truly valuable Language Forum or Welsh Language Council;
6. integrate the work of the board into the heart of government and not as a marginal department;
7. seeking to convince the public and providers to change their behaviour in response to a combination of legislation, political ideology and the effect of the education system in creating greater linguistic awareness.

The law creates opportunity, but it is daily experience as a citizen which creates the desire to make use of it. Now that we have an Assembly with law-making powers it is inevitable that Welsh-language related clauses will be included within a wide range of legislative measures.

One Wales

In the summer of 2007 the Labour Party and Plaid agreed to form a coalition government, whose broad policy aims were stated in the coalition document 'One Wales' (2007). Coalition government was perhaps an inevitable outcome of the Assembly electoral processes, but the timing and nature of this particular configuration was a novel and, at times, frustrating experience for many. What is beyond doubt, in terms of this volume's concern with governance, is that the current arrangements have set a precedence which will not be lost on either the electorate or the professional political class in Wales. In addition to the redistribution of cabinet portfolios within the ranks of the seven Labour ministers, Plaid gained three strategic areas of responsibility. Its leader Ieuan Wyn Jones became the Economy and Transport Minister, Rhodri Glyn Thomas became the Heritage Minister (which includes the Welsh language) and Elin Jones became Rural Affairs Minister. Each of these appointments allows for a fresh injection of ideas and in some policy areas will see a far greater commitment to the mainstreaming of bilingualism. Indeed if Plaid Cymru adhere to their previously announced policy then there will certainly be radical changes in the way in which the interests of the Welsh language are handled by government.

Of the many strident promises made in 'One Wales' (2007) three areas are worthy of note, they relate to Welsh-medium education, to legislative reform and to a greater recognition of the role which Wales might play within the international community. I would claim that these are evidence of the maturing of the devolution process as education suggests a different set of priorities from those which obtain in England, legislative competence suggests increased power and a more engaging international profile suggests a distinct role within the international community.

In terms of Welsh-medium education 'One Wales' states

> We will set out a new policy agreement with Local Education Authorities to require them to assess the demand for Welsh-medium education, including surveying parental wishes, and to produce a resulting School Organisation Plan, setting out clear steps to meet need.
>
> We will create a national Welsh-medium Education Strategy to develop effective provision from nursery through to further and higher education backed up by an implementation programme.
>
> We will establish a Welsh-medium Higher Education Network-the Federal College-in order to ensure Welsh-medium provision in our universities.

> We will expolore the establishment of a Welsh for Adults Unit with sufficient funding, giving priority to tutor education. (p. 22)

> It also resolves to regenerate communities, establish credit union, reduce poverty, maintain sustainable environments, support rural development, promote local food procurement, encourage renewable technologies,

On the Welsh language itself, the document confirms the thrust of Iaith Pawb and asserts that

> We will be seeking enhanced legislative competence on the Welsh language. Jointyl we will work to extend the scope of the Welsh Language Legislative Competence Order included in the Assembly government's first year legislative programme, with a view to a new Assembly Measure to confirm official status for both Welsh and English linguistic rights in the provision of services and the establishment of the post of Language Commissioner. (p. 34)

Other significant features include working in tandem with Westminster to press the case for Welsh becoming an official EU language, enhancing the use of Welsh in cyberspace, addressing the effects of population migration in-balances, promoting the representation of Wales within international agencies, draw on the collective energies of the Welsh diaspora, In other words realise a wish list of activities which give recognition to Wales's independent character and role within the wider world a la Quebec and Catalonia.

But perhaps the most revealing change envisaged within 'One Wales' is the commitment to governance arrangements, with a clear set of messages promoting greater openness and discussion within the Assembly and between it and civil society. This bodes well for democracy, especially within a small country. But it is more important to see this as a binding commitment to genuine coalition and partnership between Labour and Plaid.

Conclusion

In comparison with many of the cases discussed in this volume Wales is at an exciting juncture in its development. The principal agency of language and governance, the Welsh

Language Board, has matured to become a professional, para-public institution, an arm of government backed by UK parliamentary legislation, a champion of radical and innovative measures, and a critic of many aspects of Welsh public and commercial life. It has, in turn, been severely criticized at various junctures for its grant-allocation decisions, its prioritizing of some cultural and youth-rated activities over others and its regulatory behaviour vis-à-vis some public institutions. It has also been accused of being naive in advancing neo-liberal presumptions regarding its capacity to intervene in the marketplace, to influence the language-choice and child-rearing practices of parents and for its quango-like relationship with government. However, because of its relative autonomy of action it has forged a wide variety of enabling partnerships, at one step removed from the day-to-day concerns of government, which has given it its own legitimacy as the authoritative language-planning body. It has also mobilized a genuine discussion on the question of language rights and the establishment of a Language Commissioner. This has been the long term aim of selected political parties, Cymdeithas yr Iaith and strident language advocates. But in Wales, the style of intervention becomes almost as critical as the content of reform. The enforcement of compliance with Welsh-language schemes is dependent on action by the National Assembly for Wales. Public bodies believe that the board has far more powers than it actually has to enforce its recommendations. Consequently, the largely constructive, consensual approach of the WLB, especially when dealing with large organizations that do not have an obvious self-interest in promoting bilingualism, has paid off. Recall Dunbar's observation in chapter 5 that the board has used its investigatory powers under section 17 of the Welsh Language Act 1993 sparingly, with only six formal investigations under section 17 having been initiated between 1993–2004.

National Assembly decisions have strengthened the WLB and made more urgent its deliberations in terms of constructing a bilingual society. However, there is a certain political imperative for the Assembly government to incorporate the board as part of a routine department of state. Depending upon how the integration is handled, several features could be lost in such incorporation. The most critical is the loss of an authoritative body exercising an overview function and undertaking the strategic language planning of Welsh. The board has also exercised flexibility of action, in part because of the specialist input of the board's members and the close working relationship with a wide variety of bodies in Welsh civil society. They in turn recognize that, while the board has authority, it is not necessarily conceived to be the public face of the government on language matters.

On the other hand, the establishment of a vibrant, dynamic language planning and policy unit at the centre of government could accelerate the mainstreaming of Welsh and fulfil many of the policy initiatives identified in *Iaith Pawb* and beyond. In Catalonia and the Basque Country this is the norm, where a powerful, centrally placed department of government is answerable directly to the President and Cabinet. As in so many other matters of public life, much depends upon the relationship such a department/unit establishes both with other constituent units of the National Assembly and with the general public. Such an opportunity to influence all aspects of policy would offer an unprecedented boost to official bilingualism and may be taken by the coalition government. The horizons for Welsh may seem a little clouded at present, but some would argue that the coalition government offers a silver lining. Such ambiguity is only to be expected given the radical and incursive nature of constructing a bilingual society within part of the evolving United Kingdom.

ACKNOWLEDGEMENTS

These are personal views and do not necessarily reflect the corporate view of Bwrdd yr Iaith Gymraeg. I am pleased to offer my sincere thanks to everyone who agreed to be interviewed for this research. Special thanks to Prys Davies, Welsh Language Board, David Lambert, Marie Navarro and Wyn James, Cardiff University, Catrin Dafydd, Cymdeithas yr Iaith Gymraeg, Gerard Finn, Office of the Commissioner of Official Languages, Canada for their willingness in assisting me to understand aspects of the work.

REFERENCES

Belfast Agreement (1998) *The Belfast Agreement-An Agreement Reached at the Multi-Party Talks on Northern Ireland, Cm. 3883, 1998.* Belfast: Northern Irleand Office.

Commissioner of Official Languages (2005) '*Annual Report 2004–5*', Ottawa: Office of the Commissioner of Official Languages.

Cooke, A. (1973; 2002 2nd ed.), *Alistair Cooke's America,* London: Weidenfeld and Nicolson.

Cymdeithas yr Iaith Gymraeg (2005) *Deddf Iaith Newydd-Dyma'r Cyfle*, Papur Trafod, Aberystwyth: Cymdeithas yr Iaith Gymraeg.

Higgs, G. Williams, C. H. and Dorling, D. (2004) '*Use of the census of population to discern trends in the Welsh language*' Area, 36. 2. pp. 187–201.

Labour and Plaid (2007) *One Wales:A Progressive Agenda for the Government of Wales,* 27th June. Cardiff: Labour and Plaid Cymru Groups in the National Assembly.

Lambert, D. (2000) 'The Government of Wales Act: An act for laws to be ministered in Wales in like form as in this realm?' *Cambrian Law Review*, 30, 60–70.

Morgan, K. and Roberts, E. (1993) *The Democratic Deficit: A Guide to Quangoland*, Papers in Planning Research No. 144, School of City and Regional Planning, Cardiff University.

Morgan, K. (2004) 'Bonfire of the Quangos: The Missing Debate', *Agenda.* Winter 2004, Cardiff: The Institute of Welsh Affairs.

National Assembly for Wales (1999) *The National Assembly (Transfer of Function) Order* 1999, (S. I. 1999/672). Cardiff: National Assembly for Wales.

Rawlings, R. (2003) *Delineating Wales*, Cardiff: University of Wales Press.

Richard Commission (2004) *Report of the Commission on the Powers and Electoral Arrangements of the National Assembly for Wales.* Cardiff: National Assembly for Wales.

Shortridge, J (2004) *ASPB Reform: Circular Letter to Chief Executive Officers, Assembly Sponsored Public Bodies*, 2 August.

Wales Office (2005) *White Paper 'Better Government for Wales' by the Wales Office, part of the United Kingdom Government,* 15 June 2005. Cardiff and London: Wales Office. Can be viewed at http://www.walesoffice.gov.uk/2005/better_government_for_wales_report.pdf

Welsh Assembly Government (2003) *Iaith Pawb: National Action Plan for a Bilingual Wales,* Cardiff: Welsh Assembly Government.

Welsh Assembly Government (2006) *Consultation by the Welsh Assembly Government on the merger with the Welsh Language Board.* Cardiff: Welsh Assembly Government.

Welsh Local Government Association (2004) *The Role of Local Authorities in a Post Quango Wales.* Cardiff: Welsh Local Government Association.

Welsh Language Board (2006) *Response by the Welsh Language Board to the Consultation by the Welsh Assembly Government on the merger with the Welsh Language Board.* Cardiff: Welsh Language Board.

Welsh Office (1997) *A Voice for Wales, Llais dros Gymru*, (Cm. 3718 of July 1997). Cardiff and London: Welsh Office.

Westminster (2000) A *House for the Future (Westminster, 2000)* Cm. 45334. Westminster: House of Lords.

Williams, C. H. (1989) 'New Domains of the Welsh Language: Education, Planning and the Law', *Contemporary Wales,* Vol. 3, 41–76.

Williams, C. H. (1993) 'Development, Dependency and the Democratic Deficit', Plenary Address to the Fifth International Conference on Minority Languages, July, Cardiff University and published in the *Journal of Multilingual and Multicultural Development,* Vol. 15. 2 & 3, (1994), pp. 101–28.

Williams, C. H. (1995) 'A Requiem for Canada?' in G. Smith, (ed.), *Federalism: The Multiethnic Challenge,* London: Longman, 31–72.

Williams, C. H. (1996) 'Citizenship and Minority Cultures: Virile Participants or Dependent Supplicants?' in A. Lapierre, P. Smart and P. Savard (eds), *Language, Culture and Values in Canada at the Dawn of the 21st Century.* Ottawa: International Council for Canadian Studies. Pp. 155–84.

Williams, C. H. (1998) 'Legislation and Empowerment: A Welsh Drama in Three Acts', Proceedings of the International Conference on Language Legislation, 14–17 October, Dublin:Comhdháil Náisiúnta na Gaeilge.

Williams, C. H. (1998) 'Operating Through Two Languages', in J. Osmond, (ed.), *The National Assembly Agenda*, Cardiff: Institute of Welsh Affairs, pp. 101–115.

Williams, C. H. (2000a) 'Adfer yr Iaith' , yn G. H. Jenkins a M. A. Williams, (gol.), *Eu Hiaith a Gadwant: Y Gymraeg yn yr Ugeinfed Ganrif*, Caerdydd:Gwasg Prifysgol Cumru, tud. 641–65.

Williams, C. H. (2000b) 'Governance and the Language', *Contemporary Wales,* Vol.12, pp. 130–54.

Williams, C. H. (2004a) '*Iaith Pawb: Iaith Braidd Neb*', Public Lecture at the Welsh Institute for Social and Cultural Affairs, University of Wales, Bangor, 15 March. See institute's website for a copy of paper.

Williams, C. H. (2004b) 'Iaith Pawb: The Doctrine of Plenary Inclusion', *Contemporary Wales,* 17, 1–27.

Williams,C. H. (2005a) *Deddf Iaith Newydd. Dyma'r Cyfle a'r Ymateb.* Address to Cymdeithas yr Iaith Meeting. Urdd Eisteddfod, Cardiff 30 May.

Williams, C. H. (2005b) *Deddfwriaeth Newydd a'r Gymraeg,* lecture delivered at the Eryri National Eisteddfod and published in *Contemporary Wales*. (2007) 19 pp. 217–33.

Williams, C. H. (2006) 'The Role of Para-governmental Institutions in Language Planning', *Supreme Court Law Review,* vol. 31, pp. 61–83.

Williams, C. H. (2007) *Linguistic Minorities in Democratic Context,* Basingstoke: Palgrave.

16

New Approaches for the Empowerment of Linguistic Minorities: A Study of Language Policy Innovations in Canada since the 1980s

LINDA CARDINAL

Introduction

Over the past thirty years, principles of language policy-making and planning have been debated extensively by socio-linguists and experts of language politics (Williams, 2003; McRoberts, 2001; Laponce, 1984; McRae, 1975). Simply put, it has been argued in the main that policies should serve either to reinforce a language on its territory (the territoriality principle) or to empower individuals by granting them linguistic rights (the personality principle). Recently, such debate has been given a more explicit normative turn by political philosophers and commentators who argue for either the superiority of individual rights over collective linguistic rights or vice versa. (Patten and Kymlicka, 2003). For instance, some may advocate a purely pragmatic approach, suggesting that language policies are relevant only because a state needs to be able to communicate with its own citizens (Weinstock, 2003). In contrast, others may insist on the responsibility of the state in supporting the development of linguistic minorities. (May, 2001; 2003; Réaume, 2003; Seymour, 2004).

While such debate remains fundamental, it is impossible not to notice that despite their opposing views, commentators continue to address language issues principally from a top-down approach to policy-making and planning. Not only is it rarely acknowledged in these discussions that language policies have a history of their own which engages linguistic minorities in a specific type of power relation with the state, there is also very little concern for more empirical studies of the ways in which policies might exactly empower linguistic minorities. Pal (1993) has touched briefly on these questions in Canada in order to argue, still from a normative perspective, that official language minorities have had an excessive influence on the state for national unity reasons. More generally, he sees social movements as narrow interest groups, concerned with their own organizational interests more than with the common good. In contrast, Jenson and Philips (1996) and Smith (2005) have argued that social movements are good citizens. But none has tried to confront Pal with regards to his approach to official-language minorities and the more general debate on the role of the state in language policy-making and planning.

This chapter discusses the relationship between linguistic minority groups and the state in Canada since the 1980s. More specifically, since 1988, Canada has witnessed major changes in its policy on official languages. The federal government has adopted new legislation on official languages in which it recognized for the first time its special responsibility for the development and enhancement of official-language minorities. It was a situation which led Pal to claim that official-language minorities had too much power over the federal government. However, we will see that the implementation of the new legislation reveals a different story. Using insights from studies on the governance of public policies (Peters, 2001) and policy networks (Marsh and Smith, 2000), we will see that, in embarking on a vast project of promoting the development and the enhancement of official-language communities, the Canadian government has redefined its relationship with its official-language minorities without losing any of the powers of the state. Critics also forget that language is a defining feature of the country's politics and that since the 1960's especially, Canada has been committed to a project of a bilingual nation whether this is wishful thinking or not. Since then, official-language minorities have used every occasion as a structure of political opportunities for advancing their situation including that of their organizations. In contrast with Pal, I would argue that it is normal for organizations to militate for their own reproduction. There is no apparent contradiction between working for the common good and for a better position for an organization. To think otherwise is simply naive politics.

Thus this chapter seeks to assess whether these recent innovations in the area of official-languages in Canada have contributed to the empowerment of official language minorities. Canada is not the only country to be confronted with such questions. Debates on the status of regional languages in Europe are another case in point (Loughlin, 2005; Grin, 2003). The devolution process in Wales has led to important innovations in planning the development of the Welsh language including partnering with community groups. (Williams, 2005). Another example is the promotion of national and linguistic minorities in the democratic process in former eastern European countries. (Henrard, 2005). The role of language policies in the empowerment of linguistic minority groups is an important issue which needs to be addressed more explicitly in both normative and policy debates. First, we will present the situation of official languages in Canada. Secondly, we will give an overview of the country's official languages policy. Thirdly, we will discuss the impact of its recent policy innovations on the empowerment of official-language minorities and their implication for our understanding of language policy-making and planning.

Official Languages in Canada

English and French are Canada's two official languages. French is concentrated in Quebec and English in the rest of Canada. However, there are also approximately one million French-speakers living outside of Quebec. While the French language in Quebec is protected by the provincial governement's language Charter, Bill 101, it is the federal policy on official languages which plays this role in the rest of Canada. Both French and English are also official languages of the province of New Brunswick but elsewhere in English

Canada measures to enhance the situation of the French language are limited. Ontario is the other exception (Cardinal, 2001). That said, the future of the French language outside of Quebec is certainly not a cause for optimism. Rates of assimilation in some parts of the country are as high as 75 per cent. In contrast, English is not a threatened language in Canada but there is an English-speaking minority living in Quebec.

It is common to discuss the federal policy with regard to Quebec's language Charter (MacMillan, 1998; Cardinal, 2006). The first one is informed by the personality principle while the other is guided by the principle of territoriality. However, the study of the federal policy with regards to its objective of empowering official-language minorities has been much neglected. It has been taken for granted that French communities outside of Quebec were going to disappear gradually because of a natural concentration of langages in Canada (McRoberts, 2001). Quebec is more French speaking than ever while the rest of Canada is also more English speaking (Dumas, chapter 10; Cardinal, 2004; Castonguay, 2005). For example, from 1971 to 1996, the number of mother-tongue francophones outside Quebec increased from 926,400 to 970,207 but, during the same period, the number of those speaking French at home decreased from 675,925 to 618,522. In 1996, the difference between the two was 351,685 and a similar situation was obtained following the 2001 census results.[1] This means that practically one-third of mother-tongue francophones outside Quebec no longer speak their mother tongue. This is of course a major source of concern for francophone leaders. Fortunately, the lowest rates of assimilation in Canada are in New Brunswick where there are still important concentrations of mother-tongue French-speakers. Data from 1996 show a rate of 9 per cent assimilation among adults aged between 25 and 34 compared to 11 per cent in 1971. The rate has gone down from 12 per cent to 9 per cent among those speakers aged between 35 and 44. In contrast, assimilation is increasing in Ontario where the situation is more problematic than ever since that it is where half of all mother-tongue French-speakers outside Quebec have their home. According to the available data, the rate was

36 per cent in 1971 compared to 44 per cent in 1996. In Ottawa, the federal capital, rates have increased substantially; from 22 per cent in 1971, to 26 per cent in 1981, to 33 per cent in 1991 to 40 per cent in 1996 (Castonguary, 2002).

Furthermore, in 1996, rates of intergenerational replacement in communities outside Quebec were at their lowest, 54 per cent (Castonguay, 1999). Experts agree that the percentage is not sufficient to ensure that the population will replace itself and that even high levels of francophone immigration would not be enough to guarantee the survival of communities (Castonguay, 1999). Once again, the decline is slower in New Brunswick and in the areas close to the Quebec border. The further francophone communities are from the main *foyer* for the French language in Canada, the more at risk they are of losing their members.

However, even in areas closer to Quebec, French-speaking communities can be fragmented geographically (Cardinal *et al.*, 2005; Gilbert, 1999). For example, in Ontario, most francophones live in mixed areas, such as Ottawa where the dominant language is English and where language politics is attuned to the majority's acceptance of bilingual services and institutions. There are also those who are totally immersed in an anglo-dominant milieu such as in Toronto or in the southern part of the province. In these areas, French-speaking children can go to French school. The French language may also be used in certain social clubs or activities. However, French cannot be considered a public or a viable language as in the two other types of situation.

To summarize, statistical surveys show that francophone communities outside Quebec face significant difficulties in maintaining their numbers, even if in absolute terms they are not completely losing the battle. For this particular reason, community leaders often insist on the fact that the French language represents an added value in Canada in the delivery of services. Through their use of new technologies, they hope to compensate for their lack of a territory and their lack of power. This confirms what sociologist, Raymond Breton, has suggested: minorities, independently of their numbers, are not passive or totally disorganized in responding to their situation. For Breton, they are *mini-polities* (Breton, 1983). They create organizations in which they debate identity and strategies and suggest conflict resolution mechanisms or the best ways to increase participation in the community. They show a certain organizational capacity which they also use in order to respond to outside pressures such as assimilation or discrimination. They rely on this capacity in order to find resources which they can utilize to advance the community's institutional completedness, that is, a full set of institutions and services usually controlled by the members of the group. Thus, thinking in terms of organizational capacity helps understand how the group can maintain its numbers no matter how fragmented and dispersed the community may be. It is also an important indicator of the group's process of empowerment.

Historically, francophones living outside Quebec have relied much on the organizational capacity of the Catholic Church and on Quebec's patriotism in developing their unique institutions: schools, credit unions, radio stations, hospitals, social services. As the welfare state replaced these networks, francophones became dependant on federal and provincial governments for support. These transformations also led to a reconfiguration of their politics. For example, in Ontario and in New Brunswick especially, francophone leaders embraced community development which, in the 1970s, was understood as a politics of citizenship (Cardinal, 2001). Such politics was twofold: first, it was based on the need for grass-roots or consciousness-raising groups aimed at giving young francophones living outside Quebec a sense of pride in their own history and belonging to their own *milieux*; second, it was a politics which demanded that governments support their full development by providing francophone communities with services and institutions they could control, such as schools, universities, media, community centres, cultural centres and legal aid clinics, in order to allow them to participate in the larger political community as French-speaking citizens and Canadians. Since the 1970s francophone leaders have also asked for more reciprocity with the English-speaking minority in Quebec, especially in the area of education where the differences between the two groups are immense (FFHQ, 1980). They have been critical of the fact that English

Canadian provinces are so concerned with the rights of their English-speaking compatriots in Quebec while not supporting the official-language minority represented in their own provinces.

It is with those issues in mind that new networks in the area of official languages have evolved since the 1970s. From then on, language activists outside Quebec have regularly pressed the federal government to take their perspective into account in the development of its language policy. This became a reality in 1988, when the federal government adopted a new official language policy which included a commitment to enhance the vitality of the English and the French linguistic minority communities and to assist their development. This has been interpreted as a sign that official-language minorities had too great an influence on the direction of Canada's official language policy (Pal, 1993). Yet, it was the result of more than twenty years of debates and lobbying efforts on their part. In the next section I shall examine the 1988 official language policy before we move to a study of its impact on the empowerment of official-language minorities.

The 1980s and the Adoption of a New Official Language Policy in Canada

Before the 1960s, French–English accommodation in Canada was informed by the following three principles: federalism and the recognition of French Canada's right to self-determination; the protection of the rights of the English-speaking minority in Quebec; and the moral commitment of the English Canadian provinces towards their own French-speaking minorities (Vipond, 1991). Language policy-making and planning was restrictive and limited. In 1867, the Canadian Constitution made a specific reference to language (article 133), recognizing that French or English could be used in parliamentary debates in both the federal and Quebec legislatures, that laws would be published in both languages federally and in Quebec and that French and English were the languages of both federal and Quebec courts. However, since then, Canada has witnessed three generations of language policy-making and planning: derived from initiatives in 1969, in 1982 and in 1988.

The Official Language Act 1969, heralded the federal government's first major step on the road to institutional bilingualism. The aim of the new legislation was that all federal departments and agencies were to become fully bilingual: that government services across the country were offered in both official languages and that a fair share of public service employment be accessible to French-speakers. The Act also created the position of Commissionner of Official Languages. The notion that bilingual services would be available 'where numbers warrant only' was adopted, but the federal government also engaged in a campaign to promote bilingual education through the financing of immersion programmes. However, the requirement for numbers was not welcomed by official-language minorities and has been a sore point ever since. Leaders from official-language minority groups never miss a chance to remind the government of the inequity of such a requirement.

A second generation of language policy-making and planning was made possible in 1982, when Canada adopted a Charter of Rights and Freedoms and gave constitutional status to the French and English languages in the areas of institutional bilingualism and education. The Quebec government did not recognize the legitimacy of the Charter. It still does not and refuses to sign the new Constitution which was drafted at the time. It argues, amongst other things, that the language sections of the Charter conflict with its own language regime and that it does not recognize its specific needs and demands for a special status. For example, the Charter guarantees that 'parents belonging to a linguistic minority have the right to have their children educated in the minority language, in homogeneous schools which they can manage, where numbers warrant'.[2] This specific clause was welcomed by official-language minorities, but it was criticized severely by the Quebec government for not respecting its own criteria in the area (McRoberts, 1995, 2001; Castonguay, 2003; and

Dumas, chapter 10 above). During this period, official-language minorities were also encouraged to use the courts with the help of a Court Challenge Programme funded entirely by the federal government. It is well-known that this was a strategy which was intended to help the English-speaking minority in Quebec to fight the Quebec language Charter. Such a strategy would allow the creation of a body of jurisprudence favourable to official-language minorities. The strategy paid off handsomely: one could say that because of the programme, Canada has developed a form of minority right, especially in the area of education (Foucher, 1999). However, it has led to a very intense process of legalization regarding language issues in Canada and to the development of a culture of resistance to official-language minorities in the provinces as well as in the federal government.

Finally, a third generation of language policy-making and planning was inaugurated in 1988 with the adoption of a new Official Language Act. With this new legislation, the federal government added two new components to its approach. First, the Act recognized the right of civil servants to work in the official language of their choice (part IV). Secondly, and more importantly for our argument, the new Act states: 'The Government of Canada is committed to (a) enhancing the vitality of the English and French linguistic minority communities in Canada and supporting and assisting their development; and (b) fostering the full recognition and use of both English and French in Canadian society.' (section 41, part VII) It was not only the first time that the notion of enhancement and development was given a legislative basis, part VII of the new Act also legitimized the ongoing appeal on the part of francophones outside Quebec for a community-based approach to promote language with the aim of increasing their organizational capacity in all areas (Asselin, 2001) .

In 1993, with the coming to power of a new government, a major revision of the public service led to the adoption of a new style of governance for the delivery of services, more horizontal or less hierarchical and with the aim of being more efficient and of cutting costs. As a result, official-language programmes from 1995 to 1999 received $70–80 million less in a budget totalling $220 million, a situation which angered official-language minorities who, with the support of the Commissioner of Official Languages, were quick to remind the government that it had constitutional obligations in the area which it should consider more seriously. However, the new governance also aimed at a better integration of the different bodies supporting official-language minorities with respect to their vitality and development. Amongst those bodies, the Department of Canadian Heritage, which had the main role of coordinating the application of part VII, was given the tasks of concluding agreements with different governmental actors in specific areas such as education, school management and health in order to encourage the delivery of public services to the official-language minorities (Cardinal and Hudon, 2001). An example of such an agreement is a memorandum of understanding on the implementation of section 41 signed in 1997 between the Ministry of Canadian Heritage and the Treasury Board. The agreement was meant to encourage federal institutions to take into account, in their overall strategic planning and evaluation process, the government's commitment to the vitality and development of the official-language minorities. Accordingly, the agreement sought to promote interdepartmental coordination in the area of official languages.

Agreements with provincial governments took other forms. For example, in 1995, a federal–provincial–territorial agreement for the promotion of official languages was signed to facilitate the delivery of services to the official-language minorities in the areas of health, the economy, justice, social services and recreation, as well as for the promotion and recognition of the two official languages and their use. The content of the agreements and their methods of implementation varied from province to province.

The minister for Canadian Heritage also signed agreements with the official-language minorities. These Canada–community agreements set out a framework for cooperation between the government and official minorities. It guaranteed funding to agencies of the minority communities for a five-year period to enable them to develop programming and carry out projects in a variety of areas such as culture, the economy, communications, law, health and the rights of women and racial minorities. These agreements were also administered by a management committee that included representatives from both the Ministry of Canadian Heritage and the official-language minority communities, usually represented by a steering committee or a round table. It is the role of this round table to establish the community's development priorities and promote coordination among the agencies working on community development. Most of the community representatives sitting on the Agreement Management Committee come from provincial or territorial round tables (Cardinal and Hudon, 2001: 29–30) .

From 1998 to 2001, the federal government also signed four multilateral agreements between the various departments and public agencies and different groups from official-language minorities: a multipartite cooperation agreement on the artistic and cultural development of Canada's francophone and Acadian communities; an agreement on French-language publishing and theatre in the minority communities; a national memorandum of understanding on human resources development for Canada's francophone and Acadian communities; a national memorandum of understanding on human resources development for Quebec's anglophone community.

Despite these initiatives, official-language minorities were not satisfied with their situation and with the new governance. The implementation of part VII was moving too slowly. The Commissioner of Official Languages agreed with them and demanded that the government attend to the situation with more resolve. In response, the President of the Treasury Board was asked by the Prime Minister, Jean Chrétien, to appoint a working group with the specific mandate of making recommendation in order to improve the situation. In the end, the Prime Minister acknowledged that there was a need for better coordination of the new governance in the area of official languages. More specifically, in April 2001, the Prime Minister announced that the then Minister of Intergovernmental Affairs, Stéphane Dion would inherit the responsibility of proposing a new interdepartmental structure to coordinate action with respect to official languages, including action with respect to vitality and development. He stated that, by doing so, the government intended to exercise more 'political leadership with regard to the promotion of and respect for bilingualism and the application of laws protecting the English and French linguistic minorities everywhere in Canada' (Buzetti, 2001:) [my translation]. Following this announcement, the Minister of Intergovernmental Affairs established a secretariat for official languges within the Office of the Privy Council. He also embarked on a vast consultation of official-language minorities and other actors involved in language policy-making, planning and in community development in order to develop a plan of action in the area of official languages for the next five years.

In 2003, the plan was published and it included measures for the implementation of part VII. More generally, it proposed a modernized approach to Canada's official-language policy using a neo-liberal vocabulary and the language of 'Canadian values'. It recognized, for example, that official languages were an added value for workers and that it contributed to the country's competitevness (Canada, 2003: vii). It also acknowledged the difficulties of the French language outside Quebec and argued that official-language communities needed to be fully integrated in the Canadian project of the bilingual nation-state. It demanded, in keeping with part VII, that their needs be taken into consideration at all times in the planning of the government's policies. It announced significant investments in education, including measures to help French-speakers maintain and reinforce their ability to speak in their own mother tongue. Attention was given to five other key issues identified as priorities by official-language communities: youth, health, justice, immigration and economic development. The plan announced investments in literacy programmes for families. This is especially important in areas where francophones married to English-speakers have significant difficulties in transmitting their language to their children. Investments were also proposed in order to develop the organizational capacity of official-language minority groups and networks in education, health, justice and immigration, hoping that this would lead to projects and to more collaboration with the provinces as such areas fall within provincial jurisdiction (Canada, 2003: 44–9). Finally, the plan sought to increase the capacity of francophone communities to participate in the knowledge-based economy by giving them more access to programmes and technological infrastructure (Canada, 2003: 49). These are just a few examples of areas covered by the plan which has been very much welcomed by official language minorities.[3] It represents a clear attempt to assist the development of networks and the consolidation of the organizational capacity of official-language minorities in order for them to pursue their own development as citizens. Thus the plan clearly wants to contribute to the empowerment of official-language minorities. It makes it clear that the government is committed to working 'with' official-language minorities and not only 'for' them. Moreover, the plan increased the funding for official languages from $500 millions to $751.3 millions. This brought government's investments in the area of official languages to what it was in 1993 before it was cut for the sake of efficiency. Official-language minorities were certainly pleased with the announcement.

However, during the course of the implemention of the plan, the Prime Minister gave the responsibility for official languages to the Minister of Health, Pierre Pettigrew, while leaving the coordination of the plan in the Privy Council. In 2004, when the government in power was re-elected, as a minority government, another minister, Mauril Bélanger became responsible for the portfolio for official languages. Once more, the coordination was left to the Privy Council. Nevertheless, in the space of three years, three different ministers had been charged with the responsibility of promoting the action plan. Furthermore, official-language minorities were critical of the ways in which these ministers were more or less active in implementing part VII and demanded that the legislation be given more clout in order to force the government to take more positive measure towards their development. Following major lobbying on the part of the Commissioner for Official Languages, some key political figures in Ottawa such as Senator Jean-Robert Gauthier and official-language minorities, in 2005, part VII was amended in order to require the Canadian government to take positive measures to enhance the development of official-language minorities. The amendment also gave Canadians and more specifically official-language minorities, the right to take the government to court if it did not adopt those positive measures. It is still too early to determine what those measures will be and how they interact with the plan. Moreover, in January 2006, the coming to power of a new government meant that it will be some time before the new Act is implemented. The new Prime Minister, Stephen Harper, has also completely transformed the governance of official languages. Instead of a coordinated approach which emanated from the Privy Council, he created a new department for International Cooperation, Official Languages and *la Francophonie* and gave the coordination of the official language policy to the new minister, Josée Verner. Whether she will decide if the plan is worth pursuing is not clear. It is a document very much identified with the past government. However, the fact that her government is also a minority government might help those who want the plan to continue. Whatever her decision, she first needs to study the situation more closely and determine with her advisors what the notion 'positive measure' might mean in order to pass the legal test and persue the implementation of part VII. Then she might decide that the plan equals such a positive measure but nothing is defined at this point. One step forward on her part was to appoint, in April 2006, a Parliamentary Secretary for Official Languages, Sylvie Boucher, whose role will be to assist the minister in her role in coordinating and promoting the official language policy.

Horizontal Governance and the Empowerment of Official-Language Minorities: An Evaluation

The implementation of part VII of the Act is still not resolved and official-language minorities cannot take the situation for granted. This simple fact should help nuance the view of those who think that official-language minorities have too much influence on the federal government. It is right to argue that they have been very active at a symbolic level, such as working for some form of recognition in the 1988 Official Languages Act. They have also been successful in lobbying the government for the amendment of part VII of the Act. However, the fact that it took many years before they could reap the benefit of their lobbying efforts, and then decided to continue with such strategy despite the publication of an action plan for official languages, suggests that their influence is exaggerated. Futhermore, the government has lost no power in the process. The success of official-language minorities is due to their capacity to use institutions such as the Constitution or the courts in order to claim their rights. This in itself does not reveal any specific or exaggerated control on the state on their part. In fact, we would argue that it is precisely because they have little influence on state affairs that they mainly intervene at a constitutional or legal level. Official-language minorities are also empowered in the process but in a more limited way than would be expected. Moreover, their lobbying efforts in order to amend part VII reveal that they did not perceive its implementation as empowering with regards to their development and enhancement. A survey of evaluations of the implementation of part VII should help illustrate this point.

In 1996, the Commissionner for Official Language was already very critical of the situation. He argued that part VII had been adopted in 1988 and yet it was still the object of much misunderstanding on the part of decision-makers and public servants (Commissioner of Official Languages, 1996). In 1997, he expressed the hope that 'decision makers at all levels in the Government of Canada [would] be personally committed, and be more creative in identifying opportunities to achieve Part VII objectives.' (Commissioner of Official Languages, 1998: 73) However, in 1998, Donald Savoie, in a report for the Privy Council, the Department of Canadian Heritage and the Treasury Board Secretariat, came to the same conclusion as the Commissioner for Official Languages. In 1999, the working group set up by the President of the Treasury Board was also making the same remarks (Fontaine *et al.*, 1999). Furthermore, in his 2000 annual report, the Commissioner of Official Languages wrote that 'many government institutions are still characterized by an at best passive, if not defensive, attitude with regards to their obligations' (Commissioner of Official Languages, 2000–1: 8).

Evaluations of the different type of agreements signed between the federal government and official-language minorities also reveal that the new governance was meant mostly as a way to implement budget cuts (Cardinal and Hudon, 2001; Cardinal and Juillet, 2005). Actors criticized the fact that the rules of the game between the government and official-language minorities had not been clearly spelled out. Rules could change according to needs and political pressure. It was also not clear if the government saw itself as a partner of official-language minorities or not. Many civil servants apparently did not always know how to negotiate these agreements or which task to address. (Cardinal and Hudon, 2001: 32). They acknowledged that these agreements were often signed in haste, in a climate of widespread disinterest towards official-language minorities. These agreements also led to an intense bureaucratization of community work and not necessarily to more coordination. Creativity has often been caught in the iron cage of bureaucracy. Consideration was not even given to the long-term impact of these agreements on the development of the minorities and on the relations between the government and non-government players. In its own evaluation of the Canada–community agreements the government seems to support these conclusions (Canadian Heritage, 1997).

Players involved in the area of health, culture and economic development also confirmed the resistance of the government towards official-language minority groups (Cardinal and Julliet, 2005). For example, some did not always think that it was part of their work to develop projects with official-language minorities or they believed that expectations would be too high. In the case of economic development, actors have had structures imposed on them from top to bottom without a careful study of the communities' capacity to support these new methods. In Ontario, groups involved in economic development had work hard to convince the government that its structure was not reflecting properly the community's needs. The situation was modified but only after great effort on the part of community groups involved in the area.

Culture is the one sector where actors seem to work better together. Ironically, it was the one left out by the plan. The process has often been criticized for being too bureaucratic and too slow but at least there is an ongoing dialogue between the different partners involved and a willingness on the part of civil servants to address minorities' needs in the arts and culture. Together, they have developed a comprehensive approach to cultural development based on a bottom-up approach to the arts in which projects, once they are mature and fully supported by the community, receive support from the government. The aim is to develop a 'national' perspective meaning that only projects which can fit in a national perspective aiming at developing the arts in all francophone communities will be promoted. At the governmental level, people working in the area seem to be satisfied with the dynamism of the community in this area and can only hope to give it more support. This success in the cultural sector comes for many because networks involved in the arts are well organized, democratic and have a very strong leadership. Unlike other sectors, the new governance is also informed by a bottom-up process. It increases the credibility of the demands coming from the non-governmental actors and gives civil servants the motivation to work with them as partners in advancing their case within the different governmental bodies.

However, not all networks are so well organized and democratic and this may explain some of the resistance of governmental actors and lack of motivation to work with official-language minorities. But networks also almost 'naturally' resisted the implementation of horizontal governance. The new governance involved a change in institutional culture amongst existing networks which had been used to functioning without being accountable to anyone. Networks involved in this process were the Fédération des communautés francophones et acadienne du Canada (FCFA), a pan-Canadian organization which aims at representing all francophone minorities outside Quebec. It also included provincial associations and sectorial networks devoted to promoting the arts, women, youth and visible minorities. Critics have argued rightly that most of these groups are not always representative or democratic and that they are more involved in lobbying the government than being engaged in community development (Pal, 1993). Furthermore, Cardinal and Hudon (2001) have shown that fierce debates amongst them led many to refuse to share any of their power with other groups fearing that they would lose too much in the process. The government did not help the situation since it had identified a number of groups, such as the FCFA and provincial associations, as spokespersons for the official-language communities, without any consideration for other groups equally involved in representational activities. Its argument was that communities had to learn to work together and to solve their difficulties amongst themselves. In the meantime, structures were compressed but the associations recognized by the government were spared. This contributed to much resistance to the new governance and to the implementation of part VII.

However, a recent evaluation of the implementation of part VII revealed that official-language minority groups were more favourable towards the new governance because their working relation with the government had improved since the publication of the 2003 plan of action for official languages (Canada, 2005; Cardinal, Lang and Sauvé, 2005). They were still waiting for concrete results but at least they were better attuned to the demands of the new structure. Problems had not been solved between groups but many of them remained favourable to the principle of a more horizontal type of governance which would include their point of views and contributions (Johnson and Fontaine, 2005). Paradoxically, official language minorities were also commenting on the need to amend part VII in order for the government to take positive measures for the development. They claimed that it was important to be able to take the government to court if it did not adopt those positive measures.[4] Such pressure, they argued, would be an important reason for civil servants to work more efficiently. As mentioned, official-language minorities use a constitutional or rights discourse efficiently in order to push for their rights. This is how they feel empowered. However, in practice, the process is replete with ambiguities and difficulties due to organizational resistance and to the nature of the public service.

Our survey seems to confirm Peters's conclusion that the new horizontal governance in a Westminster system is bound to generate resistance on the part of governmental actors. Since civil servants are not accountable to groups with whom they have to work, but rather to their minister whose prime concern in this kind of system is with control, this may prevent innovation and creativity. It may also explain passivity or excess control on the part of civil servants. This type of situation has not been resolved with the implementation of the 2003 plan because the coordination of the horizontal approach by the different ministers responsible for official languages is still very much centralized and top-down. Moreover, with the exception of the justice sector, groups are consulted more than involved in any significant decision-making process. This situation also confirms Peters's view that since governance consists in setting goals or determining priorities, it tends very often to drive decisions upwards to central agencies, in spite of continuing pressures to deconcentrate and decentralize. The state continues to exercise consistent direction of policies (Peters, 2001: 38–9).

A Minister for Official Languages may help motivate civil servants and infuse a more positive attitude by them towards official-language minorities. However, our recent evaluation of the situation shows that, without any specific budget to do so, little can be done, hence the poor results in most cases despite the fact that official-language minorities think that it would be worthwhile to continue the experiment. (Cardinal, Lang and Sauvé, 2005). We have seen that the difficulties of horizontal form of governance are not attributed only to the nature of the Westminster system and its obsession with control and centralization. Resistance coming from networks show that the reproduction of their own structures of power and representation is also an issue to be taken into consideration. This seems to confirm Marsh and Smith's view that networks are institutions with their own logic of continuity and change (Marsh and Smith, 2000). Networks build on their own past institutional arrangements in order to bring changes within their own structures. It is not clear that the

2003 plan offers any solution to this situation. Governments should not be afraid to make more demands on networks to be more inclusive and democratic. If it does not do so, it might be because of past clientelist practices or simply because of a lack of sensitivity towards civil society. By providing funding to certain groups identified as spokespersons by the government, and not to others, it contributes to the reproduction of inequalities of access to power on their part. This has been particularly the case in the government's treatment of women's groups from official-language minority communities (Cardinal and Cox, 2005). They have been very much left behind and, without any government assistance, networks such as women's groups, could never be real partners in the organization of power in the area of official-languages. Their empowerment depends on the government's willingness to nourish its relationship with them. In other words, governments still have the power and official language minorities continue to depend on their good will despite constitutional obligations.

Thus, in keeping with Peter's work on governance in Canada, we argue that it is important to study the interactions between policy innovations or the new governance of official languages and the more vertical type of approach required by the Westminster style of governing in the process of the implementation of part VII. Using Marsh and Smith's insights on policy networks, we can also better capture the interactions between governmental and non-governmental actors in order to explain better their successes and failures. In the end, we argue that the implementation of part VII has had a limited impact on the empowerment of official-language minorities. They feel more empowered when they engage with the constitution and the language of rights as a tool for change. In this respect, they succeed in influencing policy-making, but official-language minorities are still waiting for concrete results.

Conclusion

We have done three things in this chapter. First, we have provided a general description of the situation of official languages in Canada. Secondly, we have discussed recent policy innovations in the area of official languages. Thirdly, we have proposed an evaluation of their impact on the empowerment of official-language minorities. We have suggested that these policy innovations have not yet been conclusive and looked at their implications for language policy-making and planning. For example, we saw that successes and failures in the area of language policy-making and planning depend on the ways in which actors interact with existing institutional arrangements at both the government and community levels. The Westminster system generates resistance which seems to be resolved only by reinforcing its tendency to centralize and control. We have also found the same to be true of networks. They are both institutions concerned with the reproduction of their own structures of power. Other factors such as the downsizing of the federal government also contribute to explaining the difficulties of official-language minorities in the short term, while the study of institutional arrangements helps us make better sense of the complexity of the process involved in policy-making and planning for their empowerment.

We have also observed that official-language minorities think of their empowerment in constitutional or rights terms. However, more legalization in the area of official language can lead to more resistance on the part of civil servant and provinces instead of a renewed commitment for the development of official-language minorities. Official-language minorities seem to think that they can still reap the benefits of such strategy but it is not clear whether constitutionalism and the legalization of official languages give better results. Moreover, the rights-based approach in Canada has already contributed to the creation of a false sense of security amongst francophone minorities. For example, studies show that after more than fifteen years of intensive constitutional and legal developments in the area of education, in Ontario only 50 per cent of francophone children have access to an education in their mother tongue (Martel, 2001). This is compounded by the fact that francophones outside of Quebec do not have much support from the Canadian population when they take the legal route. Studies reveal that English Canadian provinces support the use of the courts by the English-speaking minority in Quebec but that they take very little interest in their own official-language minority (Conlongue, 1999; Schneiderman, 1989; Vipond, 1996). There will certainly be other occasions where official-language minorities will have no choice but to use the legal route. However, to make it an everyday solution in order to improve the implementation of part VII may be a dangerous path to take.

Finally, those who debate language policy-making and planning in keeping with the original opposition between territoriality and personality principles need to update their views by looking more specifically at the way that policy innovations such as those witnessed in Canada, Wales and Europe more generally are moving the discussion in new directions. More research also needs to be undertaken in order to promote a more dynamic view of the relationship between the state and linguistic minorities than that which has been suggested so far by most commentators.

REFERENCES

Asselin, R. (2001) *L'article 41 de la Loi sur les langues officielles : portée, évolution et régime d'application*, Ottawa: Direction de la recherche parlementaire, Division des affaires politiques et sociales, 17 September.

Breton, Raymond (1983) 'La communauté ethnique, communauté politique', *Sociologie et sociétés*, Vol. 15, no. 2, pp. 23–37.

Canada (2003) *The Next Act: New Momentum for Canada's Linguistic Duality. The Action Plan for Official Languages*. Ottawa: Government of Canada. [http://www.pco-bcp.gc.ca]

Canada (2005), *Le point sur la mise en œuvre du Plan d'action pour les langues officielles*, Ottawa: Office of the Privy Council.

Canadian Heritage, (1997) *Evaluation of Canada-Community Agreements*, Ottawa: Corporate Review Branch of the Department of Canadian Heritage.

Cardinal, L. (2000) 'Le pouvoir exécutif et la judiciarisation de la politique au Canada : une étude du programme de contestation judiciaire', *Politique et Sociétés*, Vol. 20, no. 2–3, pp. 4–65.

Cardinal, L. (2001) *Chroniques d'une vie politique mouvementée. L'Ontario francophone de 1986 à 1995*, Ottawa: Le Nordir.

Cardinal, L. (2004) 'The Limits of Bilingualism', *Nationalism and Ethnic Politics*, Vol. 10, no. 1, pp. 79–104.

Cardinal, L. (2006) 'Les enjeux de la diversité linguistique au Canada et au Québec', in Palard, J., Gagnon B. and Gagnon, A.-G. (eds), *La diversité des identités au Canada et dans l'Europe des régions*, Québec and Bruxelles: Les Presses de l'Université Laval and P.I.E.-Peter Lang, pp. 93–118.

Cardinal, L. and Hudon, M-È. (2001) *The Governance of Canada's Official Language Minorities: A Preliminary Study*, Ottawa: Commissioner of Official Languages.

Cardinal, L. and Juillet, L. (2005) 'Les minorités francophones hors Québec et la gouvernance des langues officielles au Canada', in Wallot, J.-P. (ed.), *La gouvernance linguistique: le Canada en perspective*, Ottawa: Presses de l'Université d'Ottawa, pp. 157–176.

Cardinal, L. and Cox, R. (2005) *La gouvernance des langues officielles au canada et ses effets sur les femmes et les groupes de femmes francophones en milieu minoritaire : optimiser un potentiel rassembleur*, Ottawa: Coalition nationale des femmes francophones.

Cardinal, L., Lang, S. and Sauvé, A. (2005) *Apprendre à travailler autrement : la gouvernance partagée dans le domaine du développement des langues officielles au Canada*, Ottawa: Commissioner of Official Languages.

Cardinal, L. *et al.* (2005) *Francophones in Ontario: A Statistical Profile*, Toronto: Ministry of the Attorney General.

Castonguay, C. (1999) 'Évolution démographique des Franco-Ontariens entre 1971 et 1991, suivi d'un aperçu du recensement de 1996', in Labrie, N. and Forlot, G. (eds), *L'enjeu de la langue en Ontario français*, Prise de parole: Sudbury, pp. 15–32.

Castonguay, C. (2002) 'La francophonie canadienne : entre le mythe et la réalité', in Verreault, C., Mercier L. and Lavoie, T. (ed.), *Le français, une langue à apprivoiser*, Québec: Presses de l'Université Laval, pp. 19–40.

Castonguay, C. (2003), 'Politiques linguistiques et avenirs des populations de langue anglaise et de langue française au Canada', in Morris, M. (ed.), *Les politiques linguistiques canadiennes. Approches comparées*, Paris: L'Harmattan, pp. 174–234.

Castonguay, C. (2005) 'Cassure linguistique et identitaire', *Recherches sociograhiques*, Vol. XLVI, no. 3, pp. 473–494.

Conlongue, R. (1999) 'English-Canadian Culture and the Absent French Canadian', *Inroads*, no. 8, pp. 87–97.

Commissioner of Official Languages (1996) *A Blueprint for Action: Implementing Part VII of the Official Languages Act, 1988*, Ottawa: Department of Public Works and Government Services Canada. [http:www//ocol.gc.ca/vii_f.html]

Commissioner of Official Languages (1998) *Government Transformations: the Impact on Canada's Official Languages Program*, Ottawa: Department of Public Works and Government Services Canada.

Commissioner of Official Languages (2000–2001) *Annual Report 2000–2001*, Ottawa: Department of Public Works and Government Services Canada.

Dumas, G. (2007) 'Québec's Language Policy: Perceptions and Realities', in Williams, C. H. (ed.), *Language and Governance*, Cardiff University of Wales Press, pp. 250–62.

Fédération des francophones hors Québec (1980) *À la recherche du milliard*, Ottawa: FFHQ.

Fontaine, Y. *et al.* (1999) *No Turning Back: Official Languages in the Face of Government Transformations*, Ottawa: Task Force on Government Transformations and Official Languages.

Foucher, P. (1999) 'Les droits linguistiques au Canada', in Thériault, J.-Y. (ed.), *Francophonies minoritaires au Canada. L'état des lieux*, Moncton: Éditions d'Acadie, pp. 307–325.

Gilbert, A. (1999) 'Les espaces de la francophonie ontarienne', in Thériault, J.-Y. (ed.), *Francophonies minoritaires au Canada. L'état des lieux*, Moncton: Éditions d'Acadie, pp. 55–77.

Gilbert, A. (2001) 'Le français au Canada, entre droits et géographie', *Le Géographe canadien*, Vol. 45, no 1, pp. 173–179.

Grin, F. (2003) *Language Policy Evaluation and the European Charter for Regional or Minority Languages*, Londres: Palgrave Macmillan.

Henrard, K. (2005) "Participation', 'Representation' and 'Autonomy' in the Lund Recommendations and its Reflections in the Supervision of the FNCM and Several Human Rights Conventions', *International Journal of Minority and Group Rights*, Vol. 12, nos 2–3, pp. 133–168.

Jenson, J. and. Phillips, S. D. (1996), 'Regime Shifts: New Citizenship Practices in Canada', *International Journal of Canadian Studies*, no. 14, pp. 111–135.

Johnson, M. and Fontaine, Y. (2005) 'Transformations gouvernementales et langues officielles', in Wallot, J.-P. (ed.), La gouvernance linguistique : le Canada en perspective, Ottawa: Les Presses de l'Université d'Ottawa, pp. 177–193.

Laponce, J. (1984) *Langue et territoires*, Québec: Presses de l'Université Laval.

Loughlin, J. (2005) 'Les changements de paradigmes de l'État et les politiques publiques envers les minorités linguistiques et culturelles en Europe de l'Ouest', in Wallot, J.-P. (ed.), *La gouvernance linguistique : le Canada en perspective*, Ottawa: Presses de l'Université d'Ottawa, pp. 19–38.

McMillan, M. (1998) The Practice of Language Rights in Canada, Toronto: University of Toronto Press.

McRae, K. (1975) 'The Principle of Territoriality and the Principle of Personality in Multilingual States', *International Journal of the Sociology of Language*, no 4, pp. 35–45.

McRoberts, K. (1995) *Misconceiving Canada*, Toronto: Oxford University Press.

McRoberts, K. (2001) 'Les politiques de la langue au Canada : un combat contre la territorialisation', in Lacorne, D. and Judt, T. (eds), *La politique de Babel. Du monolinguisme d'État au plurilinguisme des peuples*, Paris: Karthala, pp. 155–190.

Marsh, D. and Smith, M. (2000) 'Understanding Policy Networks: Towards a Dialectical Approach', *Political Studies*, Vol. 43, p. 4–21.

Martel, A. (2001) *Droits, écoles et communautés, 1986–2002. Analyse pour un aménagement du français par l'éducation en milieu minoritaire au Canada*, Ottawa: Commissariat aux langues officielles.

May, S. (2003) 'Misconceiving Minority Language Rights: Implications for Liberal Political Theory', in Patten, A. and Kymlicka W. (eds), Language Rights and Political Theory, Oxford: Oxford University Press, pp. 123–152.

Pal, L. (1993) *Interests of State*, Montréal: McGill-Queen's University Press.

Patten, A. and Kymlicka W. (eds) (2003) *Language Rights and Political Theory*, Oxford: Oxford University Press.

Peters, G. B. and Savoie D. (eds) (2001) *Governance in the Twenty-First Century: Revitalizing the Public Service*, Ottawa/Montréal/Kingston: Canadian Centre for Management Development and McGill-Queen's University Press.

Peters, G. (2001) 'Mondialisation, institutions et gouvernance', in Peters, G. and Savoie, D. (eds), *La gouvernance au XXIe siècle: revitaliser la fonction publique*, Ottawa/Québec: Centre canadien de gestion and Les Presses de l'Université Laval, pp. 19–39.

Réaume, D. G. (2003), 'Beyond *Person*ality: the Territorial and Personal Principles of Language Policy Reconsidered', in Patten, A. and Kymlicka, W. (eds), *Language Rights and Political Theory*, Oxford: Oxford University Press, pp. 271–295.

Savoie, D. (1998) *Official-Language minority Communities: Promoting a Government Objective*, Ottawa: Report prepared for the Privy Council, the Department of Canadian Heritage and the Treasury Board Secretariat.

Schneiderman, D. *et al.*, (1989) 'Political Culture and the Problem of Double Standards: Mass and Elite Attitudes Toward Language Rights in the Canadian Charter of Rights and Freedoms', *Canadian Journal of Political Science*, Vol. 22, no. 2, pp. 259–284.

Seymour, M. (2004), 'Le droit des peuples', *Bulletin d'histoire politique*, Vol. 12, no. 3, pp. 79–88.

Smith, M. (2005), *A Civil Society? Collective Actors in Canadian Political Life*, Peterborough, Broadview Press.

Standing Committee on Official Languages. [http://www.parl.gc.ca/committee/CommitteeList.aspx?Lang=1&PARLSES=381&JNT=0&SELID=e22_.2&COM=8987&STAC=1232205

Statistic Canada website at www12.statcan.ca/francaiscensus01/products/analytic/companion/lang/Canada_f.cfm.

Treasury Board Secretariat (2000) *Official Languages: Full Sail Ahead*, Ottawa: Treasury Board Secretariat.

Vipond, R. (1991) *Liberty and Community. Canadian Federalism and the Failure of the Constitution*, New York: State University of New York Press.

Vipond, R. (1996) 'Citizenship and the Charter of Rights: The Two Sides of Pierre Trudeau', *International Journal of Canadian Studies*, no. 14, pp. 179–192.

Weinstock, D. (2003) 'The Antinomy of Language Policy', in Patten, A. and Kymlicka W. (eds), *Language Rights and Political Theory*, Oxford: Oxford University Press, p. 250 et seq.

Williams, C. (2003) 'Language Policy and Planning Issues in Multicultural Societies', in Larrivée, P. (ed.), *Understanding the Québec Question*, Basingstoke: Palgrave, pp. 1–56.

Williams, C. (2005) 'Iaith Pawb: the doctrine of plenary inclusion', *Contemporary Wales* vol.17. pp. 1–27.

NOTES

1 For details, see Statistic Canada's website at www12.statcan.ca/francaiscensus01/products/analytic/companion/lang/Canada_f.cfm.

2 Canadian Charter of Rights and Freedoms, section 23.

3 Culture was not identified a priority by the government which argued that it was already investing sufficiently in the area.

4 For details, see the debate on amending part VII of the Act during the hearings of the Standing Committee on Official Languages. http://www.parl.gc.ca/committee/CommitteeList.aspx?Lang=1&PARLSES=381&JNT=0&SELID=e22_.2&COM=8987&STAC=1232205]

17

How Quebec became a North American Region State

JEAN-FRANÇOIS LISÉE[1]

Our view of the evolution of Quebec in the last decade is generally obscured by three elements. First, from the failed attempt at constitutional reform, called the Meech agreement of 1990, through two referendums, to the resignation of Premier Lucien Bouchard in early 2001, it seems that scarcely anything but political debate has gone on in the province. Second, Quebec policies towards the rest of the world and Ottawa's response to it may seem wholly attributable not to real structural evolution, but to political posturing aimed at the next independence showdown. Third, while looking at Quebec's vital signs, the inevitable and quite relevant comparison with Ontario usually puts it at a disadvantage. As though sitting besides a giant necessarily meant that you are a dwarf.

However, beyond these elements and intertwined with them, Quebec's transformations during the 1990s, mostly coming to fruition in the second half of the decade, deserve to be weighed on their merits. As Michael Keating notes in looking at the behaviour of nationless states in the new context of globalization, it is true that nationalism predates and colours their actions and that the opening of markets provides a new opportunity for nationalistic policies (Keating, 2003). The combination of nationalist will and opening markets compounds what is, nonetheless, real and measurable change.

The view of this text is that, in the last decade, Quebec's economic and political elite, with strong popular support, *wanted* Quebec to become a region state – that is to act increasingly as a specific entity whether or not it became independent from Canada; that it *needed* to become a region state in order to achieve optimal growth; and that it was further *pushed* into becoming one by the peculiar political context.

Foreshadowing: FTA and GST

Quebec's elite made two macroeconomic decisions in the late 1980s and early 1990s that prepared the transformations to come and gave a first signal of their awareness of Quebec's economic interest in becoming a region state, well beyond sovereignists' (the Quebec term for pro-independence forces) circles.

The first was Quebec's bipartisan support for the Free Trade Agreement (FTA) between Canada and the US in 1988. (The expansion to Mexico, through the North American FTA, or NAFTA, would come in 1993). Most of Quebec's exports were destined to go to the rest of Canada, first and foremost Ontario. By then the business class was primarily francophone. Diversifying exports to the US, across the political, legal and linguistic US border should have been a more frightening challenge for them, and their electorate, than for their Ontario counterparts. As was pointed out by Canadian economist John Helliwell, 'two countries [or in this case a region and a neighbouring country] sharing a language are estimated to have two-way trade flows more than 50 per cent larger than those between otherwise similar countries' (Helliwell, 1998: 45). That is the standard he found for OECD countries. Which means that, given a similar starting point, English-speaking Ontario should do 50 per cent better than French-speaking Quebec at trading with the US. In a separate paper, Helliwell has also argued that, in 1990, based on a gravity model developed by John McCallum, Quebec's reliance on interprovincial trade over trade with US states of comparable size and distance was even greater than that of other provinces. McCallum had shown that intensity of province-to-province trade was, on average, twenty-one times greater than that between province and state. Helliwell found that, for Quebec, it was twenty-six times greater. 'National borders matter even more for Quebec than for the rest of Canada', he wrote (Helliwell, 1985: 1).

Yet Quebec's new entrepreneurs were enthusiastic in favouring free trade with the US. Politically, then Premier René Lévesque, the founder of the modern independence movement, the Parti Québécois (PQ), had given a first positive signal in a speech given in the US in 1984. Later, a risk-averse and pro-Canadian Robert Bourassa, who became Premier, joined the movement. In the election of 1988, Quebec was the only province, with Alberta, to give a majority of votes to Brian Mulroney, thus bringing the FTA into place against the wishes of a majority of English-Canadian voters.

Then came the Goods and Services Tax (GST) a value-added tax introduced by the federal government to replace the old federal manufacturing tax. The Quebec liberal government, supported by Jacques Parizeau's PQ opposition, and the Quebec business class, saw the comparative advantage in taking the sales taxes out of the structure of the manufactured product, thus lowering its cost when it crossed the border. They immediately harmonised the provincial Quebec sales tax on the same principle to lower further the cost of exported goods. There was some loss of short-term revenue – about 2 billion Canadian dollars – but it was seen as a worthy investment in the expansion of exports, and as a comparative advantage gained on Ontario, where the federal GST was furiously opposed, and where a similar provincial tax adjustment was – and still is fifteen years hence – politically out of the question.

International Exports: Time of Harvest

And expansion came. The decade started with Quebec exports to the rest of Canada exceeding its foreign exports. When the decade closed, Quebec was selling almost twice as much abroad than in Canada. By 2000, Quebec was the US's sixth most important trading partner, overtaking the UK,

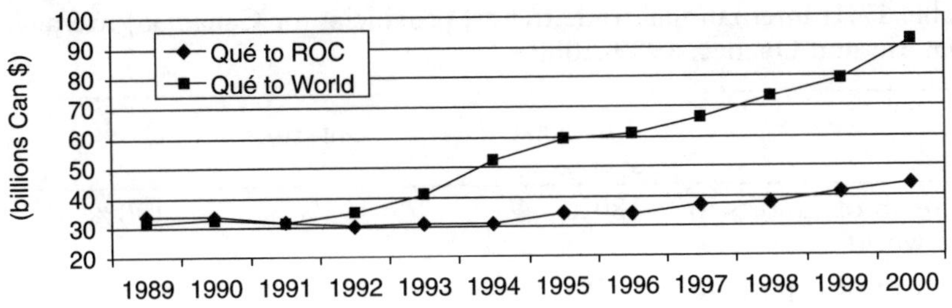

Figure 17.1: Quebec exports, 1989–2000

France, Germany, Brazil, or Russia. This amounts to a commercial 'decanadianization' of Quebec. But here interprovincial comparisons are in order. We have data that span the decade, from the previous economic peak, 1989, to what we now know to be the last peak, that of 2000. First, one has to note that Canada as a whole went from a position of near equilibrium between interprovincial trade and external exports in 1989, to a position in 2000 where international exports became twice as important as interprovincial exchanges. It is an extraordinary event in and of itself.

What is striking about Ontario and Quebec is the growth of their international exports in the decade. Compared to the very high provincial average (which is the average of the growth of the ten provinces) of 180 per cent, Quebec reached 190 per cent, Ontario 192 per cent. If corrected for population growth, Quebec's performance surpasses that of Ontario: 173 per cent over Ontario's 153 per cent. Furthermore, the change in both provinces' international trade ratio, relative to their GDP, is unmatched. Again over the very high provincial average of 74 per cent, Quebec's grew by 94 per cent over the decade, Ontario's by 90 per cent. Alberta's international exports grew by 265 per cent, driven by oil, but its international trade ratio rose by only 72 per cent.

This means that Quebec overcame both Helliwell's common OECD language-border effect, that should have imposed on it a substantial 50 per cent handicap compared to Ontario (more on this later), and its heretofore over-reliance on interprovincial trade.

Table 17.1: International trade trends, provincial (or Canadian) average, Ontario and Quebec, 1989–2000

	Provincial average	Ontario	Quebec
Growth of exports to the world	180%	192%	190%
Growth of exports to the world/per cap	152% (Canada)	153%	173%
Ratio 89/00 of world exports/GDP	23% / 40%	29% / 54%	21% / 41%
Growth of world exports/GDP ratio	74%	90%	94%
Ratio 89/99 world exports/ROC exports	1.2 / 1.9	1.3 / 2.9	0.9 / 2.1
Growth of world exp/ROC exp ratio	85%	128%	124%

Both provinces most clearly stand out in terms of redeployment of exports. Looking at the importance of international relative to domestic exports, as Ontario scholar Thomas Courchene does to measure, among other variables, the surge of a 'region state' (Courchene and Telmer, 1998), it must be said that Newfoundland and British Columbia (BC) were at the top of the chart in 1989, and remain in the top three in 1999. That demonstrates how this criterion alone cannot set the bar for what constitutes a region state. Moreover, the decade do not transform Newfoundland and BC. These provinces increased their international over domestic ratio by 18 per cent and 13 per cent respectively, far lower than the provincial average of 85 per cent. Ontario and Quebec changed theirs by over 120 per cent: 128 per cent for Ontario, 124 per cent for Quebec, both with diversified economies and exports, followed by Alberta with 123 per cent, with a late-decade surge of energy exports. Quebec went from a position below the provincial average in 1989 to a position above the provincial average in 2000.

If we were to compare Ontario's and Quebec's export ratios to other states, but by adding their inteprovincial and international exports, it would give for 1998 the figures shown in Table 17.2.

Table 17.2: International and interprovincial exports/GDP, Quebec and Ontario compared to major OECD countries international exports/GDP ratios, 1998

1.	Luxembourg	91%	Next G7 countries :	
2.	Ireland	80%	18. Germany	29%
3.	Belgium	75%	21. UK	27%
4.	ONTARIO	70%	22. Italy	26%
5.	QUEBEC	57%	23. France	26%
6.	Netherlands	55%	28. USA	11%
7.	Austria	44%	29. Japan	11%
8.	CANADA	43%		

Volume of trade tells only part of the story, although a structurally essential one. For Quebec, content of exports changed drastically. Raw materials exports have been overtaken by aerospace production and telecommunications. Quebec has moved from pulp and paper and aluminium (remaining a world leader there) to building and selling half of all the civilian helicopters in the world. In 2000, 40 per cent of Quebec's exports were composed of electronic and transportation equipment. Quebec is a net importer of raw material, to a greater extent than Ontario.

Interestingly, the structure of intra-industrial trade sets Quebec apart from its Canadian neighbours, and this could be viewed as a marker for region state status. Montreal economist Pierre-Paul Proulx has shown that the intra-industrial commerce that Ontario and the rest of Canada have with the US outweighs their intra-industrial commerce with the rest of the world. In Quebec, the reverse is true, largely thanks to Quebec's greater European connection. 'The history and role of Montreal and of Quebec as a transit point with Europe persists', he writes (Proulx, 1999).

The Decanadianization of Cross-Border Investment

If the flow of goods in Quebec became more American than Canadian in the aggregate in the 1990s, what can be said about the flow of cross-border investment? Data on investment is notoriously hard to break down into foreign and interprovincial private investment. But relying on the set of acquisition figures compiled by Crosbie and Co. for its Mergers and Acquisitions in Canada series, we see that over the 1994–9 period for which provincial data was compiled, the North-South flow was stronger than the East-West flow. It was true for all of Canada, but truer still for Quebec.

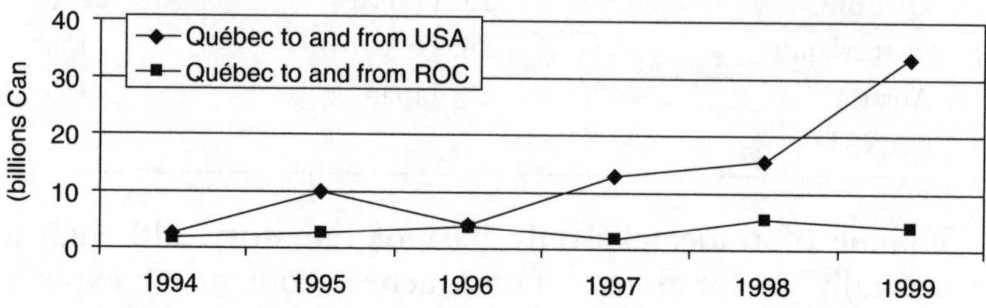

Figure 17.2: Acquisition flows, to and from Québec 1994–1999

Though it accounts for 22 per cent of Canada's GDP, Quebec's share of US acquisitions in Canada for the period reached 33 per cent. Quebec's share of Canadian acquisitions in the US reached a staggering 49 per cent. In may be partly due to the fact that Quebec corporations invested in the US 82 per cent of the $63 billion worth of acquisition they made in these five years north of Mexico. Also, in the same period, US acquisitions in Quebec were almost three times as important as those from the rest of Canada ($27 billion instead of $10 billion), a gap growing over time. This was clearly another important force in the decanadianization of the Quebec economy, thus, for example, in portfolio and real-estate investment, the Québec Caisse de dépôt is Canada's largest single investor abroad, with $37 billion worth invested at the end of 2000 (Chipello, 2001).

Quebec's Strategy, 1996–2001

Now that the score appears clearly, we can ask how much of it is attributable to the behaviour of the actors, seen here as the Quebec government and business elite, as well as the Canadian economic and political environment. Causal effect cannot be drawn with precision, and these changes are deeply rooted in more than the policy decisions taken in the latter part of the 1990s. Yet what emerges is the striking convergence between the decisions of the actors – those already mentioned on the FTA and the GST at the outset of the decade and those that we will now review – and the economic results at hand.

By mid-decade, when the structural changes in trade and investment patterns were not yet entirely visible, Quebec acted in the region-state mode forcefully. It did so with the very active participation of a business class that had not been a member of the Yes committee in the 1995 referendum, that do not wish for independence but very fervently wanted an economic revival. The participation of leaders of industry in premier Bouchard's economic summits of 1996, sometimes over the objections of federal ministers, further cemented the bond between them and the Bouchard government.

1. If You Build It . . .

Quebec's action was twofold. First, on the fiscal front, the six budgets from 1996 to 2001 would change the fiscal rules for investors. So much so that the general tax burden on businesses as a whole – meaning income, capital, sales, payroll and local taxes – in Quebec is lower than Ontario's. The Quebec Finance Department has computed that, in 2001, had the Ontario tax structure been in place in Quebec, businesses would have paid $1.4 billion more (Lecours, 2002). The burden has become markedly more favourable specifically for investors, foreign and domestic. Quebec matched its Canadian neighbours, then its American neighbours and then almost Ireland's fiscal package for investor attractiveness. By 2001, a foreign or domestic investor would have needed an extremely inept accountant to pay any provincial taxes in Quebec in the first five to ten years following the investment, including parts of the payroll tax (Price Waterhouse, 2001) Interestingly, contrary to

Quebec's website (2006) the otherwise elaborate government of Ontario website (2006) does not offer interprovincial comparisons of corporate taxes. Alberta's website (2006) is bolder, for good reason, but Quebec does well in its comparative business tax tables.

It is a clear example of the 'race to the bottom' phenomenon, albeit a targeted one. Furthermore, studies by international consultant KPMG have shown that Montreal's overall costs are consistently lower than in any other major city in Europe or North America (KPMG, 1999 and 2002) – something confirmed by similar KPMG studies proudly shown on Ontario's and Alberta's official websites. Quebec contributed to keep these costs low by freezing the cost of electricity from 1998 and until 2004.

In terms of personal income tax, Quebec's provincial burden is greater than anywhere in the continent. This measure is a poor, in fact misleading, way to assess overall real costs for individuals, since the difference is returned to taxpayers in the form of government services. In 2001, if the Ontario tax structure had been in place in Quebec, personal income tax would have been lowered by an impressive $4.2 billion. Yet, when one adds up Quebec public services not available in Ontario, one rapidly runs a tab that exceeds this amount. An Alberta-sponsored KPMG study (KPMG, 2001) shows that, in 2001, the total cost of living, including taxes, in Montreal is lower than in Toronto or Vancouver, for all cases studied (revenues from $40 to $150,000 a year). The Montrealer's standard of living is greater than that of the Torontonian at equal level of revenues. But revenue in Quebec has historically been lower, and now stands at 9 to 14 per cent less than in Ontario, whether one considers or not as a loss the fact that Quebeckers work on average one hour less a week than Ontarians, and take more vacations. When this correction is applied, Montrealers still enjoy a higher living standard than Torontonians.

Table 17.3: Compared cost of living Montreal/Toronto: Costs and taxation study, KPMG/Alberta 2001

Household	Toronto	Montreal equal revenue	Montreal revenue -14%	Montreal revenue -9%
$40,000 single	100	- 9%	Idem	- 4%
$60,000 couple, no children	100	- 11%	- 2%	- 5%
$80,000 couple, 2 children	100	- 10%	- 1%	- 5%
$100,000 couple, 2 children	100	- 12%	- 4%	- 7%
$150,000 couple, 2 children	100	- 8%	- 1%	- 4%

A similar 1998 Quebec study had shown that, at equal levels of revenue, this was true even at $250,000 a year. It expanded the comparison to the fourteen largest North American metropolitan areas. Montreal ranked first for families up to $50,000 a year, at average for other families all the way up the scale ($250,000), at average also for single persons up to $75,000 a year, never worst than eleventh (Finances/KPMG, 1998).

Still, the Quebec government has moved to reduce tax rates in the 1996–2002 period but, unable to match Ontario or the US on the overall rates, it there again targeted both foreign investors and the local high-tech industry by creating a second, specific and totally competitive regime of personal income tax for foreign staff moving to Quebec in the new economy, some financial sectors and some university research. The rule is simple: no provincial income tax for five years. So, to use Philip Cooke's terms, Quebec as a region state is trying to take both the low road and the high road to success (Cooke, 1999):

- a low road by benefiting from low costs and targeted low corporate and income taxes for investors and foreign staff.
- a high road by retaining the needed overall revenue to invest in education on a higher per capita basis than its

neighbours or the OECD (Education, 2000) and by maintaining social transfers high enough to: generate a Gini index that shows less income inequality than anywhere in the continent (Wolfson and Murphy, 2000), foster a social environment where the poverty rate is lower than its neighbours (Lanctôt and Fréchette, 2002), and implement a family and children's agenda that is unmatched (Jenson, 2002).

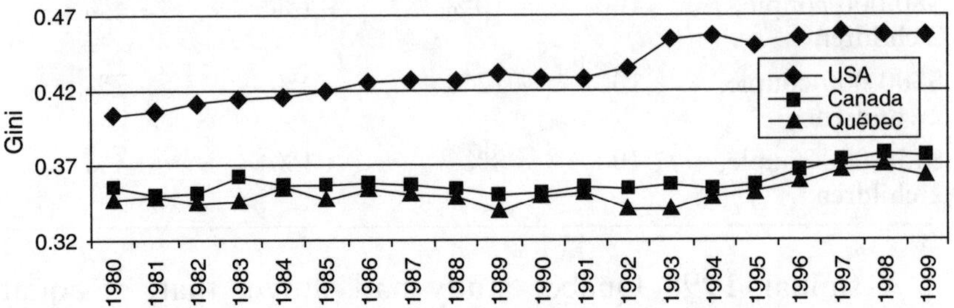

Figure 17.3: Gini index evolution, households 1980–1999

Overall from fiscal year 1995/96 to 2000/01, Quebec's own-source revenue grew by 39 per cent (Ontario 41 per cent) and its programme spending grew by 13.7 per cent (Ontario 5.4 per cent). In a nutshell, Quebec made itself fiscally competitive to investors without losing its social-democratic soul.

2. . . They Won't Necessarily Come

The second front of Quebec's action was to actively seek investors. To put it simply, the Quebec government does not think that 'if we build it – the fiscally competitive house –, they will come'. Given the linguistic, cultural, political uniqueness of the place – in an American context where this level of difference is not viewed positively – Quebec rightly feels it needs to put resources, first 'to build it', and then put more resources into bringing the client in. Clearly, it takes more energy and time to explain Quebec's distinctiveness in the US than, let us say, Ontario or BC's comparative advantages. Quebec leaders intuitively came to the conclusions reached by Helliwell and Jean-Philippe Platteau, for whom absence of shared language, values and institutions are likely to increase the costs of making and enforcing contracts (Helliwell, 1998: 45), including of course FDI.

There has always been a Toronto–Montreal rivalry but the race to US markets in the 1990s was not antagonistic – there was enough potential growth for everybody. And the fact that both regions are represented by a traditional federal state is not usually an impediment to the regions selling abroad. Though I have witnessed, during a business venture in the Philippines of all premiers and the PM (trips dubbed 'Team Canada'), the Prime Minister of Canada aggressively promoting to local economic leaders Canada's nuclear technology – primarily Ontario-based – and badmouthing oil as an unreliable product. Ontario Premier Mike Harris might have been glad, but Alberta Premier Ralph Klein, also in the room, was showing no signs of pleasure. Quebec Premier Bouchard, seated next to the Prime Minister as protocol dictates, whispered in his ear: 'Alberta'. The Prime Minister got the hint and said: 'yes, yes, Alberta, they have oil. But they don't mind, they are rich!' No wonder provincial leaders sometimes like to make their own trade trips.

But in terms of attracting investment and creating a distinctive image, region states are of course on their own. The Quebec and Ontario governments set out their marketing strategies for the US at about the same time, in the mid-1990s. Reportedly, an Ontario study had shown that, among those Americans who did not think Ontario was a county south of Los Angeles (one such county bears the same name), many believed it was a socialist state within Canada. (The centre-left New Democratic Party had been in power in the early 1990s, bringing catastrophic results.) This may not have been the exact wording of the study, but it was how it was conveyed by Premier Harris's office. Ontario acted decisively, both internally and externally, to make itself more attractive to US investors, implementing across the board fiscal measures that would make it more competitive than its Canadian neighbours – at least in the average – and, as Courchene points out, more than its immediate US neighbours.

Quebec's task was even greater. A report tabled at a major economic summit in 1996 demonstrated that, in the mind of

American economic decision-makers, Montreal had somehow fallen off the list of relevant North American metropolises in technology, education, science and the like. Site locators, essential agents for investment, had all but forgotten Quebec's existence. In the wake of the 1995 referendum on independence, Quebec's press coverage in the US was dismal. In terms of the economy and the vitality of Montreal, the coverage was way off the mark, and not only in the US press. A telling headline, on a story documenting the absence of any sign of divestment or significant level of departure within Anglo-Montrealers, was seen in the Montreal *Gazette* in July 1996. It read: 'No exodus, yet'.

In short order, between 1996 and 1998, the Quebec government expanded its investment recruitment services by an order of magnitude. A revamped agency, Investissement-Quebec, was formed and would soon win awards from American site locator publications. The Societé Générale de Financement (SGF) was also re-engineered to become much more active in seeking foreign investments thanks to its ability to take an important minority share in the investments. The combined effect on site locators, for instance, was significant. While Quebec was and still is not spontaneously put on the list of preferred North American sites for a potential investment, when it gets on, it very frequently gets right to the short list. In 2000, having reached cruise speed, Investissement-Québec organized a hundred foreign missions of prospecting and greeted 200 potential investors in Quebec. For the year, its portfolio yielded 37 new foreign investments worth 1.2 billion Canadian dollars. As for the SGF, its 2000 annual report states that the number of new foreign investments it generated went from 4 a year in 1996 to 49 in 2000, with investments going from $78 million in 1996 to $2.4 billion in 2000. Cumulative impact on direct jobs (minus construction phase) went from 800 in 1996 to 10,200 in 2000. (There is some overlap between the figures reported by the two institutions.)

Quebec made an aggressive effort of marketing, the premier travelling to nine American cities with the leaders of Quebec's business class in tow, making measurable headway in changing perceptions of economic and political decision-makers. With this 'Mission Québec' or alone, he went to the US about four times a year, meeting governors, investors, editorial boards. This effort was to know a high point in September of 2001 with the opening of a 'Quebec season' in New York, a $15 million dollar multifaceted initiative to drive the point that a new Quebec has arrived, something the last and most influential interpreter of Quebec reality in the American media, Mordecai Richler, had not entirely conveyed. The Quebec season, to be unveiled on 12 September, was postponed for obvious reasons, yet the positive coverage that Montreal and Quebec City have had since 1998 in the US and UK press in general, and the economic press in particular, is in stark contrast with that of 1995.

Ottawa and the Rest of Canada: Showing the Way

If the Quebec elite clearly worked at making Quebec a region state in the latter part of the 1990s, and if the American market and American investors provided the opportunity to redeploy the province's economic activity north–south rather than east–west, the federal government and the Canadian economy also played a part in these changes.

The internal trade picture somewhat encouraged Quebec to find growth abroad. Over the decade, interprovincial exports in Canada grew by 40 per cent in the aggregate, by 55 per cent in provincial average. For Quebec? By a smaller margin, of 30 per cent, with Ontario at 28 per cent. Of all Canadian provinces in the decade, Quebec and Ontario have had the weakest growth in interprovincial exports. Over the decade, this meant that, for Quebec and Ontario somewhat more than for the rest of Canada, economic growth laid primarily outside Canada's borders.

On the political front, it was soon understood that the task of promoting Quebec as a good investment venue in the US would be a lonelier affair than could otherwise be expected. In the post-referendum period, Canadian diplomats in the US sometimes actually fuelled the negative perception of Montreal and Quebec in briefing to investors. The example came from up high. The Prime Minister made a disparaging remark about Montreal's economy during a major speech at the New York Economic Club. The Premier of Ontario, Mike Harris, also did his share. In an interview given to the *Sun* newspaper chain in early 1998 – at a time when Montreal's economy was clearly improving – he said: 'It's tough to go to Montreal at rush hour and see no rush hour.' 'Montreal was a great city', he added, 'it is not now' (La Presse, 1998). He was reflecting the very dismissive tone of the Toronto economic press about Quebec and Montreal in these years.

The coolness was somewhat reciprocated. Quebec promotional efforts were important in the US, as we have seen, and other important missions involving the premier and representatives of the Quebec elite were organized in China, Mexico, Argentina, Chile, France and Catalonia. Yet there was scarcely any effort from Quebec to try and change perceptions, or attract investments, in the rest of Canada. Premier Bouchard travelled there almost exclusively for premiers' political conferences. Organizing a 'Mission Québec' to Toronto or Vancouver was sometimes contemplated, but the certainty that any positive economic message would be overwhelmed by the political debate on sovereignty made the endeavour not worth the investment.

This is an interesting twist where real structural change and politics combine towards a same end. Quebec was becoming a region state mainly for economic reasons. But the sovereignist premier, Lucien Bouchard, had made financial and economic growth the linchpin of his pro-independence policy. In what was then believed to be a short interval until the next referendum, Ottawa's main line of public argument at the time – from 1996 to 1998 – was that political instability was hurting Quebec's economy. (A pervasive instinctive conclusion that studies cannot confirm (Lavoie *et al.*, 2001).) An upturn would ruin this argument, and it was indeed ruined when the upturn became undeniable, starting in 1998. For a time, then, federal discourse changed. It was said that the only things that worked in the Quebec economy were those who benefited from federal policy: aerospace, pharmaceuticals. The surge of all segments of the Quebec economy gave a very short lifespan to that version of events.

It would be interesting to document how much Ottawa did, if anything, to prevent the upturn, a politically difficult wire-act to perform. The federal government was in the process of reasserting itself as an indispensable government in the life of Quebeckers, and wanted to be seen as a direct contributor to their well-being, especially in the francophone regions politically dominated by the sovereignists. At a time of reduced spending, it did that primarily by a massive effort of branding its existing contributions, and targeting dwindling resources in those activities with most visibility. Yet it refused to participate in some high-profile big-ticket items, leaving the entire tab to the Quebec government despite strong pressure from Montreal's business class. The expansion of Montreal's Convention Centre and the rehabilitation of the failed Mirabel international airport (a purely federal blunder) are the main examples. The decision of Prime Minister Jean Chrétien, a Quebecker, to approve against previous commitments the choice of a direct Nova Scotia/USA route for the new gas pipeline of Sable Island against the Nova Scotia/New Brunswick/Quebec/Ontario proposal that would have made more national sense and would have benefited Quebec, was also seen as uncharacteristic of what a 'favourite son' in power would do. The federal attempt to favour Alberta-based and bankruptcy-bound Canadian airlines over Montreal's sounder (at the time) Air Canada in the necessary restructuring of the Airline industry was also a case in point. There is simply not a single instance, during that period, when, given a discretionary choice between Quebec and another province, the Chrétien government made a major decision favourable to the Quebec economy, despite the presence of Quebeckers at almost all the economic portfolios: Prime Minister, Minister of Finance, President of the Treasury board.

These big-ticket items are marginal in the full federal presence in the Quebec economy but they gave a general tone that Ottawa was not consistently 'onside' with the Quebec elite's efforts to lift the economy up. Federal investment was also experiencing a period of contraction, due to deficit-cutting operations, which could not help but fuel this impression. From its 1994 high point to the 1998 low point, federal capital investment – Ottawa's most direct input – was reduced, overall, by 31 per cent in Canada. In Ontario, the reduction was of 19 per cent. In Quebec, the reduction was greater, of 33 per cent, going from $834 million in 1994 to $560 million in 1998. This contributed to create a greater federal vacuum in Quebec than in the ROC and in Ontario in particular.

There is no question that, if it suffers from federal under-investment on the productive side of the ledger, Quebec was a net gainer in the remedial aspect of the federal presence: equalization payments from richer to poorer provinces, redistributive characteristics of the Canada Health and Social Transfer (CHST, the main conduit for federal funding of provincial social programmes) and of unemployment insurance (UI). But even in these fields Ottawa moved to rein in the financial flow to Quebec, over and above the severe across-the-board cuts in CHST funding of that period. Quebec economist Pierre Fortin estimates that successive reforms of UI, by shifting a greater number of unemployed to provincial social assistance, added a burden of $845 million to the Quebec treasury for the 1990–7 period, and $100 million for each of the succeeding years (Fortin, 1997). In early 1999, a surprise CHST reform wiped-out Quebec's redistributive advantage therein (by folding its social assistance component on a overall per capita basis instead of a per-beneficiary basis, thus compounding the UI reform damage), and reduced Quebec's expected share of new funding by $330 million for that year alone, by $1.8 billion over five years. This structural reform, long advocated by Ontario and Alberta who got the lion's share of the new funding, coincided with a greater than expected equalization payment to Quebec, thus the timing. Both reforms also made substantial damage in the Atlantic provinces, particularly Newfoundland. This was added to previous federal discretionary financial decisions aimed at making life harder for the Bouchard government, then struggling to curtail its own deficit without alienating its referendum allies in the union and social movement. Recall that some major items had a significant impact on Quebec's public finances at this juncture: particularly the refusal to consider any compensation for GST harmonization ($2 billion) and refusal to consider any reimbursement for Hydro-Québec's losses during the January 1998 ice storm ($430 million).

For all these reasons, the Canadian environment in the late 1990s was conducive to Quebec's reducing its reliance on the Canadian market for commercial growth, its reliance on Canadian diplomacy, political leadership and business media for help in attracting investment, its reliance on the federal government for productive investment, budgetary help and remedial measures. It contributed instead to comforting Quebec's inclination to look to its own resources for strength and direction, and to look outside Canada for growth, opportunity and allies.

The Quebec Economy at the Turn of the Century

Trade and investment trends show how Quebec modified its relationship with its neighbours during the 1990s. What of the impact of these changes on the whole of the Quebec economy? Pierre Fortin has demonstrated that Quebec has been closing the historic gap with Ontario, on a per capita basis, since 1960 (Fortin: 2002). The most recent data buttress his research. Economic growth, from the 1989 to 2000 peaks, shows Ontario's GDP performing better, at 34 per cent growth, than Quebec, at 28 per cent (see Figure 17.4). Adjust it for population and you get a different picture: Ontario's per capita growth at 16 per cent, Quebec's at 19 per cent. Thus it is sometimes argued that Quebec's smaller demographic growth is a sign of economic weakness. Over the period, Ontario's population growth was greater than that of Canada as a whole (12.6 per cent) and the US (14 per cent). On the other hand, Quebec's population growth was greater than those of the states of New York, Pennsylvania, Massachusetts or Ohio, all economically very successful in the 1990s. When fertility rates, abysmally low in Quebec, are taken out of the equation, Quebec's attractiveness to immigration, though still lower than Canada's, is 40 per cent higher than the US for the 1990s, and higher than any western European country (Levine, 2002: 169). Contrary to widely held views, the rate of retention of immigrants to Quebec (some being surprised to encounter a French-speaking society) is higher than 75 per cent.

Adjusted with the GDP deflator index, real per capita disposable income growth is even more stunning: zero growth (-0.3 per cent) in Ontario, 7.4 per cent growth in Quebec. So, clearly, if you are a GDP, you did better in Ontario. On the other hand, if you are a person . . . Year by year, in real terms, Quebec's per capita GDP has overtaken Ontario's in 2000, 2001 and 2002 and predictions show this trend holding at least to 2004. Compared to the Rest of Canada (ROC) as a whole, Quebec has done better every year since 1998.

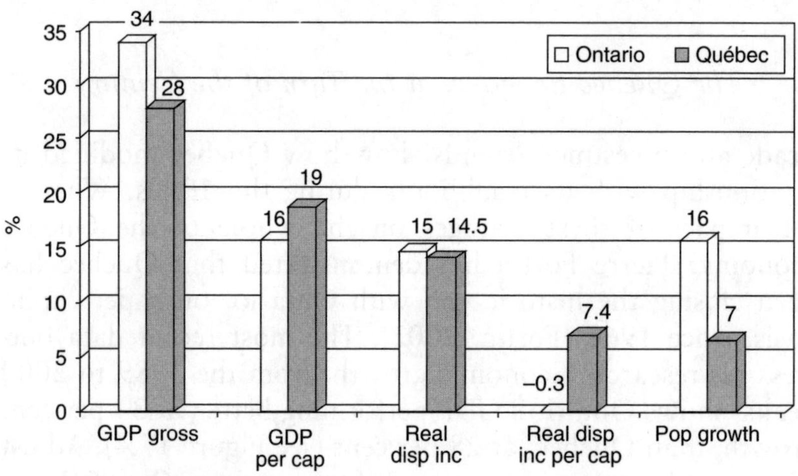

Figure 17.4: Ontario & Québec growth, 1989–2000

Comparisons with OECD states also give a measure of Quebec's progress in this period. Using the OECD's benchmark of per capita GDP, adjusted for purchasing power parity in 1995 US$, figures 17.5 and 17.6 track Quebec's progress between 1992 and 2002, relative to other industrialized countries and to the OECD average. Quebec thus jumps from 17th place to 10th in a decade, a jump surpassed only by Ireland. A recent study by Quebec's Institut de la statistique (Tran, 2001) tracks the surge of Quebec's competitiveness relative to the OECD average to an important surge in productivity.

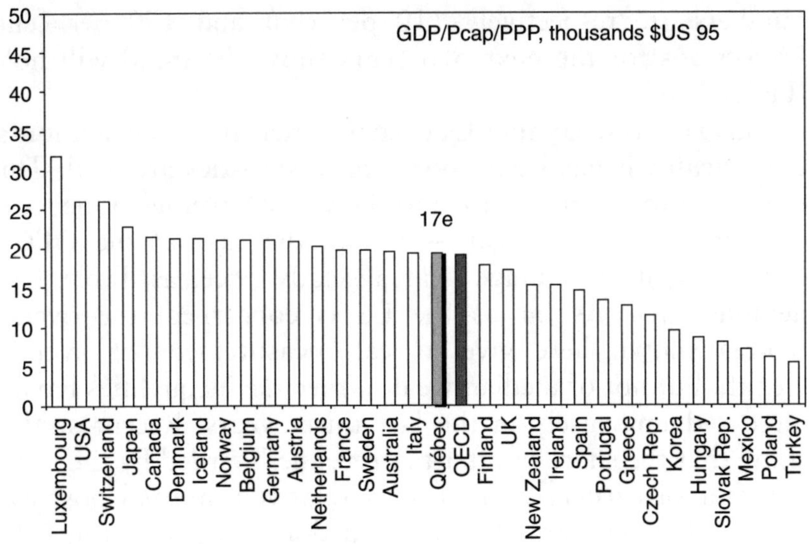

Figure 17.5: Québec in the OECD / 1992

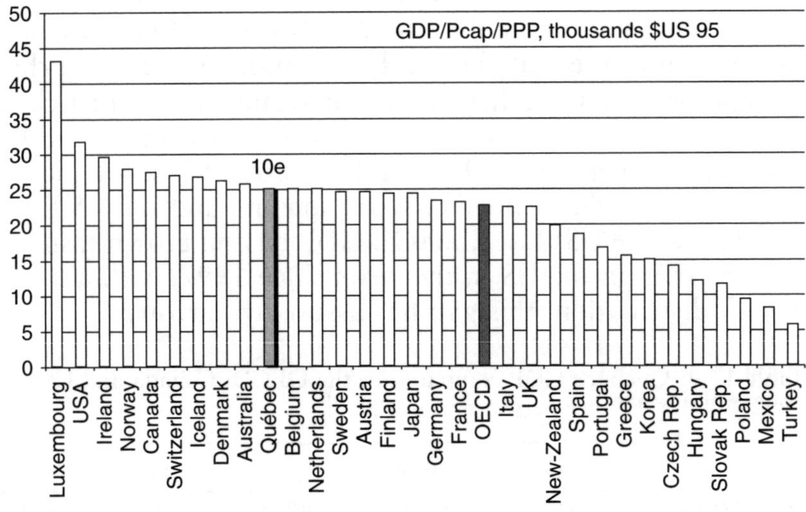

Figure 17.6: Québec in the OECD / 2002

What is striking, at the turn and in the first years of the century, is how Quebec's GDP has outperformed those of the G7 for the 1997–2002 period, growing at 210 per cent of the G7 average in gross terms, at 250 per cent per capita. If one takes only Quebec's neighbours, Canada and the US, the numbers are respectively 110 per cent and 150 per cent. Projections for the next two years show the trend will hold (Lisée, 2003).

This is not to say that Quebec is richer than its neighbours. Historically, it has been poorer since statistics are held. This even used to be true relative to the OECD average. Quebec is currently closing the gap – and in the case of the OECD expanding its advantage – at a steady pace, as Table 17.4 demonstrates. As far as the US is concerned, the overall figures shown here give a real measurement of average wealth, but not of median wealth, revenue inequalities having increased immensely in the last thirty years. Recent studies show that the share of after-tax revenue hoarded by the top 1 per cent of earners went from a relatively normal post-war level of 8 per cent in 1973 to a gilded-age 14 per cent in 1998 (Piketty, 2001) and close to 20 per cent in 2003. Granting that the US affluent class is much more affluent than elsewhere, one should note that the 25 per cent of Quebeckers at the bottom of the scale have a higher standard of living than the comparable Canadians and Americans. The yardstick of median work income is more suited to ascertaining middle-class wealth. Figures for 1997 in PPP showed Quebec slightly ahead of Canada in median work income and only 5.5 per cent below the US (Lisée, 2003). GDP having grown faster in Quebec than in the US in the years since 1997, with a better wealth distribution, this gap has assuredly narrowed.

Table 17.4: Quebec's GDP compared to the OECD, Canada and USA, 1992–2004, GDP per person and in PPP

	1992	1998	2000	2002	2004
Quebec/OECD	101%	102%	107%	111%	114%
Quebec/Canada	89%	89%	91%	92%	93%
Quebec/USA	74%	71%	74%	79%	81%

Sources: 1992–2001: OECD and Institut de la Statistique du Québec; Estimates 2002 and forceasts 2004: StatsCan, OECD, Bank of Montreal.

One could argue that the transformations we witness are driven solely by the metropolis, Montreal, and not by the whole of Quebec. It is true that some regions of Quebec did not participate in this surge. But the high level of growth was spread over all of the Montreal metropolitan area, which includes almost half of the population of the province and all or part of five of Quebec's fifteen regions. Outside that area, Quebec city is now considered by the Conference Board as Canada's fifth fastest growing local economy, and two regions that border on the US, the Beauce with almost full-employment and the Eastern Townships, have clearly participated in the internationalization of the Quebec economy in the decade. So if it is undeniable that Montreal has been the locomotive of change, there were secondary engines at play.

Although it is seldom seen as such, Quebec has become an economic powerhouse. Taken alone, its GDP went from being the twenty-third in the world in 1976 to the fifteenth in 2000, and the sixth in the Americas. Compared to G7 countries, its economy now has the highest proportion of high-tech production, just after Japan. The outlook seems promising. In the spring of 2001, the Conseil québecois de la science et de la technologie, in a report on innovation (Conseil, 2001), produced a table of fourteen indicators that are signs or precursors of innovation – investment in education, R and D spending, technological level of production, proportion of technical personnel, export rate, business financing of university research, patents, output of scientific publications, and some others. It compared Quebec's data with those of the G7. In eight of the fourteen variables, Quebec was in the top three, clearly ahead of Canada as a whole (see appendix 1). Only the US fared better overall. Obviously, Ontario would have done very well in this exercise.

These transformations have occurred through Quebec's strengthened linkage to the US economy, for sure, but that was the field on which it could flex its new R and D muscles, built up over twenty-five years of consistent fiscal cocooning. This, in turn, could not have been possible without the education revolution that brought Quebec from the lowest schooling ratio on the continent in 1961 to one of the highest in the Western world in the late 1990s (Education, 2001).

The Language Border Effect: Why It Is Not There

An essential element in this transformation, difficult to measure in pure economic terms, is what Courchene would call a 'locational externality', an advantage specific to that place and no other. In my view, Quebec's crucial externality is linguistic, and it helps explain why the linguistic border effect found elsewhere in the OECD by Helliwell is not an impediment to Quebec's commercial surge as a region state. In his research, Helliwell finds no trace of this effect for Quebec and concludes that the level of French–English bilingualism is sufficient to eliminate this handicap both for province-to-province trade and for province-to-state trade.

This is worth looking into. If there was no language border effect before the 1970s, it is simply because the people then in charge of the economic interface between Quebec and the Anglo-American continent were anglophones. In the 1960s, an absolute majority of managers of Quebec firms were members of the English-speaking minority (80 per cent of middle managers, 60 per cent of senior managers) and, most of the time; they worked only in English (Office, 1988; Levine, 1990: 181–93). Today, although anglophones still enjoy overrepresentation in management (26 per cent in 1988, given 10 per cent of the population), the French-speakers are for the first time in the majority (58 per cent, given 81 per cent of the population), allophones accounting for the remaining 16 per cent. Thus francophones are now primarily in charge of the economic interface with Anglo-America. There should have been a concomitant surge of the language border effect, instead of a clearly unimpeded surge of the ratio of exports.

What really emerged was the rise of a new business and managerial class where the language spoken is, to quote American scholar Marc Levine, 'a French-dominated bilingualism' (Levine, 2000: 366). This has little to do with Canadian linguistic policy. For the record, in Canada outside Quebec, decades of effort under the Official Languages Act brought bilingualism there from a paltry 9 per cent in 1951 and 9.4 per cent in 1971 to 10.8 per cent in 1996. The rise in the level of bilingualism of Anglos in the ROC is also partly a (perverse) result of Quebec policy, A rough estimate shows that at least 40 per cent of the new bilingual Anglos added in the rest of Canada (ROC) between 1971 and 1996 are in fact Quebec bilingual Anglos having moved out of Quebec, in part because they disagreed with linguistic and political developments in their home province. Overall, in the ROC, the proportion of Canadians who can carry a meaningful conversation in French has shrunk somewhat, from 8.2 per cent in 1951 to 7.6 per cent in 1996. See my calculations (Lisée, 2000: 134) based on Statistics Canada's sensitivity test of 1988 on what a real conversation is.

Table 17.5: Quebec and ROC linguistic evolution, active population, 1971–1996

	Quebec		Rest of Canada (ROC)	
	Bilingual 1971	Bilingual 1996	Bilingual 1971	Bilingual 1996
Total	**43%**	**50%**	**10%**	**11%**
Francophones	43%	46%	90%	92%
Anglophones	48%	74%	5%	8%
Allophones	41%	60%	5%	7%

Source: Statistics Canada, unique responses only for mother tongue

The transformation is Quebec's very own, and is a cumulative product of schooling, economic flows, migration and decades of linguistic legislation. In the fifteen years from 1971 to 1996, the proportion of the active population who knows French went from 89 to 96 per cent. The proportion that is bilingual went from 43 to 50 per cent, thanks to a slight progression of bilingualism among francophones, and a major rise among non-francophones. In the Montreal metropolitan area, Quebec's predominant economic centre, the level of bilingualism reaches 63 per cent in the active population, and 80 per cent among managers and engineers.

Somewhere between 1971 and 1996 a threshold has been crossed that has prevented the advent of a linguistic border effect, so detrimental elsewhere in the OECD. Bringing about a working population that retains, or in many cases gains,

French as a real internal functional language; expanding the use of English as an indispensable interface tool; doing this at a time when the linguistic make-up of the managerial class changes radically: that is the unheralded, bipartisan achievement of thirty years of linguistic experiment in Quebec.

There is more. When a majority of skilled francophones and anglophones are bilingual and when a majority of allophones speak three languages in a given region, there is a potent locational externality at play. This operational bilingualism enables Quebec to provide a unique, real-time connection to innovations in both French- and English-speaking Europe and the Anglo-American continent. It has effects in intra-industrial trade, as we saw, in research and development, in post-secondary education, in public policy experiments, in culture. Quebec has the ability to import, blend and re-export concepts, no outside translation required. In my view, this has only begun to pay off.

Impact on French-Speakers outside Quebec

It may be too soon to determine what impact Quebec's new-found economic strength will have on demolinguistic patterns in Canada. It is probable that combined with the weakening of the French fact outside Quebec, it will further concentrate French-speakers in Quebec.

The process is long-standing. In 1971, 88 per cent of Canadians whose home language was French lived in Quebec. In 1991, the ratio had grown to 89.9 per cent, then to 90.6 per cent in 2001. Statistics Canada published in December 2002 its linguistic results from the 2001 census showing a greater number of French Quebeckers leaving Quebec than coming into Quebec for the years 1996–2001. In the previous 1986–1996 period, however, 3 per cent of French-speakers outside Quebec had moved to Quebec. It has long been the case that there were more heirs of Acadians in Quebec than in Acadia, the French-speaking areas of the Maritime Provinces. The recent movement of French Canadians to Quebec is now notable from Ontario to the Quebec region opposite Ottawa, the Outaouais. It is interesting to note that the personal income tax differential is not an impediment to that migration.

Federal reports acknowledge that, despite real improvements since the 1970s, services rendered in French outside Quebec by the Canadian government have been eroding by about 30 per cent in the last decade. French schools are more numerous than ever before. That is largely thanks to the resilient action of federal courts overcoming the English provinces' reticence in granting French schools to an ever dwindling number of French-speakers. Yet recent reports show that 44 per cent of French-speaking children outside Quebec are not enrolled in French schools by their parents.

We now have a sufficiently long timeline to conclude that assimilation rates of French-speakers outside Quebec have not been reduced down by the very real and politically courageous Trudeau-era effort to make French a normal language all across the country. In 1971, at the outset of the Trudeau effort, the rate of assimilation was 27 per cent per generation. In 2001, after more than thirty years of official bilingualism, it reached 36 per cent. If one excludes the French region of Acadia in New Brunswick, where there is a strong French community, the rate of assimilation is 46 per cent. This means that, outside Quebec and Acadia, each generation of French-speakers will be half the size of the previous one. English Canada is thus in the process of successfully assimilating its heretofore most important minority.

Outside Quebec, among the quarter of Canadians who do not have English as mother tongue, Chinese-speakers represent 15 per cent to French-Speakers' 17 per cent. If recent trend holds, Chinese-speakers will become the second language group in importance this year (2003) or next. This is a historic event that will put an enormous strain on the politics of language in Canada. In British Columbia, minority languages other than French are spoken by fifteen times more people than there are French-speakers. It will become hard for the Ottawa government to sustain policies whereby a French-speaker, or English-speaker knowing French, has preference in hiring in the federal government, or where a

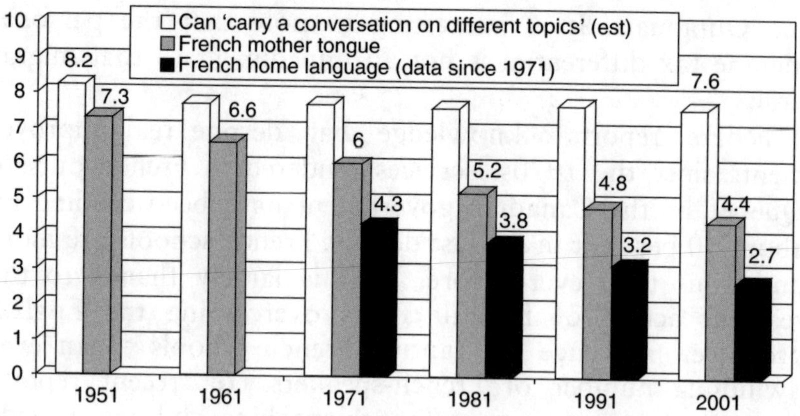

Figure 17.7: Fifty years of dwindling French minority outside Québec

French-speaker can get a criminal trial in his language, and not a Chinese-speaker.

These facts and figures are of course in sharp contrast with the image of a functioning bilingual country projected in the world by the Canadian government and its diplomacy, or by the simple fact of having had a string of Quebec-born prime ministers over the past thirty years. The most striking contrary statistic is that the proportion of Canadians outside Quebec who can carry a meaningful conversation in French is somewhat smaller now than in the 1950s. It is as though the Canadian government is reduced to presenting the preview of a bilingual country, without ever being able to produce the movie

Extraterritoriality: border half-heartedness

An important feature of region states is extraterritoriality. The internationalization of the region states' activity should translate in some cross-border political strength, as seen in some European cases. In the late 1990s, Quebec made efforts in that direction, for instance by becoming a member of the Great Lakes Governors' Conference, with Ontario following suit, as well as investing more energy in the yearly meeting of the New England Governors and Eastern Canadian Premiers.

Having participated in the planning of eight of these meetings, I can report that, apart from some minor good-will programmes, and the long-established management of Great Lakes' water intake, very little power is being held, exercised, or clearly coveted by these bodies. Quebec's willingness, for instance, more clearly to identify the remaining border irritants to trade and tourism, then lobby federal governments for quicker action to iron them out, was applauded, then went to sleep in committee. (Though some joint New York/Quebec pressure was brought to bear to expedite commercial border crossings in the wake of tightening security after 11 September, and the idea of a 'Quebec/New York' corridor was launched in 2002.)

Three reasons seem to explain the half-heartedness of these bodies and states. First, if it is true that Ontario and Quebec now have more stake in their trade to the south than in domestic trade, the same does not apply to US states. Second, US governors and Canadian premiers representing small states or provinces are clearly conscious of their lack of internal leverage, whereas governors from important states have better things to do. The governor of New York, for instance, scarcely ever attends the Great Lakes Governors' Conference, as is the case of the governor of Massachusetts for the north-eastern body. Finally, US states have less decision-making power than Canadian provinces and little time and resources to pour into external efforts.

It thus seems that, as far as North America is concerned, changes that would facilitate Ontario's and Quebec's further emergence as region states will primarily have to flow from decisions taken at the centre. And it is in influencing the centre, or putting new issues on the agenda, that the two provinces can make headway.

There are some signs that, as was the case for free trade in the late 1980s, Quebec is farther ahead in wanting a greater level of continental integration than the rest of Canada. I have no position on the common currency debate – at least until the Euro experiment confirms, mitigates or denies Andrew Rose's recent studies (Rose, 2000; Jeffrey and Rose, 2000) showing that existing common currency zones no less than triple trade flows. He computes that adopting the US currency would increase Canada's trade with the US by 111 per cent relative to its GDP, which would itself grow by 36 per cent. But it is fair to note that now Quebec Premier Bernard Landry was the first minister of Finance in Canada openly to ask for a debate on the issue, back in 1997, when it was widely seen as preposterous, if not unpatriotic. It turns out Quebec, and Ontario, would have a lot to gain (Beine and Coulombe, 2002). Dollarization is now up for debate in the most respectable of Canadian institutions. A poll released in September 2001 showed a majority of Quebeckers favourable to dollarization, a majority of other Canadians opposed. Before the 11 September tragedy, Quebeckers were also much more favourable (50 per cent, 36 per cent in the ROC) to a common North American perimeter that would allow for the outright disappearance of the Canada–US border. They were somewhat followed by other Canadians in the aftermath of the terrorist attacks (Canadian Press, 2001; Picard, 2001).

This is not to say that Quebec did not play the extraterritoriality game on its own: during the 1990s, and more so in the last part of the decade, it brought to maturity some important foreign relationships, with France, Belgium, Catalonia and Bavaria. It used France's leverage to get into international political forums to which Canada would refuse it entry.

Yet, looking for markers of region states, and allowing for the fact that Quebec–Canada international skirmishes clearly predate the last decade's structural developments, it is clear that the scope, diversity and intensity of Quebec's extraterritorial relationships exceed any other in Canada. In Europe, Quebec has developed economic and political relationships with some of the very sub-national entities that emerge as region states.

Multiple Identities, Loyalties, Voice and Exit

Sub-national communities and 'stateless nations' like Quebec show signs of multiple identities, as Keating notes. This is illustrated by the recent Quebec debate on an internal, dual citizenship, where Quebeckers would be citizens of Quebec and of Canada, something experimented with success in Finland for the Swedish minority in the island of Aland. This multiple identity also translates in multiple loyalties, as apparent in the willingness of Quebeckers to become essentially autonomous, all the while keeping ties with Canada, something Keating reports seeing in Europe's stateless nations whose sanity, there, is not put into question.

Looking at the evolution of Quebec in Canada, we see important structural change in the reality of a region's asserting itself like never before, with fewer prospect of political adjustment to accommodate this change than ever before. Recent federal polls show that only 38 per cent of Quebeckers favour the current federal system. That is less than the level of support for sovereignty. As any observer of the Canadian scene knows, no substantive reform is to be expected in the foreseeable future. At the turn of the century, it can be argued that Quebec has neither of the usual 'voice or exit' options.

No Voice

Institutional change with major impact on its political autonomy was implemented against Quebec's bipartisan opposition in a new and far-reaching Constitution adopted in 1982 and a new social union intergovernmental agreement in 1999, and in the new rules of secession law, misnamed Clarity Bill, in 2001. For a federalist view of Quebec's disappearing clout see Ryan (1999). Quebec's substantial, wide-ranging objections, sometimes unanimously voiced by its National Assembly and enjoying large popular support in the province, were simply disregarded as a variable in all three of these debates. That federal MPs from Quebec participated and, indeed, initiated these changes obviously blurs the issue. Yet other provincial governments and legislatures consented to the changes, whether or not MPs from their provinces were onside. The Quebec government and legislature did not.

Less visible but structurally important is the continuing work of the Supreme Court, whose judges, named without provincial consultation, interpreting a constitution adopted against Quebec wishes, progressively expand the paramountcy of federal laws over provincial laws: in 1988 (*Crown Zellerbach*) in commerce and environment; in 1989 (*General Motors*) again in interprovincial commerce and (*Alberta Government Telephones*) in telecommunications; in 1990 (*Hall*) in all fields of shared jurisdiction; in 1993 (*Hunt*) again expanding Ottawa's role over provincial regulations affecting commerce; and expanding the scope of the federal criminal statutes to heretofore provincial areas in the late 1990s. The cumulative impact constitutes 'a rewriting of the foundations of the Canadian federal regime' writes Jacques Frémont, dean of Law at l'Université de Montréal. He feels these changes are 'so important that we can probably say that the evolution of the division of powers has shifted more, in these last 15 years, than at any time since the start of the federation' (Frémont, 1998). Such an evolution has a particular impact on that province that is most distinct in its approach to policy and legislation, Quebec. Over a twelve-year period, the Supreme Court has invalidated 30 per cent of contested federal laws, 42 per cent of contested laws from other provinces, and fully 52 per cent of contested Quebec laws. A telling statistic on the grinding force of an outer-directed norm over one's inner-directed originality (Brun, 1991).

No Exit

The new secession legislation sets a series of discretionary and unrealistic hurdles in the road to independence, in contradiction with the more even-keeled Supreme Court decision it purports to translate into law. The Bill insists that a referendum on secession must be devoid of any reference to a desired form of association or partnership between the two future sovereign states, and even of reference to 'negotiations', although the Supreme Court's core argument was that negotiations were compulsory for both sides. In effect, with this new law, if Quebeckers were to approve, by referendum and at any level of support – say, 75 per cent – a proposal that would try and adapt to Canada the European experiment, or any experiment of shared sovereignty, the Canadian Parliament would be legally barred from entertaining the notion. Had this bill been in effect since 1980, a yes vote of any margin at the 1980 and 1995 referendum would have had to be ignored by Parliament. Had it been in effect earlier for annexations as well as secessions, the 1949 Newfoundland referendum could not have been regarded as valid by Canadian MPs.

However, if Quebeckers were to approve, by more than 50 per cent, a question deemed 'clear' by the Bill – on secession only – MPs would still be invited to determine whether or not a majority of Quebeckers really meant that they wanted to secede, and could decide that they did not – in fact would be under great political pressure to do so. Even a successful negotiation on secession would have to be approved by all provinces, several of which would have to hold referenda on the issue, thus asking their citizens to approve the break-up of their country. Any single provincial refusal could cause failure of the process – as it did for the Meech Lake Accord in 1990. Furthermore, on many counts, the law contradicts Canada-supported UN policy towards secession as formulated and applied in the 1990s in all cases at hand: Eritrea, East Timor and Western Sahara (Lisée, 2000b). Each of these efforts would have been rejected under the new norms of C-20. I like to quote Alain Noël's excellent summation of Ottawa's policy towards Quebeckers unease in the current political structure: 'Canada, love it or don't leave it' (Noël, 2000).

Prospects for Governance Change

In the short to mid-term, governance change that would espouse the structural evolution of Quebec's and Ontario's emergence as region states is highly unlikely. First, the brewing debate in the Canadian federation concerns the 'fiscal imbalance' that is emerging between the federal government on the one hand and the provinces on the other. Given the present trends of strong upward pressure on the provinces' health budgets, in particular, and the relative light pressure on the Canadian government's direct responsibilities, Ottawa is collecting more taxes than it can use, the opposite being true in the provinces.

A reassessment of the responsibilities of both level of governments and an acknowledgement of the growing power and presence of at least some provinces – Quebec and Ontario – could theoretically lead to a realignment of fiscal revenues accordingly.

The Conference Board of Canada has produced a twenty-year conservative projection for a Quebec commission on the matter (Commission, 2002). Its results were rejected on the day of their publication by the then Canadian Minister of Finance, Paul Martin. All members of the Canadian government steadfastly deny any notion of an existing or upcoming imbalance (Finance, 2002). The debate within the Canadian government hinges on the way the federal ministers will directly use Ottawa's new-found wealth.

One scheme that is favoured by some – including Mr Chrétien's successor Paul Martin – is a massive entry of the Canadian government in the funding and governance of Canada's major cities, to be done through a 'New Deal', above and beyond provincial authorities which have constitutional jurisdiction over cities. The project, unveiled in May 2002 by Mr Martin while he was Finance Minister would expand and assure federal responsibility on the engines of the two region states, Toronto and Montreal, instead of delegating power and resources on their respective provincial governments (Martin, 2002).

Prospects for more flexibility granted to provinces in their international relations are also bleak. Canadian constitutional scholar Ronald Watts cites three instances where, he feels, 'there has been some recognition of the interdependence of provincial responsibilities with issues of international relations' (Watts, 2003). The first is the consultation of provincial governments during the negotiations of the FTA and NAFTA agreements. But this was done while former Conservative Prime Minister Brian Mulroney was in power, a nine-year interregnum between thirty years of Liberal governments. Provincial participation in the current WTO round and in the talks leading to the Free Trade Agreement in the Americas is not going as smoothly, certainly not as far as Quebec is concerned. That the Quebec Premier was famously excluded from addressing America's heads of state and government who came in its capital at Ottawa's invitation in April 2001 can be seen as a purely political, transient and personal affair. Some foreign observers question the usefulness of this policy. Minister Counsellor for Political Affairs for the United States from 1992 to 1996 in Ottawa, David T. Jones, wrote that by acting in this fashion, 'Ottawa leaves the impression of constant worry and fear that separatism has not been subdued, rather than confidence in Canada's nationhood . . . The very intensity of this concern becomes counterproductive; it suggests fear that the federal success in Quebec since the 1995 referendum is ephemeral.' (Jones, 2001)

More telling, and long lasting, is Ottawa's strong international action to hinder the success of an interparliamentary association that included provincial legislators of the Americas – the Parliamentary Conference of the Americas (PCOA), whose purpose is to give national and sub-national parliamentary input in the process of integration of the hemisphere. The reason for Ottawa's opposition: Quebec is a founding and active member of the organization, was the first to host its conference in 1997 (with Jean Chrétien as guest speaker), and uses it to multiply its network of international relations in Latin America. Ottawa withdrew its support from the successful PCOA, despite the entreaties of the Quebec Liberal Party, and pushed instead for the creation of a rival interparliamentary organization open only to members of central parliaments. The inaugural meeting of this Inter-Parliamentary Forum of the Americas took place in Ottawa in March 2001.

Watts quotes Team Canada as his second example of recognition of the provincial role. It is a fair point, since Ottawa could have decided to organize these high-profile business missions (to China, Latin America, South-East Asia, Russia) without the premiers, and reap the credit with business leaders who attend. It should, nevertheless, be noted that provinces are clearly more informed than consulted in the decisions on the destination, timing and organization of these trips. In the field, premiers are mostly extras for the Prime minister's speeches and meetings. Under provincial pressure, slots of time were set aside for provincial programmes in the countries visited, however. Quebec made considerable use of this margin of manoeuvre, as did, to a lesser extent, Ontario and Alberta.

Thirdly, Watts mentions the participation of Quebec and New Brunswick in the *Francophonie* as an example of flexibility. Again, this participation was negotiated in 1984 under Brian Mulroney (and brokered by his then ambassador to Paris, Lucien Bouchard, who would become sovereignists premier) with PQ Premier Pierre-Marc Johnson, then signed with Premier Robert Bourassa. Such an accord was out of reach during the preceding Trudeau era, and it is clear to this observer that it would never have happened during the Chrétien era. In fact, Ottawa worked these past years to reduce Quebec's role in the *Francophonie*. It tried, and failed, at excluding Quebec representatives from any an all discussions among francophone members aimed at taking common or convergent positions to be relayed in other international bodies, like the UN and the WTO, where only sovereign states are invited. Other retrenchments were made in bilateral relations. In 1998, Quebec and France were prevented from signing an update to an earlier, twenty-five-year-old old, agreement on reciprocal recognition of judicial findings, in matters of provincial jurisdiction. The wording had not changed, Ottawa's rules had.

Quebec's 1999 suggestion that Ottawa adopt the German and Belgium practice of rotating the seat at UNESCO, which deals with education and culture, with representatives of interested sub-national units was rejected by Ottawa. The External Affairs minister simply refused to meet with the Quebec minister of *Relations Internationales* to discuss the issue. Watts is right in concluding that 'by comparison with such examples as Switzerland and Belgium or even Germany, participation of the provinces in decisions on foreign policy and the development of direct relations between the provinces and foreign countries is far less developed in Canada'.

One can argue that the Quebec sovereignist threat is a reasonable impediment to any extension of flexibility that would then be used by the sovereignists to further their cause. But, by the same token, one could argue that flexibility given to Quebec while it is governed by a federalist party could be misused when sovereignists return, and thus should not be granted either. The argument was used by opponents of the Meech Lake and Charlottetown constitutional reform packages, particularly on the provision that would have enabled the Quebec government to submit a closed list of candidates for the three Supreme Court judges coming from Quebec.

So if the Quebec question is driving Ottawa's unwillingness to recognize the province's new role in international affairs, it makes little difference whether or not the PQ is in power. It may be, however, that the Quebec question is a fig leaf behind which hides a more fundamental refusal, by Ottawa, to cede power in one area where it clearly dominates the agenda.

Whether it is one or the other – and it is most probably both – the federal state is currently codifying for all provinces and for the future its rigid response to Quebec's attempts at playing an international role. It would take a major reversal of policy, probably predicated on a change in the party in power in Ottawa, to start this process.

Impact on Countrywide Redistributive Policies

One last point: both Keating and Courchene note how the emergence of a rich region state weakens its basic economic advantage, ergo its willingness, to share part of its wealth with weaker regions within the traditional country. We have seen how Ontario and Alberta have pushed for a revision of the accounting of federal transfers in the past years, with considerable success. Quebec has been on the losing end of this development. Yet, if this trend continues, one could witness another reassessment, coming from poorer provinces, of the amounts of federal money pumped into Ontario's GDP, for the sole reason that the federal capital lies within its borders.

The disproportionate amount of economic activity, research, salaries and purchases made in the Ontario economy by the federal government is clearly a factor of its success. Furthermore, figures spanning the last eleven years show that Ontario's share of federal capital investment, to

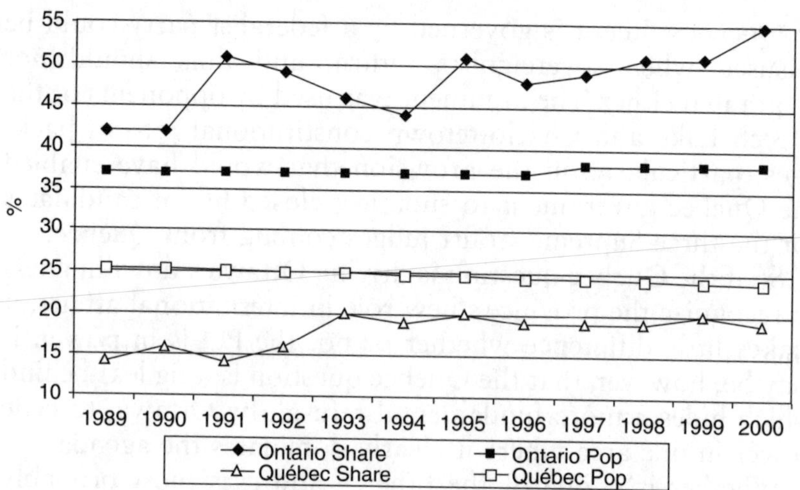

Figure 17.8: Distribution of federal capital investment Québec and Ontario, 1989–2000

look just at this piece of the puzzle, has not stopped growing, far in excess of its share of the population.

The Quebec Department of Finance has computed that, if the federal yearly investment in the economy (including capital investment, purchases, research, grants) were distributed in proportion to the provincial population, the Quebec labour market would immediately gain 30,000 jobs. This would greatly reduce the already shrinking unemployment differential between Quebec and the Canadian average. Unfortunately, in 1997 Ottawa has modified its purchase reporting with the effect of (slightly) obscuring Ontario's advantage, and give Quebec's data an artificial 2 per cent share boost. In the past, Ottawa would for instance count as an Ontario purchase an Alberta Post Office's decision to buy computers from a Toronto firm. This is now counted as an Alberta purchase. If the pressure keeps growing from Ontario to cut back on redistributive policies, it is only a matter of time before other provinces start the accounting of the structural advantages that Ontario derives from the federal state, and ask for compensation, as has already begun in Atlantic Canada (Savoie, 2001). My guess is that, for Ontario, on balance, it might be worth it. For Quebec as well.

REFERENCES

Beine, M. and S. Coulombe (2002), *Should Canadian Regions Adopt the U. S. Dollar ?* Working Paper No 0106E, University of Ottawa: Department of Economics, Faculty of Social Sciences, (revised). (at: http://www.ryerson.ca/econ/ConferencePapers/coulombeJRSversion-a.pdf)

Beaudoin, L. (2001) *Quebec's minister for International Relations, speech to Quebec's Manufacturers and Exporters association*, September 2001.Quebec:Government of Quebec (at : http://www.mri.gouv.qc.ca/le_ministere/allocutions/discours_200010918_fr.html

Brun, H. and al (1991), *Évolution de la jurisprudence fédérative de la Cour Suprême du Canada, 1978–1990*, Quebec : SAIC, Janvier 1991, 196 pages.

Canadian Press (2001) « Sondage Léger et Léger: Les Québécois sont plus ouverts à une annexion aux États-Unis¨, in *Le Devoir,* Sept 10, 2001, p A4.

Chipello, C. J. (2001) "Quebec's public-pension agency has a lot of heft – and well beyond Canada", in *The Wall Street Journal*, 1 October.

Comité interministériel sur la situation de la langue française (1996) *Le français, langue commune : enjeu de la société québécoise,* Quebec : Gouvernement du Quebec. (at : http://www.olf.gouv.qc.ca/ressources/sociolinguistique/3_3.html).

Commission on Fiscal Imbalance (2002) *Report of the Commission on Fiscal Imbalance*, Quebec. Quebec : Gouvernement du Quebec (at: www.desequilibrefiscal.gouv.qc.ca/index_ang.htm)

Conseil de la science et de la technologie du Quebec (2001), *Rapport de conjoncture 2001 : pour des régions innovantes*, mars 2001, 263 pages. (English summary at: www.cst.gouv.qc.ca/ftp/conjoncture2001/chap_3_ang.pdf entire document in French at www.cst.gouv.qc.ca/ftp/conjoncture2001/rap_conj.pdf).

CRIC (Centre de recherche et d'information sur le Canada) (2000), *Portraits du Canada 2000 – Analyse du sondage annuel de suivi effectué par le CRIC*, Novembre 2000, p. 38.

Cooke, P. and al (1999) *The Governance of innovation in Europe : regional perspectives on global competitiveness*, London: inter.

Courchene, T. J. with C. R. Telmer (1998) *From Heartland to North American Region State – The Social, Fiscal and Federal Evolution of Ontario*, Toronto: University of Toronto Press.

Finance Department, Canada (2002) *Fiscal Imbalance: the Facts,* April 2002, Ottawa: Government of Canada (at: www.fin.gc.ca/toce/2002/fbcfacts2_e.html).

Fortin, P. (1997) *L'impact des lois de l'Assurance-emploi de 1990, 1994 et 1996 sur l'Aide sociale du Quebec*, Travaux en cours CREFE, Montréal :Université du Quebec à Montréal. (at : *http://ideas.uqam.ca/ideas/data/Papers/crecrefec1.html).*

Fortin, P. (2002) *Has Quebec's Standard of Living Been Catching Up?*, Montréal : Université du Quebec à Montréal and Canadian Institute for Advanced Research Revised, January 2002, 22 pages. (at: http://www.crde.umontreal.ca/cneh/fortin-txt.pdf).

Frankel, J. A. and A. K. Rose (2000) 'An estimate of the Effect of Currency Unions on Trade and Growth', *Quarterly Journal of Economics*, available as a first draft, 1 May 2000, 37 pages (at: http://haas.berkeley.edu/~arose/FRCU.pdf).

Frémont J. (1998), ' La face cachée de l'évolution contemporaine du fédéralisme canadien'», dans Beaudoin, G.-A. et al, *Le fédéralisme de demain – réformes essentielles*, Montréal : Wilson et Lafleur, pp 45 à 68.

Gouvernement du Quebec (2006) at http://www.infostat.gouv.qc.ca/iq/section3/3_6.htm?lg=an&th=2&rt=1&cp=section3/3_6.htmshape=)

Government of Alberta (2006) (at: http://www.alberta-canada.com/locate/taxation.cfm).

Government of Ontario (2006) at http://www.2ontario.com/welcome/bc_000.asp#bctx.

Keating, M. (2003) 'The Territorial State. Functional restructuring and political change' in T. J. Chourchesne and D. J. Savoie (eds), *The Art of the State: Governance in a World without Frontiers*, Montreal: Institute for Research in Public Policy.

Helliwell, J. F. (1995) *Do National Borders Matter For Quebec's Trade?* NBER Working paper No 5215, 19 pages. (at: www.papers.nber.org/papers/W5215.pdf).

Helliwell, J. F (1998) *How Much Do National Borders Matter?* Washington: Brookins Press.

Helliwell, J. F. (2000) *Globalization : Myths, Facts, and Consequences*, C. . Howe Institute Benefactors Lecture, Toronto, 64 pages. (at: www.cdhowe.org/PDF/Helliwell.pdf).

Jenson, Jane (2002) 'Against the current : Child care and Family Policy in Quebec', in Sonya Michel, *Child Care Policy at the Crossroads : Gender and Welfare State Restructuring*, New York: Routledge.

Jones, D. T. (2001) 'Ottawa turns Landry Into a Martyr by Shutting him out of Summit', in *The Hill Times*, 16 April 2001 (at : http://www.thehilltimes.ca/newarchives/djones041601.html).

KPMG (1999) *The competitive alternative – a comparison of business costs in North America and Europe – Focus on Quebec*, September 1999, 133 pages.

KPMG (2000) *The competitive alternative – Focus on Ontario*, 21 pages.

KPMG (2001) *Facts on Alberta*, February 2001, 39 pages (at: www.alberta-canada.com/statpub/pdf/Facts_2001.pdf).

KPMG (2002) *Competitive alternatives – Comparing business costs in North America, Europe and Japan*, January 2002 (at www.competitivealternatives.com).

La Presse (1998) « Harris tente de remplacer Bouchard en Amérique Latine », in *La Presse*, January 22 1998, B1.

Lanctôt, P. and G. Fréchette (2002) *Fiche synthèses sur la pauvreté au Quebec et en Ontario, 1996–1998*, Quebec :Direction de la recherche, de l'évaluation et de la statistique, ministère de l'Emploi et de la

Solidarité sociale. (at : http://www.mess.gouv.qc.ca/francais/utilitaires/statistiques/publications/fiche_synthese022002.pdf).

Lavoie, M. and al (2001), *Les effets économiques de l'incertitude politique au cours des trente-cinq dernières années : peut-on les mesurer ?* Montréal: Université de Montréal, March 2001, 30 pages.

Lecours, R. (2002) « Le fardeau fiscal des entreprises reste moins lourd au Quebec qu'en Ontario », *La Presse,* 23 June, p A10.

Levine, M. V. (1990) *The Reconquest of Montreal – Language policy and social change in a bilingual city*, Philadelphia: Temple University Press, 285.

Levine, M. V. « L'usage du français, langue commune », in Conseil de la langue française, *Le français au Quebec – 400 ans d'histoire et de vie*, Montréal : Fides, 2000, pp 366–376.

Levine, M. V. (2002) « La question 'démolinguistique', un quart de siècle après la Charte de la langue française », in *Revue d'aménagement linguistique* numéro Hors série, automne 2002, pp. 165–181. (at : http://www.olf.gouv.qc.ca/ressources/bibliotheque/ouvrages/amenagement_hs/ral01_charte_levine_vf_1.pdf)

Lisée, J.-F. (2000) *Sortie de secours – Comment échapper au déclin du Quebec ?* Montréal: Boréal.

Lisée, J.-F. (2000) *Why C-20 is a Democrat's Nightmare*, Brief at the Legislative committee of the House of Commons examining bill C-20 on Quebec's secession referendum, Tuesday 22 February 2000 (at: http://www.vigile.net/00–9/lisee-20.html).

Lisée, J.-F. (2003) 'The Odd Couple: Mario Dumont's ADQ and the 'Quebec Model'', *Inroads*, Spring 2003. (at: http://www.vigile.net/ds-lisee/docs/Inroads-Lisee.doc).

Martin, P. (2002) Speech by the Honourable Paul Martin, Minister of Finance for Canada, to members of the Federation of Canadian Municipalities, Hamilton, Ontario, 31 May 2002. (at: www.fin.gc.ca/news02/02–046e.html).

Ministère de l'éducation (2001) 'Graduation Rates in Quebec and the OECD Countries', *in Education Statistics Bulletin,* Quebec, Janvier 2001, 10 pages (at: http://www.meq.gouv.qc.ca/stat/Bulletin/bulletin_21an.pdf).

Ministère de l'Éducation du Quebec (2000) « La dépense d'éducation par rapport au PIB en 1997 – Une comparaison Quebec – pays de l'OCDE », dans *Bulletin statistique de l'éducation,* No 20, novembre 2000, 14 p. (at http://www.meq.gouv.qc.ca/stat/Bulletin/bulletin_20.pdf).

Ministère des Finances du Quebec/KPMG (1998) *La fiscalité des particuliers et le coût de la vie – Comparaison entre Montréal et différentes villes nord-américaines,* Budget 1998–1999, février 1998, 91 pages. (at: http://www.budget.finances.gouv.qc.ca/budget/1998–1999/fr/PDF/fiscpafr.pdf).

Noël, A. (2000) 'Canada, Love It or Don't Leave It', *Policy Options/Options politiques*, vol. 21, no 1, 2000, pp. 34–36. (at *: http://www.irpp.org/fr/po/archive/po0100.htm#noel*).

Office de la langue française, *La langue des cadres d'entreprise*, (at L'Office de la langue française du Quebec website : www.olf.gouv.qc.ca/situation.html heading 3.3.

Picard, A. (2001) "Most want PM to cede sovereignty over border", in *The Globe and Mail*, 1 October 2001, p A1.

Piketty T. and E. Saez (2001) *Income inequality in the United States: 1913–1998*, NBER, 121 p. (at: http://pythie.cepremap.ens.fr/%7Epiketty/Papers/Piketty-Saez2001.pdf).

PriceWaterhouse/Invest-Quebec (2001), *Taxation in Quebec 2001–2002*, (at www.infostat.gouv.qc.ca/docs-keh/invstqc/an/pdf/fisc_2001–2002.pdf).

Proulx, P.-P. (1999) *Les effets de l'Ale et de l'Aléna sur les économies canadienne, québécoise et américaine : examen des études récentes*, Quebec : Institut de la statistique du Quebec.

Rose, A. K. (2000). 'One Money, One Market: Estimating the Effects of Common Currencies on Trade.' *Economic Policy* 15 (30): 7–46.

Ryan, C. (1999) 'The agreement on the Canadian Social Union as Seen by a Quebec Federalist', *Inroads*, June 1999, p. 27.

Savoie, D. J. (2001) *Pulling Against Gravity: Economic Development in New Brunswick During the McKenna Years*, Montreal: Institute for Research in Public Policy. 2001, 199 pages.

Tran, Q. V. and Josep, H.-C. (2001) *Regard sur la compétitivité de l'économie québécoise*, Institut de la statistique du Quebec, Extrait de la publication L'Écostat, juin 2001, 9 pages, (at http://www.stat.gouv.qc.ca/bul/economie/pdf/eco2_01.pdf).

Watts, R. (2003), 'Managing Interdependence in a Federal Political System', in T. J. Chourchesne and D. J. Savoie (eds), *The Art of the State: Governance in a World without Frontiers*, Montreal: Institute for Research in Public Policy.

Wolfson M. and B. Murphy (2000), 'Income Inequality in North America: Does the 49th Parallel still Matter?' in the *Canadian Economic Observer*, Statistics Canada, August 2000, Ct 11–010-XPB, 24 pages. (at: http://www.statcan.ca/francais/indepth/11–010/feature/eo2000_aug_f.pdf).

Appendix

Quebec's position in the world – G7 countries

Indicators Rank :	1	2	3	4	5	6	7	8
1- GDP Growth (1997- 1998)	USA	France	Canada	Germany	Quebec	UK	Italy	Japan
2a- Schooling level (postsecondary-96)	Canada	Quebec	USA	UK / Germany		France	*	*
2b-Schooling level (university-96)	USA	Quebec	Canada	UK / Germany		France	*	*
3- Technological level (HighTech-96)	Japan	Quebec	France	USA	UK	Germany	Canada	*
4- Private R&D spending (97)	USA	Japan	Germany	France	Quebec	UK	Canada	Italy
5- Private R&D staff (97)	Japan	Germany	Quebec	France	Canada	UK	Italy	*
6- Scientific + technical staff (96)	Japan	USA	Quebec	Germany	Canada	France	UK	Italy
7- Investment, machinery+equipment (97)	Japan	Italy / USA		France	Germany	UK	Canada	Quebec
8- Exports to GDP ratio (97)	Canada	Quebec	UK	Italy / France / Germany			USA	Japan
9- Exports by technological level (96)	USA	UK	Japan	Quebec	France	Germany	Canada	*
10- Number of patents (95)	USA	Japan	Germany	Canada	France	UK	Italy	*
11- Industrial funding of Univ.research (97)	Canada	Quebec	Germany	UK	USA / Utaly		France	Japan
12- Education spending (95)	Quebec	Canada	USA	France	Germany	Japan / Italy		*
13- University research spending (97)	Quebec	Japan	Germany	France / USA		UK	Canada	Italy
14- Number of scientific publications (95)	Quebec	Canada	UK	USA	France	Germany	Japan	Italy

* Missing data for some countries

Source: Conseil de la science et de la technologie du Québec, *Rapport de conjoncture 2001: pour des régions innovantes*, mars 2001, p. 78.

NOTES

1 This is an expanded and updated version of a paper presented to the conference The Art of the State: Governance in a World without Frontiers, held by Montreal's Institute for Research in Public Policy (IRPP) in October 2001 and excerpted in IRPP's December 2002 *Policy Option* magazine, under the title 'Is Quebec a North American Region-State?', 25–32. From 1994 to 1999, the author was political and international affairs advisers to Quebec premiers, Jacques Parizeau and Lucien Bouchard.

Part IV

Conclusion

18

Language Policies, National Identities, and Liberal-Democratic Norms

WILL KYMLICKA

While the chapters in this volume cover a range of issues and debates, they also reveal some common themes and trends. In particular, there appears to be a clear trend over the past thirty to forty years towards the strengthening of the legal position of minority or non-dominant languages. A corner has been turned in debates over language policy. The basic principle that it is legitimate, perhaps even obligatory, for states to protect and promote non-dominant languages is now firmly established. Indeed, it is increasingly enshrined in international law, such as the language rights provisions of the Council of Europe's Framework Convention for the Protection of National Minorities (1995), the European Charter for European or Minority Languages (1993) and, at the global level, the Draft Declaration for the Rights of Indigenous Peoples (1993) (see Dunbar, chapter 5 above).

Throughout much of the nineteenth and twentieth centuries, the presence of minority-language rights in a country was seen as an anachronism or sign of backwardness – as evidence that a country had not become fully modernized. Today, however, acceptance of minority-language rights is seen as evidence of a country's political maturity and openness to difference. States that cling to the model of 'one nation-one language-one state' are seen as outmoded, trapped in a nineteenth-century model of political community, unable to adapt to the complexities of the modern world.

This shift has caused some confusion in the post-communist states of central and eastern Europe. In the past, the fact that the Habsburg and Ottoman empires had failed to assimilate large pockets of linguistic minorities was often said to be evidence that they were not real countries or viable modern states, and that it is was therefore appropriate to break them up. When countries in the region acquired (or re-acquired) independence after the collapse of communism in 1990, they naturally assumed that in order to be accepted internationally they had to show that they were capable of successfully assimilating their minorities. They were surprised to discover that the international ethos had changed, and that their linguistic assimilationist projects were now seen as primitive and backward.

The chapters in this volume focus on two important examples of this trend – namely, the strengthening of the status of the French language in Canada, and of Celtic languages in the United Kingdom and Ireland. While these two cases testify to the global trend, they also (implicitly) reveal that this trend is a targeted one – that is, it applies only to historic language groups, rather than immigrant groups. This is true not only in Canada, the UK and Ireland, but also in international law. The legal conventions I noted earlier are limited to 'national minorities' (in the European context) and 'indigenous peoples' (in the United Nations). Although there is no agreed legal definition of either of these terms, they are typically understood to refer to groups that have been living on a territory for centuries – a territory they view as their homeland – and more specifically were living on this territory before it was incorporated into a larger state. Put another way, national minorities and indigenous peoples did not come to the state (as with immigrants), rather the state came to them through some process (voluntary or involuntary) of territorial expansion.

None of the chapters in this volume focus on the case of language policy towards immigrant languages. If they had, a different story would have emerged. Although there are some interesting bilingual primary education programmes using immigrant languages in some jurisdictions, there is no move in Canada, the UK or Ireland towards granting official-language status to any immigrant languages, and nothing akin to the 'Official Language Commissioner', 'Welsh Language Act' or 'Gaelic Language Board' for any immigrant languages. There is no government commitment to increase the number of immigrant-language speakers, or to enhance the spheres within such languages can be used.

Indeed, the overall climate regarding the retention of immigrant languages is generally hostile. Throughout Europe today, there is a growing concern – almost paranoia – that immigrants are too attached to their native tongue, and are not making enough effort to learn the official language. Moreover, acquisition of the national language is typically understood as a subtractive process: properly to master the national language they (and their children) must abandon their immigrant language. In short, while assimilationist projects with respect to historic minorities are now largely delegitimized, the same cannot be said of assimilationist projects regarding immigrants, at least in respect of language.

It is an interesting question why there is such a sharp variation, in both domestic policies and international legal norms, between immigrant and historic linguistic minorities. The explanation cannot be size: several immigrant groups in the UK outnumber the 60,000 Gaelic-speakers in Scotland, or the 167,000 Irish-speakers in Northern Ireland. Similarly, while French is by far the largest linguistic minority in Canada as a whole, there are several provinces of Canada where immigrant groups outnumber the local French-speaking community. And certainly many immigrant groups are larger than Canada's indigenous-language communities.

So why are historic language communities being singled out for legal protection? I suspect there are a number of factors at work here. One factor relates to linguistic survival. Even if immigrant languages disappear in the diaspora, they presumably will survive in the country of origin. The Bengali language will survive in Bangladesh, even if it disappears from the Bengali immigrant community in Britain. By contrast, if Gaelic disappears from Ireland and Britain, it will disappear entirely: this is its homeland. So too with indigenous languages in Canada. Insofar as we wish to maintain linguistic diversity around the world, we have to give special protection to languages in their historic homelands.

This undoubtedly is part of the explanation. But it cannot be the whole explanation. After all, even if French disappeared in Canada, it would continue to thrive in France. So too with many other historic linguistic minorities, such as the German minority in Denmark, the Hungarian minority in Romania and Slovakia, or the Turkish minority in Bulgaria, all of whom are protected by emerging international norms regarding the language rights of national minorities. The trend towards strengthening the linguistic rights of historic minorities applies whether or not their language is also securely protected in some other country.

Another factor concerns consent. It is sometimes argued that immigrants chose to come to a new country, knowing that this would involve living and working in another language. Linguistic shift is simply part and parcel of what it means to be an immigrant. People who find this prospect intolerable can remain in their country of origin. By contrast, historic minorities did not choose to leave their original community. Instead, their community has been incorporated (usually involuntarily) into a larger state, turning them into linguistic minorities. One could argue that such processes of incorporation should not result in the diminishing of the right of a people to continue to use their language on their historic homeland.

This too is surely part of the explanation. Yet here again it cannot be the whole explanation. The idea that newcomers have understood and accepted that they are leaving one language community for another may apply to some immigrants, but not to all. Refugees in particular did not 'choose' to leave their homeland: they were fleeing persecution. Indeed, in some cases, they were fleeing persecution precisely because they belonged to a linguistic minority (for example, the Kurds in Turkey). In such cases, one could argue that refugees left precisely in order to be free to maintain their language, which was under attack in their country of origin.

A related factor concerns the role of historic injustice. In every case discussed in this book, and in most other cases around the world, historic linguistic minorities can plausibly claim that they have suffered some injustice at the hands of the larger state, and that their language would be in a stronger position today were it not for that injustice (that is, there would be more speakers of the language, often over a wider territory, and more cultural products and publications in the language). The state arguably has some obligation to acknowledge that injustice, and perhaps to redress some of its effects. By contrast, most citizens of Western democracies do not feel they have any comparable historic debt regarding the language of newcomers.[1]

No doubt there are many factors that explain the variable treatment of immigrant and historic minorities in terms of language rights. In any event, it is important to note that this differentiation is not limited to issues of language. We see a similar differentiation regarding other forms of minority rights, including issues of self-government, legal pluralism, political representation,and (in the case of indigenous peoples) land claims. On all of these issues, we find systematic differences between immigrants and historic minorities, both at the level of domestic policies and international law. Within the broad category of historic minorities, there are important differences between 'indigenous peoples' and 'national minorities' (Kymlicka, 2001).

This systematic differentiation is linked, I believe, to the way that historic minorities have been able to draw upon ideas of 'nationhood'. Both national minorities and indigenous peoples have described themselves as 'nations' or 'peoples', even if their national homeland is now incorporated into a larger state, and to demand various rights and powers in virtue of that status. Such claims to nationhood were historically rejected by most Western states, but have become increasingly accepted, as have the more specific claims that are seen as flowing from nationhood, such as regional autonomy, the maintenance of distinct educational and legal systems, and the protection and use of national languages (Keating, 2001; Kymlicka, 2001).

Language policies, therefore, are one component of a much broader phenomenon of the revindication of ethno-national identities in the post-war era, and the rebirth of the 'nations within' as self-consciously political actors and movements. Despite predictions that they would disappear as a result of modernization or globalization, national identities and nationalist ideologies have remained powerful sources of political mobilization in the contemporary world.

The role of language within such nationalist projects varies immensely. In some cases, as in Quebec, language is the central marker of an individual's national identity, and ensuring the dominance of the language on the national territory is the central goal of collective nationalist mobilization. In other cases, such as Wales and Ireland, language is a widely accepted symbol of nationhood, and concern for the language is a widely accepted goal of national political action, but proficiency in the language is not necessarily a marker of individual national identity (many people who identify themselves as Welsh or Irish do not speak Welsh or Gaelic). Moreover, while collective political action aims at the reproduction and promotion of the language, it does not aim to establish its dominance (that is, Welsh and Gaelic are being promoted alongside, but not in place of, English, which will continue to be hegemonic). In yet other cases, such as Scotland, language is controversial even as a symbol of nationhood (since Gaelic was historically used primarily by the highlanders, not all Scots), and it is disputed whether the language should be seen as a 'national' issue, as opposed to, say, a more diffuse issue of 'diversity' disconnected from the larger Scottish nationalist project (Williams, 2007).[2]

While the centrality of language issues to national projects varies, in all of these cases there is an implicit or explicit assumption that it is up to the relevant national community to decide on its own language policy. The Welsh, Irish, Scots and Québécois should be free to decide whether, or to what extent, they wish to adopt collective policies to promote their historic language. And, in order to make such decisions, the national community requires some form of self-government. Indeed, one of the most widely accepted arguments for devolving power to 'nations within' is that they need some degree of self-government over issues of language and culture.

This in turn raises interesting questions about the complex linkages between language policy and national autonomy. It is often said that national groups require self-government in order to maintain their language and culture. But the causal relationship can also go the other way. According to Rainer

Baubock (2000: 384), 'rather than self-government being a means to preserve cultural difference, this difference is more often preserved as a means to justify the claim to self-government'. This applies not only to linguistic differences, but also, for example, to distinct legal traditions (as in both Scotland and Quebec). Ethno-national groups are continually required to explain why they deserve self-governing powers, and having a distinct language or legal tradition provides one possible answer.[3]

This may help explain the otherwise puzzling fact that there is broad public support in Wales (and Ireland) for official bilingualism and linguistic revitalization policies even amongst people who have no serious desire or intention of increasing their competence or use of Welsh (or Gaelic). These policies help to reinforce a sense of national distinctiveness that provides legitimacy to claims of national self-government. Even if the vast majority of the society remains English-speaking, and does not really wish to change this fact, the visible public commitment to Celtic languages helps to make clear that this is not just a province of England, but the homeland of a different national group. This not only supports claims to national self-government, but also reminds newcomers to the region that they have entered a distinct national community, and are expected to identify with it.

Many language activists in Wales and Ireland complain that these revitalization policies are half-hearted. Yet perhaps that is what one should expect if the public perceives these policies as primarily an instrument for symbolizing and affirming nationhood. Many English-speaking citizens want just enough linguistic revitalization to secure their claim to nationhood, and to remind newcomers of that fact, but not so much revitalization that they would actually have to change their language repertoire or language use.

In short, the trend towards greater recognition of non-dominant languages must be seen as part and parcel of a broader trend towards the resurgence of ethno-national identities and nationalist projects, although the connection between the two is complex. Language may be the substantive core of these nationalist projects, or merely symbolic of them (or both). Similarly, national self-government may be demanded in order to adopt better language protection, or better language protection may be adopted in order to justify self-government claims (or both). Whatever the precise connection, in all of these cases, language policies have been carried along by broader nationalist political projects.

Of course, this simply pushes the puzzle back a level. If increased support for non-dominant languages is tied to the growing strength of ethno-national projects, why have ethno-national projects become stronger? The chapters in this volume suggest a range of answers, including the delegitimization of older ethnic/racial hierarchies, as well as neo-liberal restructuring of the state, which has (unexpectedly) created opportunities for non-dominant groups, particularly through ideas of decentralization and subsidiarity.[4] But the main change is the gradual recognition that these nationalist projects, including their linguistic aspects, are often wholly consistent with basic liberal-democratic values. This is an important shift. In the past, it was widely assumed that ethno-national projects were inherently illiberal or undemocratic, grounded in reactionary (and ultimately futile) attempts to preserve community traditions from the inevitable changes brought about by modernization, education and individual mobility. Today, however, it is increasingly recognized that such ethno-national projects can fully respect liberal-democratic constitutional principles, can be open to the world (for example, in terms of support for free trade, or European integration), and indeed in some cases are actually leaders in terms of progressive social policy (for example, in areas of gay rights, immigration, women's rights, deliberative democracy, or social justice).[5]

The idea that the political projects of the 'small nations' or 'nations within' can not only embody but even advance liberal-democratic values remains contested. The chapters by Dumas and Lisée reveal the extent to which Quebec must continually struggle against misperceptions and double-standards regarding its nation-building projects, and the fear of being labelled illiberal is present in many of the chapters by Welsh policy-makers. But, while non-dominant groups must continually defend themselves against such charges, the reality is that these defences have been reasonably successful.

There is in fact widespread public acceptance of the basic legitimacy of the Quebecois national project within Canada, and of Scottish and Welsh nationalism in Britain.

However, here we reach an important difference between Canada and the British/Irish cases. In Canada, the legitimacy of the Quebecois project stems in part from the fact that it relies on a fairly familiar model of a national political community, defined by a common language that is dominant over a particular territory. The Quebecois simply insist that there are (at least) two such national communities within Canada, and that Canada must therefore be understood as a binational (or multinational) state.[6] Official bilingualism at the federal level, on this model, is necessary to ensure that both language communities are equally represented in the central government, and equally able to access its services. But the assumption is that most individuals will continue to live their lives in relatively monolingual societies, each of which is institutionally complete. There is a francophone society in Quebec (and part of New Brunswick), and an anglophone society in the rest of the country, each with its own full set of economic, educational, media, legal and political institutions, and each with its own robust public debates. Keeping a country together with two parallel, institutionally complete and territorialized language communities is not easy, but part of what holds it together is precisely the fact that each community can see the other as forming a separate but 'normal' liberal-democratic national political community built around a common language and territory.[7]

In the Celtic cases, by contrast, the main goal of language policy is not to create two parallel and largely monolingual societies – a separate Welsh-speaking or Gaelic-speaking society alongside the English-speaking society.[8] Rather, the goal is to encourage greater bilingualism in everyday life, so that most citizens will feel comfortable operating in either language in a wide range of functions. In his chapter, Dunbar describes this as a more 'thoroughgoing' conception of bilingualism than in the Canadian case. It is in any event a quite different conception, one that clearly makes sense given the history and demographics of the Welsh, Scottish and Irish cases.

Viewed in this light, the Celtic cases offer the promise of a genuinely new model of a single bilingual national political community (in contrast to the sort of binational federation of two distinct monolingual political communities that we see in Canada or Belgium). Various chapters in this volume express the hope that this new model will not only be feasible and enduring, but will also create forms of democratic inclusion, provide new scope for a more deliberative politics and create more empowered citizens. It seems too early to tell whether such hopes will come to fruition. We do not yet have either the practical policy experiences or the normative political theories that would identify the potential benefits and hazards that are likely to arise in the building of such new forms of bilingual democratic practices. But the essays in this volume are surely an important step in that exploration.

REFERENCES

Baubock, R. (2000) 'Why Stay Together: A Pluralist Approach to Secession and Federation', in Will Kymlicka and Wayne Norman (eds), *Citizenship in Diverse Societies*. Oxford: Oxford University Press.

Keating, M. (2001) *Plurinational Democracy: Stateless Nations in a Post-Sovereignty Era*. Oxford: Oxford University Press.

Kymlicka, W. (2001) *Politics in the Vernacular: Nationalism, Multiculturalism and Citizenship*. Oxford: Oxford University Press.

Kymlicka, W. (2004) 'Justice and Security in the Accommodation of Minority Nationalism: Comparing East and West', in Alain Dieckhoff (ed.) *The Politics of Belonging: Nationalism, Liberalism and Pluralism* New York: Lexington, pp. 127–54.

Williams, C. H. (2007). *Linguistic Minorities in Democratic Context*, Basingstoke: Palgrave.

NOTES

1 Citizens in the West may feel some obligation to remedy the injustices of colonialism, particularly if they are former colonial powers, but this is unlikely to extend to assisting ex-colonial immigrants to maintain their native tongues.

2 As Williams (2007) notes, the promotion of Gaelic in Scotland is sometimes seen as a 'minority' or 'multicultural' issue, rather than a matter of Scottish national identity.

3 In the Canadian case, for example, the presence of the civil law tradition in Quebec not only provides an argument why Quebec should have autonomy, but also provides an argument why Quebec

needs three of the nine seats on the Supreme Court (which sometimes has to rule on issues of civil law). If Quebecers gave up the civil law tradition, they would lose a central argument for autonomy and judicial representation.

4 One factor not mentioned in the chapters is the 'desecuritzation' of state-minority relations – that is, the fact that national minorities in the West are no longer seen as potential fifth columns for some neighbouring enemy. For a discussion of how such security fears have dissipated in the West with respect to national minorities (but not necessarily immigrants), and how it remains a powerful obstacle to greater accommodation of national minorities in much of the rest of the world, see Kymlicka (2004).

5 Catalonia is often pointed to in this context, as its policies on many of these issues are more liberal than that of the Castilian majority throughout Spain. The same is true of Quebec, at least on issues of women's equality, which are more progressive than those in the rest of Canada.

6 Whether Canada is understood as binational or multinational depends, in part, on whether indigenous peoples are seen as 'nations', or whether their self-governing communities are described in other terms.

7 The Official Languages Act can be seen as attempting to diminish the perceived territorialization of Canada's two major language communities, by insisting that francophones and anglophones can receive federal services in their language 'from sea to sea to sea'. But this (commendable) approach has not changed the widespread public perception that for most purposes, including political decision-making, French is the language of public life in Quebec (and parts of New Brunswick), and English is the language of public life in the rest of the country.

8 Apart, of course, from the Gaeltecht and the few counties in Wales where native-speakers remain a local majority. Sustaining these linguistic enclaves is an important goal in both Wales and Ireland, but is not the main focus of the language revitalization plans, which are precisely concerned with enhancing the status of Gaelic and Welsh in those parts of the country where it is no longer the language of daily life.

Index